MW01152249

SIERRA PACIFIC
A FAMILY HISTORY

Copyright ©1991 by J. "Bud" Tomascheski

All rights reserved. No part of this book may be reproduced or utilized in any form or by any means, electronic or mechanical, including photocopying, recording or by any information storage and retrieval system, without permission in writing from the Publisher. Inquiries should be addressed to J. "Bud" Tomascheski c/o Creative Type, 1703-B Giuntoli Lane, Arcata, California 95521.

Library of Congress Cataloging-in-Publication Data

Tomascheski, J. "Bud"
        Sierra Pacific: A Family History / J. "Bud" Tomascheski
ISBN 0-9630947-1-8

91-66688
  CIP

Printed in the United States of America

BOOK PRODUCED AND DESIGNED BY CREATIVE TYPE, ARCATA, CALIFORNIA

▪ FROM A FORESTER'S PERSECTIVE ▪

A Family
SIERRA PACIFIC
History

PUBLISHED BY
J. "BUD" TOMASCHESKI

PRODUCED BY
CREATIVE TYPE
ARCATA, CALIFORNIA

Dedicated
to
Emily (Emmerson) Thorpe

Mother of A. A. Emmerson

A gracious lady, who lived in early-day Oregon, and raised her
children with little access to the amenities of life.
She and her husband, Raleigh H. Emmerson, survived many trying
years in the timber industry and endured its disappointments.
She persevered with devotion to God and her church.

ACKNOWLEDGEMENTS

How do I begin to acknowledge all those who have contributed to writing a history such as this? Perhaps it is safest to start with my wife, Norma, who might harbor irritations from seeing me spend long hours in front of a computer screen when I could have been doing something more "productive." She should be near the top of the list and, since I will spend most of my remaining years with her, it is best that she receive proper recognition so that she will think kindly of me.

In all efforts at writing acknowledgements there is the danger, indeed the probability, that someone's name will not be included; someone who is very important to the story. To those whose names have been omitted inadvertently, I apologize profusely in advance.

When beginning the research for this story, I distributed short questionnaires to many employees of Sierra Pacific Industries, both present and past. To those who responded, my sincere thanks. To those who did not respond, I apologize if they find their names omitted. The mistakes of omission are mine, as well as the mistakes of commission. I take responsibility for factual errors, as well as for misinterpretation of facts.

With those niceties out of the way, I reiterate my debt to my wife. She put up with disrupted schedules, the receipt of strange bills that required payment, and countless arguments over the wisdom of driving long distances for a short interview of a key person. Although she is not an early riser, she tolerated strange sounds in the early mornings as I attempted to capture an elusive thought before it disappeared into the back of my mind, never to be thought again.

Next, I thank all of the Emmerson family. Red, in particular, has my greatest appreciation for furnishing some of the facts about his early life, correcting some of the faulty information I had gathered about his family and his company, and, most of all, for providing me with sufficient economic security so that I could devote some of my retirement to my "project."

Ida Emmerson was most supportive. She helped with my questionnaire, found old family pictures, loaned me her scrapbook and told me many funny stories about the family. The Emmerson children, George, Caroline and Mark were very helpful. Mark, especially, found hundreds of photographs depicting company operations which he loaned to me.

Marlin Emmerson, Curly Emmerson's brother, and his wife, Augusta, were gracious in providing pictures and information. Naida Emmerson, Chet Emmerson's widow, also provided pictures and stories about Chet's involvement in his brother Curly's early sawmill ventures.

Orvamae Emmerson, Curly's widow, told stories of her life with Curly. She gave me many pictures of her irrepressible husband, to be used as I needed them. Her frankness and support were evident.

My admiration and respect goes to Emily Thorpe, Red Emmerson's mother, who, at 90 years, corrected an early draft of my description of her life with Curly. Her manner was forceful and direct, exhibiting a quick mind and a prodigious memory. She was especially sensitive to the image for which she would be responsible if I slanted the information she gave me the way some journalists seem to do. She was afraid present day Emmersons would think unkindly of her if that were so. I hope she will not be disappointed by the results.

R. L. "Dick" Smith was extremely helpful, doing many hours of research of old company records, making copious notes, then correcting my efforts at interpreting them. He was a tough critic and explained some of the finer points of corporate maneuvering which took place at several points in the company's early life. Without his advice, the economic data given in this book would be sketchy at best.

Many key people at Sierra Pacific Industries were helpful, particularly Ron Hoppe and Ron Stevens who spent several hours with me answering questions. Ray Lowry, Corporate Controller, aided my efforts in running to ground information and photographs. Steve Gaston, Data Processing Manager, set up my computer, helped me learn how to turn it on, and found things that I erased from its memory from time to time. He was a patient teacher.

Laura Montagna, of Creative Type in Arcata, coordinated the proofreading by Margo Coleman and art work by Joan Grytness, and did the typesetting herself. She found Peter Palmquist, who advised all of us in the matter of preparing manuscripts, publishing them, and in preparing photographs. Both Joan and Peter are master craftspersons and spent long hours at their work.

Laura, in one sense, was the publisher. She and her husband were building a log cabin in the hills above Kneeland and she drove back and forth each day; sometimes with a load of hay for their farm animals. She knows how to work; and I gained a great deal of respect for her commitment to the project. Whether wielding a hammer or saw, doing farm chores, or running her business she was always cheerful and outgoing. Meanwhile, she was pregnant with their first child.

Two photographers granted permission to use their pictures. David P. Bayles, a portrait photographer and a real artist from Seal Beach, California, graciously said yes when I contacted him. Mark Fator, from Redding, California, let me use a number of aerial shots of Sierra Pacific facilities he took in 1987. I appreciate their contributions very much.

Those who submitted to my inept questions during interview sessions are thanked profusely, particularly Don Riewerts, Moose Mathews, Audrey Griffith, Mike Albee, Gordon and Shirley Amos, Dorothy and Bob Anderson, Velma Peterson, Burr Coffelt, Tony Zanze, Toots Gahart, Dennis Gomez, Fritz Hagen, Phil Heckenberg, Liz Hoaglen, Otto Peters, George Rogers, Gary Shaffer, George Sharp, Sam Witzel, Arnie Jepson, Sue and Bill Kleiner, Jim Laier, and Tim Mason.

George Craig gave me advice early in the project, read some of the early efforts, and sent them back with caustic comments. Bill Dennison, agreeing to write the Foreword, did not have time to do so, but took the time anyway. I count both George and Bill among my best friends and admire their tenacity and commitment.

Then there are other members of my family who took the time to read and criticize some of the stories. Daughters Dolores Blanc, Liz Adams, and especially Ann Heikkila took time to read some boring chapters and made helpful suggestions to improve them. Ann especially, was instrumental in getting the manuscript completed, did much of the typing for revision of the manuscript, and helped with the coordination of photographs and text. She did the indexing - a monumental task. Son, Dan, took up where I left off, writing the final chapters to bring the story up to date. I have great admiration for his abilities in managing a forestry business in very difficult times.

To a degree this was a family effort, and I am grateful for the opportunity to be the nominal head of my own family. They were supportive all the way. The Sierra Pacific foresters, my extended family, deserve thanks for providing information and photographs when I requested them. They also taught me much about forestry and made my job easier and more rewarding.

This "history" is not the end of the story of Sierra Pacific Industries. At some future time, another history of the company should be compiled which should be professionally researched and written. I hope that, when that time comes, this effort will provide the future authors with some needed information about the early days of the organization and the family that founded it.

FOREWORD

This book is more than the story of Sierra Pacific Industries (SPI) and the development of its owner and president, Red Emmerson, into an industry leader. As the author, Bud Tomascheski, leads us through the important history of the forest resource industry, the story serves to remind us of the dedication of thousands of men and women who made our industry great.

Whether intentional or not, the review of SPI's history has served another important role. As you read The Beginning; and then about Curly's early life in Oregon; the fires that destroyed two of his mills; Red Emmerson's early years and his developing management philosophy; the lean and profitable years leading up to the current issues of appeals, litigation and community upheaval; you are reliving a simple era turned complex. Those of us who were part of that period can appreciate the fact that change cannot be stopped, only guided.

As you follow those changes, from the 1940s through the 1980s, the rate of change has accelerated. Some in our industry have been unable to keep up. They will be part of our history, but not our future.

I was pleased to be asked to write a foreword to this book for several reasons. First, I have a great respect for Bud that is shared by so many of his peers. His leadership has provided guidance and drive over the years which is sorely missed.

I am also pleased to be able to be even a small part of a work that helps portray the importance of our great industry, as well as uphold the truths and dispel some of the myths of this tumultuous period.

Bud's 1980 presentation to the SPI directors showed the insight for which he became known. "We are being choked to death by wild and scenic rivers, California Wilderness Bill, air quality requirements and on and on and on..." That prophesy is being fulfilled, if measured in terms of available timber supply.

Bud Tomascheski has written in much the same unassuming manner in which he has led the industry for the past 22 years. After listening intently to both sides, he would often begin his analysis of a situation with, "I don't know what I'm talking about, but...," then he would provide an explanation of the problem and at least one reasonable solution.

Bud has served us well in clearly relating the important history and current problems of our industry. It is up to many of us who read his story to develop the solutions in the months ahead.

William N. Dennison
(President, California Forestry Association)

TABLE OF CONTENTS

TABLE OF CONTENTS

PART THREE

SIERRA PACIFIC INDUSTRIES

THE PRIVATE COMPANY

(1975 - 1982)

PART FOUR

SIERRA PACIFIC INDUSTRIES

POST DEPRESSION ERA

(1983 - 1989)

PART FIVE
EPILOGUE

INTRODUCTION

Prior to my retirement in February, 1990, as Vice-President and Manager of the Forestry Department for Sierra Pacific Industries, I had decided to write a book about the company and the people who were associated with it.

The following pages represent a combination of research, records, reflections, personal experiences and thoughts. As such, they exhibit a lack of sophistication in writing such a work. The cardinal sin of mixing first person with third person dialogue is committed many times, even though I have been advised by many knowledgeable persons to refrain from doing so. I hope the readers will not be too inconvenienced by switching mental gears as they go along, or worse yet, become disenchanted with the whole thing and give up reading.

There have been many histories written of lumber companies and timber companies, of logging outfits, and of timber barons. Many of them were authored by historians or professional writers, and bore the mark of extensive research and access to large portfolios of pictures. Most of them were written for a specific audience or intended to be used by historians of the future. Some may even have been produced to make a profit for the author.

This story of Sierra Pacific Industries is written by a rank amateur and is none of the above. My purpose in writing it is even unclear to me. When I was beginning to talk about the project with several of my respected friends, one of the first questions asked of me was "Who are you writing it for?" My answer was, "I don't know, perhaps for myself." One question that kept recurring was, "How many pages will it be?" Again my answer was "I don't know, and I won't know until it's finished."

Peter Palmquist, prominent author, historian and photographer, of Arcata, California, once asked me why I wanted to write such a book. I told him I wished to do it for the Emmersons, my former employers, for the men and women who worked for the company over the years, and lastly for myself.

When I sent my first poor efforts at writing a couple of chapters to George Craig, a good friend and former magazine editor, he advised me to look in the library for a book on grammar. He then mailed me several excerpts of books dealing with punctuation. The few pages that I sent him were returned with so many notes on them that, running out of room for more, he suggested I telephone him so we could discuss the project in some detail. I sincerely appreciated his candor.

For me to tell the story was a challenge that I could not ignore. I intended not only to provide some historical facts but to give some feeling for the kinds of men and women who devote their lives to providing wood products for the people of the country. I also developed considerable respect for the owners of the company, and believed their story should be told by someone who knew most of them.

As my research began, I found there were many humorous stories associated with the people who made Sierra Pacific Industries successful. The founder R. H. Emmerson was a humorous individual; and I came to the realization that it would be well to try to tell some of the funny stories I uncovered. Whether I have succeeded remains to be seen.

Several more points came to light as I proceeded. The lumber industry was always plagued with fires, some of disastrous proportions. Why? As research progressed, there seemed to be an inordinate number of fires that affected the success of the company, not always adversely. Why were there so many? What started them?

I remembered a number of fires that occurred at several operations where I was employed prior to beginning work for Sierra Pacific Industries. The sawmill at Loyalton, before its purchase by Sierra Pacific, was saved by the prompt response of the Loyalton Volunteer Fire Department to a fire in its filing room. Several years ago, the sawmill at Sloat, then owned by Ken Metzker, had been completely destroyed by fire, then rebuilt.

Many lumbermen believed the causes of such fires were easy to explain. Since few had researched their causes and documented them in one place, their theories may be too simple.

Sawmills were usually constructed of wood. Over the years the wood became dry and, in some cases, saturated with oils or lubricants. Hydraulic lines or compressed air lines ruptured occasionally, flooding the floor with hot oil. Sawdust or shavings, particularly from the planing of dry lumber, was flammable. Old sawdust, whipped into cracks by the wind, became dry as time went by. All that was needed was a source of ignition to produce a fire.

In the "old" days, there was always a debris pile that was being burned. Later, it was the tepee burner that provided the spark. And there was always the welder or cutting torch used in maintenance that could set off a conflagration.

Upon ignition in the old days, before the advent of the sprinkler system, most fires were never contained. The mill burnt to the ground. With modern fire control systems and fire fighting equipment, control is more successful. But even today an occasional fire can get out of hand.

When a story such as this one is pieced together, the various fires seem to occur quite often. In describing the early years, a fire seems to occur every few pages. Old-timers believe that was not unusual; it was part of being in the lumber business.

My research into some of the later years focused attention on an unrelated phenomenon. It seemed that most of those in the timber industry hated those who worked for the U. S. Forest Service, or other government agencies. Was that fact or fiction?

After discussions with acquaintances both within the agencies and within the industry, I concluded that there had been a decided change in government agencies, particularly in the U. S. Forest Service in California.

The agency had shifted from hiring professional foresters to hiring specialists schooled in various disciplines. Additionally, their management objectives had changed as well. The bureaucracy had changed from a "producing" stance to a "planning" or "saving" stance.

Most old foresters, particularly, believed the U. S. Forest Service was a good organization as far as government agencies went. Foresters who were employed there were, for the most part, hard-working and competent. While there was considerable argument and conflict between industrial foresters and government foresters, most was good-natured banter. Serious disagreements were usually settled peacefully.

The Forest Service of today is a different organization. It seems to be managed now by public consensus instead of by professional foresters. The agency is a rudderless vessel being pushed first one way then another by the whims of a fickle populace. Many good employees have taken early retirement and have found other things to do. The morale of those remaining is very, very low. The country has lost something as a result.

Thus, the stories making up this history, as it unfolded, were many and varied. Sometimes they seemed inconsequential and unrelated to the real story of the company's success. However, I thought some of them were important enough to be included, to provide the flavor of the environment in which the workers toiled in the lumber business.

It was difficult to work all of the stories in at the proper times and to show their relationship to the whole. Some of the first efforts were failures, and perhaps the final story will be confusing to many. I was a forester, not a historian nor an author. I spent my adult life in the woods cruising and appraising timber and timberlands, buying logs and timber, contracting logging and road construction, and doing all the things private industry foresters do.

I derived great satisfaction in doing all of these things. I watched the raw materials I procured being delivered to the various sawmills, and knew that the people who worked in the mills depended upon those logs for their livelihood. More important, however, was the knowledge that those raw logs were being turned into products that the citizens of the country could hardly do without.

During the many years spent in the timber industry, I came across many unique and caring individuals, some coarse and some refined, some educated and some not. Most could be described as "real" people, pridefully doing the work they loved. They were, almost without exception, hard-working and committed.

This story will concentrate on the forestry side of the company. Thus, the manufacturing arm of Sierra Pacific Industries will not be given the emphasis it deserves. This is not meant to demean other parts of the business as less important than forestry, but it will provide me a degree of comfort in discussing those things about which I know a little, versus those things about which I know virtually nothing.

The reader must understand that "real foresters" love the woods. They can tolerate sawmills, plywood plants, and remanufacturing plants only because they are a necessary part of the timber industry. Such facilities are noisy, dirty, and often run by individuals who love them. So be it; those individuals, almost without exception, are the salt of the earth. But to a forester, the real timber industry begins in the woods, and is

the woods. The rest of the process is only the frosting on the cake, albeit a necessary part of the whole.

In the forty odd years I spent doing the things that foresters enjoy, I never regretted choosing forestry as a profession until the closing years of the 1980s. It became clear to me that during the 1970s, the leaders in the timber industry had lost touch with reality. The system of turning a raw material into various products that were essential to the citizens' life and comfort was coming increasingly under attack by various individuals and organizations. To most of the industry's leaders, it was business as usual. They were having too much fun making lumber or plywood out of logs, or logs out of trees, to believe the environmentalists would seriously threaten them.

The forester was the first to feel the pressures of their attacks; but his voice became only a whisper in the winds of change that were about to engulf the industry. The Chief Executive Officers (CEOs) of the companies were not listening or, most likely, were too far away from the issues to realize the gravity of the peril they faced. Most were optimists who could not fathom the fact that their industry was in real danger. They had faced many serious threats before and something had always come along to bail them out. But this time would be different.

Many foresters became politicians. They began to spend more time fighting those who were trying to kill the industry. Some became the boy in the theater crying "fire," but no one paid any attention. Thus, many foresters who loved the woods could find no time in which to do the things they loved. Those who were able to do so, quit their jobs and went on to other pursuits. Some are still in the trenches fighting a losing battle. They deserve our deepest respect.

A history of Sierra Pacific Industries must show that the company has always made the best of any adversity. In fact, it has prospered when others in the industry were in decline. It will be interesting to watch the evolution of the company as it attempts to operate in the business climate that now infests California and the nation.

My first impression of the company was

gained as a competitor for timber when I worked for DiGiorgio Corporation. Sierra Pacific Industries was then a publicly-owned company. At that time, it was known as an outfit which had to be watched carefully, since it operated barely on the edge of legitimacy. When dealing with it, one needed to keep one's hand on the wallet, and get everything in writing.

Upon closer association with it, I discovered that the reputation was ill-deserved, and stemmed more from a lack of knowledge of it than from shady business practices. The company, and particularly A. A. Emmerson, its CEO, believed in tough, open negotiation. Their people usually knew more about the deal being negotiated than their competitors, and that knowledge gave them an advantage. Those who lost in such negotiations did not take kindly to that fact; thus, the reputation.

It was my good fortune to have been acquired by Sierra Pacific Industries, along with several junk sawmills. It was also my good fortune to become acquainted with R. L. (Dick) Smith, the controller for the company. In a number of conversations, and a good number of arguments, I learned that Dick Smith was a gentleman who had an opinion about everything, even those things about which he knew nothing. However, Dick had an extremely quick mind and was committed to making the company a legitimate member of the business community. While there never was a conspiracy, or a definite plan to do this

together, there was an implied understanding, on my part perhaps, that the two of us would attempt to change this image of a high-flying company for the better. We worked at this project diligently.

As time went on, the company changed tremendously. It became too big for one man to manage by himself, and it matured to become the premier lumber producer in California. Many people, including the author, grew with it.

As this occurred, there was a subtle change taking place in management philosophy. Whereas before emphasis was placed on the manufacturing facilities, now the emphasis was being placed on the acquisition and management of timberlands. This did not always set well with those within the company who were in charge of those facilities. It is to the credit of A. A. Emmerson that, even though he loved sawmills more than almost anything, he became aware of the changes taking place, and the need to secure an adequate timber supply.

With these points in mind, the reader is requested to think charitably about the efforts of an amateur involved in the task of recording information about a unique company and some unique individuals. The experiences gained in working for Sierra Pacific Industries were invaluable and rewarding. The associations and acquaintances developed within the company, and within the industry, are valued, and sorely missed.

PROLOGUE

Sierra Pacific Industries, SPI, was eventually to be the largest lumber producer in California, and one of the largest in North America. In some respects, the story illustrates how one lumber company responded to some important issues that affected the whole lumber industry during the past 80 years. Its owner in later years, A. A. Emmerson, became one of the industry's leaders.

The story began in the first part of this century when a segment of the Emmerson family moved from the Lake States to the Pacific Northwest. By the early 1990s (some 80 years later), the descendants owned a company with nine sawmills, four millwork plants, and nearly three-quarters-of-a-million acres of timberland, all in northern California.

At one time, shares of the company were traded on the American Stock Exchange. Whether the company was public or private made no difference in one respect — a principal owner was always named Emmerson. Raleigh Humes Emmerson was considered to be the founder, although his father George had owned a sawmill. Raleigh had two brothers of which one, Chet, would also spend much of his life in the sawmill business.

Raleigh's son, Archie Aldis, was the person who later took over a faltering business from his father and made it what it is today. Along the way, a number of people became associated with the younger Emmerson, and contributed to the success of the company.

This story is about some of them.

The founding of such a company, and its success story, probably could not be repeated today. There were several elements that had to come together at the proper time and in the proper sequence for things to turn out the way they did. Although a certain amount of luck was necessary, it was hard work, tenacity, and the willingness to assume risks that were the principal ingredients in the recipe for success.

One of the first ingredients that was present at the outset of the Emmersons' endeavors was the climate, both economic and political. For example, when Raleigh began in the business, his father George had already begun a small sawmill operation. George was probably forced into this venture because of economic conditions and the need to support his family. Timber to saw was readily available on his own farm, and permits and lengthy reports were not required for entering the business. Political forces had not yet begun to deter business activity.

A will to work extremely hard and a small amount of capital was needed at that time. To enter the mill business today would still require a considerable amount of the former, but far more of the latter.

Also at the time, there were countless people who were able and willing to work. Indeed, they had to work or starve, as they did not have the opportunity to live on unemployment insurance benefits or welfare. That is not the case today.

The tax climate was totally different when Raleigh Emmerson began his climb to the top. He and his company got to keep a far larger percentage of their income than they would be able to keep today. Both real property taxes, and income taxes, were far less (or nonexistent) when measured as a percentage of their gross income. The economic incentive was there for anyone committed to succeed and willing to risk everything to do so.

People who were in the timber industry in the earlier years, even up into the 1960s, were usually recognized as legitimate entrepreneurs and good citizens. They provided for their employees and their families, and contributed to their communities in numerous ways. Today they are erroneously portrayed by many as rapers of the land who are interested only in profits.

Thus, today there is less incentive to do what Raleigh and his son Aldis did. Economic rewards are less, social acceptance is limited, and it is difficult to find committed employees who will work hard enough to help owners succeed. Such employees would be required to work almost as hard as the Emmersons did; and their numbers are limited.

The ingredients mentioned above provided the Emmersons' "luck." A certain amount of luck was indeed necessary; but in some respects the Emmersons made their own luck through their ability to recognize opportunities and to adapt to change.

At the turn of the century, the lumber industry was centered in the Lake States where the most valuable species being utilized was Eastern White pine. Lumber production had peaked there in 1892 but had begun to decline. The industry was moving south to take advantage of the extensive stands of Southern pines that were available there. Lumber production would peak in the south in 1909.

However, by 1900, lumber was becoming a very important industry in the Pacific Northwest. There, the vast stands of Douglas fir were attracting the lumbermen who had seen the decline of the availability of their raw materials in the Lake States, and those who foresaw the limited supply of pines in the south. They were moving west where the timber stands of Washington and Oregon seemed limitless. The nation was crying for building materials at this time.

There were stands of Ponderosa pine on the eastern side of this region and Douglas fir on the western side. Douglas fir was the most plentiful and would attract the greatest attention from the lumbermen. The other species associated with these two, such as the true firs, would long be considered of only minor importance.

This is the era in which the story begins.

PART ONE

OREGON

(1908-1941)

Raleigh H. Emmerson with draft horses, Barney and Queenie. Location and date of photo are uncertain, estimated to be early 1920s. Photo from A. A. Emmerson.

chapter one

THE BEGINNING

It was the spring of 1908, and George and Ida Emmerson decided to move west. They were leaving Wisconsin to take the long journey to the Oregon country to make a new life for themselves and their family.

At this time, we do not know what prompted their move, nor do we know if George was one of those who made his living in the lumber industry. We do know that he was a good farmer, and it is far more likely that he was heading west to find suitable farming land. The year 1907 was not a good year for the economy in this country, and that also may have contributed to their decision to move.

The family consisted of two boys: Raleigh, the oldest, and Marlin, some six years younger. Marlin at the time of the move was only 13-months-old. The family settled near Newberg, Oregon, where George worked at whatever job he could find to make ends meet. Some seven months after arriving, Ida gave birth to a third son, Chet.

The Emmerson family had roots in Scotland and England. Emmerson (spelled with two m's) was a large clan, and several of them settled around the Newberg area southwest of Portland. Most had come from Wisconsin and Minnesota.

Many married into religious families, and some became members of the Seventh Day Adventist Church. There was a rather large group belonging to this denomination in that part of Oregon. These people were very strict and family-oriented, took care of their children and elderly, and worked very hard to make a living. The church was the center of their existence.

George was a typical father of that era. Stern, broaching no nonsense from his sons, he instilled in them a sense of duty to work to get ahead. He was not a Seventh Day Adventist, but his wife was. His sons learned to be respectful and not to argue with their father. Work was far more important to them than was schooling.

Raleigh, the oldest, did not particularly enjoy school. He was large for his age, and had a quick mind. At an early age, he could do ciphering with no difficulty, and exhibited an aptitude for repairing anything mechanical. He liked to work, but the regimentation of the classroom left him cold. He found himself in a one-room school, which he was to attend for eight years.

When Raleigh finished the eighth grade, his parents decided to send him to the Seventh Day Adventist Academy near Gaston, Oregon. The principal of the school had a reputation for helping students attain their potential. Raleigh was not enchanted with the school, nor the principal. It didn't matter; his parents sent him there anyway.

It was not long before George and Ida got a letter from their son telling them that he wanted to come home; and if they did not

Raleigh H. Emmerson (on left) and his brother Marlin just prior to leaving for Oregon.
Photo taken in New London, Wisconsin, circa 1908.
From Marlin Emmerson collection.

George R. Emmerson and Ida with (from left) sons Marlin, Raleigh and Chet, Yamhill County, Oregon. From Naida Emmerson collection.

consent, he was going to run away. Raleigh's parents talked this development over and decided that their son was, indeed, serious. Besides, George could use help around the place. Ida was selected to bring him home; and Raleigh was delighted to see his mother coming for him with a horse and buggy.

The family spent about two years in Newberg, then moved to a place on Chehalem Mountain. For the next several years, Raleigh was to live and work there with his father. From their place they could see the lights of Hillsboro to the north.

George's father had evidently settled in the same area. We do not know whether he had come to Oregon before George; but we know that George had, with the help of his father, bought 50 acres. The elder Emmerson had also purchased 50 adjoining acres, and the two set out to make a living off the combined farms. This was to be a short-lived partnership, however, for George's father died just a short time later. George and Ida inherited his 50 acres.

Now George had a sizeable tract of land, but no money with which to make payments, or to feed his family. He decided to sell 20 acres to reduce the debt, and to log a little of the timber on the remaining 80 acres. He built a small mill and set it up on the property, logged the timber, and sold the lumber on the open market. Marlin remembers there was "quite a bit of old growth on the property, but there was also a lot of second growth." Practically all of it was Douglas fir.

Raleigh was a welcome addition to the crew. He was home from school, was large and healthy, and liked to work. What more could a father ask?

The other Emmerson sons were still too young to be involved in the budding lumber business. They were going to school and helping their parents around the farm while Raleigh and his father worked in the mill. Much of the logging was done with horses; and Raleigh learned to love the big animals used for skidding the logs to the mill and hauling the lumber to town.

It wasn't long before George had installed a small planing mill alongside the sawmill, and they were selling some of the lumber surfaced. All of it was green, however. Raleigh was working hard and learning the lumber business from the ground up. As he matured, he found that people liked him. He was a big, curly-haired boy who could work most men into the ground. He also found that he did not get along very well with his father.

At the same time, another family was beginning a new life in the West. Chris Aebischer was born in Bern, Switzerland. When he was 12-years-old his mother died, and he was sent to France to live with an uncle. The two of them immigrated to Chicago when Chris was 16.

There he worked for a carpenter as an apprentice, and learned the trade quickly. He was frugal and saved his money. In 1894, he headed west and, with the money he had saved, bought 120 acres on Chehalem Mountain near Sherwood, Oregon.

This homestead was covered with timber, with only an acre or so cleared where the original homesteader had a building site. Chris began to clear the rest of the land and to build a house. Today, that house is listed with the Oregon Historical Society as a Historical Site.

Two years later, he married Emma Birkemeier. The marriage produced eight children; the third oldest was named Emily. The family continued to farm, and Emily remembers that her father was an excellent farmer. Six of the Aebischer children are still living.

Though the Aebischers did not belong to the Seventh Day Adventist Church, they were religious in their own way. The observed Sunday rather than the Saturday Sabbath. Emily's father was also very strict; and the family never missed attending church on Sunday. Their church was the only one in their neighborhood.

As the children matured, the church was the center of their social life. At some point, Emily Aebischer and Raleigh Emmerson met and became friends. Raleigh occasionally would go to the same church where Emily and her family went. Emily thought that the very handsome young man would be just right for her. He worked very hard, seemed to like her, and sometimes went to church.

George R. and Ida Emmerson with (from left) Marlin, Raleigh and Chet in front of house on Chehalem Mountain, Oregon. Dog is unidentified. From Emily Thorpe collection.

Raleigh H. Emmerson and Emily Aebischer on their wedding day in 1923, Yamhill County, Oregon. From Naida Emmerson collection.

They were married in 1923. Soon after the marriage, Raleigh quit going to church. Emily believes that he had gone to church only to be near her. By that time, Raleigh was able to purchase 40 acres from his parents. Raleigh and Emily set out to be farmers.

They grew strawberries and raspberries on the farm, and had a few cows. Raleigh tried very hard to be a good farmer. Emily remembers that he had a great deal of difficulty with this occupation because things did not grow fast enough for him. He was always in a hurry. Then, too, his first love was the sawmill business.

While Raleigh was waiting for crops to grow, he began to log poles. He would buy a patch of timber, move in his equipment (usu-ally horses), log the timber, and sell poles and sawlogs. In the beginning, it was mostly second-growth Douglas fir that he logged, and there were more poles than sawlogs. His father helped with the selling of the poles on the first purchase, but did not finance the purchase of the timber. Raleigh and Emily used the income from these operations to make payments on the farm.

Raleigh was impatient. He began to think the lumber business was the best place for him to make a decent living. He never did wish to work for someone else; he wanted his own business. He had learned how sawmills worked while working for his father. It was time for him to try to be a lumberman on his own.

```
--------------------------------------------------------------------------------
   (31469)        O. B. RIPPEY ET. AL. TO GEORGE R. & IDA EMMERSON    WARRANTY DEED
--------------------------------------------------------------------------------
  KNOW ALL MEN BY THESE PRESENTS, That O. B. Rippey, Widower & single, of Portland,
Oregon, and A. O. Smith and Orelia Smith, his wife, of Omaha, State of Nebraska, in
consideration of Ten ($10.00) Dollars, and other valuabe consideration, to us paid by
George R. Emmerson and Ida Emmerson, his wife, of Oregon, State of Oregon, have bargain-
ed and sold, and by these presents do grant, bargain, sell and convey unto said George
R. Emmerson and Ida Emmerson, husband and wife, their heirs and assigns, all the
following bounded and described real property, situated in the County of Yamhill and
State of Oregon: and more particularly described as follows to-wit:

  The South East quarter of the North West quarter of Section ten (10) Township No.
two (2) South of Range four (4) West of W. M. containing 40 acres,

together with all and singular the tenements, hereditaments and appurtenances thereto
belonging or in anywise appertaining, and also all our estate, right, title and interest
in and to the same, including dower and claim of dower.
  TO HAVE AND TO HOLD, the above described and granted premises unto the said George
R. Emmerson and Ida Emmerson, their heirs and assigns forever. And O. B. Rippey and
A. O. Smith, said grantors above named do covenant to and with George R. Emmerson and
Ida Emmerson, the above named grantees, their heirs and assigns that we are lawfully
seized in fee simple of the above granted premises, that the above granted premises are
free from all incumbrances, and that we will and our heirs, executors and administrators,
shall warrant and forever defend the above granted premises, and every part and parcel
thereof, against the lawful claims and demands of all persons whomsoever.
  IN WITNESS WHEREOF, we the grantors above named, have hereunto set our hands and seals
this 14" day of April, 1923.
Executed in the presence of
        Caroline Leth      ) as to A.O. and      A. O. Smith        (Seal)
        W. L. Idell        ) Orelia Smith         Orelia Smith       (Seal)
        John T. Whalley    ) as to signature     O. B.Rippey        (Seal)
        E. H. Horner       ) of O. B. Rippey
```

Warranty deed for forty acres in Yamhill County, Oregon in 1923. One of the first land transactions appearing on the public record involving George and Ida Emmerson.

chapter two

RALEIGH'S FIRST SAWMILL

Raleigh's first sawmill was built from used machinery. It is probable that some of this came from his father's stash of spare parts and junk. Every sawmill to this day has a "junkyard" connected with it. Used parts, scrap steel, chain, shafting and assorted machinery are stored there. Most of the machinery found in the piles has been cannibalized for usable parts. Most sawmill owners hate to get rid of anything faintly resembling something they might need in the future; and over the years, rust and weeds invade the storage yard.

No one knows for sure where Raleigh got the parts for his first mill. Emily remembers a place in Portland called Front Street where she believes he went to obtain used parts and machinery. Chet remembers the area not only as a street but as a district. Used parts and supplies could be purchased there, and "things that the ladies would not approve of." The latter could be anything from drinking establishments and cardrooms to whorehouses. Raleigh knew his way around there, and knew where to go to find what he needed to keep the mill running.

He began to cut railroad ties in his mill on Chehalem Mountain. Such mills are simple operations, usually consisting of a circle saw powered by a used automobile engine. In the old days, logs suitable for cutting ties were usually small. They could be bucked into the required lengths by hand, although later models used a powered bucking saw. The tie "bolts" could be loaded on the carriage and turned by hand. Work was strenuous and dangerous.

Waste from the operation (sawdust and slabs) was usually run out a conveyor and dumped over the end. In many cases, the mill was situated on the edge of a draw or on the side of a hill to facilitate getting rid of the debris. This pile was rarely burned on purpose, although there were frequent fires that would ignite either slab pile, or mill, or both. It is doubtful that Raleigh's first mill consisted of more than the bare essentials.

The operations were highly portable. There were usually no buildings of any permanence. A makeshift roof usually was constructed to shelter part of the crew from the rainy season, but even that was not common. In many cases, there was no crew.

The Oregon woods were full of similar operations, where for many years the forest echoed with the sound of unmuffled automobile engines. In later years the engines became noisier with the advent of the two-cycle diesel engine. These could be heard for miles, and indicated that a more sophisticated mill than those built in the '20s was running.

Raleigh would do what many of the small mill owners did in those days. He would negotiate a price for a patch of timber that was suitable for his mill, then make a down payment, and pay the remainder as the lumber was cut and sold. Of course, that required a certain amount of negotiating skill, and a reputation for paying bills on time. Reputations for shady dealings travelled far and fast.

The Emmersons had developed a reputation for paying promptly, and of doing what they said they were going to do. Raleigh was able to trade on his father's reputation; and he did so from time to time. The attention to business, and his integrity, would be put to good use in the years ahead.

Emily was seldom able to visit the sawmill operations since, in many cases, they were past the end of a road suitable for travel by automobile. During the winters, the walk to the mill seemed especially long.

They had an old Model T Ford with no fenders that they called "The Bug." Emily had learned to drive this machine. It had the seat lowered onto the frame, and she was able to reach the pedals from this lowered perch. Raleigh hated to see her drive it since the brakes were not very good.

Emily says that none of Raleigh's vehicles had good brakes. Of course, the brakes of that day were mechanical, and none were ever very good; but Raleigh's were worse than most. She attributes this to his penchant for always being in a hurry and driving fast. Brakes on vehicles were not important to him, as his priorities lay in getting places fast, and in keeping sawmill machinery, not cars, repaired.

As time went on, Raleigh was gone from home quite a lot. The mill was eventually modified to cut more timber in less time, and could be moved from one timber patch to another. He would move it wherever he could find timber available. He was home as often as possible, since he hated to leave Emily alone at night.

Emily thinks today that he was almost "over-protective;" he worried too much about her. He was working so hard that they gradually slipped out of the habit of going to church. Raleigh usually found something that had to be done around their place on Sunday, or he had to go to see "a man about business." He would take Emily with him on those occasions.

Raleigh's priorities were being set, and Emily soon found that sawdust was in the Emmerson's blood.

chapter three

ADVERSITY

Raleigh and Emily had their first child, Margaret, on December 19, 1924. Raleigh's grandmother was named Margaret Humes, and the new little girl was named after her. Raleigh had moved the mill to a timber stand some distance from their place on Chehalem Mountain, and now he had additional family responsibilities.

By that time, they were really not working the farm very much. Emily had a big garden, and it "was a good one." She would spend a lot of time there while Raleigh was tending to the mill business. She was very busy with the new baby and the garden, canning what she could for the long winter ahead.

Afterwards, she was always thankful for that garden because disaster struck. The mill that Raleigh had built and improved caught fire and burned. There was not much they could do to save it; and there was not much left when the fire was out. Both of them were stricken with grief and concern. Their fledgling business had gone up in smoke, and they had a little one to care for.

Emily is not sure of the exact location of that mill. She knows that it was on Chehalem Mountain. She describes the area as more of a series of ridges than a single mountain, with valleys and meadows in between. They lived on one part of it, and the mill was situated on another part.

Raleigh salvaged what he could from the fire and took off for Front Street. It is not recorded whether he stopped at one of the saloons to calm his nerves or to plan his strategy. Emily thinks that, since he was so committed to the mill business, he did not have time to waste drinking. Few would have blamed him if he had.

In later years, Raleigh said that he never had a drink before he was 26 years old. With his religious background, stern father, and family orientation, that is probably so. However, those who knew him in later years find it hard to believe.

Somehow, he made arrangements to secure the necessary used parts and machinery, and began to rebuild the mill. He had become a skilled mechanic by that time, and worked day and night on the project. If he could not find the right part, he made do with something else. He had to make numerous trips to Front Street; but after several weeks the mill was finished.

His father might have helped in securing credit; but Emily does not think so, since Raleigh seldom asked for help. It may have been that Raleigh, having become somewhat cool to his father, never even asked him for help. It did not matter, for they were back in business.

Their second daughter arrived in September of 1926. They named her Bernadine Ruth. By that time, the family had moved to Newberg, Oregon; and Raleigh worked on nearby timber patches. He could drive to the

Raleigh and Emily Emmerson with daughters Margaret (on stool) and Bernadine in 1927, Yamhill County, Oregon.
From Emily Thorpe collection.

mill every day, but was always home at night.

Raleigh finally located a sizeable tract of timber near Carlton, northwest of McMinnville. It was too far to drive from Newberg every day, so the family moved to an apartment in Carlton. Even from there, the mill was difficult to drive to; and Raleigh could make it home only on weekends, and usually once during the middle of the week. Emily remembers that he and one of the employees "batched" at the mill in a "poor kind of shack." He worried about his family living in Carlton without him.

Raleigh was dealing with a lumber company located in Portland at that time. He convinced the company that he was a hard-working individual, and that "he had a wife who did not buy things on credit, or run up big bills." He was able to get an advance payment on lumber as he sawed it. For each lot, the company would advance a percentage of the value; and Emily remembers that it only seemed to be enough to pay the help and expenses. There was precious little left over with which to buy groceries; but it did help through the winter months.

This arrangement permitted him to saw all winter while roads were impassable. The lumber was piled up awaiting the spring thaw that would allow the roads to dry out enough to haul the lumber to market.

By the winter of 1927-28, the mill was somewhat stationary and cutting dimension lumber. It was no longer just a tie mill. It appeared to the Emmersons that business was looking up. The lumber business was good, they had managed to rebuild after surviving the fire, and they were looking forward to continued success.

And then the second disaster struck even more devastatingly than the first. After working nearly all winter, the mill again caught fire. It was a huge fire. Along with the mill, most of the lumber inventory went up in smoke. The mill was so remote that they had no help in fighting the fire; about all they could do was watch it burn.

The Emmersons had no mill, no lumber to show for a whole winter's work, no money, and a debt to be repaid. Things were, indeed, bleak.

As it turned out, the company that had

advanced them money on the lumber inventory had secured insurance on it. Emily does not recall the name of the lender; but she remembers the relief they both felt upon learning that their creditor would be paid off. However, things were still bad. Raleigh had lost everything. He had no mill, and no prospects for securing the necessary funding and machinery to begin again. There was very little they could do to rebuild at that time.

Consequently, Raleigh secured work at a sawmill just outside of Sheridan, Oregon. Emily does not remember the name of the sawmill, but the company was happy with the new employee. Raleigh was a hard worker, knew mill machinery, and he got along well with the other employees. But he was not happy.

The routine bothered him. He was a young man who had owned his own business. He had always been independent, doing things **his** way. At Sheridan, he was just another employee doing what he was told to do. Emily relates that he was very difficult to get along with at that time; and to make matters worse, they lived in a mill shack, and she was again pregnant.

(2467)   G. W. McCLAFLIN ET UX. TO RALEIGH HUMES & EMILY EMMERSON   WARRANTY DEED

THIS INDENTURE WITNESSETH, That we, G. W. McClaflin and Viola M. McClaflin, his wife, for the consideration of the sum of Ten Dollars, to us paid, have bargained and sold, and by these presents do bargain, sell and convey unto Raleigh Humes Emmerson and Emily Emmerson, his wife, the following described premises, all situated in Yamhill County, State of Oregon:

All of Lot Seven of the Jesse Hodson Fruit Land Subdivision and being a part of the Andrew Harvey and wife Donation Land Claim in Township Three South of Range Three West of the Willamette Meridian, as platted and recorded in the office of the Recorder of Conveyances for said County and State, in Book of Town Plats, Volume 1 Page 6.

Also the following described premises: Situate, lying and being in Yamhill County, Oregon, and being a part of the Donation Land Claim of Matthew Hall and Malinda Hall, his wife, Claim No. 72, Notification No. 1775, in Township Three South of Range Three West of the Willamette Meridian in said County and State, and the part thereof hereby conveyed being described as follows:

Beginning at the Southwest corner of that certain tract or parcel of land particularly described in deed made and executed on April 22nd, 1907, by John D. C. Koberg to Catherine Wind of record in the office of the Recorder of Conveyances in and for Yamhill County, Oregon, in Book of Deeds Vol. 51 page 242; running thence East 2.29 chains; thence North Three chains; thence West 2.29 chains to the West line of said tract described in said deed, and thence South Three chains to the place of beginning, and containing .687 of an acre, more or less.

TO HAVE AND TO HOLD the said premises, with their appurtenances, unto the said Raleigh Humes Emmerson and Emily Emmerson, their heirs and assigns forever.

And the said G. W. McClaflin and Viola M. McClaflin do hereby covenant to and with the said Raleigh Humes Emmerson and Emily Emmerson, their heirs and assigns, that they are the owners

Deed to lot in Fruitland Subdivision and .687 acres in Matthew Hall Donation Land Claim sold to George and Ida Emmerson.

chapter four

A Son

The Emmersons stayed at Sheridan only three or four months. Raleigh was not happy; but Emily was more contented than she had been for a long time. They had a steady income and her husband was home every night. They "lived in a shack with four walls that had a good wood stove, and they kept warm." Even though the living conditions were rather grim, she accepted them. There was one problem: Raleigh's paycheck went to pay bills, or was saved. There was no money for anything except the necessities.

Their third child was born on April 10, 1929; this time, a son. They called him Archie Aldis. Emily says that Raleigh picked the name Archie because he liked it. She did not particularly care for it, but she went along, thinking she would get used to it. They eventually called him "Sonny" when he was still little.

Sonny it was, until it was time for him to go to school. At that point, his mother asked him which name he would like to go by. He told her Aldis, and that is the name he used while he was growing up. A few old-timers still remember him as Sonny. Raleigh was not worried about names at that time; he was trying to figure out how to get back into the lumber business.

It bears repeating that Raleigh's sawmills were not elaborate installations. If a sawmill similar to the ones he constructed were to be found in operation today, they would be a source of concern for those involved with public safety. There were few safety features included in their design; and unguarded sprockets, chains and conveyors were in abundance.

Since logs are heavy and round, they can roll without warning, crushing whatever is in their path. Lumber piles or heavy timbers can cause serious injury to those who are careless or inexperienced in working around them. By the time Aldis was born, Raleigh was an experienced sawmill man. He knew what he was doing, and he believed he could build a better mill than those he had lost.

He built another mill from the usual sources of parts and junk that he always returned to when he needed something for a mill. He had found another patch of timber, not too far from Newberg, where he began to erect the mill. We do not know where he got financing for the venture; some of it, no doubt, came from the wages Emily had stashed away while they lived at Sheridan. A good portion was probably borrowed.

In the latter part of 1929, the Emmersons moved back to Newberg. Margaret was nearly five. Raleigh's mill was bringing in a little money, so they moved into a comfortable home on Cherry Street. Since his mill was not too far away, he could drive there every day.

But Raleigh had bigger ideas. He had always wanted to have a sawmill located where there was easy access to the railroad. He had

Archie Aldis Emmerson in late 1929.
From Emily Thorpe collection.

Marlin Emmerson's donkey near Oregon City, Oregon, circa 1935. Although the little boy is unidentified, he very much resembles Aldis.
From Marlin Emmerson collection.

found a good location for such an operation close to Newberg, and he wanted to get started. He began to plan for a mill at Springbrook.

He enlisted his brother Chet's help in the venture. With the Emmersons' reputation, by then well-known in the area, they were able to secure the necessary financing. While it was still built largely with used parts and re-conditioned machinery, it **was** located on the railroad where they could load lumber on freight cars. Logs would be trucked to the mill. This turned out to be a substantial operation that could not be picked up and moved.

As construction progressed, they continued to scrounge used machinery, parts, lumber and funds. They borrowed money against the inventory even before they were in production. Raleigh was often back on Front Street putting deals together.

Chet had followed in Raleigh's footsteps, working for their father. Several years younger than Raleigh, he was far more easygoing. He put up with the elder Emmerson longer than Raleigh had, had owned his own sawmill, and saved a little money. He and Raleigh became partners in the Springbrook mill. Chet moved in with the Emmersons on Cherry Street.

Even though Raleigh's other brother Marlin was older than Chet, he had not been as involved in the family lumber businesses. He describes himself today as mentally and physically lazy; but perhaps this was in comparing himself to Raleigh. Marlin can remember visiting the Springbrook operation only once.

Emily and Marlin do not remember if George, Raleigh's father, was a partner in the Springbrook mill. Both think not. It is possible that George had some money invested in the mill, but it would have been a loan. Raleigh was definitely the principal partner in the venture.

Emily recalls that George Emmerson may have wished to go into business with Raleigh, but the son did not think this a good idea. The two just did not have the same ideas about conducting a business. Raleigh had very defi-

Deed to
lots in Home Acres
Subdivision, Newberg,
Oregon, 1932.

```
- - - - - - - - - - - - - - - - - - - - - - - - - - - - - - - - - - - - - -
(28376)        B. F. HAWLEY, ET UX   TO    R. H. & EMILY EMMERSON      W. DEED
- - - - - - - - - - - - - - - - - - - - - - - - - - - - - - - - - - - - - -
    THIS INDENTURE WITNESSETH, that we, B. F. Hawley and Mary E. Hawley, his wife, for the
consideration of the sum of Ten DOLLARS, to us paid, have bargained and sold, and by these
presents do bargain, sell and convey unto R. H. Emmerson and Emily Emmerson, his wife, the
following described premises, to-wit:
    Tracts numbered Five and Fifteen, in Home Acres, a Subdivision of a part of the Donation
Land Claim of David Ramsey and wife, in Yamhill County, Oregon, according to the plat of said
Subdivision recorded and now of record in the office of the County Clerk, for Yamhill County,
Oregon.
    TO HAVE AND TO HOLD the said premises, with their appurtenances, unto the said R. H.
Emmerson and Emily Emmerson, their heirs and assigns forever.
    And the said B. F. Hawley and Mary E. Hawley do hereby covenant to and with the said R.H.
Emmerson and Emily Emmerson, their heirs and assigns that they are the owners in fee simple
of said premises; that they are free from all incumbrances, and that they will warrant and
defend the same from all lawful claims whatsoever.
    IN WITNESS WHEREOF, We have hereunto set our hands and seals this 27th day of September,
A. D., 1932.
Done in the presence of
    R. H. C. Bennett                                   B. F. Hawley          (Seal)
    Dorothy Chenevert          50¢ Revenue             Mary E. Hawley        (Seal)
                               Stamp cancelled.
                        ACKNOWLEDGEMENT

STATE OF OREGON,    )
                    )  ss.
County of Yamhill   )
    On this 27th day of September A. D., 1932, personally came before me, a Notary Public in
and for said County and State, the within named B. F. Hawley to me personally known to be the
identical persons described in and who executed the within instrument, and acknowledged to
me that they executed the same freely for the uses and purposes therein named.
    WITNESS my hand and Notarial Seal this 27th day of September 1932

        (Notary Seal)                          Dorothy Chenevert.
                                               Notary Public for Oregon
                                               My commission expires: April 9, 1933

STATE OF OREGON,    )
                    )  ss.
County of Yamhill   )
    BE IT REMEMBERED, That on this 5th day of October A. D. 1932, before me, a Notary Public
in and for said County and State, personally appeared the within named Mary E. Hawley who is
known to me to be the identical individual described in and who executed the within instrument,
and acknowledged to me that she executed the same freely and voluntarily.
```

nite ideas; and he did not think that he could work with his father very long.

The Springbrook mill was moderately successful. All of Raleigh's ventures had been underfinanced, and he always plowed every nickel back into the business. Springbrook was no different. While the operation made more money, it took more money to make it go. It seemed to Emily the pattern would never change; the family always lived on a shoestring. Emily was finding that hard to accept, because she had three children to raise, and their needs were increasing.

She wanted the children to get out more often, especially Margaret. Emily would take all three of them to church on Sunday; but Raleigh objected to that. Instead, he would take them to church on Saturday unless he had work to do. Eventually, he got too busy to even do that, so Emily continued to take the children to the Seventh Day Adventist Church. Raleigh saw to it they always had

transportation since it was too far to carry a baby and walk.

Ida, Raleigh's mother, must have had some influence on him. He wanted his family to be raised as Adventists. He also insisted that the children go to "church school." The current Emmerson family finds it hard to believe that Raleigh would take the children to church; but Emily stands by her account. Of course, there were good Christian relatives close by who might have thought ill of Raleigh had his family not gone to church. Perhaps it was their influence that put pressure on him to see that his family had the opportunity to attend services.

When Aldis was two, he would go to "Sunday School" with his mother. She discovered that he had a quick mind and a long memory. Even though he had not yet learned to read, he remembered the lessons that were being taught there. He could recite the answers from memory.

Meanwhile, things were not going well for the mill at Springbrook. The Great Depression was approaching, but no one knew that at the time. Lumber prices began to drop, slowly at first, then accelerating downward.

The Emmersons tried to keep the mill running, but it was losing money. Day after day, it was the same old story. Not only were prices at rock-bottom, in most cases there were no orders. No one was interested in building, so no one was interested in buying lumber. Other mills were shutting their doors, but the Springbrook mill hung on.

Finally the mill could not be kept at full production. The Emmersons spent many sleepless nights discussing strategy for mini-mizing their losses, trying to figure out how to keep things going on a reduced schedule. Perhaps there was a way to run on shorter shifts; they were already running only one shift. There was no way they could see to re-duce the size of the crew; it was just large enough to run the machinery.

Nothing seemed to make sense to them; they struggled along for a time, but finally had to give up. They thought afterwards that they had kept the mill open too long, and could have salvaged more by shutting down sooner.

One can imagine the discouragement that Raleigh and Emily felt. They had survived two disastrous fires, had lived a precarious exist-ence for several years believing that they had a chance to be successful, and now the dream was shattered for good. In addition, they had three children to care for.

They found enough money to purchase an acre of land near Newberg. Emily calls this "Home Acres," and it seems to have been an early subdivision. They built a garage on it and moved into the garage.

Raleigh had bought some timber in the Milwaukie area, and he became a logger. He logged the timber, dumped the logs into the Willamette River, and rafted them downriver to the mills. The venture went quite well and they were making good money, but he was not in the sawmill business.

Raleigh worked with a crew on the wa-terfront. With saloons close by, there was ample opportunity to have a drink, keep warm and dry on occasion, and swap stories with the crew. He began to run around with them.

Emily would like to forget those times. She says that Raleigh did not lie to her; he told her what was going on. Pressures were continuing to build since it was the early 1930s. The logging job was about over, and there was little money to live on. Those were discouraging times, and Raleigh drifted away. She thinks that at one point he tried to build a mill in the Portland area, but she is not sure. He did not come back to her.

There is no way of telling what was on Raleigh's mind at that time. One part of his life was over. His world, the sawmill business, was no longer available to him. Man, being a creature of habit, finds it very difficult to adapt to change; and Raleigh's life had cer-tainly changed in a few short months. He would **have** to adapt.

Perhaps all of these factors affected Raleigh's perspective. The fact that he was no longer available to be a father to the three children would undoubtedly affect them, and their mother as well. It was up to Emily to keep the family together and to provide for their security. It would take a considerable amount of mental toughness on her part to take on the job. She had no choice but to ac-cept the responsibility.

The children were growing up; and it ap-peared to Emily that her world had come to an end. There were many people facing simi-lar circumstances; but to her, the uncertain-ties seemed enormous. She was lucky to have "family" close by to help weather the storm.

chapter five

UNCLES MARLIN & CHET

Aldis's uncles, Marlin and Chet Emmerson, spent part of their lives in the sawmill business, confirming Emily's suspicion that sawdust was in the Emmersons' blood.

Marlin had left Oregon in 1927 to begin work in a grocery store that was located in Loma Linda, California. This store was owned by one of their relatives. There he met a young lady named Augusta, and they "chased around together" for two years. He could not save enough money to ask her to marry him, so he went back to Oregon. Augusta went on to become a registered nurse.

Back in the Northwest, Marlin, single and with no money, found work as a truck driver delivering vegetables to stores in the Roseburg area. He worked there for about three years, and later went on to become a logger and sawmill owner.

His parents, George and Ida, had by that time "rented" a dairy farm near Coos Bay on what was called "Kentuck Slough." Marlin found work in an alder mill nearby. There he lost a finger to a 60" circle saw. A missing finger was a sort of badge that many lumbermen carried in the early days of the industry. Many times the badge was a missing hand or leg, and Marlin considered himself lucky to have lost only a finger.

He finally built a two-man, portable tie mill. It was constructed on a trailer and could be hauled from site to site. He was following in Raleigh's footsteps, but was never as successful as his big brother. At one time, he had

a mill that employed 20 to 25 men. All of these operations were in Oregon, where he married and had a son, Leroy.

After the Springbrook operation went broke, Chet built a number of sawmills, and worked them in various locations in Oregon. One was at Lincoln City near the coast. At one time, he had a mill in Montana, and Marlin went back there to be the sawyer. They ran mills near White Sulpher Springs and near Bozeman, Montana. Marlin was a part-owner of some of these mills.

Marlin finally sold his interests, moved back to Oregon, and built a motel and grocery store at Rice Hill, north of Roseburg. He married twice, was divorced from each wife, and finally remembered Augusta back in Loma Linda. He found her through school records where Augusta had graduated. In 1983, he married his old sweetheart. Now retired, he lives in Sun City, California, with his new wife.

Chet married Naida in 1946. Raleigh had left Oregon by that time, and neither brother was closely associated with him thereafter. Chet died in 1986, and his widow Naida lives at Myrtle Creek, Oregon. She keeps track of some of the Emmersons, particularly Marlin.

George and Ida Emmerson, who started it all, eventually moved back to Newberg where George passed away in 1946. Ida lived on until 1961. They were hard-working pioneers and, to the end, were proud of their three sons. They had every right to be.

George R. and Ida Emmerson in 1941.
From Naida Emmerson collection.

chapter six

GROWING UP

Raleigh was gone, and Emily was concerned with raising the three children. She was close to her family and friends, and that helped. She was particularly close to Chet and Marlin and their wives. The children were reasonably well-behaved and in school. Aldis liked his Uncle Chet very much. Chet became his favorite uncle.

At one time or another, Aldis attended both public and "church" schools, having gone to the first grade at Milwaukee, a public school. Grades two, three and four were spent in the public school at Dundee. In one sense, he was a good student. He was very quick, particularly with numbers; but he did not really apply his energies to school. It seemed to Emily that he had inherited his father's aversion to the classroom, and he hated homework. He was getting poor grades in deportment, a fancy name for behavior in those days.

At one point, when he was in the third grade, she arranged for him to take piano lessons. He didn't take to music any better than he did any other type of school work. He did have a good voice and could carry a tune; but he was too embarrassed to sing where anyone could hear him. She remembers that when he was just big enough to drive a tractor, he would do so at every opportunity. He loved anything mechanical. While driving the noisy machine, he would sing at the top of his voice, believing that no one could hear him

over the roar of the tractor. She, particularly, enjoyed listening to the harmony from the fields.

Emily thinks Aldis was a "better young man than most." She saw how some of the other boys put things over on their parents; and she was sure that Aldis was doing the same thing to her. However, she could never catch him lying, and he always seemed to be very honest. Her friends were always complimenting her on what a fine boy Aldis was. She wishes now that she had complimented him more when he was growing up.

The biggest criticism that Aldis's mother had was his lack of interest in school work. She recounts a day early in his schooling when he came home from school with instructions from his teacher to ask his mother for help. He was having trouble with spelling. She worked with him on three successive evenings. It appeared to her that once he memorized the spelling of a word he never forgot it. His problem was that he hated to study the words. It was too boring, and there were always other things that interested him.

Emily decided that it would be better to have Aldis in a Seventh Day Adventist school. Therefore, grades five, six, seven and eight were spent in "church" schools. Aldis hated this development. The schools were strict and there were no diversions such as sports.

Most youngsters develop a few special

Aldis Emmerson (on fender) and best friend, Willie Rogers. From Emily Thorpe collection.

friends during childhood. Aldis was no different; he developed a special friendship with a boy named Willie Rogers, and they were together constantly. Willie was just the opposite of Aldis. He was slow and deliberate, while Aldis was quick and always on the move.

When Aldis and Willie were in the seventh grade, Elder Rippey was in charge of building a new church not far from the school. He had retired and was working full-time on the construction project. He had taken a particular shine to Aldis because he worked so hard at whatever he did. He enlisted his help at the construction site.

During their lunch hour the two boys would jump on a bicycle and ride double to the new church. They would eat their sandwiches on the way so there would be more time to work when they got there. Elder Rippey would have them help measuring pieces, or steadying them while he sawed. They would run errands and help clean up scraps. He used this time together to talk to the two youngsters about their duties and opportunities. He was a good influence on the two, and Emily was glad that Aldis had an adult male friend.

To make a little extra money, Willie and Aldis would pick berries or other fruit in the summers. Aldis would ride part-way to work with his Uncle Chet, unload his bicycle from the truck, and ride the rest of the way by himself. Willie and Aldis enjoyed working together, and developed fond memories of the times they spent in Oregon. Willie now lives in Canada and the two friends seldom see each other, but they do keep track of what each is doing.

One summer, Aldis, then nine-years-old, picked cherries for Roe Robinson near Dundee, Oregon. Emily was afraid that he would get tired of picking cherries, give up, and get into trouble because there was no adequate adult supervision. She needn't have worried.

She remembers one instance when the group Aldis was with included a Mrs. Silvernail, who had brought her two sons with her. Mrs. Silvernail picked from a ladder, but Aldis and the boys had to climb the tree. Picking there was a lot harder, for the cherries were not as abundant as near the ends of the branches, and the footing was precarious. Aldis was not impressed by the amount of work done by her boys.

At noon, they sat on the grass by the prune drier to eat their lunches. It was a social time, and the group would visit and laugh at the youngsters' antics. They would discuss church activities and local politics. After the noon break, it was time to go back to work. Some of the youngsters would take naps or play with the others. The afternoons could be warm; and on a full stomach, it was harder to work up enthusiasm for the rest of the day's work.

After three days of picking, Emily heard that her Aldis had taken Mrs. Silvernail to task. He told her that she had better teach her sons to work because "if they did not learn to work now, they would never learn to work." He was already committed to spending most of his time working. This was to be the pattern of his life; labor was his hobby.

When Aldis was in the eighth grade, Emily got a job teaching school at Rose Lodge, close to the Oregon coast near Otis Junction. Aldis attended the same school, but did not like this school any better than the others.

In Rose Lodge, Emily met and married Harry Thorpe, who was in the real estate business and a part-time preacher. He was several years older than Emily. The year was 1942.

The school at Rose Lodge burned down before Aldis was out of the eighth grade. The cause was not determined, and Aldis was not accused of setting it afire; but he was glad to see it go up in smoke. That did not solve his school problems though, because he was sent to live with his grandparents at Lafayette to finish school. He spent the last two or three months of the eighth grade at Newberg, riding his bicycle the six or seven miles to school.

The summer after the eighth grade, Aldis went to live with his Uncle Marlin and Aunt Bernice. At the time they owned a stud mill near Rose Lodge, and he pushed logs on the pond and fed the mill. The studs were hauled to McMinnville and were sold green. Aldis was not permitted to work inside the mill since he had just turned 14, and minors could not legally work there. This was his first sawmill job.

Harry and Emily soon bought a farm near Boardman, east of Portland, and they farmed there for a couple of years. By that time, Aldis had entered Laurelwood Academy southwest of Hillsboro near Gaston, and he would work on the farm when he was not in school. Aldis remembers that Harry was not a very good farmer, so Aldis tried to teach him when he came home for the summer vacations.

Aldis tells a story of Harry not being "too ambitious" and his "habit of wasting time." On one occasion they were haying, and had been for several days. The work was hard and the weather was hot. They were almost finished with the job, but the end of the day was fast approaching. If they kept at it, they could finish before dark.

Harry was tired and hungry, and wanted to stop work for the day. Aldis would have none of that. He wanted to finish so they would not have to get the machinery out and waste time for a few hours work the next day. Harry, being the boss, won out; but Aldis never forgot that Harry did not have the commitment to be a good farmer.

Harry's next farm was near Hermiston; and two acres were set aside where Aldis could grow watermelons. Aldis would work on the farm during summer vacations; however, he was having continuing problems with his behavior in school. He especially did not like religion; and would sneak off to attend the movies in Portland whenever he could.

About that time, the Seventh Day Adventist Church was opening a new school at Spangle, Washington (a few miles south of Spokane), and they needed students. The school, named Upper Columbia Academy (UCA), was situated in the rolling hills at the north end of the Washington Palouse region. Aldis was sent there — one of about 200 young men and women. Emily wishes now that he had been left at Laurelwood, because he did not like being so far away from home.

Aldis did not particularly care for this arrangement either, and his deportment did not improve. He was still a hard worker, and could not wait until school was over so that he could go to work and earn a little money. Emily remembers that Harry treated Aldis well, and tried to work with him to teach him how to be a good farmer and citizen. Of course, Aldis and Harry had different definitions of what a "good" farmer was. Aldis now believes that he should have been more receptive to his stepfather's suggestions; but he still remembers him as being somewhat lazy.

Emily remembers Aldis's watermelon patch. While this was **his** patch, his stepfather helped him from time to time, especially when it was time to load them for the trip to town. They would take a truckload and peddle them to stores in the vicinity. Some of them would end up at the church or school, of course. The watermelons that belonged to Aldis provided spending money for him during the next school year, and paid his tuition. Even though it did not amount to a lot of money, Aldis was one of the few youngsters who had any at all. He made the most of it.

He would loan small sums to his friends and classmates. Emily does not think that he charged interest, but he required security for the loan. This was usually in the form of a knife, or marbles, or some other object. The borrower got it back when the loan was repaid. This may have been one of the first pawnshop type operations to take place at a Seventh Day Adventist school.

BUD WAGNER   JEANNINE BOLYARD   ALDIS EMMERSON   AUDREY WAHNER
PAT WAGNER   JOHN NORD   BETTY BLAKE   GLENNA McGEE
RONALD TURNER   WANDA CLYMER   CORINNE PFLUGRAD   BETTY ST. CLAIR
CLAYOMA FINNEY   LUCILLE JAUSSAUD   LaVONNE HENYON   RICHARD MORPHIS

Page from the 1946 yearbook at Upper Columbia Academy in Spangle, Washington, when Aldis, upper right, was a junior.

Aldis became an entrepreneur. Because he was one of the few students who had a driver's license, he was permitted to go into town to pick up supplies for the school. Since he had a little money of his own, he managed to pick up other things as well, and he was soon doing a brisk business in his room.

He somehow acquired a hot plate and began to make hamburgers. He brought sodas from town, as well as tobacco (usually in the form of "snoose"). All of these things (caffeine, beef, and tobacco) were frowned upon by the church. In addition, he was breaking the rule by having a hot plate in his room. He was also learning that each enterprise involved a certain amount of risk.

At the Academy, Aldis was soon the class treasurer. He was learning to handle his own money, as well as some that belonged to others. Emily was proud of her son, but wished that he would spend more time studying. She doesn't think he had time for girls, since he was always working. Girls just took up too much time.

To those who knew him in later life, that may be difficult to accept because he certainly seemed to like girls. Perhaps he **was** putting something over on his mother. One thing is certain; Aldis was turning out to be a worker like his father.

One of the teachers at UCA in Spangle liked Aldis, and he would stand up for him if he got into trouble. The trouble was not usually serious, but he was involved in the kind of mischief active boys usually get into. His biggest problem was his dislike for the religious side of the Seventh Day Adventist community. He had never really accepted their tenets; and that did not set well with the school officials. He appeared to them to be somewhat rebellious and unable to fit into the role of a good Spangle student.

Between his junior and senior years, he went to Omak, Washington, where he worked for Sam Smith, who owned a cattle ranch nearby. He built fences, helped with haying, and did general ranch work. He hated to see the summer end with the prospect of another year at Spangle facing him.

By the time Aldis began his senior year at Upper Columbia Academy, he was practically on his own. He worked full-time on the school

ROSTER

ANDERSON, AGNES	Box 98, Millwood, Washington
ANDERSON, ALICE	520 Alder St., Missoula, Montana
BABCOCK, DONNA	Rt. 5, Box 170, Port Orchard, Washington
BEANE, MARILYN	Box 135, College Place, Washington
BECRAFT, MARGARET	29 E. Palm, College Place, Washington
BENNETT, JEANINE	Freewater, Oregon
BERGMAN, JIM	Viola, Idaho
BERGSTROM, ELEANOR	Lewiston, Idaho
BIGGAR, DONNA MARIE	Rt. 2, Colville, Washington
BISCHOFF, MARVIN	Ruff, Washington
BLACK, JUANITA	Rt. 5, Box 315, San Jose, California
BLAKE, JOSEPHINE	Greenacres, Washington
BLAKE, BETTY	Greenacres, Washington
BOCK, DOUGLAS	Box 1034, College Place, Washington
BOGAR, LORRAINE	Deary, Idaho
BOHLMAN, GLENNA	Hermiston, Oregon
BOICOURT, VERYLE	Marcus, Washington
BOICOURT, GALVIN	Marcus, Washington
BOLYARD, JEANNINE	Rt. 3, Wenatchee, Washington
BOOMER, JOHN	Box 89, College Place, Washington
BOORMAN, JEANICE	Greenacres, Washington
BOWHAY, ALONZO	Box 464, College Place, Washington
BROCK, GEORGE	Pendleton, Oregon
BROMGARD, VERN	Rt. 2, Wapato, Washington
BROWN, WILLIAM	1014 S. W. Fraizer, Pendleton, Oregon
BROWN, FARRELL	Rt. 2 Box 118A, Springfield, Oregon
BROWN, FRANCES	S. 219 Howard, Spokane, Washington
BRINEGAR, DORIS	Edgemere, Idaho
BRUCE, HERBERT	College Place, Washington
BUDD, ORPHEUS	Freewater, Oregon
BURKE, DERALD	418 Church St., Sandpoint, Idaho
BYRD, CHESTER	Tonasket, Washington
CAMERON, DONALD	Washtucna, Washington
CAMERON, DOREEN	Washtucna, Washington
CAMPBELL, STANLEY	Tonasket, Washington
CARMAN, MERLIN	Omak, Washington
CARLSON, RAMONA	214 E. Fourth, Moscow, Idaho
CHURCHMAN, LILA	Box 406, Tonasket, Washington
CHURCHMAN, WANDA	Box 406, Tonasket, Washington
COPPERNOLL, SHIRLEY	Box 1003, Coeur d'Alene, Idaho
CUMMINS, JOYCE	College Place, Washington
DANIELS, THELMA	Rt. 1, Cashmere, Washington
DE FORD, WINTON	502 N. Farr Rd., Opportunity, Washington
DERTING, FAYE	Touchet, Washington
DERTING, AUDREY	Touchet, Washington
DEVEREAUX, ROBERTA	Rt. 3, Yakima, Washington
DORNER, LEE	Rt. 1, Sunnyside, Washington
DRAIN, HALLIE	Priest River, Idaho
DUTCHER, PAT	Rt. 1, Wapato, Washington
EDWARDS, OTTIS	Rt. 1, Prosser, Washington
EMMERSON, ALDIS	
FINNEY, CLAYOMA	1311 Garland, Spokane, Washington
FRANKS, BETTY LOU	617 S. E. 4th St., Pendleton, Oregon
FISHER, MERRIE	Box 200, Washtucna, Washington
FRYMIRE, ZELMA	146 S. W. 20th, Pendleton, Oregon
FIELDER, RUTH	Rt. 2, Box 59A, Pendleton, Oregon

Portion of roster for Upper Columbia Academy, 1946, showing missing address for Aldis Emmerson.

farm and was well liked there because of his work habits. Upon the school's purchase of a new truck, Aldis had even more freedom to go to Spokane. He became the truck driver on a steady basis. His pay had risen to $1.00 per hour; and he paid all of his tuition and expenses for his last year at Spangle. Of course, he was still attending classes on a full-time basis too.

However, he felt inferior at the school. His grades were not good and he had few clothes. He remembers that he had only one sweater to his name and, in cool weather, wore it nearly every day. He was, for all practical purposes, without a home address. Emily was living in Alaska, and Raleigh was in California. The school at Spangle was his address.

Just a couple of months before graduation from UCA, he was in trouble again. This time he coerced one of his classmates into hanging a condom on the school bulletin board. He claimed that it was not blown up, "it was just hanging there, limp." Evidently someone told on them, for that night at about 11:00 P.M. Aldis was hauled out of bed and questioned about his involvement in the affair. He was expelled from school and denied the opportunity to graduate with his class.

There, in the middle of the night, Aldis did a lot of growing up. He did not have a home to go to. He resented the school official who expelled him, and would carry the resentment for the rest of his life. He had only one friend who he could turn to; Bob Christianson, the farm manager. He put in a call to him.

The Christiansons took Aldis into their home. When they moved to Omak a short time later where Bob had secured work at the Columbia Concrete Pipe Co., Aldis went with them. They asked Aldis to stay with them while he finished school.

Bob Christianson was one of the most influential men in Aldis's young life. Ever after, Aldis would remember him as the individual who had kept him out of serious trouble. Aldis never forgot him.

That summer, Aldis resumed working for Sam Smith. He met some of the other ranch hands in the area, many of whom were Native Americans. He began to run around with some of them, learning to have a beer or two on occasion. It was a good thing that the Christiansons were there and able to keep him under control. His life could have taken a bad turn at that critical time.

In the fall, he entered Omak High School and found the studies easier to master than at Spangle. In 1948, he graduated from Omak High, and today claims that it took him five years to get through high school. That was to be his last taste of formal schooling, and he was glad his school years were behind him.

Another important incident occurred at Omak. Sam Smith wanted him to stay at the ranch and share in his ranching business, in effect becoming a sharecropper. Aldis could not be talked into such an arrangement and wanted to leave that part of the country. He had other plans, though at the moment he did not know what they were.

Sam Smith liked this young man, and had given him a nickname which was to be his "official" name for the rest of his life. He would no longer be known as Aldis, nor Archie, both of which he hated. Because of his red hair, he was **Red** Emmerson, and he was about to embark on a distinctive and fruitful life.

chapter seven

OREGON & WASHINGTON REVISITED

In January, 1991, my wife Norma and I travelled to Oregon, to visit some of the places where Raleigh, Emily and their children had lived so long ago. We stayed at Newport and at McMinnville while touring Chehalem Mountain and the surrounding country.

Chehalem Mountain is a long ridge that runs northwest and southeast, perhaps 1200 feet in elevation at the top. At the northwest end a peak, called Bald Mountain, sticks up higher than the rest of the ridge. Off to one side of a grassy area is a small State Park with a few picnic tables scattered in a little patch of Douglas fir timber. The trees appear to be perhaps 100-years-old, and quite tall for ridge top timber.

Off to the southwest, we could look down on the rolling hills of Yamhill County. Young stands of Douglas fir grow on these low hills. On the flatter ground are vineyards, apple and nut orchards, and farm crops. The elevation on the flats is about 200 feet. The soil between the low hills looks black and rich. The hills are not rocky; and as the roads cross from one flat area to another, the cut banks expose deep red soil that resembles high-site timberland on the coast in California. The young growth is tall, thick and straight. Christmas tree plantations are everywhere.

On a day that was cold and sparkling, we shared a bottle of Oregon chardonnay, cheese and crackers, and some pastrami at one of the tables in the park. Through the trees to the

east we could see Mt. Hood, to the northeast Mt. St. Helens, and farther, a big one that I took for Mt. Rainier. Along the spine of Chehalem Mountain runs a good road, paved for part of the way and graveled the rest. Stub roads run off to access homes and small ranches of every description. Those situated on the paved portion to the northwest are expensive homes built to capture the view of the mountains. Those constructed on the lower slopes are more modest.

The timberland is not what I had expected. The ground is not steep when compared to Humboldt County or southern Oregon. Today, it is very accessible, with numerous good roads going in every direction. This is country that had been inhabited for a long time, and is not the deep Oregon woods of long ago. Of course, when Raleigh was running a "brush mill," the roads were dirt or mud, or even nonexistent.

All of the towns that Emily had described were almost within sight of where we sat on Chehalem Mountain. They were not very far apart. At the base of the mountain lies Newberg, a big "small" town with Springbrook a part of it. The railroad runs very close to the high school and, just to the east of the school, is the only location that now appeared to be industrial. The rest is residential, or devoted to small businesses of every description. I did not find any evidence of a sawmill ever having been at Springbrook.

Main building at Laurelwood Academy, Laurelwood, Oregon, January, 1991. Photo by author.

Stand of Douglas fir in state park on Bald Mountain, Oregon, part of Chehalem Mountain. Norma Tomascheski at picnic table setting up lunch, January 1991. Photo by author.

At the foot of the mountain in the other direction (northwest) is Laurelwood. The academy is still there, but has fallen upon difficult times. The buildings and grounds appear to be well-maintained, but quiet. It had been closed for lack of students. Recently some of the alumni have bought it and are trying to reopen it; but currently there are only 15 students. The buildings and grounds are quite attractive, but its heyday is obviously over. A small millwork plant is located adjacent to it where many of the former students used to work while attending the school. At one time over 100 of them worked there.

Farther along to the northwest, perhaps 10 or 12 miles, is Gaston. One of the places that George and Ida Emmerson owned is only a short distance southwest of the little community. They had purchased the 40 acres from O. B. Rippey, a widower, in April of 1923. A big onion field is close-by, filling the air with its pungence. A long blink of the eye and a traveler would miss Gaston altogether.

We looked for Sheridan where Raleigh and Emily had lived in the mill shack, and where Aldis was born. It is another of the nearly identical small towns located ten or so miles from each other. There are signs of shutdown sawmills in many of them, but nothing to distinguish one from the other. Occasionally, there is an operating veneer plant (Boise Cascade has one in Sheridan), or a pole-treating plant operated by one of the larger corporations of today. Nowhere is there evidence that this was timber country. Except for the patches of young growth on the low hills, it could be mistaken for the Napa Valley, or some parts of the mid-west.

Dundee is almost a suburb of Newberg, and Carlton is a cross-roads a few miles north of McMinnville. Again, there is nothing to distinguish them. They all seem so close together that, even in the old days, everyone must have known each other, particularly if they attended one of the many churches that are still scattered across the countryside.

The mill at Rose Lodge where Aldis first pushed logs around on the pond is long gone. A young man who owns a little country market along the highway told me that he knew of someone who might remember where it was. I called the number, but got no answer.

The young man also told me he thought there had been a stud mill a little way up Bear Creek. There was no sign of a mill there, only thick young-growth fir and spruce. This may have been the location where Aldis had his first job in a sawmill.

I found an old-timer, Virgil Herndon of Lincoln City, who remembers the mill that the Emmersons owned near Otis Junction. He is certain that the mill was not a stud mill, but cut random-length lumber. A house now sits on the site of the mill pond, and the rest of the site is occupied by an RV park. Prior to the trailer park, there was a restaurant at that location called Pixie Kitchen.

Herndon remembers that an occasional high tide would stop the operation when the tidewater would back up the Salmon River that runs nearby and flood the mill. He remembers the owner left for Montana when the sawmill was closed. It would appear that this was Marlin's mill where Aldis worked at one time. Today, there is no sign of a mill ever having been there.

We spent a couple of days in the Yamhill County courthouse searching the public records for locations of properties that might give us some feel for the country that the early Emmersons knew. We found a copy of a marriage certificate indicating that Raleigh and Emily were married by Rev. H. E. Abel on September 8, 1923. Their witnesses were Lloyd Bigelow and Esther Abel.

The records also revealed a warranty deed executed by Raleigh Emmerson by which he conveyed to Emily the two lots in Home Acres subdivision on September 10, 1935. The words of the first paragraph are poignant and revealing perhaps. They say that "Raleigh H. Emmerson, of Milwaukie, Oregon, in consideration of Ten Dollars, **love and affection and other valuable considerations,** ($10.00) dollars, to me paid by Emily Emmerson .... do bargain, sell and convey unto said Emily Emmerson" .... the two lots at Home Acres. The words pretty well closed a chapter in the lives of both of them.

Several months later, on Memorial Day, we visited Spangle, Washington to look for the campus of Upper Columbia Academy. It was a sunny, warm day, and the land was greening with new grain just a few inches high. One could see for miles across the rolling hills and, here and there, a buzzard circled in the cloudless sky.

Warranty Deed from Raleigh Emmerson to Emily Emmerson for lots in Home Acres Subdivision, Newberg, Oregon, dated September 10, 1935.

Girls' dormitory at Upper Columbia Academy, Spangle, Washington, in 1991. Photo by author.

The school sits to the east of the old highway, now bypassed by a newer road. Indistinguishable from many others towns nestled in the countryside, Spangle lies within shouting distance of the campus. Perhaps a half-dozen automobiles sat in the parking lot in front of the main building.

A new Seventh Day Adventist church had been built across the road from the school. It was not there when Aldis Emmerson trod the hallways. A few students walked from one building to another, but there did not seem to be much activity anywhere on campus.

Upon entering the Administration building, I could see classes were in session. One of the instructors, Don Perkins, graciously answered my questions and led me to the basement where the "alumni room" was located. We searched for old school records, particularly yearbooks from the 1940s. The one for Aldis's senior year exhibited no sign of Aldis. It was as if he had never been there.

The 1946 yearbook was another matter. It seemed to be a typical record of high school years; and the students pictured in it could have been in any school in the land. Aldis's picture was at the top of one page; on another, the class roster showed he had no home address. His was the only one omitted. I wondered about the apparent insensitivity of those who put the yearbook together.

We stayed long enough to take a few photographs of the campus. The buildings appear to be well maintained and as austere as in the days of old. The grounds are attractive and also show good care. Although it was a school obviously more active than the one at Laurelwood, we wondered about the quietness and the classes being held on Memorial Day.

PART TWO

CALIFORNIA

(1942-1974)

R. H. (Curly) Emmerson in 1941 photo taken at Timberline Lodge, Mt. Hood, Oregon.
Naida Emmerson collection.

chapter eight

CURLY

Information concerning the years immediately after Emily and Raleigh split up is sketchy. It is believed that sometime in 1939, Raleigh had been injured in an accident. Marlin reports that this was an automobile accident, but others say that it was a logging accident. They remember that it was a cable or choker that caught a limb or a sapling and nearly killed Raleigh. This account seems more likely. They also remember that Raleigh's arm was immobilized in a cast that held the arm nearly head high. In later years, this old injury would cause him a great deal of discomfort.

In any event, during his recuperation, he studied to be a "body and fender" man. There is no real evidence that he ever pursued this career seriously, although he may have considered the possibility of doing so. No one could have blamed him if he had left the lumber industry after all the adversity he had endured, and with a life-threatening injury to top it off.

For some time he had known a woman named Myrtle Emmerson who had been married to a distant cousin of his. Naida Emmerson believes Raleigh and Myrtle were married sometime in 1940. Naida says that the Adventist community was a sort of extended family with everyone knowing each other, their problems, and their frailties. She believes that everyone in this "family" got along reasonably well together - even the "exes."

There is stronger evidence that Raleigh married Myrtle in 1942. That is the way the Emmersons of today remember it because it was, in their opinion, the war years when they were married.

About that time, the lumber industry was going through another of its transitions. There were a number of circumstances that were foretelling change. The demand for wood products was increasing at an ever-expanding rate. The exploitation of the great Northwest forests was nearing its zenith, and the lumbermen of the time were looking for raw materials elsewhere.

Many in the environmental community today decry "the good old days" when there were countless small sawmills employing a great number of workers. They cite the decrease in the number of persons employed in the timber industry as evidence that the industry is in decline, and that it is now dominated by huge national firms that have no compassion for the workers. Most of them would recommend a return to the small, inefficient mills that used to be situated behind every stump, or no mills at all, even though today the operations are far more environmentally sound.

The work in the small mills of old was hard and dangerous because there were few

Raleigh Emmerson and Myrtle Emmerson about the time of their marriage in the early 1940s.
From Marlin Emmerson collection.

environmental controls, and few safety precautions were observed. The owner would do much of the work himself. There was, for many years, no workmen's compensation law, nor unemployment insurance. Families of workers did not have health insurance; or if they did, it was not provided by the mill. Most of the people who worked in them were, nevertheless, happy to have a job.

There was an abundance of available timber to supply the mills; and many of the men who built the early operations had only limited education. The lumber business was one of the few ways open to them to escape poverty.

As the industry consolidated, the smaller, inefficient mills were being phased out. The remaining mills were larger and more stable. They utilized a greater portion of the tree and they produced a better product. The days of the "brush mill" were limited.

Times were changing, indeed; and Raleigh Emmerson, recuperating from his injury, was not comfortable observing the industry instead of participating in it. While there were still some portable mills scattered around in the "brush," more and more of them were being crowded out by the better financed operations. Raleigh was looking for something to do.

Sometime during those years, his name became "Curly." No one seems to know who gave it to him. It may be that he gave it to himself, since he did not like his given name at all. He did have curly hair and was a handsome man. The ladies took to him easily, and Curly was a charming individual to be around. From this time on, he would be known as Curly Emmerson.

Somehow he made his way to California. The year was 1942, and there was timber available in Humboldt and Del Norte Counties. There, and in southern Oregon, could be found patches of timber that were available for purchase. A mill could still be set up rather quickly.

Humboldt Bay was the center of the lumber industry in California, and the location of a number of large companies that had been in business for over 50 years. A considerable portion of their production was centered on redwood.

Curly was a "fir" man. He knew and understood this species very well. At that time, the high-grade Douglas fir logs were being utilized by plywood plants. There were several of these in the Humboldt Bay area, and they could pay a lot more for these logs than a sawmill could. Usually the only logs left for a small mill were those rejected by the plywood plants.

However, in those days the plywood plants did not use good #2 grade sawmill logs. They were reaching down into this grade for plywood core stock, but only took the high end of the #2 grade. They called these logs "peelable mill" or "select peelers." The rest of the lower grade logs were left over for people like Curly to make lumber from. Some of them did very well at it.

Curly came to Humboldt County with no money, but with a will to work. He also had a talent for finding timber and for finding people to finance him. No one is sure where his first mill in California was located, nor what he did to survive when he first arrived here.

Audrey Griffith, a long-time employee of the Emmersons, says that Curly told her when he arrived in California he had only one pair of "dress" shoes to his name, and they had holes in both soles covered with cardboard. Others say that when he first got to California, he worked for Lenwood Speier. He had met Speier in Portland and thought he would become a partner in Speier's sawmill business. After working for him for several months, the partnership did not pan out. Curly, on his own, constructed a mill just west of the present Highway 101 near Humboldt Flakeboard.

The story that I have heard several times is that Curly arrived in Crescent City in a beat-up old car that was nearly out of gas. Somehow, he borrowed 50 cents for gasoline to continue his journey to Humboldt Bay. If that is so, it is certain his benefactor was repaid.

Mike Albee, who is a friend of the Emmersons, says Curly told him that when he first came to Humboldt County, he worked

Curly Emmerson with his parents, George and Ida, standing in front of Carson Mansion in Eureka in early 1940s.
From Naida Emmerson collection.

Curly and Myrtle Emmerson, photograph dated July 4, 1944, location unknown.
From Naida Emmerson collection.

equipped sawmill, including:
> *One Caterpillar Diesel power unit*
> *One 42" 3 block carriage Head-rig; two*
> *48" Hoe saws, with arbor and shafting*
> *One 42" 3 saw edger*
> *One gas Caterpillar tractor*
> *One double drum gas donkey with lines*
> *and blocks now in use*

The agreement goes on to state the purchase price was $12,000, with $1 down, and the remainder to be paid in monthly installments of $800 beginning November 5, 1944. The Chiltons also agreed to pay Curly the sum of $5 per thousand board feet (MBF) for all lumber produced, and that this sum would be credited to their total indebtedness of $12,000. Moreover, R. H. Emmerson was to receive an additional $1 per MBF, over and above the purchase price, for all lumber produced by this mill. This arrangement was to continue until the full purchase price was paid.

The sawmill that Curly sold to the Chiltons was situated in Section 35, Township 7 North, Range 4 East, of Humboldt Meridian which would put it a mile or two west of Willow Creek, California.

Of significance here is the fact that R. H. Emmerson had arrived in California in 1942, broke and looking for work. Some two years later, he had acquired and sold a sawmill for $12,000 or more. Of course, we do not know how much he owed on the mill at the time of sale.

The next transaction that appears on the record is the purchase by Curly of the timber on 40 acres owned by Charles and Evelyn Flockhart for the sum of $1,500. This occured on February 26, 1945, and he had three years in which to remove the timber. The property was located just north of Highway 299 near Lord Ellis Summit.

From these records, it appears that Curly Emmerson did not waste any time in getting back into the lumber business once he reached California. There has been no evidence uncovered indicating how he accomplished this feat, nor where the money came from with which he made the acquisitions. It serves as another example of the Emmerson traits of tenacity and ingenuity that would prove to be an important element of their success.

in a body and fender shop on Alliance Road in Arcata. There, in his spare time, he built a portable mill behind the shop. One day a man saw the mill almost finished and asked him what he wanted for it. Curly quoted him a price, and a short time later the man came back with a certified check and hauled it off.

One of Curly's early mills was reported to have been on Bald Mountain (not the more familiar Bald Hills), and it was a tie mill. No one knows for sure what year that mill began production, but it is certain it was the same type mill that Curly had in Oregon. It cut Douglas fir.

Upon searching the public record in Humboldt County, the first recorded document involving Curly that could be found was a Conditional Contract of Sale between R. H. Emmerson, of Arcata, and J. E. and Norman Chilton, of Humboldt County. This instrument indicates that Curly sold the Chiltons a sawmill consisting of the following items:

The various elements constituting an

THIS CONDITIONAL CONTRACT OF SALE made and entered into this 20th. day of September 1944, by and between R. H. Emmerson of Arcata, County of Humboldt, State of California, hereinafter referred to as vendor, and J. E. Chilton and Norman E. Chilton, of the same county and state, hereinafter referred to as vendors.

WITNESSETH:- Vendor hereby agrees to sell to vendees, and vendees agree to purchase from vendor the following described personal property situate in the County of Humboldt, State of California, on land owned by J. E. Chilton and Vernie Chilton, being located on Section 35, Township 7 North of Range 4 East, Humboldt Base and Meridian, and consisting of the following principal items, to-wit:-

The various elements constituting an equiped saw-mill, including, one Caterpillar Diesel power unit (Serial No 2-E-83)

One 42 inch 3 block carriage.

Head-rig-two 48 inch Hoe saws, with arbor and shafting complete;

One 42 inch 3 saw edger;

One gas caterpillar tractor;

One double drum gas donkey with all lines and blocks now in use in connection with the same;

All saw mill equipment now on said premises and used in the operation of said saw mill. for the total purchase price of twelve thousand dollars, lawful money of the United States, and the vendees agree to pay the vendor the said sum at the times hereinafter mentioned and in the following manner, to-wit: One dollar on execution of this conditional contract of sale, the receipt of which is hereby acknowledged; beginning on the 5th, day of November 1944, the sum of eight hundred dollars or more, and in monthly installments thereafter on or before the 5th. day of each and every month the sum of eight hundred dollars or more, until the total purchase price of twelve thousand dollars has been fully paid and satisfied:

It is understood and agreed between the parties hereto, that for each and every one thousand feet of merchantable lumber sawed and produced in the operation of said saw-mill, vendees herein shall pay and account to the vendor the sum of five dollars, said accounting and payment to be during the month said lumber is shipped and invoiced, for all of which payments vendees shall receive credit on the purchase price, and vendor shall have access to all invoices sent through any bank to determine the amount due to him; and it is further agreed that vendees shall account to vendor for all lumber sold by them for local consumption on the same basis on the 5th. and 20th. day of each and every month and shall permit the vendor to inspect their account books to determine the number of thousand feet so sold.

It is agreed between the parties hereto that for all lumber delivered to or invoiced by R. H. Emmerson, Vendor herein, an additional charge of one dollar per thousand feet will be made by said vendor which sum is not to be considered a part of the purchase price herein and shall not be credited on the monthly installment payments provided herein above; and that for all lumber so invoiced through the office of R. H. Emmerson, vendees shall receive full payment for the same according to the market price then prevailing, less the five dollar charge and the one dollar charge for invoicing as stated above.

In addition to the payments regular and otherwise to be made herein, vendees agree to pay all taxes which may hereafter be levied or assessed against the within described property; and to make all payments herein provided promptly and punctually at the times and in the manner provided; and vendees agree that in no instance will they permit any lien for materials furnished or labor rendered or otherwise to be filed;

Witness our hands the date first above written.

R. H. Emmerson   J E Chilton
      Vendor
                                                  N. E. Norman E. Chilton
                                                        Vendees

State of California, (
) S. S.
County of Humboldt.   (

Conditional Contract of Sale for real property and sawmill near Willow Creek, California, dated September 20, 1944.

AGREEMENT FOR SALE OF MERCHANTABLE TIMBER.

THIS AGREEMENT, made the 26th. day of February 1945, at Arcata, County of Humboldt, State of California, by and between Charles E. Flockhart and Evelyn A. Flockhart, owners of the land and timber hereinafter described, referred to herein as first parties, and R. H. Emmerson, of Arcata, hereinafter referred to as second party,

WITNESSETH:

That the first parties in consideration of the covenants and agreements on the part of the second party, to be done, kept, and performed, hereinafter contained, agree to sell and do hereby sell, and the second party agrees to buy and does hereby buy, all merchantable timber on the real property situated in the County of Humboldt, State of California, and more particularly described by metes and bounds as follows, to-wit:-

The southeast quarter of northeast quarter of Section 5, in Township 6, North of Range 5 East of Humboldt Meridian, and including all trees and timber now remaining thereon: and also all the rights of way and other rights thereupon.

for the sum of fifteen hundred ($1500.00) dollars, the receipt of which is hereby acknowledged.

It is further agreed between the parties hereto, that second party herein shall have immediate possession of said described land and shall retain uninterrupted possession of said land for the purpose of felling and removing the timber on said premises until the 26th. day of February 1948, unless second party voluntarily surrenders possession of said property to first parties prior to that date.

It is further agreed between the parties hereto that second party during all times that he is in the exclusive possession of said described premises may at his own expense construct any and all roads on said property as he sees fit for the purpose of hauling and removing logs and timber therefrom; that in the construction of said roads he may at all times use and pass over logging roads situated on adjoining land owned by first parties herein; that said second party at his discretion may construct logging roads on and over adjoining lands belonging to first parties; that second party may use all gravel found on the above described premises in the construction of roads and may likewise make use of all gravel found on adjoining lands now belonging to the first parties.

And it is understood, that the stipulations aforesaid are to apply to and bind the heirs, administrators, executors, and assigns of the respective parties hereto.

IN WITNESS WHEREOF, the parties hereto have executed these presents in duplicate the day and year first above written.

Charles E. Flockhart
Evelyn A. Flockhart
First Parties
R. H. Emmerson
Second Party.

**Agreement for Sale of Timber
dated February 26, 1945.**

chapter nine

GROWTH

The California timber industry, as in the Northwest, was undergoing significant change in the early 1940s. The first Certified Tree Farm was established by Weyerhauser Timber Company in Modoc County in 1942. In 1943, a bill was introduced in the California Senate that prohibited the cutting of any conifer tree less than 18 inches in diameter for conversion to lumber. This was the forerunner of the Forest Practice Act that would regulate the management of private forest lands in the State.

On January 14, 1946, nine major producers of redwood lumber were affected by a strike of union workers (A.F. of L.). The strike was to last more than two years. Lumber production in Humboldt County dropped from 418-million board feet in 1945 to 271-million board feet in 1946 as a result. By 1947, base wages in the industry would raise to $1.25 per hour.

Curly Emmerson was not involved in these labor disputes. He disliked the unions, believing that they promoted inefficiencies and prevented good men from working very hard. He hated the bureaucracy created by the unions, believing it interfered with direct access to his men.

He had always treated his employees well. He usually paid them better than union mills paid their employees. He did not lead his men from the office; he led them by working with them in the mill. As a result, most of his employees developed strong loyalties to him and to the company he owned.

During the time of labor unrest, Curly was busy buying timber and logs. He was running various mills that he owned, the locations of which are difficult to pinpoint at this time.

He undoubtedly purchased several stands of timber in those days, but the pertinent documents may not have been recorded. There is also a strong possibility that many agreements were verbal. During the early days of the lumber industry, this was common. Many old-timers were proud of their reputations for reliability, and of their ability to make a deal involving thousands of dollars that was sealed with nothing more than a handshake.

On May 3, 1946, Raleigh and Myrtle Emmerson deeded to Jalmer Berg 11 parcels of property situated in Humboldt County. Most of these parcels were timberlands located between Arcata and Willow Creek. Some of them were near Brannan Mountain and Three Creeks Summit. Additionally, there were 320 acres near Low Gap Creek just north of Highway 299 and east of Berry Summit, and another 320 acres south of Bald Mountain off the Snow Camp Road. A parcel along the Northwestern Pacific Railroad near Arcata was included in the sale.

Present-day Emmersons remember that Curly had a sawmill at one time located on Bald Mountain. The parcel described previ-

Arcata sawmill where crane was wrecked. Note single-drive truck at brow log, dumping logs in pond. Driver is unidentified. From Naida Emmerson collection (who believes year was about 1944).

Crumpled log crane lying on damaged rails with sawmill building in background. Photo taken at Arcata sawmill, date unknown. The man on crutches is identified by Naida Emmerson as Curly Emmerson. From Naida Emmerson collection.

ously may have been the location of that mill. They also remember that the mill on Bald Mountain was moved to Arcata. It is possible that Curly sold the properties to Jalmer Berg and moved the sawmill machinery to Arcata, although it is unclear if the property along the railroad described herein was at that location.

Berg and Emmerson formed a partnership during that period. We know that such a partnership existed because on May 5, 1947, a bill of sale was recorded by which R. H. Emmerson sold to Emmerson and Berg Lumber Co., "a copartnership consisting of Berg Lumber Co., and R. H. Emmerson," a certain sawmill and sawmill equipment situated near Arcata. At the time, the sawmill was being operated under the name Emmerson Lumber Co.

It is interesting to note that the list of properties sold included the following:

A complete sawmill, including building, machinery and equipment
Log storage pond, machinery, and equipment
A spur railroad track
Various items of office equipment and furniture
Two welding outfits & equipment
A blacksmith outfit
Sundry tools
One Ross lumber carrier

It is believed that this mill was located just south of where the old Highway 299 and Highway 101 intersected north of Arcata.

The November 1947 issue of the *West Coast Lumberman* contained a story titled "California Operator Cutting More by In-Line Sawmilling." There are several pictures accompanying the story, and a notation that the mill was located "just north of Arcata" and "owned by R. H. Emmerson." This was very likely the same mill described in the May 5, 1947 bill of sale, since the stories appearing in the magazines were typically several months late.

The story goes on to say that a "bottleneck" in the trimsaw department was corrected when "he purchased an Allis-Chalmers air gang trimmer, formerly in use at Plant 2, Hammond Lumber Co., Eureka. The trimmer was rebuilt, and is now a 24', 13-saw machine.

Installation of the new trimmer stepped up production about 5M' per day."

The story notes that "lumber is sawed with a double circular head rig of two 48" saws driven by a 125-hp steam engine. Steam is provided by a 250-hp locomotive-type boiler." Emmerson also developed a log turner that "increased the cut about 8M' per day. Friction is used on the log turner, which is also powered with a small steam engine." The article stated the mill employed 16 men and cut "40M' per shift."

At the time of the article, Harry Poff was the sawyer, and Clifford DeMille rode the carriage.

There is an old snapshot showing a substantial mill building in the background. Standing in the foreground on crutches is Curly Emmerson. There is a crumpled log crane that had turned over, ruining the tracks on which it ran. It evidently was used for decking logs, and Curly may have been injured when it went over. No one seems to know what injury Curly sustained. According to the Emmersons, the mill is the same one located near Arcata that Berg and Curly owned. The buildings are difficult to identify, but they very well may be the same buildings with photographs taken from different angles.

Jalmer Berg was a shrewd business man. Francis Mathews, a prominent local attorney, remembers him as a man "who never sold much of anything he ever acquired unless he got a good deal in the bargain." He especially hated to sell timberland. Somehow the two men, Berg and Emmerson, became associated in a number of transactions. There is evidence that Berg had the money, and Curly had the know-how to build and operate sawmills.

On April 10, 1948, the Emmerson and Berg Lumber Co. sawmill was sold to Arcata Timber Products. Included in the sale were a number of parcels of timberland, along with a long list of equipment and rolling stock. Emmerson and Berg took back a first mortgage on all of this property to secure the indebtedness of $917,500. This was to be paid by Arcata Timber Products in annual installments

on or before each of the following dates: October 4, 1948, 1949 and 1950.

Berg and Emmerson still owed money on the timber that went with this mill. They intended to pay off the indebtedness with proceeds from the sale. Arcata Timber Products, the new owner, was a co-op. The timber involved in the transaction was the Stover Ranch, and the Stovers were still owed a considerable sum of money. The co-op was to pay for stumpage as the timber was cut; but Curly and Jalmer Berg were responsible if there was a default on their deal with the Stovers.

In those days, there were a number of co-ops that operated plywood plants. Not many were running sawmills. They were owned by the workers who, in effect, had bought themselves a job when they purchased a share in the company. Each worker usually had one share that entitled him to a job if he wanted it. Some were well managed; but many were run by the workers themselves through an elected board of directors. In many cases, the people elected to the boards had little experience in running any business, much less a sizeable operation like a plywood plant or sawmill.

For some reason, it wasn't long before the co-op was in financial trouble, and they were falling behind in their payments. The operation struggled along for a time, getting farther and father behind. Finally Curly Emmerson and Jalmer Berg repossessed the mill. It was subsequently sold to George Van Vleet who ran it for another three or four years. He finally shut it down and auctioned off the machinery and assets.

At that particular time, Curly was as busy as ever; but much of his time was spent playing, not working. As a result of the sale to the co-op, he had received more money than he had ever had in his whole life. He was beginning to think about getting into the ranching business, a business that had always interested him. He was also drinking more than was good for him.

BILL OF SALE

KNOW ALL MEN BY THESE PRESENTS:

That I, R. H. EMMERSON, of Humboldt County, Californa, do by these presents grant, sell, bargain and convey unto EMMERSON & BERG LUMBER CO, a coparternship consisting of Berg Lumber Company, a Deleware Corporation, and R. H. Emmerson of Arcata, California, the following described person property, to wit:

That certain sawmill and sawmill equipment situated near Arcata, Humboldt County, California, operated under the name and style of Emmerson Lumber Company, including the following:

Log storage pond machinery & equipment

1 complete sawmill, including building, machinery and equipment

1 Spur railroad track

Office furniture and fixtures, as follows:

1 Remington Rand portable adding machine

1 Marchont electric calculator

1 LC Smith typewriter

1 4 drawer steel filing cabinet

1 4 drawer wood filing cabinet

Desks, chairs and sundry furniture

Shop machinery and equipment, as follows:

2 welding outfits & equipment

1 blacksmith outfit

Sundry tools

1 Ross Lumber Carrier

IN WITNESS THEREOF, I have set my hand this 5th day of May, 1947.

R. H. Emmerson

STATE OF CALIFORNIA,)
) SS.
COUNTY OF HUMBOLDT.)

On this 5th day of May, 1947, before me, ARTHUR W. HILL, JR., a Notary Public in and for said county personally appeared R. H. Emmerson known to me to be the person whose name is subscribed to the within instrument, and acknowledged to me that he executed the same.

WITNESS my hand and official seal.

(SEAL)   Arthur W. Hill Jr.

NOTARY PUBLIC in and for the County

of Humboldt, State of California.

4919   Recorded at the request of Hill & Hill May 26th, 1947, at 20 minutes past 12 P. M., in book 7 of Miscellany page 487 Records of the County of Humboldt.

Emma A. Cox, Recorder.

Paid $1.00   By Bernice Starr, Deputy.

Compared: *Pat Bailon* Compared:

Bill of Sale for a sawmill and sawmill equipment from Curly Emmerson to Emmerson & Berg Lumber Co., a copartnership, dated May 5, 1947.

MORTGAGE OF REAL PROPERTY AND
MORTGAGE OF CHATTELS

THIS MORTGAGE made this 10th day of April, 1948, by ARCATA

TIMBER PRODUCTS COMPANY, a corporation, by occupation a business cor-

poration engaged in the manufacture and sale of lumber and lumber

products, MORTGAGOR, and R. H. EMMERSON and JALMER BERG, a copartnership

doing business under the firm name and style of Emmerson & Berg Lumber

Company, of Arcata, Humboldt County, California, MORTGAGEES,

W I T N E S S E T H

That the Mortgagor mortgages to the Mortgagees all of that

certain real and personal property situated in the County of Humboldt,

State of California, described as follows, to wit: ————————————

The east half of the southeast quarter of Section 7;
The north half of the southeast quarter, the southwest quarter
of the southeast quarter, the southeast quarter of the southwest
quarter, and the west half of the southwest quarter of Section 8;
The northwest quarter of Section 17.

The following land in TOWNSHIP 7 NORTH of RANGE 2 EAST,
Humboldt Meridian:
The south half of the southwest quarter of Section 24;
The west half of the northeast quarter, the east half of the
northwest quarter, northwest quarter of the southeast quarter, and
the northeast quarter of the southwest quarter of Section 25.

The following land in TOWNSHIP 7 NORTH of RANGE 4 EAST,
Humboldt Meridian:
The south half of the southwest quarter of Section 26;
The west half of northwest quarter, the northwest quarter of
southwest quarter and the southwest quarter of southeast quarter of
Section 27;
The southwest quarter of the southwest quarter and the north-
east quarter of the southeast quarter and the southwest quarter of
the southeast quarter of Section 28;
The east half of the southeast quarter of Section 29;
The east half of the northwest quarter, the northwest quarter
of the northeast quarter, the northwest quarter of the northwest
quarter, the east half of northeast quarter and the east half of the
southeast quarter of Section 33;
The north half of the northeast quarter, the southeast quarter
of the northeast quarter, the south half of the southwest quarter,
the northeast quarter of the southwest quarter and the southeast
quarter of the northwest quarter of Section 34; and
The west half of the northwest quarter of Section 35.

TRACT C

The following land in TOWNSHIP 11 NORTH of RANGE 1 EAST,
Humboldt Meridian:
Lots 1 and 2, the south half of the northwest quarter and the
east half of the southwest quarter of Section 16.
Excepting therefrom that portion thereof lying within the
boundaries of the mining claim patented to John G. Chapman et al,
by United States by patent dated November 20 1891 and recorded in
Book 14 of Patents page 288.

**Mortgage dated April 10, 1948, from Arcata Timber Products Company to Emmerson & Berg
Lumber Company.**

TRACT D

All timber standing, lying or being on the east half and
the southwest quarter of Section 36, TOWNSHIP 7 NORTH of RANGE 4
EAST, Humboldt Meridian.
Subject to the reservation of all timber standing or remain-
ing on said land after 5 years from November 15-1946, made by
Leonard Ketchum in Agreement made November 15 1946 to R. H. Emmerson.

TRACT E

All timber standing, lying or being on the southeast quarter
of the southwest quarter of Section 31 in TOWNSHIP 5 NORTH of RANGE
4 EAST, Humboldt Meridian.
Subject to the reservation of the timber standing or remaining on said land after 5 years from August 22 1946, made by Leno
Anna Gilmore in deed recorded January 26 1948 to R. H. Emmerson.

TRACT F —

All timber, except tan oak and redwood, standing, lying or
being on the land in TOWNSHIP 3 NORTH of RANGE 2 EAST, Humboldt
Meridian, described as follows:
On the southwest quarter of southwest quarter of Section 2;
The south half of southeast quarter and southeast quarter of
southwest quarter of Section 3;
The northeast quarter, the east half of southeast quarter and
northwest quarter of southeast quarter of Section 10;

3

DESCRIPTION

All that real property situated in the County of Humboldt,

State of California, described as follows:

TRACT A

The following land in TOWNSHIP 8 NORTH of RANGE 3 EAST,
Humboldt Meridian:
Lots 1 and 2, the south half of northwest quarter and the
southwest quarter of Section 2;
Lots 1, 2, 3 and 4, the south half of northwest quarter and
the south half of northeast quarter and the southeast quarter of
Section 3;
The east half of Section 10;
The west half of northeast quarter, the west half of southeast
quarter and Lot 3 and the west half of Section 11;
The northeast quarter of northwest quarter and the west half
of northeast quarter of Section 14.

The following land in TOWNSHIP 9 NORTH of RANGE 3 EAST,
Humboldt Meridian:
The southwest quarter of southwest quarter and the east half
of southwest quarter and the southeast quarter of Section 27;
The southeast quarter of southeast quarter of Section 28;
The east half of Section 33;
All of Section 34.

TRACT B

The following land in TOWNSHIP 5 NORTH of RANGE 3 EAST,
Humboldt Meridian:
Lots 1 and 2, the south half of the northwest quarter, and the
northwest quarter of the southwest quarter of Section 2.

The following land in TOWNSHIP 6 NORTH of RANGE 1 EAST,
Humboldt Meridian:
To find a point of beginning first commence at the northwest
corner of Section 21 in Township 6 North of Range 1 East, Humboldt
Meridian, and run east on the section line 1338 feet and then south
8¼ degrees west 57 feet to a point which is the point of beginning
of the parcel to be herein described. Said point of beginning is on
the west line of the parcel of land heretofore conveyed to James T.
Hemm and wife, by deed recorded January 3 1941 in Book 248 of Deeds
page 243, Humboldt County records;
thence along west line of Hemm parcel south 8¼ degrees west 350
feet to southwest corner thereof;

thence east 1½ rods to the center line of the old Arcata-Scottsville County Road;
thence along same north 27 degrees east 215 feet and north 76 degrees east 208 feet and north 30 degrees 50 minutes east 89 feet to a point that bears south 84 degrees east from the point of beginning;
and thence north 84 degrees west 303 feet to the point of beginning. Containing 1 acre, more or less.

The following land in TOWNSHIP 6 NORTH of RANGE 3 EAST, Humboldt Meridian:
The southwest quarter of the southwest quarter of Section 35.

The following land in TOWNSHIP 6 NORTH of RANGE 4 EAST, Humboldt Meridian:

The west half of southwest quarter of Section 11 except that portion thereof lying east of the County Road.
Subject to the reservation of the timber standing or remaining on said land after 5 years from July 1 1947 and to the covenants and conditions, all as contained in the deed from Luther W. Libley to Emerson & Berg Lumber Co. dated July 1 1947 and recorded March 18 1948, Humboldt County records.

TRACT G

The timber on the following land in TOWNSHIP 4 NORTH of RANGE 1 WEST, Humboldt Meridian:
That portion of the northwest quarter of the southwest quarter of Section 2 that lies south of the gulch which runs easterly through said Subdivision and east of another gulch which runs southerly through said subdivision from its intersection with first mentioned gulch; being the land lying between the gulches named.
That portion of the southwest quarter of the southwest quarter of Section 2 that lies east of the gulch which runs from the north line to the south line of said subdivision.
That portion of the southeast quarter of the southwest quarter of Section 2 that lies west of the gulch running northerly and southerly through the same.
That portion of the southwest quarter of the northeast quarter of the southwest quarter of Section 2 that lies south of the gulch last above referred to.
That portion of the northwest quarter of Section 11 that lies between the two gulches above referred to and running northerly and southerly through said subdivision.
That portion of the east half of the southwest quarter of Section 11 that lies east of the gulch which runs from the north line of said subdivision southerly to the south line thereof except however the portion east of another gulch near the east line of said subdivision intersecting said east line at about 10 chains south from the northeast corner thereof.
Subject to the reservation of all timber standing or remaining on said land after 5 years from July 12 1946 made by Dunn and Robinson in Deed to R. H. Emmerson dated April 1 1948.

TRACT H

PARCEL ONE
Beginning at the quarter section corner in the center of Section 32 in TOWNSHIP 6 NORTH of RANGE 1 EAST, Humboldt Meridian;
running thence along the quarter section line south 89 degrees 59 minutes east 521.2 feet, more or less, to Butcher Slough;
thence northerly following Butcher Slough to a point which is 300 feet due north from said quarter section line;
thence parallel to said quarter section line north 89 degrees 59 minutes west 803.8 feet more or less to the east line of the railroad right of way of the Arcata and Mad River Railroad Company as defined in deed from Elias Sharp dated January 6 1876 and recorded in the office of the County Recorder of Humboldt County in Book W of Deeds page 570;
thence south 23 degrees 45 minutes west 35.6 feet to the north point of the parcel of land conveyed by William N. Campbell to California and Northern Railway Company by deed dated November 1 1901 and recorded in said Recorder's Office in Book 77 of Deeds page 75;
thence along the easterly line of said parcel south 13 degrees 59 minutes west 275.2 feet more or less to the southeast corner of said parcel which corner is situated on the above mentioned quarter section line;
thence south 89 degrees 59 minutes east 303 feet to the point of beginning. Containing 5.63 acres, more or less.

PARCEL TWO

The right for an electric power line, of poles and wires, extending from the north line of above described land north across the next 300 foot strip, and thence northeasterly on a line as near as practicable to the west line of the Axel Anderson tract of land to a connection with power lines in "I" Street near Fourth Street of Arcata; being the same right granted to R. H. Emmerson and Myrtle A. Emmerson, his wife,

by deed from Axel Anderson and wife dated June 18 1946 and recorded in the Recorder's Office of Humboldt County, California on February 13 1947.

PARCEL THREE

Beginning at a point on the westerly line of H Street as produced southerly from the city limits of Arcata where said line intersects or crosses the south line of the southwest quarter of the northeast quarter of Section 32 in Township 6 North of Range 1 East, Humboldt Meridian;

running thence north along said west line of H Street 300 feet; —

thence west along a line parallel with said section line to the east bank of Butchers Slough;

thence southerly following the meanderings of said Slough to said south line of the southwest quarter of the northeast quarter of said section; and

thence east along said line to the point of beginning.

Excepting therefrom the rights, privileges, and easements, deeded by Arthur A. Tomlinson and wife to the City of Arcata by deed recorded August 14 1923 in Book 164 of Deeds page 500, Humboldt County records.

PARCEL FOUR

The right of way to construct, maintain and use a single-track —
railroad spur to connect between the Northwestern Pacific Railroad Company's Main line south of Arcata and the land of grantors situate in the southeast corner of the southeast quarter of the northwest quarter of Section 32 in Township 6 North of Range 1 East, Humboldt Meridian, the route of said spur being set forth in the deed for same executed by Ralph W. Bull and wife to R. H. Emmerson and wife recorded February 13 1947 in Book 5 of Official Records page 110, Humboldt County records.

Also all rights incidental to the use thereof and any and all other rights granted by said deed to the grantors herein, their heirs and assigns.

TRACT I

Beginning at the quarter section corner in the center of Section 32 in TOWNSHIP 6 NORTH of RANGE 1 EAST, Humboldt Meridian;

thence along the quarter section line running east and west through the center of said section north 89 degrees 59 minutes west 295.3 feet to the east line of the railroad right of way conveyed by R. W. —
Bull and wife to R. H. Emmerson and wife by deed recorded in the office of the County Recorder of Humboldt County, California, in Book 5 of Official Records at page 110;

thence following said east line south 11 degrees 33 minutes west 94.7 feet to the intersection of said east line with the east line of the right of way of the Northwestern Pacific Railroad Company;

thence following the east line of said right of way on a curve to —
the left with a radius of 3786.83 feet the chord of which bears south 12 degrees 30 minutes east 109.8 feet to a point which is situated south 200.0 feet and at a right angle from the said quarter section line;

thence parallel to said quarter section line south 89 degrees 59 minutes east 792.0 feet to the center of Butcher Slough;

thence following the center line of said slough north 44 degrees 03 minutes east 172 feet;

thence north 48 degrees 26 minutes west 115.2 feet to the above —
mentioned quarter section line;

thence along said quarter section line north 89 degrees 59 minutes west 535.0 feet to the point of beginning.

TRACT J

Beginning on the east line of the 66 foot right of way strip belonging to Northwestern Pacific Railroad Company at a point 200 feet south from the north line of the northeast quarter of the southwest quarter of Section 32 in Township 6 North of Range 1 East, Humboldt Meridian, said point being the southwest corner of the parcel of land conveyed by Ralph W. Bull and wife to Emmerson and Berg Lumber Co. by

deed dated June 11 1947 and recorded in Book 16 of Official Records page
281, Humboldt County records;
     and running thence southeasterly along the easterly boundary
of said railroad strip on a curve to the left about 1600 feet to
the middle of Butcher Slough;
     thence northerly following the middle of Butcher Slough to a
point 200 feet south of the quarter section line being the southeast
corner of said parcel conveyed to Emmerson and Berg Lumber Co. as
aforesaid;
     thence along the south line of said parcel north 89 degrees 59
minutes west 792 feet to the place of beginning.

- - -

PERSONAL PROPERTY

SAWMILL

1   7 ft. Klamath Ban Head Rig powered by 300 h.p. electric motor
1   6x54 Klamath Edger
1   24 ft. Air Controlled Gang Trimmer
1   60" Screw Block Carriage
1   1200 cu. ft. Ingersoll Rand Air Compressor
1   9" Air Shot Gun Carriage Feed
1   Electric powered Water Spray System for washing logs
1   Electric Automatic Water System Fire Protection
1   54" Yates Resaw complete
1   Yates No. 14 Timber Sizer and 100 h.p. electric motor
1   Ross Carrier Serial No. 875
1   40 ft. Slab and Sawdust Burner
1   Filing Room, equipped with tools and grinders
1   Shop with spare parts and repair equipment for maintenance
1   Log Haul Conveyor
1   Sawdust conveyor - main
1   Sawdust and slab conveyor
1   100 ft. Green Chain
1   Electric Log Unloading Machine
1   Electric Pond Drag Saw
1   Electric 4" Water Pump for pond

TRUCK AND LOGGING EQUIPMENT

		Year	
1	½ ton Chevrolet Pickup Truck	1940	Engine #K 2697990
1	½ ton Ford Pickup Truck	1942	Engine #18-6871974
1	1½ ton Chevrolet Dump Truck	1940	Engine No. T-3220089
1	1½ ton Ford Dump Truck	1938	Engine No. DN-30520
1	3/4 ton International Pickup Truck	1940	Engine No. HD 213D1078
1	2 ton Reo Flat bed Truck		Engine No. 2028894
1	Kenworth Diesel 2-axle drive Truck	1944	Engine No. 44225
1	Fruehauf 2-axle Logging Trailer	1944	" C-9946
1	Kenworth Gas 2-axle drive, Log Truck	1942	Serial No. 51532
1	Frehauf 2-axle Log Trailer	1942	Serial No. C6434
1	M.D. 7 Caterpillar Tractor		Serial No. 7M 5797-SP

   equipped with hyster single drum and cable powered dozer
2   4-speed BU 30F Skagit 3 drum Loading Donkeys with Fair
    leads, sleds, cable and steel roof Serial No. 30-1019 and
    30-1020
1   4-speed BU 30 Skagit 3 drum Loading Donkey equipped with line
    Serial No. MOH 30-1670
1   Carco Logging Arch for D-7 Tractor - Model LS - Serial No. 417
1   Link Belt 3/4 yd. Crawler Track; log loading Crane, equipped
    with two booms; No. K952

With all new and used parts, tires, rigging blocks, guy lines,

shackles, marlin spikes, chockers, climbing gear, fire equipment,

loading tongs and all other tools, equipment and supplies now on

hand for use in connection with said trucks and logging equipment.

As security for the payment of promissory notes of which the following are copies:

$917,500.00   Eureka, California,   April 10th, 1948

ARCATA TIMBER PRODUCTS COMPANY, a Washington Corporation, promises to pay to R. H. EMMERSON and JALMER BERG, a copartnership doing business under the firm name and style of Emmerson & Berg Lumber Company, or order, at Eureka, Humboldt County, California, the principal sum of $917,500.00 in lawful money of the United States with interest thereon in like lawful money from the date - hereof until paid at the rate of four percent per annum, payable currently at the time of the installment payments on the principal as follows:

$305,833.33 or more on or before October 4, 1948,
$305,833.34 or more on or before October 4, 1949, and
$305,833.34 or more on or before October 4, 1950.

Interest shall be payable in addition to the principal sums above set forth, computed upon all balances remaining unpaid. Advance payment of portions or all of the unpaid balance of this note may be made at any time without penalty.

AND the undersigned further agrees that in case of default in the payment of any of said installments in the manner aforesaid, then such installments shall bear interest from the date of maturity until the date of payment at the same rate as the principal sum; and at any time during such default the entire unpaid balance of said principal sum and the interest thereon, shall at the option of the holder of this note be due and payable, of which election notice is hereby expressly waived. In case suit is brought to collect this note or any part thereof the undersigned promises and agrees to pay all costs of said action, including such reasonable sum for attorney fees as may be set by the court.

This note is secured by a mortgage of real property and mortgage of chattels.

                                        ARCATA TIMBER PRODUCTS COMPANY
                                                 a corporation

                                        By____H. J. GOODRICH_____
                                              First Vice-President
         (SEAL)

                                        By____D. W. BURWELL_____
                                              Assistant Secretary-Treasurer

$30,000.00   Eureka, California,   April 10th, 1948

Ninety days after date, for value received, ARCATA TIMBER PRODUCTS COMPANY, a corporation, promises to pay to the order of R. H. EMMERSON and JALMER BERG, a copartnership doing business under the firm name and style of Emmerson & Berg Lumber Company, in Eureka, California, Thirty thousand Dollars, in lawful money of the United States, with interest thereon from date at the rate of four per cent per annum until paid, payable at maturity in like lawful money, and if the interest is not punctually paid it shall become a part of the principal and thereafter bear the same rate of interest as the principal debt, and the whole sum of principal and interest shall be due

D E E D

R. H. EMMERSON, sometimes written Raleigh H. Emmerson, and MYRTLE A. EMMERSON, his wife, hereby grant, sell, bargain, and convey to JALMER BERG, all of that real property situated in the County of Humboldt, State of California, described as follows, to-wit:

PARCEL 1: BEGINNING on the east line of the Northwestern Pacific Railroad right of way (acquired as Eureka and Klamath River Railroad Company, by deed recorded in Book 60 of Deeds page 397) where the same intersects the north line of Section 21, Township 6 North, Range 1 East, Humboldt Meridian; and

running thence southerly along the said right of way line a distance of 400 feet;

thence leaving railroad and running east parallel with the said section line a distance of 300 feet;

thence northerly parallel with said railroad right of way 400 feet to the section line; and

thence west along the section line 300 feet to the point of beginning.

PARCEL 2: The south half of the southwest quarter of Section 24 and the east half of the northwest quarter of Section 25, all in Township 7 North of Range 2 East, Humboldt Base and Meridian containing 160 acres more or less.

PARCEL 3: The West half of the northeast quarter; The northwest quarter of the southeast quarter; and the northeast quarter of the southwest quarter of Section 25, in Township 7 North of range 2 East, Humboldt Meridian;

Containing 160 acres.

PARCEL 4: Lot Number One (1), the South half of the Northwest quarter and the Northwest quarter of the Southwest quarter of Section Two (2), in Township Five North, Range Three East, Humboldt Meridian, in California, containing 156.54 acres.

PARCEL 5: Lot numbered 2 of Section 2 in Township 5 North of Range 3 East and the Southwest quarter of the Southwest quarter of Section 35 in Township 6 North of Range 3 East of Humboldt Meridian, containing 76.59 acres, more or less,

PARCEL 6; The west half of the southwest quarter of Section eight and the east half of the southeast quarter of Section seven in Township Six north of Range four east of Humboldt Meridian in said California, containing one hundred and sixty acres, more or less, according to the Official Plat of the Survey of the said Lands returned to the GENERAL LAND OFFICE By the Surveyor General.

Being the same premises according to Certificate No. 9441 of the UNITED STATES OF AMERICA, given and granted to Ward Richardson, May 16, 1906, under the seal of the General Land Office and signed by T. Roosevelt, the then President of the United States, by F. M. McKean, Secretary.

This conveyance is made subject to all the conditions, reservations and restrictions set forth in said Certificate No. 9441.

PARCEL 7: The southwest quarter of the southwest quarter of Section 28; the east half of the southeast quarter of Section 29; and the northwest quarter of the northwest quarter of

Deed from Curly and Myrtle Emmerson to Jalmer Berg dated May 3, 1946, covering the sale of several parcels of real property in Humboldt County, California.

Section 33, all in Township 7 North, Range 4 East, Humboldt Meridian.

PARCEL 8: The south half of the southwest quarter, the northeast quarter of the southwest quarter, and the southeast quarter of the northwest quarter of Section 34, and the east half of the northeast quarter and the east half of the southeast quarter of Section 33, all in Township 7 North, Range 4 East, in the County of Humboldt, State of California, containing 320 acres more or less.

PARCEL 9: The northwest quarter of Section 17, Township 6 North, Range 4 East, Humboldt Meridian, being the property acquired by grantors from Dake.

PARCEL 10:   The southeast quarter of the southwest quarter and the west half of the southeast quarter and the northeast quarter of the southeast quarter of Section 8, Township 6 north, Range 4 East, Humboldt Base and Meridian, being property acquired from Dunscum.

PARCEL 11: The south half of the southwest quarter of Section 26, and the west half of the northwest quarter of Section 35, Township 7 North, Range 4 East, Humboldt Meridian, being the property acquired by the grantors from Grinsell.

IN WITNESS WHEREOF, the parties have set their hands this 3rd day of May, 1946.

R. H. Emmerson

sometimes written

Raleigh H. Emmerson

Myrtle A. Emmerson

115.50

STATE OF CALIFORNIA,)
)SS.
COUNTY OF HUMBOLDT.)

chapter ten

A Young Man In California

Soon after graduation from Omak High School, Red Emmerson made his way to California. His mother was living in Craig, Alaska, where Harry Thorpe had purchased an old fish cannery, possibly for the real estate. Red's sister Bernadine was with her mother. The other sister, Margaret, was married and living in Portland. Red headed south to be with his father. Curly, his wife Myrtle, and her two children by a previous husband, were living in Arcata.

In 1948, Red arrived in Arcata. He had purchased a 1937 Ford convertible with money he had saved working at Omak. Since they had not built automobiles during World War II, the car "had a lot of miles on the speedometer." He still may have owed money on it when he arrived in Arcata, but he was certainly proud of his machine. It was yellow, and seemed to attract all kinds of attention, especially from unattached young ladies of the day.

The first two nights in California, he stayed with his father and his family at their home on G Street. Curly had not adopted Myrtle's two children, and there seemed to be instant friction between Red, Myrtle and the children. It seemed to Red that he might be the source of irritation, so he quickly found an apartment in Arcata. He had spent a grand total of two nights in his father's house after so many years without him.

He soon found work with Jim Rynearson at Arcata Timber Products (the same mill that Curly had sold to the co-op). Jim had recently graduated from college and was an engineer for the firm. Red liked him, and the two worked well together. Red remembers at one time staking out a new plywood plant while working for Rynearson.

Red and Jim worked together for a short time; but Red soon became disenchanted with the amount of money he was making. He had learned that men made more working on the green chain than he did. It was still 1948, but he could see that he was not doing very well in the lumber business. He decided that this problem deserved critical attention.

He remembers going to the manager of the company, telling him that he would have to quit because of the pay problem, and that those on the green chain made more than he was making. He actually had tears in his eyes because he had never quit a job in his life, and the prospect upset him. He forthwith found himself on the green chain. He worked there for about three weeks.

The company at the time was looking for a ratchet setter. Skilled help is always difficult to find in any sawmill, and it was no different in those days. Red was aware of the job opening, but had no experience on a sawmill carriage.

A ratchet setter was a person who rode on the carriage that holds the log as it moves back and forth against the head-saw. The carriage moved very quickly on the back stroke, and more slowly as the saw bit into the log on the forward stroke. In some mills the saw cut on both the forward and the back strokes, and the carriage moved more slowly. If the carriage drive was a steam shotgun, it moved very quickly, and was similar to the action of a steam catapult on an aircraft carrier.

The ratchet setter responded to signals from the sawyer as to the thickness of cut, when to turn the log, and to operate the "knees" that allowed the log to be positioned in relation to the saw. The two worked as a closely coordinated team, to get the most out of every log. Each was a skilled position; but the ratchet setter rode back and forth all day long on the monster of a machine just inches from the saw. At the end of the day, the ground seemed to continue to move, and the ratchet setter walked like a sailor who still had his sea legs. Today, there are no ratchet setters; the job has been eliminated by automation (automatic set-works).

Red decided that he could handle the task since it paid more than the green chain. He had never ridden a carriage in his life, but had observed many of them. He understood how they worked, and he had never been known to be afraid of taking a chance. **And he was not a quitter.** He asked for the job.

He was given a trial run, and in no time he had mastered the intricacies of ratchet setting. In that job, he learned how the sawyer recognized grade and defect in the logs; and before the summer was over, he was in the "box" running the head rig. He worked there for about five months. Then the mill shut down because of financial problems.

Red next went to work for Precision Lumber Co. that had a mill on Old Arcata Road. It was owned by Bob Halvorsen (75%) and Maurice Thorpe (25%). Red started out riding the carriage as he had at Arcata Timber Products; but in a short time he was doing other jobs as well. Before he was through at Precision Lumber Co., he had mastered every other job in the sawmill. He worked there about eight months, and was learning the intricacies of lumber manufacture.

During this time, he met and worked with a man who he describes as a "confirmed alco-

holic." He was the head millwright, and Red worked for him for a short time. In order to get overtime work, Red was expected to drink with him, and he had to supply his own bottle to boot. Red maintains that he never did get tipsy on the job, and that his bottles lasted a long time since he would pretend to drink but would only swallow a sip. He also believes that this man was one of the best millwrights that he had ever known, and that he learned a great deal from him.

During all that time, he lived by himself in an apartment in Arcata. He would visit with his father often, but their contacts were largely social. Invariably they would discuss sawmilling and their prospects of getting into business together.

Finally, in June of the following year, Curly and Red leased the Olson Mill near Jacoby Creek. It was diesel-powered, cutting primarily young-growth Douglas fir. There was no electricity in the facility. Red sawed, millwrighted, and did every other job required to keep the mill running.

The affiliation was significant. The year was 1949, and a formal partnership was formed from the transaction. The name of the partnership was R. H. Emmerson & Son. It was to endure for a long time.

Production from the mill was about 25 MBF per shift, and it ran only one shift per day. The lumber was custom-surfaced at a planing mill named Arcata Lumber Services, and sold surfaced-green. They ran the mill for little over a year before finding new opportunities in the lumber business.

At the time, Mike Crook owned a sawmill just north of Arcata near the Highway 299 overpass. He had a partner in this venture, and the two were having a serious disagreement. As a result, Mike Crook took over the operation, and hired Curly and Red to run the mill for him.

The company bought open-market logs, not having any timber of its own. Red did not saw in the mill, but he did everything else. He was the "push" that kept everyone working to capacity. That summer, Red and Curly made about $25,000 for some three months work, considered to be big money in those days. The year was 1950.

While they worked there, they were dis-

R. H. Emmerson & Son sawmill shortly after construction. Exact date of photograph is unknown Samoa Road (then called Navy Base Road) crosses bridge at left. At the time, the log pond was a part of Humboldt Bay.
From Lynne Ivey Daugherty collection.

cussing getting into business for themselves rather than working for Mike Crook. They decided to build a planing mill, and selected a location on the Samoa peninsula. The site was nothing but a "mud flat." They purchased a piece of property from A. K. Wilson and started to build the planing mill. Even in the 1950s, there were few permits required, and no red tape to hinder their progress. Red would probably have built without permits anyway, securing them afterwards only if they were demanded by the authorities. They worked very closely with Mike Crook while the building project got underway.

Mike had a son, John, who was away at college at the time. As soon as John gradu-

ated, he went to work for his father running the same mill formerly run by Curly and Red.

When the Emmersons' planing mill was finished, they opened for business. At first, they surfaced mainly redwood lumber. Their specialty was custom surfacing for anyone who needed their services and who could pay their bills. Business was good.

In the spring of 1951, they began to construct a sawmill on the same site as the planing mill. They worked diligently on the project; and by the time November rolled around, they began producing lumber. They owned no timber, and logs were purchased off the open market. That sawmill is still running today at the same location.

In those days, open market logs were rather plentiful. It was not uncommon for mills to post their log prices on a sign at the front gate. Many of them advertised in the local newspapers and quoted prices openly. Logs were bought by grade; and many mills subscribed to a log scaling and grading service operated as a non-profit organization for that purpose. Both buyer and seller of logs paid equally for their services. Of course, some mills did their own scaling; but the sellers of logs seemed to distrust the scale at such locations.

There were many loggers of that era who purchased blocks of timber from ranchers and landowners of every description. There were some government timber sales on which they, as well as mill owners, bid; but there were far more private logs available. The logs produced from these sources were labeled "open-market logs." They were sold to the mill that offered the best price and had the best scale, especially if that mill paid their bills on time.

The operation at the Samoa location did well. The "bugs" had been worked out of the new mill, and the two Emmersons were hard at work. Times in the lumber business were relatively good, and prospects for further growth for R. H. Emmerson & Son were good. Red, by that time, had done every job there was in the mill and he was running the crew. He was the boss when just 22 years old.

Then Red Emmerson got some bad news. The Korean War was in progress, and he was a healthy male of the right age. He was drafted into the U. S. military.

chapter eleven

THE MARINES

It was March of 1952 when Uncle Sam called Red Emmerson to duty. Another young man from the north coast, Mike Albee, was also drafted at the same time. They were soon notified to report to the induction center in the San Francisco Bay Area. Transportation would be provided for them.

Greyhound was on strike at the time, so service was provided by a local bus line. This bus was not quite as nice as those usually provided by Greyhound, but it was adequate to transport a load of inductees to San Francisco.

Some of the men had attended going-away parties in their honor on the day of departure, and were slightly sloshed by the time they boarded. Red was among them. There was a store of Scotch in the back of the bus, and it wasn't long before the driver couldn't hear himself think over the noise.

They headed down Highway 101, and were scheduled to travel most of the night. As usual for the coast, it was raining. By the time the bus got to Leggett Hill, it was snowing hard, and the bus could not make it up the hill. They were all unloaded, and those who were able, had to push the bus over the top.

The first night, they were put up at the YMCA. This was a good chance to party some more, and most of the men took the opportunity to do so. However, Red had done too much partying the day and night before, and he could not make it to the celebration honoring their last night as civilians.

The men had no idea where they were going, nor in which branch of the military they would be assigned. Upon reaching the induction center, they were told to line up. Every third man was picked for the Marines. According to Mike Albee, he and Red Emmerson were two of the 64,000 ever drafted into the Marines.

Marine boot camp was no picnic for either man. Red and Mike had no choice but to behave themselves while they learned to be good Marines. After boot camp, Red was assigned to be a mechanic on tanks, and Mike was to become a PBX operator.

Mike Albee was married, but Red was not. Mike was 24-years-old, and Red was 22. After boot camp, the two were stationed at Camp Pendleton; and Mike brought his wife to Oceanside where they rented an apartment. Red was living on the base in a tent at the time; but two or three nights every week he would get off and stay with the Albees. They were there 15 months.

Mike thought that Red had a funny sense of values. Red had an automobile (an Oldsmobile 88), that he was permitted to keep on the base. He would get a bucket and wash this car himself; he would never pay to put it through a car wash. However, he would send his laundry out instead of washing it himself. Evidently, Red thought more of his automobile than of his laundry.

Red Emmerson (on right) with two Marine friends, 1953. Gordon (Mike) Albee is at center, Marine on left is unidentified.
Photo from Ida Emmerson collection.

Red Emmerson and unidentified Marine buddy in Japan, 1954. Photo from Ida Emmerson.

Mike says that the two friends had some "pretty wild times" together. They did their share of drinking, and one of their favorite haunts was the Ship Ashore in Oceanside. This hangout had the "greatest martinis in the world." Red drank Early Times bourbon, but switched to gin because of the martinis at the Ship Ashore. However, martinis seemed to bother his arthritis so he eventually gravitated to scotch.

Mike and Red were in separate companies, but they were both at Camp Pendleton. Red's company commander was Captain Jack Reed. Mike always thought that the only reason Red was able to make sergeant, and stay a sergeant, was because Reed was a friend of Red and his father. Captain Reed had been in World War II, but had been called back to the service when the Korean War broke out.

Curly would come to Oceanside several times to visit with his son. Mike remembers that on one occassion Red had been drinking on the base and had rolled his automobile. A group of Marines saw the accident; and before Red could get out of the car, they tipped it back on its wheels. It was badly bent-up, but driveable. Red did not want Curly to see what he had done to his Oldsmobile, fearing that he would be severely scolded for bending up a machine like that. He would always try to park it out of sight, and walk quite a distance to meet his father.

Red had a 3-day liberty two or three times a month. On those occasions, he would take off for Arcata. Mike did not know what Red was up to in Arcata, but thought he had a girl friend. He was right, of course; but there was also a sawmill there that had been entrusted to his father. Red thought it might need a little looking after.

chapter twelve

IDA MITCHELL

There was a young lady in Eureka whom Red Emmerson remembered having met. He had trouble forgetting her. Her name was Ida Mitchell. She and a Frank Powers had gone to Walt's Club in Eureka. Red was there with another date.

Ida was 19 at the time and had been dating Powers off and on. Red remembers this meeting very well; she made quite an impression on him. Ida does not remember the incident; and it is evident that he made no impression on her on that occasion.

Ida was born in Eureka on January 11, 1932. She was the youngest of five children, her three sisters and one brother being several years older than she. She says that she was a "change of life'" baby. Her father had been a baker, but in later life had gone to work in the mills. Eureka was well-populated with mills and plywood plants, and they paid better wages than the bakery business.

She attended local grade schools and graduated from Eureka High School. She turned into a beautiful young lady, small-boned and petite, with dark curly hair. She did not lack for dates. After graduation, she had found work at Pacific Gas and Electric, doing office work and bookkeeping. She subsequently found a better job working in a clothing store in Eureka.

Ida had made friends with two women several years older than she. One was Arnie Jepson's wife, Thelma. (Arnie was the first bookkeeper hired by Red and Curly.) The other was a woman whom Thelma and Ida liked very much. Curly also knew her. The three women would have lunch or dinner together occasionally; and unattached males, attracted by Ida, would buy them a drink. The two older women enjoyed this little game at Ida's expense; and Ida was glad that her mother did not know about it.

Curly and Thelma were always trying to arrange a date for Red with Ida when Red came back to Arcata on his scheduled liberties. Ida was not really interested, since for her, it would be a blind date. She did not remember Red. After persistent pressure, she finally agreed, and they all went to the Ingomar Club for dinner on the first date. Ida was 20; it was 1952.

The next day, Red called for a date since he was going back to San Diego on Monday. She was not too impressed with this brash young man, but he was insistent and sent a cab to pick her up. They went to Everett's Club in Arcata. Ida was still not impressed, and complains that he was "too pushy."

As the weeks went on, she was receiving telephone calls from San Diego quite often. Their early relationship was rocky from the start, but Red would not give up. Mike Albee remembers that Ida did come to Oceanside to see Red, and that the Albees went out with them. Ida would travel south with Curly and Myrtle. Curly would visit with his old friend,

Red and Ida Emmerson on their wedding day, 1955, in Eureka, California.
Photo from Ida Emmerson.

Captain Reed, on occasion when in southern California. He would combine the social visit with a party for the young Marines.

Finally, Mike Albee and Red were ordered to Korea. They were to land in North Korea, but would have one last fling before they left. Red called Ida to see if she would come to San Diego this last time before he shipped out. Curly and Myrtle were to come, too. Ida was very reluctant to get so involved, since she had been engaged to a serviceman before, and did not want to have another long-distance romance.

She finally agreed, and Red sent her a ticket to fly down for the weekend. She boarded a DC-3 and met Curly and Myrtle at San Diego, since Curly was a reluctant flyer. She and Red stayed in adjoining rooms in Oceanside. Ida says that Red tried "awfully hard" to stay in the same room with her, but was unsuccessful.

The next day they went to Tijuana. Everyone in the party was trying to get them married, but Ida would have none of it. Curly threw a big party for them that evening, and a Marine colonel was there along with Captain Reed. It was quite a party.

They left San Francisco for Korea. When they were a few days out, the truce ending the war was announced, and the ship was diverted to Japan. Mike and Red ended up in Japan for several months, both of them itching to get back to the U.S.A. Red had written to Ida quite often, and she had responded on occasion.

Finally, the two Marines were sent back to Treasure Island for discharge. Red called Ida to meet him there; but she already had a date for that evening and would not be talked out of it. Red was very disappointed. He was met by Curly and Mike Crook and they, along with Mike Albee, began by celebrating at the 365 Club. It was another first-class party; and the two ex-Marines would remember it for a long time. It was February, 1954.

After discharge, they headed back to Arcata. Red and Ida would date off-and-on for several months. Thelma would meet Ida when she got off work, and they would go to Roy's Club where they would meet Arnie and Curly,

who would have been there for some time. Red had learned after returning to Arcata that the business was not going well and was losing money.

Curly had received "several hundred thousand dollars" in cash when he and Jalmer Berg had sold their timber to Mutual Plywood. Curly had not had that kind of money before; and while Red was gone, Curly was not attending to business very well. He was drinking heavily, and he was breaking up with Myrtle, his second wife. His heart was not in the business.

Red went back to work with a vengeance. They installed a pony rig, and replaced the circle saws on the head rig with a band saw. Curly had never wanted to run two shifts; but Red prevailed and they began the second shift.

Curly was spending more and more time being a rancher. He had purchased a ranch in Del Norte County above Crescent City. To Red, this seemed to be Curly's first love now, and he seemed to have tired of the sawmill business. Curly seemed to like horses and cows more than the smell of sawdust.

Red was working most of two shifts, and trying to date Ida in his spare time. The relationship, as far as Ida was concerned, was still rocky; but Red was the most persistent man she had ever met. In addition, she was learning that he would be a success at whatever he decided to tackle. Within two years after he returned to Arcata, the mill was back in the black. He was becoming a man of means; but she still considered him to be "too pushy."

Finally Ida agreed to go steady with Red. The arrangement went along for about eight months before they decided to get married. They had a big church wedding, with Mike Albee as the best man. The reception was at the Eureka Inn; and Mike recounts that Red seemed to want to party all night. The date was June 5, 1955.

From then on, Red would have a stable home life and a great deal of support from someone he loved. This would help him forge a company that one day would be very successful.

Circular saws of the kind Curly Emmerson operated. Saw filer pictured is unknown.
Photo from Lynne Ivey Daugherty collection.

chapter thirteen

UNDER NEW MANAGEMENT

With Red back from the service, married and settled down, the business began to prosper. Red began to make most of the business decisions; but he always conferred with Curly, particularly on "important" matters. There were only a few minor disagreements between them; and the people who were close to them have said that they never disagreed in public. To their employees and business associates, they were close partners.

One of their minor disagreements occurred when it was time to build a new office. The office, at the time, was a very small (about 6 X 8 feet) lean-to with a shed roof. It sat close to the front gate. There was not room enough inside to sit down; it was standing room only. When Red insisted that they had to have office help and some place to put them, Curly "raised hell" about the extravagance. Red persisted; and finally a small building was constructed at the present location of the office.

When he first came back from the service, Red was not as well liked by the employees as Curly was. Red was harder to get along with, and probably was considered the new kid who did not know what he was talking about. He was still awfully young to be running a mill complex. Red has said that his father could get more work out of an employee than any man he ever knew. However, he did not do it the way most bosses did.

Curly was a friend to the employees in-

stead of a superior. He understood them and their problems, and he understood the business. He worked with them on the job, and could work harder than they could. To top it all off, he drank with them on the premises. In one respect, he was a father figure to them; in another, he was a comrade. Red took lessons on how he did it.

Arnie Jepson came to work for R.H. Emmerson & Son in 1950 as the accountant and office manager. He worked in the little plywood office that he describes as about 10 X 14 feet. He was recommended to Curly by Mike Crook through Pacific Fir Sales' relationship with Lenwood Speier.

Arnie was born in Denmark on October 3, 1906, and his family brought him to this country when he was three-years-old. His father operated the kilns in the manufacture of building bricks. At first, they lived in New Jersey, then Kansas, where his father found work in the same occupation.

Arnie moved to California where a brother had preceded him. He enrolled at Cal-Berkeley to study accounting, but only spent two years pursuing an education. He left to find work with The Pacific Lumber Co. at Scotia in what he calls their "bungalow office," doing general office work; then moved to do accounting work for Len Speier, where he attracted the attention of Mike Crook.

From top left,
Red Emmerson and son George in 1957.
From Naida Emmerson collection.
George and Caroline Emmerson, April, 1960. From
Ida Emmerson.
George and Mark Emmerson, April, 1960.
From Ida Emmerson.
Ida Emmerson and first-born son, George in 1957.
From Naida Emmerson collection.

He was to become one of the key people to work for Curly and Red in the early years. He became one of the "family," as so many of the early employees describe their employers. He drank with Curly at the Alibi in Arcata before the new office was built where there would be room for a bar in the kitchen.

Arnie notes, "The head guy sets the tone of a company, and drinking was a part of the company's policy back then. Curly was the head guy, and the finest gentleman I ever met."

Curly and Red arranged for Arnie's pay to be based on a share of the profits, if there were any. Because of the arrangement, he was able to retire after 15 years of employment (October 19, 1966). He and his wife, Thelma, now live in Oak Harbor, Washington, where at 84-years-young, his weight is down to 115 pounds as a result of throat cancer.

In the year immediately after Red and Ida were married, they moved into an apartment at 1330 E Street in Eureka. Red surprised her by buying new furniture for their first home. It soon became more than a home for them, however; it became a meeting place for the mill management.

After work, Arnie Jepson, Red, Curly and others from the mill would drop by for a drink and to discuss business. On some occasions, Ida would feed the group before they headed back to the mill to work on maintenance or to solve some other problem. She enjoyed the company; but the pace was faster than she had anticipated, and she had to work awfully hard to keep up. She was learning what it meant to be an Emmerson.

During that time, a pattern developed that was to become typical behavior for Red and Ida in their marriage. Ida became personally acquainted with the business problems, and with the discussions that occurred relating to the solving of them. She also became acquainted with the people who worked for the company, and became closely involved with most of the activities that took place. Red would confide in her more and more as the years went by. Ida was a "team player;" she knew what was going on.

The pattern was set, and the mill had finally "turned the corner." The company was still dependent upon open-market logs, but was learning to compete with the plywood plants for the better logs. Red, especially, had become expert at looking at timber or logs, and could judge their worth with unerring accuracy. Their mill was operating with fewer employees than others with similar production. They had few supervisors on the payroll. The two Emmersons were the supervisors, and every penny they made was plowed back into the company.

Red and Ida purchased a house on the corner of Dolbeer and Harris in Eureka, where they would live for about five years. Their home was still the meeting place. Soon Ida became pregnant. George was born on November 17, 1956, and two other babies would follow: Caroline on January 4, 1959, and Mark on February 1, 1960.

I got to know Ida in later years and developed a great deal of respect for her and her role in the company. She once told me that her husband was "pretty wild" in his early years, and that she, at one point, had become worried about Red not having enough time to spend with their children. Then she got a hard look in her eye, looked straight at me and said, "I decided that I was going to make him the best damned father in the world, and I think I succeeded." I was surprised by her vehemence, but I believed her; and I think she was at least partially responsible for doing just that.

On Easter Sunday, 1957, a fire occurred in the machine shop at the mill on Samoa Road. Millwright Carl McKinney and two others were cleaning up around the green chain when the fire was noticed. The fire spread so quickly they could not put it out. The fire department was called immediately.

Several acetylene tanks exploded when the fire reached them. News accounts of the incident put the damage estimate at $100,000. One firefighter, Reno Orlandi, suffered a back injury and was hospitalized.

There is a picture in one of the papers of Red, wearing a hat, on a dead-run toward the building that was on fire. The picture shows the corrugated metal roof of the building beginning to buckle. Another picture, taken later, shows one end of the mill with the roof entirely burned away.

The mill was insured and was back in business in a very short time. The sawmill crews worked around the clock to rebuild the damaged portions. Both Curly and Red Emmerson directed the rebuilding and, for several days, they went with very little sleep.

There is a story that was told by several people about Curly's ability to go without sleep if there was work to do. I do not know whether the fire of 1957 was the incident that triggered the story or not. The time and place are probably not important.

In any event, the mill was shut down and needed parts, or machinery, or some other device that was necessary for it to run. Curly drove all night from Arcata to Portland to find that the part was not available in the Portland area as he had been told. Without stopping to rest, he got back in his vehicle for the drive to San Francisco where he had been assured he could obtain it. He arrived there, loaded it, and drove all the way back to Arcata without sleeping. On today's roads, the total mileage is in excess of 1500; quite a feat with no sleep.

Red had become a very busy man. The sawmill was running as well as any sawmill ever runs, but there were always breakdowns. Also, the company was beginning to purchase timber. The first significant purchase was a tract of timber from Georgia Pacific Corp. R.H. Emmerson & Son bought cutting rights, but not the land.

This was an acquisition of about 100 MMBF on the Eel River near a place known as Camp Grant. They paid $250,000 as a down-payment; and the rest was to be paid on a perthousand board foot basis as it was cut. Willits Redwood Co. would buy the Redwood, and R. H. Emmerson & Son, the Douglas fir. Red thought the down-payment was "all the money in the world."

On July 5, 1957, Gordon Amos came to work at the mill at Samoa. Gordon's stay, with one interruption, was to be a long one, lasting until his retirement in 1985.

Picture postcard of R. H. Emmerson & Son mill on Samoa Road. Note burner and new office at lower left. Date of picture unknown but probably mid-1950s.

Gordon was born in Nebraska in 1930, and had grown up there where his parents were farmers. After graduating from high school, he had heard of the higher wages, up to $6 per hour, available in the Pacific Northwest. He and a cousin headed for Oregon where they found work near Sheridan, pulling lumber on the green chain at McCormick's sawmill, one of the several mills located nearby. One of the mills may have been the same mill where Curly worked for the few months prior to the birth of his son, Red.

Gordon worked at various jobs in the mill, finally learning to grade lumber. He worked at that occupation, both before and after World War II. However, he was to become an unwitting player in a labor dispute.

The lumber industry had become unionized to a great degree since Curly had begun as a lumberman. Gordon ran afoul of the rules when he attempted to operate a crane; such work was not considered to be a part of his lumber-grading duties. He was threatened with having a 2 X 4 wrapped around his neck, and decided that a union job was not that important to him.

By that time, Gordon Amos was a certified lumber grader, so he went to work for the West Coast Lumber Inspection Bureau. The graders worked much the same as log scalers did, working for a "disinterested," third-party organization. They were to grade lumber as they saw it, free of outside pressures from either buyers or sellers.

Gordon came to Arcata where he worked as a grader at Van Vleet's sawmill. He spent about six months there, then heard about a job at Emmerson's Samoa sawmill. He applied for the job, got it, and sent for his wife and family.

He had married Shirley McGaha on October 6, 1951. They had three children, two of whom (Gordie and Anita) would also work for the Emmersons at Arcata. Gordon was still working for the Bureau when he began grading at Samoa.

On July 3, 1957, Gordon reported for work. Superintendent Runar Anderson ran the mill and Gordon, even though a Bureau employee, came under his direction. He was told to report for work the next day, according to Gordon's thinking, usually a holiday. Red and Runar were getting acquainted with the new grader.

Gordon said, "Tomorrow's the Fourth of July."

"Yeah, and the next day is the fifth," said Red, "then it's the sixth, and so on."

Runar said, "Today's the third."

"You guys don't take holidays off?" asked Gordon.

"I thought you wanted a job, not a holiday," Runar replied.

Early on the Fourth of July, Gordon went to work at Samoa. The next day, July 5th, stands out in his memory.

As Gordon was walking by the office after work, he met a distinguished, white-haired gentleman who approached him.

"Son, I hear you went to work for us yesterday. Come on in and let's get acquainted," Curly said.

"Well, I went to work here yesterday, but who are you?" Gordon asked.

"My name's Emmerson; friends call me Curly," he said. "Come on; I'll buy you a drink."

Gordon was not much of a drinker; but he knew jobs were hard to come by, so in he went. Curly poured him a big water glass of straight bourbon whiskey. Runar already had his half-finished, and Red was sipping on his. They sat around the kitchen table in the lunchroom, kidding each other, and getting acquainted with the new lumber grader.

Soon Gordon had to call Shirley for a ride home. He could barely make it to the door. His three friends helped Shirley get him in the car and off they went.

The next morning, Gordon came to work at the usual time - early. He felt awful. His job was to climb on top of a lumber pile and grade the heavy pieces, as two men, one on each end, turned them over for him. After a few minutes, it was plain for all to see that he would not make it very long without getting off to throw up. Runar stood alongside the lumber pile watching the performance, and making wise remarks

about his lack of drinking ability.

Finally, seeing that perhaps the lumber grades might be suffering, Runar relented. He told Gordon he had something better for the two men to do, and Gordon could grade lumber on the green chain.

This required Gordon to stand on top of a moving chain full of lumber, looking down, and watching each piece as it moved along. That was worse than being on top of the lumber pile; now the whole world was moving beneath his feet. He had to hop off occasionally to retch over the side of the green chain.

Runar watched this part of the Amos initiation for a short time, then sent him home for the day. Gordon Amos never forgot his first week on the job. He would say that Runar Anderson was the only man he knew who could keep up with Curly in the drinking department.

A year later, on July 5, 1957, Gordon left the Bureau to begin work as a full-time employee of R.H. Emmerson and Son. For most of the first four years, he was a grader; then he worked in the shipping department under Sam Witzel. He would go on to spend most of the next 28 years working at the sawmill on Samoa Road. The rest of his story comes later.

In 1958, R.H. Emmerson & Son purchased a tract of timber in Cappel Creek, near Weitchpec, from Rich Brunello and Jim Berry. There was about 60 MMBF on about 2,500 acres. It was excellent old-growth Douglas fir. They paid $75,000 down, with the rest to be paid as the timber was harvested. Included in the sale was a stud mill located at Weitchpec, and a deck of mostly cull logs.

Curly thought it would be a good idea to saw the culls into studs without the added cost of trucking them to another mill, so the mill was run for about a year cutting culls and low-grade logs. Curly managed it for a couple of months. It really was not much of an operation, but it required someone to look after it. Paul Allen, a long-time employee, was recruited to run the mill for Red and Curly after the first two months, and did so until it was closed.

By that time, the sawmill at Samoa was specializing in old-growth Douglas fir. It was cutting large timbers and also concentrating on cutting to maximize vertical grain products. The company had a good reputation for producing a quality product, and had developed customer loyalty. It also paid its bills on time. The latter trait was recognized as being somewhat unique for a company of its size.

The first "forester" the company had was Red, himself. As the workload increased, it was evident that he could not do everything by himself, so they utilized a log scaler who worked for them as a log buyer. There were two men who filled the position at one time or another: one was Bob Voight, the other was Roy Byers. Neither was formally educated as a forester, but both knew logs.

In 1961, the Davis & Brede tract was purchased, involving some 5,400 acres and 60 MMBF of timber, primarily Douglas fir. It was scattered in the fir belt, mostly south of Willow Creek and in the Snow Camp area. The downpayment was $500,000, with the remainder to be paid as the timber was cut. They bought the Van Duzer tract on the Klamath River, and found enough Port Orford cedar on it to pay for the whole tract. It was beginning to take big money to stay in the lumber business.

Otto Peters came to work for R. H. Emmerson & Son in 1961. By that time, it was necessary to hire someone whose talents included forestry as well as log buying. Otto fit the bill. Roy Byers was kept on as log buyer under Otto; but Red thought that both of them together were "bad news." Each of them were cast in the Curly mold; they knew how to drink. Red thought that Otto was better for the company, so they kept him.

A team was being formed that would contribute to the successful operations in Humboldt County for a long time to come. Otto would be one of the key members along with Arnie Jepson, Sam Witzel, Gordon Amos and Runar Anderson.

chapter fourteen

SAM, PETE, & RUNAR

Sam Witzel was one of the key players in the early days of R.H. Emmerson & Son. He was born in Yelm, Washington May, 1924.

He was raised in Yelm, Tacoma and Seattle, Washington, and finally Glendale, Oregon. He attended many schools, gaining a degree from none of them. These included Willamette University, University of Colorado, Cal-Poly, Saint Mary's and the University of Georgia.

In 1958, Sam was working for Twin City Lumber Co., a wholesaler in San Rafael, California. He and his wife, Sharon, lived in Santa Rosa; but Sam spent 50 weeks a year travelling in California from Redding to Bakersfield. In March of 1958, Sam made a "mill trip" to Arcata, and had dinner with Red and Ida. Red approached him about coming to work for R.H. Emmerson & Son selling lumber.

Sam's wife did not wish to leave Santa Rosa, so Sam declined the invitation. On Easter Sunday, the fire at the Samoa sawmill triggered another call from Red for Sam to come to work. There is no indication that the fire had anything to do with the call; but Sam remembers the date in reference to it. He asked for a week to think about it.

Monday after Easter was a "lousy day" for Sam. At this point, no one knows whether the "lousy day" meant at home or at work. (Sam was, in later years, to lose his wife through divorce.) In any event, he phoned Red and

accepted the job. He says that his wife was "very, very angry."

Sam went to work at Arcata the last week of April. He knew Runar Anderson and Arnie Jepson by that time through his travels to the various mills while working for Twin City. At the Samoa mill, Curly Ashby was in charge of the dry kilns, Bob Harrison was "pond monkey," June Scott worked in the office, and Gordon Amos was the shipping clerk. John Murphy and Devere Lake were car loaders, and Ruben Salazar was tailing at the edger. Jim Tucci was the millwright. Sam fit into the team at once.

Witzel recognized early in his career at R.H. Emmerson & Son that Curly Emmerson was "satisfied with the status quo, but Red had visions." Sam's first obstacle was Arnie Jepson, who thought that he might be "treading on his territory." After Arnie decided that the new man "was capable, there were no further questions." Sam maintains that after the first few weeks of his employment, the group was "really one big family." They "worked, partied, hunted, fished, entertained; all together. Those were good days."

Sam Witzel remembers that in 1958 their total sales amounted to less than $4,000,000, since their sales average was roughly $78 per MBF. He also recalls the first timber purchased from Georgia Pacific at Camp Grant. The logs produced such good lumber that the mill was able to cut an order for a carload of

12 X 12 and wider, 16' and longer, "C" and Better boat lumber in one night-shift.

When Sam first went to work, Pacific Fir Sales (the Crook family) had an exclusive sales agreement with the Emmerson mill. Jack Ivey ran the Crooks' Arcata office, and P.V. "Bud" Allen was in charge of the sales office in Ukiah. Allen would later move to Arcata where he became a close friend of Curly and Red. He could "always get a rise out of Curly by calling him Raleigh or Humes."

Witzel recalls the mill at Weitchpec and the day it burned in 1965. John and Dorothy Crook had left with Red and Ida for a European vacation the day before. At 1:00 a.m., Sam Witzel got a call from Paul Allen that the mill was burning and it would be a total loss. Paul could not find either Red or Curly to tell them of the catastrophe.

Then Sam remembered that on Fridays Curly usually went to San Francisco to see Orvamae Oncken. He immediately called her number to tell Curly of the problem at Weitchpec. Orvamae answered the telephone.

At Sam's inquiry she replied, "Oh, Sam, you just missed him."

Sam said, "I'm trying to find him because the mill burned down, and I'm trying to locate Red."

There was silence on the other end. Then Curly came on the line.

"Well, Sammy boy, what seems to be the problem?" Curly asked.

Sam explained what he had just learned about the fire.

"Sammy," said Curly, "Leave the boy alone, he needs a vacation. I'll tell you what you do. When he calls in to ask for the production figures, dummy up some good ones. Don't tell him about the fire; just give him the usual figures. I'll handle that boy when he gets home. Understand?"

When Red came home two weeks later, he was angry.

"I'll never know what the hell went on here the last two weeks," he said. "Why didn't you try to call me, or at least tell me about the fire?"

Sam had to tell Red that he was under orders from Curly to do what he had done. As far as the rest of the people in the company were concerned, that was the end of it. No one ever heard what Red and Curly said to each other about the incident.

Sam also remembers an incident that occurred sometime after the above confrontation. It involved Curly and a couple of celebrities.

Sam had arranged for Y. A. Tittle and Matt Hazeltine of the San Francisco 49'ers to attend a meeting of the local Hoo Hoo Club as guests. This was a fun-loving club organized to promote wood products and camaraderie among those in the trade. Many of the members were sales people.

Sam brought the 49'ers out to the sawmill to show them the operation, and for Curly to meet them. After the introductions and a few minutes of conversation, Curly asked, "What kind of work are you fellows in?"

Y. A. said, "We play football."

Curly responded, "Seriously fellows, what do you really do? I mean for a living."

Sam was responsible for Gordon Amos' leaving the employ of R.H. Emmerson & Son for a period of less than two years during which Gordon worked for Eel River Sawmills at Fortuna. Gordon was the superintendent of the planing mill there.

The dispute arose over an incident that occured in 1965 when Gordon was in charge of shipping and Sam was the sales manager. An order was "over-shipped" to a good customer, who complained. At this time it is unclear whether it was Sam who authorized the over-shipment (which Gordon claims), or Gordon who did it (which Sam claims). Gordon says he quit over the incident, and Sam says Red fired Gordon. Whatever happened, both Sam and Gordon worked for many years for the Emmersons after Gordon's "sabbatical" in Fortuna. It appears to have been a family squabble that was patched up over the years.

Other members of the early "family" were Runar Anderson and Glen Peterson.

Runar (Swede) Anderson was cut from the same mold as Curly. Most of Runar's friends never did know his first name. He was a native of Humboldt County, his father having worked for Hammond Lumber Co. Runar, after graduating from high school, had gone to work for the same company. He had become an excellent carpenter in Hammond's employ, making $1.75 per hour.

The mill went on an extended strike, and Runar did not want to cross the picket lines to go to work. He needed work though, so he found work at Len Speier's sawmill. In a few weeks, he was a shift foreman; and during his stay there he built the mill into an efficient operation. Curly Emmerson had heard of him and approached him to come to work for R.H. Emmerson & Son. The Emmersons were still adding to the mill. It was 1952, and Runar went to work as a foreman.

There he met Glen "Pete" Peterson, Emmersons' saw filer. The two would become close friends; and they and their wives (Dot Anderson and Velma Peterson) would eventually become involved in the close association that key employees had with Curly and Red Emmerson and their wives. When Red went away to the Marines, Runar was made superintendent.

At the time Runar went to work at Samoa, a good shift's production was 55 MBF. In order to attain that lofty goal, the logs had to be just the right size, and there could be no breakdowns.

Runar, Pete, Otto, and the rest of the crew continued the reputation the Emmerson crew had for partying. Of course, Curly was the chief partier. The rule was no drinking before 5:00 p.m.; and at one session, Runar received a watch from Curly that had no numbers on its face but fives.

Dot Anderson remembers many of the parties very well. She remembers particularly that Otto would invariably get soused first; and he and his wife, Myrt, would usually get into some kind of an argument before the party was over. When Curly was married to Myrtle, the two of them would argue after a few drinks, but not nearly as soon as Otto and Myrt.

At one of the parties, Ida pushed Otto and Myrt out the front door of their home and locked them out. The rest of the party-goers could hear the two of them on the front porch hollering and banging on the front door to get back in. Ida would not relent; she thought it was time for them to go home. It was a good lesson for all of them; when Ida said "go home" it was time to go home.

When the mill in Weitchpec was in production, Runar, Sam, and a man named Chris Nicholas, formed a trucking firm to haul the green studs to the mill at Samoa for finishing. After the mill burned, the truck was used to haul lumber to other markets in California. They only owned one truck. The firm was named Nicandwit Trucking Co. after elements of each of the three men's names. It gradually came to be known as the Nitwit Trucking Co.

Pete Peterson worked primarily for the mill at Samoa. In later years though, when there were saw filing problems at some of the other Emmerson mills, he would be called upon to lend his expertise to solve them.

Runar and Dot Anderson had a son, Bob, who worked at the mill during the summers while pursuing his education at Humboldt State where he graduated in Forestry. Bob remembers that Red would visit the mill at all hours, driving through the mill yard in the middle of the night. Occasionally, he would be critical of a grade mark on one or more pieces of lumber; and he would change the grade, undoubtedly never to a lower grade, but to a higher one.

In 1963, Runar Anderson suffered a stroke and became disabled. Jim Long took his place as superintendent. Eventually, Swede went to a nursing home for extended medical care, where Pete Peterson would often visit him. Pete quit work in 1970. They were a part of the original R.H. Emmerson & Son crew that Red and Curly Emmerson would always remember with affection and respect.

Otto Peters - SPI's first professional forester.

Myrta Peters who met Otto at Oregon State University and considered him the best ballroom dancer at the school.
Photos from Mrs. Doug Peterson

chapter fifteen

OTTO

To those who worked for the Emmersons between 1960 and 1980, the name Otto meant only one person. There was only one Otto Peters. Even if one did not know Otto personally, the stories about him were so provocative and widespread that most felt they knew him, particularly if they worked in the Humboldt County timber industry.

Otto was born on December 23, 1914, in South Dakota. His parents were farmers; and they came to Oregon in 1924 to settle near Eugene. They eventually moved to Redmond, where Otto's father got into the trucking business hauling potatoes, wheat, cattle feed, and anything else that needed hauling. Otto grew up there.

In 1936, he went to Oregon State College at Corvallis to study forestry. He graduated, took the Junior Forester examination for the U. S. Forest Service, and flunked it. He felt that his world had come to an end with the notice of failure; and he went back to Redmond to work for his father. He also began applying at various places for forestry work.

Finally, in 1941, Weyerhauser Timber Co. hired Otto along with a number of other young men to staff their forestry department. He stayed there until 1946 when Hill Timber Co. hired him to work in the Sweethome, Oregon area, surveying property lines. This company was a successor to the Northern Pacific Railroad, and owned alternate sections of land paralleling their right-of-way in Or-

egon. By that time, Otto had studied for his Land Surveyor's license, taken the test, and passed it.

In 1948, Roddiscraft, successor to Humboldt Plywood Co., brought Otto to California. This company had acquired timber cutting rights on the Wiggins Ranch, near Maple Creek, and on a large tract of land north of Orick. They were actively trying to acquire more Humboldt County timber.

Roddiscraft had negotiated an option to purchase the Hunter Ranch situated on the upper reaches of the Mad River. One of Otto's first jobs for Roddiscraft was to cruise the timber on the ranch. This took him nearly a year and, after finding only about two percent of the volume consisted of peeler logs, the company turned it down. Shortly after, Roddiscraft sold out to Weyerhauser.

Otto, meanwhile, had decided to go to work for R. H. Emmerson & Son. The company was growing and help was needed in acquiring logs and timber. Otto had considerable experience with Douglas fir, the company specialty. He was the first formally-educated forester that the company hired. The year was 1961.

When he first went to work for R. H. Emmerson & Son, most of his time was spent searching out logs that might be for sale. He was simply a log buyer. The company by that time had developed expertise in sawing old-growth Douglas fir, and had entered the

Red Emmerson and Otto Peters, both full of Christmas cheer, at SPI Christmas party in 1974.

market for the products made from it. A good portion of the production was being sold for export as "export clears."

This enabled the company to compete effectively with the plywood plants for high-grade logs. Technology had by then progressed to the point that lower grade logs could be peeled, the knot holes patched, and an acceptable grade of veneer produced. R. H. Emmerson & Son would buy #1 and #2 Peeler logs from the plywood plants, and sell back the lower grades. The sawmill at that time began paying more for the peelers than the plywood plants would.

Otto remembers that in the early 1960s, #2 Peelers were going for $70 per MBF, while #1 Peelers were $80. At one point, he remembers, they got as high as $120 for #1 Peelers, and Otto thought the market had gotten completely out of hand. He would be aghast today to see the prices hovering in the $1,200-$1,400 range.

As time went on, Otto began to cruise and appraise government timber sales. The company had been aggressively trying to purchase the high-grade Douglas fir that grew among the redwoods. It was common knowledge that the best logs came from these areas, for the redwoods would grow tall, forcing the firs to reach for the sky along with them. At lower elevations along the coast, the better growing sites were occupied by these two species, and the result was extremely high-grade Douglas fir.

The supply of these logs was limited, however, since they were mostly owned by private companies that cut them themselves, or sold them to the highest bidder. The government owned large stands of good Douglas fir, not up to par with that associated with redwood, but perfectly acceptable for R. H. Emmerson & Son. It was decided to go after timber from these sources. Otto remembers the first government timber he cruised, and purchased, was owned by the Bureau of Indian Affairs.

It wasn't long before they were also bidding on timber offered for sale by the U. S. Forest Service. These sales were primarily on the Orleans District of the Six Rivers National Forest. The Douglas fir at the higher elevations near Orleans was slow-grown, and the fine grain was desired in the markets that the company served. The Snow Camp area south of Highway 299 also produced good grade fir logs.

Otto worked hard at acquiring timber sales and timberland that would fit the company's needs for old-growth fir. He also played very hard.

Bob Harrison, who worked in the R. H. Emmerson & Son mill yard, and Otto were initiated into the Hoo Hoo Club in Eureka. The ceremony was quite bizarre and enjoyed far more by the initiators than by the victims. The ritual was followed by dinner and drinking; a considerable amount of the latter.

After the party, Otto and Bob Harrison climbed into Bob's pickup truck for the ride home. They had dressed for the occasion in suits and ties. As they made the sharp turn at the foot of Fourth Street in Eureka, Otto's door flew open. Out he rolled into the street, breaking his glasses and tearing a gash in the shoulder of his suit.

Harrison applied the brakes and came back to see if Otto was still alive. He was not only alive, he was angry. He stood unsteadily in the street and shouted at his friend.

"What'n hell am I going to tell my wife when I go home looking like this?" he asked. He had nothing but a skinned nose, a torn suit and no glasses. He was so full of booze and relaxed that the pavement had barely dented his composure.

"Otto, you'd better tell her the truth. Myrta can be awful tough if you lie to her," Bob said.

"I can't do that," Otto said, "She'd kill me".

They got back in the truck and headed for Otto's home, discussing their story as they went. When they got there, they found the house dark and the door locked. Myrt had gone to bed and locked Otto out. He knew he was in deep trouble.

Bob propped Otto up by the front door, rang the doorbell, and headed for the bushes to watch the fun. Otto stood swaying by the door in his torn suit. Finally the porch light came on and the door opened a crack.

"What happened to you?" Myrta asked in a suspicious tone of voice.

"Oh Christ, Myrt," Otto said, "That was the damndest initiation I ever went through. I'll never join another club as long as I live."

"Oh honey," Myrt said, "Come in here and I'll fix you up. You look terrible."

Bob Harrison, back in the bushes, had just seen a masterful performance by an expert.

There are hundreds of stories about Otto Peters and his escapades. He was well-liked by those who knew him and, to some extent, he became a minor legend in forestry circles in Humboldt County. Otto could party well into the night, get up early the next morning, work hard in the "brush" all day, and do the same thing all over again the next night. He could out-walk his peers even as he got older, but he began to have trouble out-drinking them.

Otto retired at the age of 63 and, with his beloved Myrta, lives in Magalia, California. He contributed significantly to the success of the company.

Old-growth Jeffrey pine stand in eastern Plumas County. Photo taken in early 1900s is one of several found in attic of old Clover Valley Lumber Co. office.

chapter sixteen

EAGLE LAKE TIMBER CO.

By the early 1960s, Curly and Red Emmerson and Mike and John Crook had been involved in several business relationships. Mike Crook owned Pacific Fir Sales, with main offices in Los Angeles, California, and a local office in the Lumbermen's Building located on the east side of the town square in Arcata. From there, they bought and sold the lumber produced by many of the small mills located in Humboldt County. They also financed many of the operations by advancing them money and securing the loans with liens on the lumber they produced. It is reported that in 1948, there were 265 sawmills in Humboldt County, and Pacific Fir Sales handled a significant amount of their production.

During the early 1940s, Curly Emmerson had developed a number of customers for the products that his mill produced. The lumber from Curly's operation was sold by Pacific Fir Sales. The firm would take a percentage of each sale as a commission. Red did not particularly like the arrangement, but the procedure was common. In order to sell the lumber any other way, it was necessary to add salespersons to the payroll. Red did not like that prospect either; and he tolerated the business relationship as the lesser of two evils. Then, too, the Emmersons and the Crooks got along very well together; the four men were good friends.

Mike Crook also owned a sawmill at Happy Camp and a moulding plant at Yreka, which they had acquired in the 1950s. They ran the moulding plant under the name Siskiyou Mouldings. The Crooks were quite successful; and the Emmersons, with their sawmill at Samoa, were becoming so.

Adjacent to the Emmerson mill to the east was another sawmill, Brightwood Lumber Co. Working there as the superintendent was a young man, Burr Coffelt, with whom Red had become acquainted when Red advertised a used Buick for sale. Burr was interested in the car. As a result, the two met when Burr came to look at it.

Burr thinks the Brightwood mill was a good operation, and that Red, by observing it, learned a great deal about mill efficiency and the cutting of logs. Red also seemed impressed by the young Burr Coffelt. When it came time for the Emmersons and Crooks to expand, he hired Burr to help with the expansion.

Burr was born at Sixes, Oregon, in 1927. His grandparents owned the ranch that stretched upstream from the Highway 101 bridge over the Sixes River. Burr's father had worked on the construction of the highway, then gravitated to the trucking business; and the family moved to Lorane, Oregon, where his father hauled lumber. Burr grew up in the timber industry, working with his father in the trucking business.

After graduating high school, and a stint in the Army Air Corps from 1945 to 1947, Burr came to Eureka, again to work with his father. It was there that he went to work for Brightwood, beginning on the green chain; and by the late 1950s, had worked his way up to superintendent.

Burr Coffelt began a long career with the Emmersons and Crooks in 1964. He would retire in November, 1981, still a young man, and move to Arizona where he and his wife, Dee, live on a golf course. Burr spends much of his time in his machine shop, where he is constructing an automobile, doing all the work himself. His wife is "down to playing golf only five days a week."

Burr remembers that when he first began working for the Crooks and Emmersons, they were looking for an operation to acquire in the Sierra. One of the first they looked at was Zamboni's mill at Round Mountain, just east of Redding. While it was for sale, it was not what they were looking for, and they turned it down.

While employed in the search, a mill at Susanville was brought to their attention. There they found the complex owned by Fruit Growers Supply Co. The mill was an old one and quite inefficient. There were the usual accouterments, such as dry kilns, dry sheds, a power house, a planing mill, and an inventory of spare parts, which was huge. There was also a small subdivision located near the mill where modest homes for the employees had been constructed. The Emmersons and the Crooks opened negotiations to buy the whole thing.

Included in the package was a sizeable tract of timberland and approximately 80,000 MBF of timber. These timberlands were scattered in the mountains west of Susanville and grew mainly White fir timber. The fir was to be paid for at the rate of $6.50 per MBF as the timber was cut. They agreed to purchase everything, although the old mill was not running at the time.

In preparation for the purchase of Fruit Growers, the Crooks and the Emmersons formed a partnership and named it Eagle Lake Timber Co. Each of the four men owned 25% of it. Then a corporation was formed, named Eagle Lake Lumber Co., which would be owned by the partnership. The partnership would own the timber and timberlands, and the corporation would own the sawmill complex and real estate. The Timber Co. would sell logs to the Lumber Co.

Up until that time, neither John Crook nor Red Emmerson had been a substantial investor in their respective companies. With the acquisition of Fruit Growers on September 1, 1964, they would become heavily involved both financially and in the management of the operations. It is reported that John and Red each put up $75,000 as their part of the deal.

Fruit Growers had insured the mill properties and the houses for several million dollars. At closing, R. H. Emmerson & Son kept the policy in force by paying a pro-rata share of the premium, as the policy only had a few months to run before expiring.

Burr Coffelt was hired as manager. After going to work for Eagle Lake Lumber Co., one of his first duties was to tear down the old mill, and prepare the excess machinery and spare parts for auction. The auction of the parts inventory and machinery took three whole days.

Burr sold the houses to California Northwest Capital, which was an investment business that used government funds to loan to small businesses. This firm, in turn, sold the houses to employees and others interested in purchasing them.

The next order of business was to begin to construct a new sawmill on the site. Curly was in charge of the construction project. With the proceeds from the auction of the machinery and parts, and the sale of the real estate, the company had considerably reduced its investment in the properties. The new mill was designed to fit the species and size of logs that were available in that area.

The Lassen National Forest, located just west of Susanville, had a sizeable sales program, and much of the timber consisted of high-quality old-growth Ponderosa and Sugar pine. Competition for the timber was keen, and bid prices were high. However, the Emmersons believed they could successfully compete with anyone when it came to buying logs or timber.

Sawmill at Susanville. Picture was taken in 1975 long after the fire, and shows the crane shed and planing mill (large building in right center with office attached). Note old powerhouse with four smokestacks. Old log pond was not being used to store logs by this time.
Photo from SPI collection.

Curly and Burr Coffelt got along well together. For weeks at a time, Curly would live in one of the old company houses as he looked after the construction project. Burr was busy helping with the construction, as well as looking after the sale of surplus properties and cleaning up the old mill site.

The new sawmill was completed; and in April 1965, the first lumber was produced. Burr was the manager for the new sawmill, and sold the first lumber in June. A new planing mill was to be constructed next.

John Crook spent a considerable amount of time at Susanville also, but Red was there almost continuously. Ida and the family were there for days at a time, living in one of the company houses.

Then on June 13, 1965, another disas-

trous fire struck a sawmill in which the Emmersons were involved. The planing mill under construction caught fire; and since the sprinkler system was inoperative because of construction, the fire burned fast and hot.

At 1:13 a.m. the Susanville Volunteer Fire Department received the first call, and two engines were dispatched. Fire Chief Ever Bangham took one look at the glow in the sky and called for help. The California Division of Forestry, U. S. Forest Service, Bureau of Land Management, Sierra Army Depot at Herlong, and the California Conservation Center sent men or equipment, or both.

When it was all over, between 4:00 and 5:00 a.m., only the new sawmill, the power house, and a number of small storage sheds were saved. Lost were the dry kilns, lumber transfer equipment, unstackers, planing mill, trimmer, monorail shed, machine shop, three lumber carriers, a service truck, and 90% of the finished lumber inventory. The inventory was said to have been seven MMBF.

At the time of the fire, Red and attorney Francis Mathews were attending a party in Yreka. They were notified that the planing mill was on fire. They hurried to the airport and took off for Susanville early in the morning hours. As the plane climbed out of the valley at Yreka, they could see the red glow in the sky over Susanville.

Newspaper pictures in next day's issue show an extremely hot fire and smoking ruins. The photographs seem to show an area resembling the aftermath of the London blitz. There were eyewitness accounts that the fire was so hot, convection currents tossed corrugated roofing sheets over a mile from the mill site.

The sawmill went back into production the following Monday on a limited basis. Twenty-five to thirty men still had sawmill jobs. Many of the rest of the employees were put to work cleaning up the mess and rebuilding the facilities.

The insurance policy that had been taken over by the new owners contained a clause that required the buildings to be protected by an operable sprinkler system **or** an alarm system. Most policies require both. Francis Mathews, attorney for the Emmersons, read the policy carefully and confirmed that the wording was very specific. The alarm system was operational, but not the sprinklers.

Don Riewerts and Curly Emmerson were selected to meet with Lumbermen's Underwriters who carried the policy. They met in San Francisco to negotiate settlement of the claim. Don reports that Curly, in his slow, gruff manner of speaking, lead the negotiating. After about an hour, they settled for $2,250,000 which included $250,000 for the lost inventory.

The proceeds of the settlement enabled Eagle Lake to rebuild the planing mill and a dry shed that contained a large overhead crane for handling units of lumber. It was one of the first of that type of lumber transfer systems in California.

A new office was added, attached to the planing mill-crane building. It was a vintage Emmerson building, somewhat spartan by today's standards. The manager's office had a big window on one wall from which a large portion of the operation could be seen. Sawdust easily infiltrated the structure, so the occupants were constantly reminded they worked for a lumber company. If they had any doubts about that, frequent rumblings from the crane could be heard that occasionally resulted in a jolt resembling a small earthquake.

The competitors for timber in the Sierra knew they had new neighbors at Susanville. Bid prices for government timber had escalated after the new owners took over, and before they were even in production. Higher prices were yet to come.

chapter seventeen

ANOTHER ACQUISITION

At one time, Jim Laier owned the sawmill just east of Arcata that is now Blue Lake Forest Products. Robin Arkley managed the mill for Jim, and lived next door to Bob Johnson who was a manager for Weyerhauser. Through this friendship, Arkley found that Weyerhauser might like to leave Humboldt County. He told Jim Laier about it. It was 1965.

Laier had once owned a sawmill at St. Helens, Oregon. He had met Curly Emmerson sometime in the 1930s when Curly "operated a mill southwest of Portland" (probably the Springbrook mill). The two were only casual acquaintances at the time, but Jim Laier remembered Curly. The two men became reacquainted after they both moved to California.

Jim Laier, by 1965, owned considerable timberland and, in addition to the mill at Blue Lake, a sawmill at Cloverdale. The mill was called Cloverdale Redwood Co. Harry Merlo, the present chief executive of Louisiana Pacific Corp., managed a sawmill located adjacent to it. His mill was owned by Rockport Redwood Co.

Laier was interested in purchasing the Weyerhauser holdings in Humboldt County, but felt that it was too large an acquisition for him to finance by himself. He approached Merlo about the possibility of a joint venture to buy out Weyerhauser. Merlo was in favor of the venture; but after presenting the details to his superiors, could not get a decision from

them. Laier gave up and contacted Red and Curly Emmerson.

Red was very much interested. He talked the situation over with Curly; but Curly could not see how they could participate in such a venture, considering the size of the Weyerhauser holdings and the amount of money it would take to acquire them. Weyerhauser owned considerable timberland in Humboldt County, along with a particleboard plant and a plywood plant. The whole package was for sale, and it would take a lot of money to buy it.

Laier had a partner named Henry Trione who, after World War II, founded a mortgage banking firm in Santa Rosa. It grew to become Sonoma Mortgage Company and merged with Wells Fargo Bank in the early 1970s. In about 1963, he had purchased an interest in Laier's sawmill in Cloverdale. Trione's banking background and Laier's lumber background provided a good combination, and the two had been quite successful.

This small group got their heads together to figure out how to structure an offer that they could afford, and that would be interesting to Weyerhauser. They contacted Simpson Timber Co. to pre-sell some of the assets to them. With so many entities involved in the purchase, negotiations became quite complicated.

The group agreed to split the properties several ways. Simpson was to purchase the timberlands and the Mad River Plywood plant. Laier, Trione and the Emmersons were to get ten years' cutting rights on the timber growing on the properties, along with the particleboard plant. Simpson was to pay cash for their part of the deal.

Laier, Trione and the Emmersons then formed a corporation, Humboldt Flakeboard. The corporation would own only two assets: the cutting rights and the particleboard plant. R. H. Emmerson & Son bought their half of the plant for $500,000, and Cloverdale Redwood purchased the other half for the same amount. They agreed to divide up the cutting rights on the property so that each party would have their own areas on which to operate. The package (cutting rights and flakeboard plant) was to cost R. H. Emmerson & Son $2,500,000 for their share. They did not have that kind of money.

Red remembers calling Frank Keene at the Bank of America in San Francisco. Frank was in charge of the Commodity Loan Department that handled all of their lending functions to the timber industry in California.

Frank wanted to take a look at the proposed acquisition. He asked Red to pick him up at the Arcata airport, and Red did so in his 1965 Thunderbird. They took off for the woods in this machine. It was probably quite a ride for Mr. Keene.

One quick look and a short conversation with Red was all Frank Keene needed to approve the loan. He told Red to "deal as if you have the money." He guaranteed that the Bank of America would come through with the funds.

Red was a little uneasy in making commitments without the money in his pocket, but he took Frank Keene at his word. When the negotiations with Weyerhauser were finished, the money was waiting for them. They had agreed to borrow $2,500,000 and to pay it off in five years. The loan was actually paid off in three.

Newspaper stories of December 7, 1965, noted the sale of Weyerhauser's 36,000 acres of timberland in Humboldt, Del Norte and Mendocino Counties. Also included were the particleboard plant, plywood plant and logging equipment. Laier at the time was the president of Molalla Forest Products, and Trione was the president of Sonoma Mortgage Co. The Emmersons were partners in R. H. Emmerson & Son.

C. E. Goll, Weyerhauser's Arcata manager, was quoted as saying the reason for the sale was the uncertainty in acquiring a long-term wood supply for their operations. He cited pressures from both federal and state agencies to acquire forest areas for park purposes as the primary reason Weyerhauser found it necessary to leave the Arcata area. The same story would be repeated by other departing companies again and again in the years ahead.

The transaction put R. H. Emmerson & Son on the map in Humboldt County. It also began a long relationship with the Bank of America, and established what was to become known as the Emmerson "track record" in paying back loans. Jim Laier and Red Emmerson also began an association which is still in existence at this time.

Frank Keene was to stay at the Bank of America until 1977. He and his wife, Patty, became personal friends of Red and Ida. They would often attend the annual meetings of the company as honored guests. Frank would make a presentation to management at each of these meetings, describing economic conditions as he saw them, and projecting opportunities for the future. Red considered Frank's advice to be invaluable and valued his friendship highly.

chapter eighteen

FURTHER EXPANSION

After the acquisition of the Weyerhauser holdings in Humboldt County in late 1965, R. H. Emmerson & Son concentrated on running the sawmill at Samoa and, with Laier and Trione, managing Humboldt Flakeboard. The first order of business was to run a profitable organization so that the debt owed the Bank of America could be promptly paid off.

The operation at Susanville was also occupying a great deal of the Emmersons' attention; and the settlement of the claim with the insurance company had provided some much needed capital. However, this money had to be reinvested within two years or be subject to taxation as income.

In 1967, in the little town of Hayfork, California, there were two separate lumber operations. One, on the east edge of town, was a sawmill owned by Ed Head. The other, on the west end, belonged to American Forest Products (AFPC).

Ed Head had owned a grocery store at Happy Camp, but always wanted to be in the sawmill business. He had sold out at Happy Camp and built a small mill at Hyampom, a few miles west of Hayfork. In 1962, the Hyampom mill burned. Head then built a new mill at Hayfork, using some of the machinery that was saved from the fire.

The new mill had an 8-foot Klamath head rig, a 7-foot vertical resaw, a 4-saw edger and a trimmer. It produced about 130 MBF per shift, lumber tally. While it was considered to be a big mill, there were quite a number of mills of that size scattered across northern California.

Production in a sawmill can be described in various ways. Foresters usually like to describe mill production in terms of the amount of logs the mill consumes per shift, or per year. Sawmill managers like to describe it in terms of the amount of lumber produced from the logs per shift. The former is called log scale; the latter is called lumber tally. The two numbers vary considerably due to a number of factors.

Log scale is a measure of the number of one-inch boards that can be sawn from a log of given diameter, with an allowance for the thickness of the saw (which turns that part of the log into sawdust).

The log is not usually sawn exclusively into one-inch boards. It is sawn into thicker boards, cants, timbers, or other products. Thus the portion of the log made into sawdust is less when the log is sawn into thicker pieces. Even the measurement of these various products is not in full inches. For example, a "2X4" is not two inches by four inches; it is somewhat less. However, when sold, the mill "takes credit" for selling the full "2X4." To complicate matters even more, each species of log is sawn to different thicknesses. Describing production can be a very confusing project unless the basis of measurement is specified.

The difference between log scale and

Liz Hoaglen at Hayfork office, 1991.
Photo by Pat Gustafson.

lumber tally is termed overrun (or underrun) in the trade. It can be useful for measuring the efficiency of the operation. Lumber tally also is good for describing the size of an operation in terms of the amount of wood produced. This can be easily translated to dollars, since lumber is sold on a lumber-tally basis.

Since the measurement of the size of an operation can be based also on log scale, it is often used for that purpose because it is quite constant from one operation to another. The basis for describing the production of an operation should always indicate whether log scale or lumber tally is used.

In the mid-1960s, timber supply was becoming a problem for Ed Head, for he was competing with American Forest Products for timber sales on the Hayfork District of the Shasta-Trinity National Forest. The Emmersons and Crooks knew this, and thought that Head's mill at Hayfork might be for sale. He was approached and indicated interest in listening to a proposal. The acquisition was made in March of 1967.

There were only a few logs at the mill then; and Curly Emmerson wanted to know why anyone would want to buy a sawmill with no logs and no timber behind it. Red by that time was actually running most of the Emmerson operations. Curly was concentrating on construction activities and looking after his ranching interests.

Red thought the company could compete with anyone, particularly a large publicly-held company, because they usually were bound up with procedural matters and had too many employees trying to make decisions. In his opinion, that always resulted in excessive production costs and an inability to move quickly when an opportunity presented itself.

After buying the mill, the new owners rebuilt the "front end" so that logs could be fed from the opposite side of the mill. This facilitated a better flow of logs, and allowed for feeding the mill from a point closer to the log storage area. A Klamath carriage and a 7-foot pony rig were also installed.

Liz Hoaglen, the accountant at the Hayfork operation today, was working in the office there in 1967. She remembers that Red spent a great deal of time in Hayfork when the building project was underway. Curly used to be there quite often, "to check up on Red" as she put it. Curly was in charge of the construction, and Red had assumed management of the production facilities. This was perfectly acceptable to Curly as he was bowing out of actively making management decisions.

John Crook also spent considerable time there. Liz says that he rarely came to Hayfork with an overnight bag or a change of clothes. She would be directed to buy him the necessary clothing at Earnie's in downtown Hayfork. Red and John got along very well during those days, and spent a lot of time together. They succeeded in getting thrown out of both the restaurant and the hotel in Hayfork on the same day. Liz did not specify what the offense was.

Curly would drive to Hayfork from either Arcata or Susanville. Flying was not for him. After several hours, or several days with Red and John, he would ask Liz to take him to town for cheeseburgers. After eating, he would want her to drive him to her place where she kept several horses that she owned. This was his way of relaxing away from the pressures of Red and John. He loved just to be around animals; and the two of them would sit there and discuss horses and ranching.

Liz had a new 1967 Mercury Cougar which she was very proud of. She would drive this automobile to the airport to pick up either Red or John when they arrived. On one of the first occasions after purchasing it, she went to get John Crook. As was her custom, she slid over onto the passenger's seat to let John drive to the mill. Instead, he took off for the grassy field at the airport and spun circles in the mud while she hung on in terror. She says that "John was a real character."

After the mill was rebuilt, the first manager was Luther Stienhauser. Luther had come to Hayfork from somewhere in Oregon. He managed the operation until the latter part of 1970. Other key people were Walt Caples, the accountant, and Vern Matson, who was the forester from 1967 until January of 1971.

At the same time, AFPC, at the opposite end of town, was running out of timber on the property they owned on the shoulder of South Fork Mountain west of Hayfork. This property was known as the University Hills tract. They

Trimmer being placed in new Hayfork sawmill building, 1965. Photo from SPI archives Hayfork.

Modernization of Hayfork sawmill, 1965. Head rig and carriage in foreground, pony rig can be seen in background. Photo from SPI archives Hayfork.

Pouring concrete for the new mill at Hayfork in 1965. The men pictured are Fred Weinzinger, Jim Swearingin and Guy Scruggs.   Photo from SPI archives Hayfork.

had selectively logged much of the timber that was considered of merchantable size for their mill. There was still a considerable quantity of small White fir timber there, but they considered it inferior to the other species.

The mill was old and becoming obsolete and, with little assured timber supply for the future, there was insufficient incentive to modernize the mill. However, an effort was still being made to run the mill with Forest Service timber. The two mills at Hayfork, and others in nearby communities, competed for the limited resources available.

The Crooks and Emmersons knew this; and with their purchase of the Head mill, the competitive level was raised. Bid prices were going up.

Early in 1968, AFPC was approached to see if they would be interested in getting rid of their old mill and the headaches that went

with trying to supply it with logs. A short time later, the dickering began in earnest. Finally, an agreement was reached, and the sawmill was purchased in March of 1968. The timberland on Southfork Mountain did not go with it.

The AFPC mill had better planing facilities and dry kilns than those at the old Head sawmill on the other end of town. It was decided to tear down the old AFPC mill and upgrade the planer and kilns. This was done in 1968, and the operations were consolidated under one manager. Lumber would be sawn east of town, and trucked to the other end where it was dried, surfaced and shipped. The office was consolidated at the AFPC office, which was an old two-story frame building.

If Red and John Crook thought they were buying out some competition for timber, they were only partly correct. One competitor was gone, but many more showed up to take its place. Bid prices did not go down. There was a difference though; the surviving mill in Hayfork competing for timber was a far more efficiently-run outfit than the two that had been there before.

About two years later, Luther Stienhauser, the first manager, left Hayfork because of dissatisfaction with a change in his method of compensation. He had participated in a company program of remuneration based on the profitability of the operation he managed. John Crook did not like that arrangement, and prevailed in attempting to change it. He asked Luther to accept an increase in salary in lieu of an incentive. Luther promptly quit.

Fritz Hagen replaced Luther in October of 1970. Fritz would stay with the company for a long time, and would be a valued employee and involved in major expansions still to come.

For most of his life, Conrad Hagen had gone by the name Fritz, his father's name. He was born in Los Angeles in 1928, and showed good sense in picking parents who would bring him to Coos Bay when he was only one-year-old.

Fritz attended schools at North Bend. He had less than one year of college, but secured an appointment to West Point Military Academy. Failing the dental requirements for admission, Fritz refused to have his dental problems corrected. As a result, he spent two years in the Navy as a radarman.

He married Gloria Holland in 1951 and went to work in the Coos Bay sawmill industry, becoming a Certified Lumber Grader. In 1955, he went to work for Bob Monson at Alderpoint, who used to take some of the key personnel on deer hunting expeditions to Nevada in season. On one of those excursions, Fritz met Red Emmerson and John Crook.

Fritz went to Colorado for a short time to

Sawmill complex owned by American Forest Products Corp. and later purchased by SPI in 1968. The office is small building at lower left center. The dry kilns and planing mill were all used by SPI for several years after the mill was closed. Photo from SPI archives Hayfork.

help build a sawmill; but the owners backed out when the lumber market began to deteriorate prior to the mill beginning production. Fritz was left high and dry in Colorado. He remembered Red and John, contacted them for a job, and was assigned to be a shift foreman at the mill recently purchased at Susanville.

Later, Fritz was transferred to the Happy Camp sawmill, where he worked for about two years. When Luther Stienhauser left SPI, Fritz and Gloria moved to Hayfork and he became Hayfork's second manager.

Lumber sales at Hayfork were handled by Paul Treub. He began in 1967. Liz Hoaglen and Paul did not get along well. She fought him from the beginning. Red thought that both of them were partly to blame for that state of affairs; but they were both good for the company. He knew that one of them would eventually have to go if matters did not improve. Finally, John Crook drew Liz aside and asked her to "be a little nicer" to Paul. She complied with his request; but it was very difficult for her to do so. The two of them barely tolerated each other during the time Paul was there. He was the only salesman Hayfork ever had, and transferred to Redding in the late 1970s.

There were a number of logging contractors who delivered logs to the Hayfork operation over the years. Hollenbeak Logging Co. was one of the first; it was managed by Eddie Murrison. Hollenbeak had a truck shop located near the site of the present office. Glenbrook Lumber Co., owned by Bill Kershaw and Bob Mead, were big loggers there in the early 1970s. Timber Contractors, owned by Vic Masters, was also a major logger in the Hayfork valley.

About the same time, at Eagle Lake, a young forester was hired who would have a lasting impact on the company. His name was Gary Shaffer; he came to work in September 1968.

Gary had graduated in Forestry from Humboldt State some four years earlier. He had worked for U. S. Plywood in Humboldt County during the summers and accepted a job with them upon graduating. At U. S. Plywood, he worked for Leonard Lindberg, a civil engineer, who would go on to manage the Northern California Log Scaling Bureau in later years.

Gary did a lot of surveying while at U. S. Plywood. He met Bob Kleiner while doing that, since Kleiner was also a surveyor. Gary left U. S. Plywood in 1966, taking a job with Sam Arness who owned Humboldt Fir at Hoopa. In September 1968, Kleiner recommended him for the job at Susanville with Eagle Lake. Gary was glad to leave the brush and wet climate in Humboldt County to head for the dry, flat ground of the east side.

Gary probably had much to do with instituting the image that Emmerson foresters would assume in the coming years. His strong suit was cruising and appraising timber. He had an excellent business head, and would aggressively stand up for the position the company took in all forestry matters. He was a "company man" to the core.

Thus, in the late 1960s, there was a sawmill and particleboard plant at Arcata, a sawmill at Susanville and another at Hayfork. The Emmersons owned some of these operations themselves, but had partners in several of the ventures. The business was becoming quite complicated and extensive; and major expansions were still to come.

chapter nineteen

THE EARLY ADVISORS

During an approximate 20-year period, beginning about 1950, there were two men who had considerable influence on the direction the Emmersons' business would go. Red, of course, ran the show, but he listened to these two and took their advice more often than not. One was an attorney, Francis "Moose" Mathews; the other was a Certified Public Accountant (CPA), Don Riewerts.

As the name implies, Moose was a big man with a big voice. He always wore soft black shoes that made his feet look enormous. He had an imposing courtroom presence. He was also very smart, knew the law, and he could be very cagey when it came to business.

Moose was a bird-watcher of the first order. He was an expert at his avocation, and would take trips to places like the Aleutians or Africa to watch birds. He also was a wine aficionado and loved to play chess. He was an interesting man to be around.

Moose had grown up in Oakland and Berkeley, and had graduated from Cal-Berkeley. He studied for the bar, passed it, and intended to stay in the Bay Area to practice law. At that time, he had an uncle who lived in Lafayette, where he stayed immediately after graduation. He discovered that it took almost an hour-and-a-half to get home in the evenings, and that soured him on getting anything done if he worked in the city. His working time would be too short, and he was a workaholic.

He decided to head north since, in the late '40s, the timber industry in the Eureka-Arcata area was booming. He thought there would be opportunities there for a new lawyer. In 1947, he arrived with his wife Minette and opened an office. In a short time, he was a busy man.

Moose is not the usual attorney who gets to the office at 9:00 or 10:00 a.m. He arrives at 5:30 or 6:00 a.m., and he is there until late in the evening. If there is something to be prepared, he will work all night at it. He has a special knack for dictating agreements, letters, or other documents without referring to notes or references. Many attorneys will promise a finished document in a week or so. Moose will prepare it while you wait, or have it ready the next morning.

By the time Red got his discharge from the Marines, Moose had met Curly. Curly was divorcing his second wife, Myrtle, and he was representing Curly in the proceedings. He met Red for the first time when Red arrived home from the service.

The Emmersons discovered that Moose was an excellent attorney who would work tirelessly for his clients. They began to use him in their business dealings. His trait of getting to his office at 5:30 a.m. endeared him to Red. Soon he was considered the company attorney, although he was not on the payroll.

One of the first problems the Emmersons

Moose Mathews on bird-watching expedition to Galapagos Islands, 1988.
Photo from Francis Mathews.

brought to Moose involved a parcel of timberland for sale in the Snow Camp area that appeared to be "land locked", i.e., there was no right-of-way over which logs could be hauled. Since the owners wished to sell, they were willing to take a deep discount because of the lack of access. No other buyer would take the chance of purchasing something that was of little use to them. The Emmersons asked Mathews to review the documents. It appeared to them that access was blocked by the adjacent property owner, Abe Rochlin.

Moose studied the papers carefully. He determined that Rochlin did not control the road, and that it could be used for hauling logs from the property the Emmersons wanted to buy. He advised them accordingly; and the property was purchased at the discounted price.

Moose, of course, was correct. The Emmersons were impressed. He could make them a lot of money. As time went on, they would use the young attorney more and more.

The Mathews and Emmerson families became close friends, particularly "Butch" Mathews and George Emmerson, the elder sons of each family. Minette and Ida would spend a great deal of time together in the summers, entertaining their children while their husbands were tending to their respective businesses. Moose remembers that their families would, on many occasions, spend an entire afternoon in the swimming pool at the Ingomar Club; in many cases they would be the only ones there.

When he was quite small, Mark, Red's youngest son, was good at a game called Four Square, which Moose considered to be a good mind game. He decided if Mark was good at Four Square, he would be good at chess, so he taught him how to play.

In no time, Moose was "having to pay attention" or Mark would beat him. After a few months playing together, Mark was beating him "about 50% of the time." Moose was impressed with the young man's intelligence.

Along with Moose, Don Riewerts was also an early advisor. He, too, had been raised in the Bay Area. He had grown up in Oakland; and, in the fall of 1942, enrolled at Berkeley.

The war was on by that time, and Don entered the Navy V-12 program for another year at Cal. Then he was sent to Harvard; and after a year there, received his commission as an Ensign. He was stationed aboard ship as a disbursing officer. After the war, he went back to Berkeley where he graduated with a degree in Business Administration.

After a couple of years as an accountant, Don was sent to Humboldt County by his employer, a predecessor of Arthur Young and Co., one of the big accounting firms. This firm had several large accounts: one being The Pacific Lumber Co.; the other the Russ family, pioneers in Humboldt County. The firm was opening a new office in an area that was enjoying the postwar boom. Don arrived in 1947 to open the new office.

In 1950, he took the CPA exam and passed. The same year he began to do some auditing work for the Emmersons' operation on Samoa Road. There he became acquainted with Red, Curly and Moose. In 1952, he bought an accounting practice owned by Alf Westenberg, and continued to do accounting work for the Emmersons. His business prospered.

The two men, Moose and Don, were quite different. While Moose's manner was more polished, his appearance was rumpled and he affected the style of a country lawyer. He would listen carefully to what one had to say. Even though on many occasions he "shot from the hip," his pronouncements were usually well-thought-out and accurate.

Don, on the other hand, did not project a polished manner. He chain-smoked, spoke with a grating voice, and did not listen very well. He was brash, opinionated, noisy and somewhat overbearing.

The two probably had far more in common than they had differences. Both were experts in their fields. Both worked for their clients tirelessly; and they would do everything legally possible to further their clients' interests. To some, it might appear that their zeal in that respect overstepped the bounds of propriety. Not to the Emmersons; they considered the two men priceless. They were consulted on many of the transactions that the Emmersons undertook, and on the problems they encountered along the way.

Don Riewerts in 1991. Photo from Don Riewerts.

Robert E. Kleiner on old log landing, as most of his friends and co-workers knew him.
Photo from Sue Kleiner (one of Sue Kleiner's favorite photos of her husband).

chapter twenty

R.E. KLEINER

Whenever SPI was considering the purchase of a substantial tract of timberland, Red always turned to an old friend for advice. Bob Kleiner owned Western Timber Services (WTS), which he founded in the early 1950s. The offices were located in the Lumbermen's Building in Arcata. Bob, Sue and their two sons, Bob and Bill, were all involved in the family's forestry consulting business. The Kleiners became personal friends of Red and Ida Emmerson.

Red and Curly became acquainted with "Kleiner" when Bob first came to Arcata. They hit it off immediately. Bob could drink with the best of them; and the Emmersons, in those years, were among the best. The Emmersons developed a great deal of respect for "Kleiner," not only for his drinking ability, but for his attention to business. Bob would be in the office at 5:30 or 6:00 a.m. Usually, if he were in town, he observed the 5:00 p.m. cocktail hour in his office, or at one of the watering holes on the Arcata Plaza. He was in the office on Saturday and Sunday, if he wasn't in the woods or out of town. He was always accessible to either Red or Curly.

Early in the 1950s, WTS hired young foresters who would become well-known in forestry circles. Besides "Pop" Givens, there was Frank Schmidt, who would work for the State Board of Equalization in California for many years. Al Devoe, after leaving WTS, ended up working for the old Western Pine Association. Dick Johnson later became the company cruiser for Roseburg Lumber Co. until his retirement in the early 1980s.

The two Graham brothers, Bobby and Brian, were with WTS for many years; Brian is still there. Davey Meyer and Ned Simmons were associated with WTS. Al Nielsen was a partner of Kleiner's at one time, and Jerry Cone was an associate. The list looks like the Who's Who of Humboldt County foresters.

Red, especially, respected Bob. He told me that "Kleiner" could not be bought. Bob made it a practice of never being a principal in a timber transaction. He felt that a cruising, consulting and appraisal service should not be in the business of competing with clients for the purchase of land or timber.

Bob was born in 1919 in Illinois. He hitchhiked to Seattle to go to college and enrolled to be a forester. He was in the R.O.T.C. program and took time off from school to fight a war. After WW II, he went back to earn a Masters Degree in Forest Engineering at the University of Washington.

Both my wife and I had known Bob before he migrated to California from Oregon. I had met him in 1951 when he worked as a forester for Douglas County in Roseburg, Oregon. At the time, he was unmarried and a budding character.

As a young forester, I was spending a

good portion of my working hours cruising timber for Fir Manufacturing Co., my employer. Occasionally it would be necessary to consult the county assessor's office for information about land ownership, or the surveyor's office about property corners. Bob would be helpful in those endeavors, and would do cruising work besides. He was a "field forester," first and foremost. On occasion, as the years went by, I would call on their firm to do cruising or appraisal work.

Late in 1951, Bob and Everett Givens, one of Bob's associates at Douglas Co., stopped by the office where I worked. They had quit at Douglas Co., and were on their way to Eureka to begin a consulting business. They had a bottle of Old Forester with them to toast their hoped-for success. It was early in the morning; but in a couple of hours, the bottle was nearly empty. That day, the forestry crew at Fir Manufacturing Co. did not accomplish much that could be considered productive.

From the day I met Bob, he had a "butch" haircut. He was given the nickname "Mumbles" because he talked very quietly without moving his lips. On first impression, he seemed to be about as dumb as a person could be. He wasn't.

I watched him one day, several years later, in a courtroom where he was qualified as an expert witness. Francis "Moose" Mathews had hired him on behalf of a client; and I watched as Moose questioned him on the witness stand.

Bob spoke very quietly into the microphone, his eyes never leaving the attorney's face. He did not elaborate. He would pause to carefully consider a question, then answer in short concise sentences. His choice of words was outstanding. Because of the microphone, he could be heard, and everyone listening was impressed.

When it was time for attorney Bob Dedekam to cross-examine Bob, Dedekam said, "I have no questions, your honor."

At the noon break, as we streamed out of the courtroom, I overheard Mathews ask Dedekam why he had not cross-examined Bob Kleiner. Dedekam's answer made a lasting impression on me.

He said, "Francis, I've seen your witness operate. I'm an attorney, and Kleiner is an expert forester. He's carved up attorneys from the witness stand before. I'm not going to give him a chance to do it to me."

As SPI grew and more foresters were hired, Red still consulted with "Kleiner." It was disconcerting for SPI foresters to have their judgments questioned by Red after he got an opinion from Bob. Red would describe the situation as he saw it; the two would discuss it, and Red would come back to the SPI forester either in agreement or not. In this way, WTS had a great deal of influence on forestry decisions made at SPI.

While Red liked WTS's work, he did not like their billings. The bills would be deposited on the forest manager's desk. Red would complain about the size of them, saying that if Bob Kleiner had learned anything about being a consultant, one thing he had learned well was how to charge clients. Of course, the bills were always paid on time, and Red always went back to WTS for more advice.

Unlike many forestry consultants, WTS was field-oriented. While other firms farmed out their field work to become expert at interpreting the work done by others, and in producing long reports and beautiful maps, Bob would not do that. In his view, faulty field work resulted in faulty conclusions. He insisted they do the field work themselves, or have it done under their immediate supervision.

WTS was among the first to advocate heavy use of 100% cruises and the climbing of trees to measure form class (the ratio of the diameter at 16-1/2 feet above the ground to diameter at 4-1/2 feet). Such attention to basics took hard work; but it produced accurate timber cruises and appraisals. There was none better at it than WTS.

Bob worked in the woods until the last. He was cruising timber on Prince of Wales Island in Alaska when he had a heart attack and died on June 21, 1989. The ground on his cruise strip was steep and brushy. The rest of the crew found him dead. He had died, at 70 years, a field forester to the end. Red lost a good friend, a hunting and drinking buddy, and an expert forester.

Bill Kleiner and his mother, Sue, carry on at Western Timber Services. They continue Bob Kleiner's commitment to field forestry, and SPI makes good use of their talents. Bob also taught them well how to bill clients.

chapter twenty one

SIERRA PACIFIC INDUSTRIES

In the late 1960s, it became popular in the business community to discuss ways of "having your cake and eating it too." One of the theories advocated the formation of a publicly-owned company. The new enterprise could be structured in such a way that the owner of a private company would have public financing, but would still control his company.

John Crook had read about these possibilities. The ideas intrigued him; and with the knowledge gained from his reading and discussions with others, he suggested to Red they take their operations public. John was quite enthusiastic about the prospects, but Red was lukewarm. Red finally was convinced by John and others that he could probably make more money if the company were public than he could if the company were private and he owned it. That sold him.

They decided to investigate the procedure in depth, and contacted several brokerage firms in the Bay Area to advise them. White, Weld and Co. was one of them. John and Red were told it would be necessary to clean up some of the various ownerships of the divisions that might go into a package for public ownership. Humboldt Flakeboard was still owned in part by Laier and Trione. It would not be desirable to have only a portion of a company owned by the public. As a result, an independent, third-party appraisal was made to value Humboldt Flakeboard; and it was offered for sale to Permaneer Co., who agreed to buy it.

It was also necessary to prepare financial statements for the past three years that were, in effect, pro-forma statements for the entities which would make up the new company. These statements would show how the various endeavors had done financially, had they been operated as one public company.

The next step was to select an accounting firm. After considerable discussion, they selected Jim Maxwell, from the firm of Ernst and Ernst, to prepare the necessary financial statements and to certify the results. Don Riewerts was heavily involved in this endeavor. The task was quite difficult, since it was necessary to value the portion that each family owned for each of the parts, and to value all of the assets on a common basis.

After the dust settled, it was determined that the Emmersons had more value than the Crooks. Of course, Pacific Fir Sales, Mike Crook's sales company, was not included. In order to even-out the value each family owned, Curly Emmerson would be issued $2,500,000 of subordinated debentures.

On January 31, 1969, most of the separate businesses that made up the Emmerson and Crook interests were brought into one. The new company was called Sierra Pacific Industries (SPI). The name was selected through a contest held among the employees of the various divisions at the time. Lloyd Bailey, Sales Manager of Humboldt

Flakeboard, was the lucky winner. The prize was $100.

After dickering with Permaneer for the sale of Humboldt Flakeboard, Sierra Pacific had decided to purchase the Laier and Trione stock for themselves. SPI paid Cloverdale Redwood Co. $3,500,000 for their half-interest in Humboldt Flakeboard. That took Laier and Trione out of the company.

There was an attempt made to obtain the letters SPI as the abbreviation designating the new company on the stock exchange. That was not possible, since those letters were already in use, so a compromise was reached. The letters "SIP" were adopted to label the new company for trading purposes.

The principal subsidiaries making up the new company were:

Eagle Lake Lumber Co.
Humboldt Flakeboard Log Transport Inc.
J and R Millwork Sales
Siskiyou Mouldings Inc.
South Fork Timber Products Inc.
R. H. Emmerson & Son

A couple of the enterprises above-named were somewhat obscure and were largely inactive; however, they were still legally in existence at the time SPI was formed. All of them were owned in varying proportions by the Crooks and the Emmersons. There may have been some minor stockholders involved in some of them. South Fork Timber Products was the Hayfork operation. Siskiyou Mouldings at the time included the Happy Camp sawmill, as well as the plant at Yreka.

With the value of the debentures issued to Curly Emmerson deducted from the total value of the assets, the resulting Emmerson and Crook interests were equal. As a result, John Crook and Red Emmerson each owned 50% of the new company. The company was then poised to go public.

On April 24, 1969, the Board of Directors of Sierra Pacific Industries met to approve a set of by-laws, and to elect members to the Board. Those elected were:

Arthur B. Adams, Lawrence Warehouse Co.
M. W. Crook, Pacific Fir Sales
R. H. Emmerson, R. H. Emmerson & Son
Fortney Stark, Jr., Security National Bank, Walnut Creek

In addition, the Board confirmed the election of the following to office:

A. A. Emmerson, President
John B. Crook, Executive Vice-President
Donald Riewerts, Secretary and Treasurer
M. W. Crook, Vice-President
R. H. Emmerson, Vice-President

On June 11, 1969, a press release was issued informing the public that White, Weld Group offered 700,000 shares of Sierra Pacific Industries common stock at $18 per share. The release described the company as having four sawmills, a particleboard plant, and a millwork plant, all located in northern California. The company believed it to be among the 12 largest lumber producers and the ten largest particleboard manufacturers in the United States.

A few days after SPI stock became available to the public, Dwight Eisenhower suffered a heart attack. As a result, there was an immediate sell-off in the markets, and SPI stock closed at $16 two days later.

No matter; the paper work connected with appraisals, financial statements, filings with the Securities and Exchange Commission, underwriting documents, by-laws, and similar matters were finally finished. The pertinent documents were bound into an official book about four-inches thick. Supporting papers filled several filing cabinets in several offices. That part of the procedure was finally over.

Life was to be far more complicated for Red Emmerson from that day forward. While he and John Crook still controlled the company, they had public stockholders who were protected by law and various regulations. All financial details would be a matter of public record. They would be required to file, with various government agencies, numerous reports and documents which were not required before. On top of it all, they still had several plants to manage to show a profit for their new stockholders.

On September 19, 1969, the Siskiyou Mouldings plant at Yreka caught fire while it was undergoing modernization, and a portion of it burned. The loss was estimated at up to $1,500,000. At the time, 35 to 40 people were employed there.

Ron Stevens was in charge of the plant. A

new re-saw system had been installed only the week before the fire. Two loaded railroad cars were destroyed; but firemen managed to save the office building and a shed full of high-grade lumber just south of the plant. There were some bright spots evident in the situation: the buildings and contents were insured; and the company was large enough to withstand the loss of production and profits while reconstruction got underway.

The 1969 Annual Report listed net sales for the year ended December 31, 1969, at $38,113,734, of which 77% came from lumber, 12% particleboard, and 11% from other products (chips, logs, etc.). Net income was reported at $5,078,277, or $1.45 per share. At that time, the stock was owned 40% by John Crook, 40% by Red Emmerson, and 20% by the public.

The Annual Report also listed John B. Crook as **Chairman** and A. A. Emmerson as President. Kenneth LaBoube had been hired as Vice-President, Administration and Planning. Mike Crook had resigned from the Board.

Notes on the last page indicated SPI consisted of:

Coachmate, Inc.	Redding
Eagle Lake Division	Susanville
Emmerson Division	Arcata
Humboldt Flakeboard	Arcata
Inyokern Division	Inyokern
Lassen Wood Products	Susanville
Siskiyou Mills Division	Happy Camp and Yreka
South Fork Division	Hayfork

The report noted that 50% of Humboldt Flakeboard was purchased in January, and $6,800,000 was invested in improving existing facilities. Humboldt Flakeboard was a recipient of part of the funds to increase its production 20%, to a rated annual capacity of 90,000,000 square feet on a 3/4" basis.

While the report listed Lassen Wood Products and Coachmate as owned by SPI, it also stated that they were acquired in 1970. Evidently the report was printed after those acquisitions were made the following year.

In the report, there is a full-page photograph of the two top executives of SPI standing before an extremely knotty tree that appears to be a pine. Red and John are dressed in conservative blue suits with shirts and ties. They both look like up-and-coming young entrepreneurs ready to set the business world on its ear. The company was poised to do just that.

THE COMPANY

Sierra Pacific Industries (the "Company") was incorporated under the laws of the State of California in January 1969 for the purpose of centralizing the ownership and management of eight corporations and two partnerships engaged primarily in the manufacturing and marketing of lumber and particle board. These businesses were founded or acquired over the past 17 years by John B. Crook and A. A. Emmerson, now officers, directors and the principal shareholders of the Company, and members of their families. The most significant of these companies were Eagle Lake Lumber Co., R. H. Emmerson & Son, Humboldt Flakeboard, Siskiyou Mills and South Fork Timber Products, Inc. The Company believes that this consolidation under a centralized management will permit economies in various aspects of the Company's business.

The Company produced approximately 258 million board feet of lumber and approximately 57 million surface feet, ¾ inch basis, of particle board during 1968. The Company believes that it is among the ten largest lumber producers and among the ten largest particle board manufacturers in the United States.

The Company's principal office is located in Arcata, which is on the California coastline approximately 300 miles north of San Francisco. Unless the context indicates otherwise, the term "Company" as used herein refers to Sierra Pacific Industries, its wholly-owned subsidiaries, and its predecessor companies.

CAPITALIZATION

The following table sets forth the capitalization of the Company at April 24, 1969:

Debt:

Short-term notes	$ 353,206
Long-term notes①	2,144,202
Subordinated debenture②	2,500,000

Capital stock:

Preferred stock, $1 par value, 2,000,000 shares authorized	None
Common stock, $1 par value, 15,000,000 shares authorized	3,500,000 shs.③

① See Note E of Notes to Financial Statements.

② Bearing interest at the prime rate and due in February 1983. See "Management—Transactions with Affiliated Persons."

③ Excludes 200,000 shares reserved for issuance upon exercise of options granted or to be granted under the Company's Qualified Stock Option Plan. See "Management—Qualified Stock Option Plan."

DIVIDENDS

No dividends have been paid by the Company. It is the present intention of the Board of Directors to reinvest earnings for the expansion of the Company's business and the payment of cash dividends is not contemplated. Should the Company in the future adopt a policy of paying dividends, the declaration and payment thereof will depend on earnings, the financial condition of the Company and other factors.

Pages from SPI's 1969 annual report to stockholders.

CONSOLIDATED STATEMENT OF INCOME

The following statement of income includes the results of operations of the various companies combined in the organization and formation of Sierra Pacific Industries, which was incorporated on January 31, 1969. This statement, for the three years ended December 31, 1968, has been examined by Ernst & Ernst, independent accountants, whose report with respect thereto appears elsewhere in this Prospectus. The statement for the years ended December 31, 1964 and 1965 and the three month periods ended March 31, 1968 and 1969 has not been audited, but in the opinion of the Company includes all adjustments, consisting only of normal recurring accruals, necessary to present fairly the results of operations for those periods. Operating results for the three months ended March 31, 1969 are not necessarily indicative of results for the entire year. This statement should be read in conjunction with the other consolidated financial statements and notes thereto appearing elsewhere in this Prospectus.

	Year Ended December 31					Three Months Ended March 31	
	1964	1965	1966	1967	1968	1968	1969
	(Unaudited)	(Unaudited)				(Unaudited)	(Unaudited)
Income:							
Net sales	$10,978,813	$11,572,882	$12,098,372	$17,046,473	$25,372,044	$5,531,375	$10,030,890
Other income	8,748	139,511	156,087	155,092	137,852	28,867	41,043
	10,987,561	11,712,393	12,254,459	17,201,565	25,509,896	5,560,242	10,071,933
Costs and expenses:							
Cost of products sold	9,215,541	9,570,652	10,143,990	13,730,798	18,192,488	4,197,908	5,798,442
Selling, general and administrative①	801,050	900,253	973,125	1,243,064	1,458,750	331,081	693,394
Interest:							
On long-term debt	56,548	70,133	73,815	55,557	51,283	15,810	33,695
Other	29,534	31,115	33,615	88,396	81,661	10,294	5,617
	10,102,673	10,572,153	11,224,545	15,117,815	19,784,182	4,555,093	6,531,148
Income before income taxes, equity in income of 50% owned company and extraordinary gain	884,888	1,140,240	1,029,914	2,083,750	5,725,714	1,005,149	3,540,785
Income taxes①	391,300	493,051	378,991	915,134	2,768,664	442,305	1,777,728
Income before equity in income of 50% owned company and extraordinary gain	493,588	647,189	650,923	1,168,616	2,957,050	562,844	1,763,057
Equity in income of 50% owned company②	—	—	104,044	(45,463)	195,616	7,584	37,356
Income before extraordinary gain	493,588	647,189	754,967	1,123,153	3,152,666	570,428	1,800,413
Extraordinary gain, less applicable deferred income taxes③	—	773,728	—	—	—	—	—
Net income	$ 493,588	$ 1,420,917	$ 754,967	$ 1,123,153	$ 3,152,666	$ 570,428	$ 1,800,413
Per share of Common Stock④:							
Before extraordinary gain	$.12	$.16	$.19	$.30	$.87	$.16	$.51
Extraordinary gain	—	.22	—	—	—	—	—
Net income	$.12	$.38	$.19	$.30	$.87	$.16	$.51

SIERRA PACIFIC INDUSTRIES AND SUBSIDIARIES

CONSOLIDATED BALANCE SHEET

Assets	December 31, 1968	March 31, 1969 (unaudited)
CURRENT ASSETS		
Cash	$ 2,076,808	$ 1,305,675
Commercial paper—at cost (which approximates market)	1,142,501	2,689,673
Trade accounts receivable, less allowance of $11,306 at December 31, 1968 and $13,306 at March 31, 1969 for doubtful accounts	1,025,062	2,942,868
Due from affiliates and stockholders	495,698	37,626
Inventories—at lower of average cost or market:		
Lumber and related products	1,981,356	2,112,976
Logs and related costs	3,409,790	1,868,580
	5,391,146	3,981,556
Prepaid expenses	289,405	359,278
Deferred income taxes—Note D	69,000	116,872
TOTAL CURRENT ASSETS	10,489,620	11,433,548
PROPERTY, PLANT, AND EQUIPMENT—on the basis of cost—Notes C, E, and H		
Timber and timberlands	—	384,302
Land and land improvements	366,600	408,100
Buildings	924,110	1,757,382
Machinery and equipment	7,339,938	12,103,137
Construction in progress	199,563	428,162
	8,830,211	15,081,083
Less allowances for depreciation	3,792,073	4,869,309
	5,038,138	10,211,774
OTHER ASSETS		
Timber cutting rights—at cost	115,521	99,976
Investment in and advances to Humboldt Flakeboard—50% owned company—at cost, plus equity in undistributed income—Note A	894,197	—
Miscellaneous other assets	118,390	162,516
	1,128,108	262,492
	$16,655,866	21,907,814

See notes to financial statements.

SIERRA PACIFIC INDUSTRIES AND SUBSIDIARIES

CONSOLIDATED BALANCE SHEET

Liabilities and Capital	December 31, 1968	March 31, 1969 (unaudited)
CURRENT LIABILITIES		
Notes payable	$ 268,494	$ 355,383
Trade accounts payable	2,338,555	2,084,823
Employee compensation	270,561	563,764
Other accrued expenses	170,875	374,684
Income taxes—Note D	1,900,540	3,697,895
Portion of long-term notes due within one year	284,727	277,431
TOTAL CURRENT LIABILITIES	5,233,752	7,353,980
DEFERRED INCOME TAXES—Note D	695,542	1,044,362
LONG-TERM NOTES, less amount due within one year—Note E	1,060,327	2,042,814
SUBORDINATED DEBENTURE—due February 1, 1983; bearing interest at prime rate; subordinated to all other obligations; callable at 7% premium, decreasing ½% each year to maturity	2,500,000	2,500,000
CAPITAL—Notes A, G and H		
Preferred Stock—$1 par value:		
Authorized 2,000,000 shares; none issued or outstanding	—	—
Common Stock—par value $1 a share:		
Authorized 15,000,000 shares; issued and outstanding 3,500,000 shares	3,500,000	3,500,000
Retained earnings	3,666,245	5,466,658
	7,166,245	8,966,658
COMMITMENTS AND CONTINGENCIES—Notes A and H		
	$16,655,866	$21,907,814

See notes to financial statements.

John Crook and Red Emmerson, two young executives dressed for the boardroom, as pictured in SPI's 1969 annual report to stockholders.

chapter twenty two

THE GO-GO YEARS

The late 1960s and the 1970s were to see diversification and acquisitions abound in corporate America. It was the age of the conglomerate. Numerous large corporations would use their power and money to gobble up competitors, other profitable companies, or companies that might have assets that could be sold off to pay for the acquisition. Many of the acquisitions involved companies that were in an entirely different business from the acquiring company.

For some, the idea was to reduce the cyclical nature of their own business. For instance, the lumber industry had always been profitable at the top of each building cycle. At those times, it was nearly impossible to lose money, no matter how poorly managed the company was. The trouble was, the down-part of the cycle usually lasted longer than the up-part; and there was a lot of money lost in the industry when the housing market collapsed periodically.

To some extent, prices for lumber would even fluctuate on a monthly basis. Usually prices would increase early in the year as the spring building season got under way. They would decrease with the onset of winter, particularly for lumber shipments to the east and midwest. Labor strikes and other causes for reductions in production would affect the price of lumber, and consequently profits.

Particularly in publicly-owned companies, it was desirable to show two things: sustained growth and quarterly profits. A company losing money in a quarter was bad enough; losing money in two or more consecutive quarters made stockholders uneasy. Many companies would resort to "creative accounting" to show profits quarter after quarter, so that dividends could be paid on a regular basis.

Predicting business cycles is a hazardous occupation, and there may have been as many wrong guesses as right. However, it seemed wise at the time to fill in the expected down-cycles by acquiring companies that were not so cyclical in nature, or those whose cycles were opposite from those in the building products business.

In any event, the year 1970 was a growth year for the new company. Early in the year, SPI made a number of acquisitions.

All of the stock of Lassen Wood Products was purchased from Wilbur Christiansen for $210,000. This was a small moulding plant three or four blocks from the Eagle Lake sawmill at Susanville.

On March 30, 1970, SPI purchased 51% of Coachmate, a vinyl wrapped moulding plant owned by Bob Ahrens, Ron Hoppe and Robert Vorhies, at Chico.

Chico Millwork was under construction by SPI at a cost of $1,200,000. A 10-year contract for the export of 100 tons of wood chips annually was signed with Oji Paper Co. of Japan.

SPI formed, and had a 51% interest in, a

Main building of Chico millwork plant in 1990.
Photo by author.

Chico millwork plant's wood-waste storage and truck- loading bins in 1990. Photo by author.

new company called Reeve Investment Co. Earl Reeve was the minority stockholder. The purpose of the venture was to buy and lease-back industrial properties. Only one property was purchased: a parcel where a shopping center was built. The shopping center consisted of one large building that promptly caught fire and burned.

A new stud mill at Inyokern, California was constructed and began production on a limited basis. The establishment of that mill in the desert on the east side of the southern Sierra Nevada is a story in itself.

The Baugh brothers had owned a sawmill at Bishop, California for a number of years. It was a pine mill, and had been constructed to take advantage of the Ponderosa and Jeffrey pine that grew near there. It subsisted mostly on Forest Service timber from the Inyo Forest. However, at the time, pine timber was becoming scarce and White fir made up a larger share of each sale offered. Sometime in the 1960s, the mill closed.

The Baughs had operated a log re-load at the upper end of Nine Mile Canyon, several miles north of the little town of Inyokern. There they decked logs during the summer that were hauled to the site via Forest Service roads on trucks that were overweight for normal highway travel. They fed their mill from this deck in the winter months, or as needed.

After the Bishop mill closed, there were few purchasers for the timber sales on the Inyo Forest. There was interest in the sales; but all of the competitors for the timber owned sawmills far removed from the Inyo. Some of the sales were sizeable - 25 to 30,000 MBF or more. They were being bid at prices low enough to reflect the cost of hauling logs long distances to the existing mills.

Red Emmerson and John Crook knew of the situation. Timber was timber to them, particularly to Red. The closeness to the southern California lumber market was well-known to both of them. Howard Finn, a long-time acquaintance, was interested in the possibilities he saw there. He wanted to bid the timber sales and needed a market for the logs.

Sometime in 1969, it was decided to build a stud mill at Inyokern if SPI could bid successfully on a very large sale that was advertised. The timber was purchased quite easily, and mill construction began soon after.

Inyokern was an odd place for a sawmill. It was in the desert where the wind could blow fiercely, and often did. There was nothing there but sand and sagebrush. They chose a site for the mill just over the line in Inyo County, where they thought the business climate was better, and where it was easier to obtain building permits. There was no town; but China Lake, primarily a Navy town, was only a few miles away.

The mill was never very successful. One of the problems identified later was with the White fir timber itself. It did not lend itself to the manufacture of studs very well. It was old timber growing on poor sites. While it was large in diameter, the trees were short; and the large limbs produced knots in the upper logs that were bigger than the studs were wide.

That was not the only problem. It was extremely difficult to find good help at that location. Wives especially hated the place. SPI management-level employees who were sent to Inyokern felt they had been banished to Siberia; wives felt the same way.

Gary Shaffer was in charge of the forestry activities at Inyokern in the early years. He also hated the place. In 1969, he learned to fly an airplane that at one time was owned by Pacific Fir Sales. It was an old Cessna 180 which Burr Coffelt used to fly to the various operations SPI had. It took Gary 22 hours to solo, and almost a year to get his pilot's license because of all of his other duties; but the plane was a good way to get from Susanville to Inyokern.

Gary remembers being up at dawn in Inyokern to have breakfast with John Crook. John was ecstatic about the sunrise in the desert. He asked Gary, "Don't you just love the desert?"

Gary replied, "John, I hate this place and you know it. It's hotter 'n hell, the wind blows every day, and there's not a tree in sight. I'm a forester, not a damn sourdough. This is the lousiest place for a sawmill I've ever seen. You and Red must be nuts." John didn't reply.

There were several other foresters who were hired to look after the mill's needs there. Bill Bockman was probably the first; and he was there for almost two years. John Marshall and Jerry Burke came after him. Burke was the only one who seemed to like Inyokern.

Southern California was getting some other attention from SPI at that time. A lumber distribution center was established in Ontario, California to handle production principally from the Inyokern mill. It opened for business in 1970.

By the end of its first full year in business, SPI had 850 employees and a net worth of $12,168,000. It had also posted a net loss of $76,316. Perhaps some of the 2,912 shareholders (as of December 31) were a little unhappy with the performance of their company. The loss was two cents per share.

The annual statement noted that lumber prices were off considerably from a year earlier. Douglas fir was off $23 per MBF from $80 a year earlier. White fir was down $24 from $70 a year earlier. The Inyokern mill had incurred higher than anticipated start-up costs, and had only limited production in 1970.

However, the Company had 703,000 MBF of timber under contract, and lumber production, on a lumber tally basis, was as follows:

Arcata	73,000 MBF
Happy Camp	62,000 MBF
Hayfork	65,000 MBF
Susanville	67,000 MBF
Inyokern	22,000 MBF

Although the lumber market in 1970 was poor, SPI had done quite well considering the times. Still, the management team was less than satisfied with the loss the company had sustained. Discussions centered around what to do about it.

Red, in particular, cannot stand a financial statement written in red ink. At the first hint that an operation is not profitable, the telephone rings at the offending division to find out how bad the loss might be. This might occur shortly after the first of the month when the data for the financial statement is ready, and before the statement has

SPI's then new Inyokern sawmill, as pictured in SPI's annual report to stockholders, 1969.

actually been prepared and typed. In some cases, there may have been only a forecast made by the accountant that things did not look good.

In a short time, perhaps in an hour, Red roars in (by plane or car) to discuss what went wrong. The manager of the offending operation is consulted, as is the accountant in charge. The consultations under these circumstances are dreaded by those involved. Voices are seldom raised; but there are no doubts about the seriousness of the situation.

Shortly after the reasons for the losses were identified in 1970, the controller for SPI was replaced by R. L. "Dick" Smith, who had been working at Masonite. After Dick's first interview, John Crook thought he was too old for the job, but Red prevailed in offering him the job. It may have been the single, most significant thing Red ever did to assure the

success of the company. Dick Smith was to have a profound and long-lasting effect on the operations of the company and its profitability.

SPI continued its acquisition program in 1971. Bill Main had owned a sawmill just south of Redding on Branstetter Lane, west of old Highway 99. On El Cajon Blvd. in Central Valley, he also owned and operated a planing mill. Both carried the name Heron Mills after Main sold out. SPI purchased these facilities from the Pughs Bros., and began to run the Branstetter mill.

Chuck Seago managed the Branstetter operation for SPI until January 1, 1974. The mill had actually been purchased for the deck of logs that was stored there in 1971. The plan was to shut the mill down after the logs were sawn to reduce competition for logs and timber. As the deck was being sawn, Red discovered the mill was consistently making a profit, and decided it would be wise to purchase logs and continue to run it.

When it was decided to keep the mill open, Burr Coffelt was put in charge of the day-to-day management of the facility, and Gary Shaffer became the forester. Both Gary and Burr spent most of their time at Susanville, but traveled to Redding as necessary.

With the purchase of a sawmill in the Redding area, SPI had secured a position in another timber/log market. The company now had access to timber, or logs, that could be delivered to Susanville, Redding, Arcata, Happy Camp and Hayfork. Practically all of the timbered counties in the northern part of California were within reach of their sawmills.

On July 1, 1971, SPI acquired Pan American Gyrotex Co. Ltd. The firm was located in Franklin Park (near Chicago), and had a plant in Jacksonville, Florida. There were distribution warehouses in Elkhart, Indiana; Marshfield, Wisconsin; Tulsa, Oklahoma; Ocala, Florida; and Lancaster, Pennsylvania. They manufactured plywood overlaid with hardwood veneer, much of which had to be imported.

On July 9, 1971, Johnson Sawdust Inc. was purchased for 15,841 shares of SPI stock worth about $200,000. The plant was at Paramount, California, and made soil additives. It was to be operated by SPI as a subsidiary.

In August, the company acquired Gage Products in Anaheim, California. This company made pre-hung doors. Annual sales for Gage were $114,000. The acquisition turned out to be a bad deal, as it cost about $25,000 to buy it and considerably more to get rid of it later.

A big step was being planned in 1971. SPI was considering entering the retail lumber business in a big way. The first retail store was planned for a grand opening in 1972. The stores were to be quite elaborate structures, where everything a builder or a do- it-yourselfer needed could be found under one roof. John Crook thought this would be a good way to integrate their manufacturing know-how with the selling of their own products - a value-added operation.

Company operations were far-flung as the year drew to a close. It was increasingly difficult for Red and John to personally look after everything that was going on in the operations, for they were scattered all over the country.

Red, particularly, was becoming uneasy about the expansion into lines that he knew very little about. It was a far cry from the little lean-to office on Samoa Road, where R. H. Emmerson & Son had started, to the corporate office in Walnut Creek. It was necessary to hob-nob with bankers and politicians and to dress in a suit and tie more often. Red and Ida, each having a high school education, may have felt a mite inferior with all of the posturing and trappings of power that were evident in the corporate world. If they did, they did not show it, and they need not have worried anyway. They were becoming recognized as a force in the business world.

At the end of 1971, SPI had over 1,000 employees, 10% of whom were represented by a union. There were 2,228 shareholders, and total sales were over $58,000,000. There was 676,000 MBF of timber under contract, and 350,000 MBF of lumber was produced on a lumber tally basis. Total assets were almost $34,000,000.

The company was poised to grow some more.

SIERRA PACIFIC INDUSTRIES

Directors

Arthur B. Adams, *President,* Lawrence Warehouse Co.
John B. Crook
M. W. Crook*
A. A. Emmerson
R. H. Emmerson
George H. Pfau, Jr., *Partner,* White, Weld & Co.
Donald E. Riewerts
Fortney H. Stark, Jr., *President,* Security National Bank

Officers

John B. Crook, *Chairman*
A. A. Emmerson, *President*
R. H. Emmerson, *Vice President*
Kenneth T. LaBoube, *Vice President, Administration
    and Planning*
Donald E. Riewerts, *Secretary-Treasurer*

Transfer Agents

Bank of America N.T. & S.A.
San Francisco, Calif.

Bankers Trust Company
New York, N.Y.

Registrars

Wells Fargo Bank, N.A.
San Francisco, Calif.

Morgan Guaranty Trust Company
New York, N.Y.

Sierra Pacific Industries

Coach-Mate, Inc.	Redding
Eagle Lake Division	Susanville
Emmerson Division	Arcata, Calif.
Humboldt Flakeboard	Arcata, Calif.
Inyokern Division	Inyokern
Lassen Wood Products	Susanville
Siskiyou Mills Division	Happy Camp & Yreka
South Fork Division	Hayfork, Calif.

CORPORATE OFFICES:

822 G Street, Arcata, California 95521

REGIONAL OFFICE:
45 Quail Court, Walnut Creek, California 94596

*resigned October 30, 1969

Decking logs for future conversion.

Hayfork, in Northern California's Coast Range.

27

A page from SPI's 1969 annual report to stockholders.

chapter twenty three

ANSWERMAN AND MORE

The year 1972 was relatively quiet for SPI after the expansion of the previous two years. However, a significant event occurred with the opening of the first retail, building-supply store owned by the company: the Answerman store in Orem, Utah. There would be more of them to come, all in the western states. Each store would be similar, i.e., large, well-stocked and in a prime location. The second one was opened soon after the first, this one in Sacramento.

Several months after the store in Sparks, Nevada, opened for business, I had occasion to visit it. Since I lived in the community, I drove by it nearly every morning on my way to work. Being curious, I wanted to see what the new place had to offer, and found it was a unique and intriguing place to shop for building materials. At the time, I did not know that it was owned by SPI.

The building was new and quite large for a building supply store. It appeared to be a supermarket. Inside were bright lights, aisles filled with hardware, paints, fixtures and gadgets of every description. Lumber was displayed, stacked vertically, with each board labeled with a price sticker. However, some of the employees were far more interesting.

The great majority were attractive young ladies. They were attired in shorts and blouses. In the idiom of the day, the lower portion of their costume could be labeled "hot pants." At that time, in the Reno-Sparks area, the costume was probably not out of place; many women affected the style on the streets. Today their costumes would be considered to be inappropriate in a business establishment, for they might be construed as sexist. In that era and in that location, it was not considered to be bizarre. There was one problem, however.

Most of the employees had little training or experience in the building trades, or in household repairs. For example, it was very difficult to explain to many of them what I was looking for, because they had no idea what I was talking about. They were very friendly and polite; but it was not quite the same as the old friendly lumber yard where the clerk knew what one wanted almost before a full description was given. Some customers, including me, went back to the old familiar establishments for the needed supplies.

Elsewhere at SPI, it was business as usual, which meant continued change. Lassen Wood Products was sold in 1972, since it had never made money. At Inyokern, a portion of the log deck caught fire; and it was impossible to control, since the usual winds were of hurricane velocity. The result was a pre-tax loss of $600,000.

Near year-end, the stock of Lamb Bros. was purchased as a joint venture with Harwood Investment Co., and then liquidated. Lamb Bros. was a ranching business with property located primarily in Humboldt County, east of Hydesville and north of Highway 36. There was also significant acreage located not far from Ruth Lake in Trinity County, and a few parcels scattered in other locations. A good deal of the property was grassland, but there was good timber growing in a number of locations.

Bud and Virginia Harwood owned sawmills at Branscomb and Willits. They concentrated on sawing redwood, but used Douglas fir and other species on occasion. They also owned timberland in the vicinity of their mills. Theirs was a family-owned business much like the Emmersons' before SPI was formed. Their son Art was active in the business, too. It was natural for the two families to become close friends. However, Red could never understand why the Harwoods always voted as Democrats.

The agreement reached between Harwood and SPI included a division of the timber, giving Harwood all of the redwood and SPI the Douglas fir. Each company would log their species from the land, which was owned in common. Incidental amounts of the opposite species would be delivered by the logging party to Harwood or SPI as the case might be. The land was owned 50% by each party as an undivided interest. As a result, a long association began between Harwood and SPI.

As 1972 came to a close, SPI had 1,350 employees, and 688,000 MBF of timber under contract. There were six mills operating with a production of 353,000 MBF lumber tally. There were 1,950 shareholders and assets were some $47,000,000.

Early in 1973, the Branstetter mill was still running as an SPI sawmill. It existed mostly on "farmer logs," which are bought off the "open road" from small loggers and/or landowners. In many cases, the logs are small and low-grade from second-growth timber, usually reasonably priced.

Jerry Gromacki was the forester/log buyer for the operation, having been hired away from the California Division of Forestry (CDF). At the time Jerry was hired, Shaffer was still looking after the forestry activities for the Branstetter mill, and Jerry was an inspector for CDF.

Jerry was born in 1940 in Canonsburg, Pennsylvania, where his father worked as a salesman for Wholesale Foods Company. In 1951, the family headed west and settled in Pittsburg, California, where Mr. Gromacki worked on the docks at the Port Chicago Naval Base. Jerry attended local schools and graduated from high school there. He met Claire Runckel in high school, and they were married in 1963.

After attending Diablo Valley Junior College, Jerry worked at several jobs in construction and at an automobile manufacturing plant. Eventually he enrolled at Humboldt State University. He graduated with a degree in Forestry in 1964. While at Humboldt State, he met Gary Shaffer and Ken Bird who were also in the forestry program.

Jerry remembers Burr Coffelt would often show up at the sawmill to make sure everyone was busy. In Jerry's words, "He would fly here in his airplane, stay just long enough to stir things up, cause all sorts of problems, then quickly leave, leaving the problems behind."

SPI then had a Forestry staff consisting of Otto Peters, Gary Shaffer, Bill Bockman at Inyokern, Jerry Gromacki, and Bill Swarts at Hayfork, soon to be replaced by Ken Bird. Peters, Shaffer, Gromacki and Bird would be considered the SPI foresters for the next several years. They epitomized the forestry program that concentrated on timber and log acquisition, in which the company was strong in that era. All were very competent people, were field-oriented, and worked extremely hard.

The next acquisition, in January 1973, was noteworthy. This was the purchase of the Watt tract of timberland northeast of Redding. It was the first tract of forest land of any size purchased by SPI east of Humboldt County. It involved over 16,000 acres of well-stocked, cutover land. The property was, for all practical purposes, in one block, well-roaded, and for the most part, high-site-growing land. Purchase price was $3,260,000. There was supposed to be some 30,000 MBF of merchantable mixed conifer timber growing there, and 27,000 MBF of "pre-merchantable" timber.

The tract was put up for sale, under sealed-bid procedures, by the owner, R. G. Watt. The second-high bidder was Baxter Pole Co.

Many companies at that time would not purchase cut-over land unless it supported enough merchantable timber to permit early harvest and help pay for the acquisition. This reduced the carrying charges of holding the property to maturity of the next crop. The carrying charges could be excessive when the time it takes to grow a crop of trees is considered. Up until then, the Emmersons and the Crooks had not invested significantly in land that had little merchantable timber. There was a lot of merchantable timber on the Watt property, but it was quite young and small.

Properly managed, the Watt tract would supply wood forever. It was possible to harvest some of the timber to reduce the size of the investment; but it would have to be done carefully and conservatively. Red agreed to such a program.

SPI harvested some poles and small sawlogs the first year after purchase. For the following few years, a selection system of cutting was used. Jerry Gromacki was in charge of the management of the property. Many small trees were cut to thin the stands so that the remaining trees could put on added growth.

Jerry found it was nearly impossible to harm the high-site land, since it was so well stocked that the small trees would grow into merchantable size while the initial harvest went on. After the first few years, an excellent stand of young merchantable timber was left to grow. A re-cruise in the late 1980s showed there was over twice as much timber growing there as when SPI bought it.

Even in the earlier years, Red hated to cut timber that the company owned "in fee." It was difficult to get him to spend money on land, even good land, if it did not support timber that could be cut immediately. But if a parcel was found that fit these needs, it was easy to convince him to purchase it. In fact, he

Jerry Gromacki after a couple of drinks at one of his birthday parties, 1989. SPI foresters arranged for several birthday parties every year for Gromacki because he enjoyed them so much. He eventually forgot how old he was, but the parties afforded an excuse to toast his good health as he aged.
Photo by author.

was very aggressive when it came to buying timber. The problem was that in the early years there was little money available to invest in timberland.

Once a large part of the initial investment was recovered, however, he wanted to let the rest of the timber grow, and cut timber owned by someone else. It was wise, he believed, to buy government timber and save your own. Even today, 30 years later, the company is still cutting some of the old-growth Douglas fir that was growing on the Davis and Brede land when it was purchased in 1961. This reflects the good judgment, conservative management, and commitment to long-term investments in the timber business typical of

Red Emmerson.

By 1973, the Answerman stores were not doing well, with three stores in operation, one under construction at Sparks, and one in the planning stage at Chico. Dick Smith believed that SPI was not familiar with the management of a retail business. They were lumber manufacturing people, and they were forced to depend upon others with retail experience for advice in running the stores.

Dick Smith described a couple of other acquisitions in 1973 as "pain-in-the-rear purchases." Both were located in Denver. One was W. C. Sutton Division, a distributor of particleboard. The other was Rocky Mt. Stairs that manufactured stair steps. The latter was operated for a short time under SPI ownership, and "given" back to the original owner when it was found to be unprofitable.

The company was growing; but things were not going well. Relations between the two principal owners were becoming strained. The corporate office was now in Walnut Creek, removed from the main operations; and the retail stores were a headache. Ken LaBoube, Vice-President, Administration and Planning, was still looking for more sites on which to build stores, with the goal of constructing ten per year until there were 50 or 60 in operation. There were added complications when LaBoube circulated a suggestion to the Board of Directors that Red be relieved of his duties as President because he was not qualified to hold such a position.

Some of the proposed acquisitions seemed bizarre to Red. One was a Japanese-style nursery located under a power line in southern California. To some members in management this appeared a good business to purchase. The pitch made at one of the meetings was that the plants grown on the site took three years to reach marketable size, in effect tripling in size in that time. Since they were grown from seed which cost very little, the company could nearly triple its money in three years.

According to Don Riewerts, the company actually bought a plywood plant that was to be installed on an ocean-going barge. The barge was to be towed across the Pacific to the Philippines where a sawmill would be constructed on another barge, and the two would then be towed to Indonesia. There they would be anchored together where Indonesian logs could be obtained close by. The whole facility then could be easily moved to additional locations to take advantage of log resources as they became available. Gary Shaffer was sent there to look into the venture. He did not think much of the idea.

In 1973, Harry Merlo, of Louisiana Pacific Corp. (LP), became interested in SPI. He took a look at the company for possible acquisition. However, John Crook would not speak to Merlo; they had never liked each other very much.

In any event, Red, with Controller Dick Smith conducted a tour of the SPI facilities for Merlo. They met him in Texas, flew in the LP jet to Franklin Park, Illinois, then to Jacksonville, Florida, on to Denver, and finally to Portland. Merlo did not like what he saw, and no deal was made.

In the meantime, LP personnel had inspected some of the records of the company at Susanville, Arcata and other locations. This caused a general feeling among some of the SPI employees that they were being sold down the river. Morale was not good. At the top, John Crook was angry, claiming that he had not known about the potential sale of the company to LP.

By the end of the year 1973, SPI stock was selling for about $9.00 and there were 3,520,000 shares outstanding. There were six sawmills, a particleboard plant, a millwork plant, three plants for prefinishing paneling and moulding, and three retail stores operating. The company had 1,500 employees. Lumber produced was 370,000 MBF lumber tally. There were 168,000 MBF of logs (and timber) owned by the company at year-end, with another 687,000 MBF of timber under contract, mostly government. Total sales were $123,000,000, and assets at year-end were valued at $62,000,000.

Also at the end of the year, Johnson Soil Amendments, another of the acquisitions, was closed. Andy Johnson and Burr Coffelt were fighting regularly, and the operation was not profitable. Red Emmerson was not looking forward to the new year with a great degree of confidence. However, no one had ever known him to give up.

chapter twenty four

OPEN CONFLICT

The two principal stockholders of Sierra Pacific Industries were discovering early what others might take a long time to learn. Purchasing new businesses about which one knew very little was quite risky.

They learned, too, that fast growth can be addicting, and there were dangers associated with it. Unless growth was sustained indefinitely, at some point the acquired businesses had to be managed effectively, and each had to pay its own way. This took competent people to run them; and it was increasingly difficult for John Crook and Red Emmerson, as owners, to personally check each operation on a daily basis.

Red tried to do this. Liz Hoaglen, at Hayfork, has said that Red would call every day to get daily production figures and volumes of lumber shipped. That was typical behavior for him; it seemed when he wasn't in the air, he was in a telephone booth. Once at a party, before the age of cellular telephones, he was given a portable telephone mounted in a briefcase. It was given somewhat in jest, but the message was clear. He had developed a reputation for having a telephone growing out of one ear.

The company continued to expand. Early in 1974, SPI had an option to purchase land on the Chicago River in Illinois, on which plans were made to build a vinyl overlay plant under the Gyrotex label. At the time, Gyrotex was importing veneer and hauling it by truck from Florida, where it had arrived by ship, to the plant at Franklin Park. John Crook thought it would be a better idea to build a plant on the river and barge the veneer up the river, thus reducing the cost of transportation.

Local people, who knew the neighborhood, thought the people at SPI were dumb to try to build in that end of town. SPI was told they would never be able to hire good people to work there; crime and vandalism were too prevalent. Bob Ahrens was sent to Chicago anyway, to begin construction and to oversee the project. He ordered machinery and the building began.

By 1974, the sawmills and the particleboard plant were the only operations making a reasonable profit. The others were either losers, or close to it. Red was becoming very bitter; and the two top executives were beginning to fight publicly, causing a split among the other members of the management team.

On one side were Red Emmerson, Don Riewerts and Burr Coffelt; on the other, John Crook and Ken LaBoube. Dick Smith was somewhere in the middle, since John Crook, Chairman of the Board, was Dick's superior. Dick, however, could see that Red was the manager of the SPI operations which were making money. He felt that, in his position as controller, he could not win.

As chairman, John was in charge of preparing the agenda prior to Board meetings.

The meetings had become very structured and formal, and had become a source of conflict.

Red did not like the corporate maneuvering at all. To him, the company was in trouble, and it was unwise to stand on protocol and procedure. He was always direct; and if something needed to be done, he spent little time talking about it. It used to be common to see the motto, "Either lead, or follow, or get the hell out of the way" hanging on an office wall. The motto fit his philosophy just right.

He had decided SPI should build a cogeneration (cogen) facility at the mill in Susanville. At the time, there were not many of those facilities at sawmills in California. He had researched the costs and benefits, and intended to bring up the matter at the next Board meeting.

At the next meeting in Walnut Creek, Red tried to discuss the cogen project. The subject had not made it onto the agenda; and when Red persisted in trying to discuss it, John Crook got up and walked out. Red Emmerson was furious.

He reflected on the Answerman stores, in his opinion a disaster, and the fact that Ken LaBoube, one of John's men, was responsible for them. He thought of the various businesses that SPI had purchased, and of the many that were losing money, or had already been sold. He saw where they sat in fancy offices, the men in business suits, amidst the alien world of traffic in the city, while their company needed them in Arcata, or Susanville, or Hayfork. The irritations became unbearable.

The situation deteriorated into a "you buy my shares or I'll buy your shares" argument. The two old friends were shouting at each other. Some of those present thought they were about to come to blows.

After they calmed down, they discussed the possibility of one buying out the other. John Crook felt he could not swing the funding to buy out the Emmerson interests. Some who were there that day thought he might have had reservations about his ability to run the sawmills and other plants that SPI owned. He did not have the total dedication to the sawmill business that Red Emmerson had. In the final analysis, Red agreed to take John Crook out of SPI. John would never forgive Red for the way it turned out.

Saying it and doing it are two different things. The company was a public company. There were public shareholders to consider, and there were laws that protected their interests. The breakup would be a bitter pill for both John Crook and Red Emmerson to swallow; but the process to take SPI private began.

chapter twenty five

THE BREAK-UP

A number of events occurred that assured the break-up of the company. The arguments over the agenda and construction of the cogen plant were partly responsible. But there was one item, in particular, which probably had more to do with the break-up than any other.

A few miles up Elk River, just south of Eureka, is a tract of redwood timberland that was known at one time as the Cheney tract. It consisted of nearly 10,000 acres in one block, and was owned by an old-time lumber firm that owned property and sawmills in parts of the west. They owned a mill at Crescent Mills in Plumas County, had operations near Medford, Oregon, and had owned the Elk River tract for many years.

The Elk River property was high-site land supporting mostly second-growth redwood. It was some of the best timber-growing land in Humboldt County, and Red Emmerson heard it was for sale.

Red, with Don Riewerts, had met with the Cheney interests in Portland to negotiate the purchase. The price was $18,000,000. Red considered that an excellent price to pay for such a property.

The acquisition was brought up at the next Board meeting of SPI. Red was enthusiastic about the purchase; John was not. Ken LaBoube was in charge of acquisitions, and the Answerman stores were at the top of his list. He sided with John Crook. Discussions became heated, and the two sides again

nearly came to blows.

The objections were based on several facts and assumptions: the timber was mostly redwood, and logs would have to be sold since SPI did not cut redwood; and the $18,000,000 could be put to better use somewhere else in the company. Some thought it would not be wise to incur more debt at the time. Red was equally adamant. The investment could be recouped many times over in a very short time; and there might never be another opportunity to acquire that kind of land in one block again.

Red lost his case. He was told that if it was such a good deal, he and Curly should buy it themselves. The Emmersons did not have $18,000,000 readily available.

On the way to the airport after the meeting, Red stopped at a telephone booth. He called his old friend and partner, Jim Laier, to arrange a meeting a short time later the same day.

On the way back to Arcata, Riewerts and Red stopped at Santa Rosa to meet with Laier. Within thirty minutes, they had an agreement in principal to buy the Cheney property. Laier and Trione, in effect, would guarantee the loan. The next day they formed Elk River Timber Co., with Laier and the Emmerson family as partners.

In hindsight, Elk River was one of the best timber deals Red Emmerson ever made. The property was paid for long ago. It is managed today on a "sustained-yield basis" and produces seven to ten MMBF of logs every year. By 1990, the Emmersons owned 58% and the Laiers 42%.

The open conflict over the purchase of the Cheney tract and the cogen argument resulted in the agreement for Red to buy John Crook's interest. Thus, in May 1974, the break-up of the company began in earnest. The company requested that trading for shares of SPI be stopped on the American Stock Exchange. Shares were trading at $10.25 when the request was made, and trading stopped on May 20. After announcing that the company would be taken private, trading was to resume some three weeks later.

An article appeared in the *Wall Street Journal* on June 6, 1974, describing the rift between John Crook and Red Emmerson. The article noted that all or parts of the profitable forest products operations might be sold. There was speculation that a major forest products company was negotiating to acquire all or parts of SPI. That would have been Louisiana Pacific Corp. and Harry Merlo.

The *Journal* reported that LP had negotiated earlier in the year to purchase SPI for $68 million; but talks collapsed in March when details could not be worked out. It went on to detail that Mr. Emmerson was unhappy over the company's poor showing in its retail operations in the first quarter when earnings plunged to $1.8 million, or 51 cents per share.

Some two weeks later, the *San Francisco Chronicle* reported that the company planned to buy back all of its 704,000 publicly owned shares for $18.00 per share. SPI had also agreed to repurchase the 1,403,662 shares held by Crook and his family for $17.60 per share.

When news of the takeover became known and trading resumed, the price of the stock began to rise. At the same time, the lumber market was beginning to deteriorate, and John Crook wanted out. He did not want any hitches to develop in the break-up of the company. Dick Smith did not want to be caught in the middle of all of the maneuvering going on; but on August 21, 1974, reorganization of the company took place.

On the same date, a class-action lawsuit was filed that halted the reorganization.

Newspapers on the following day carried details of the litigation. A local attorney, Tim Murphy, filed the action on behalf of Atilio Mossi, some of the shareholders, and the corporation itself. Mossi owned 100 shares. Named in the suit were Crook, Emmerson, Riewerts, Dick Smith, Warren Sanborn, Arthur Adams, and the Bank of America as trustee.

It was alleged that Crook and Emmerson had sold SPI the right to remove timber on certain Forest Service sales for more than they had paid for it. The timber involved was from the North Beach sale near Inyokern, the same sale that Howard Finn had promoted purchasing. His involvement in the North Beach timber sale was questioned.

It was also alleged that the Cheney tract in Humboldt County (Elk River) had been wrongfully diverted from SPI and its shareholders to benefit the main stockholders, Crook and Emmerson. There were several minor counts included in the filing. The plaintiffs asked for compensatory damages of $15 million, plus interest, and an additional $15 million for exemplary and punitive damages.

The suit was settled out of court. Finn had originally come up with the idea of forming a partnership (named F.E.C.) for the purpose of purchasing the sale. At the time there was no mill at Inyokern. Since Finn had no relationship to SPI, the later purchase of the logs by SPI was considered to be an "arms-length" transaction at fair-market value.

Since the Elk River tract had been offered to SPI, the minutes of the Board meeting noted that fact, and that the purchase was turned down. The lawsuit was over.

SPI and Louisiana Pacific began negotiating for LP's purchase of Humboldt Flakeboard. Harry Merlo and Red Emmersom met on Mother's Day to finalize the deal. They settled on a price of $11 million, plus the value of inventory. This would result in a taxable gain for SPI since the property was valued on the books for $3.5 million. To minimize taxes, they decided to distribute the assets to John Crook so John could sell it to LP. It was touch and go for a while, however; John would still not talk to Harry Merlo.

The company reported the sale by John

Crook to the Internal Revenue Service (IRS), but they would not accept it as a legitimate transaction. Later, after much wrangling with the IRS, agreement was reached at the appellate level. SPI would pay half the tax due on the gain, and Crook would pay the other half.

Pan-American Gyrotex was another bone of contention. Neither Red nor John wanted it; in fact, nobody wanted it. There were attempts made to sell it, but there were no takers. Upon close examination, Gyrotex had made money in 1972-73, but it was profit made on the inventory of veneer. The company had a very large inventory of Luan veneer that increased in value during that period. It was determined that more money could have been made by selling the veneer, rather than manufacturing it into panels and selling the panels.

John Crook agreed to take $17.60 per share, which was less than the public was offered, if the company would keep Gyrotex. Crook would also receive the Watt property; but Red agreed to repurchase the land from him, and to repurchase the timber on a cutting contract over a four-year period.

When it was all over, SPI offered to purchase the outstanding public shares. Over $11.8 million was paid to those shareholders who accepted the tender offer. John Crook got his $17.60 per share for the shares he owned. He was paid in cash, notes and assets that involved the four retail stores, the Watt tract and the particleboard plant. Red got the sawmills, the moulding plants and Gyrotex.

Late in 1974, SPI, now private, sold the Inyokern sawmill to LP. Red negotiated the sale with Harry Merlo over the telephone. The dickering took less than ten minutes.

In December, it was decided to either sell or liquidate Gyrotex. There were no buyers, so the company wrote off the book value ($2.8 million).

Even with the company in disarray, the sawmills continued operating and changes were made in personnel assignments. The most significant of these was Deke Fairchild's transfer from Hayfork to run the Branstetter mill.

The Branstetter mill was still cutting mostly farmer logs. It was not much of a sawmill by SPI standards, but it was still making a little money.

At the end of the year 1974, there were 1,100 employees, and sales were some $72,000,000. Red Emmerson owned 97% of the shares of the company, and total assets were in excess of $42,000,000. Red was relieved that the public phase of SPI was over; but he was working harder than ever, and there were problems still to be solved.

The Emmerson family in 1977. Mark, George, Red, Ida and Caroline. Photo from Ida Emmerson.

chapter twenty six

THE FAMILY

Ida and the children had to contend with all the turmoil that had occurred over the past several years. Red was extremely busy, particularly from the time the company had gone public. With the break-up, he was feeling better about the future, but the strain had been severe.

Ida, especially, had felt "awful" about the end of the friendship between Red and John Crook. Dorothy Crook, John's wife, and Ida had become very close. Years later she would say, with a catch in her voice, that Dorothy had been one of the best friends she ever had. Even then, it was hard for her to accept the split.

Of course, she had the children to take care of; but with her involvement in the company on a daily basis, it was not easy to put business problems out of her mind. By the time SPI was again owned by Red and his family, George was 18 years old, Caroline was 15 and Mark was 14.

The Emmersons still lived at the east end of 12th Street in Arcata, in the home that Curly and his wife Myrtle had built. In 1961, Ida and Red had traded their home on Harris and Dolbeer for the house in Arcata. Curly, at the time, still had a mortgage on the place, and Red and Ida succeeded in paying it off. Ida remembers crying at the prospect of moving from their home in Eureka. She hated the house in Arcata - the drapes and the furniture. It wasn't hers.

The children grew up there. It was home to them; and Ida eventually grew to like the place since it also became home to her. The children went to elementary school at Sunny Brae, and to Junior High at Stewart. They fondly remember their life in Arcata and the friends they made there.

All three of them were taught the value of work and the value of a dollar. It is difficult for people who do not know them to believe that. They were also taught to respect people who were older than they. It was disconcerting for some within the company to be called "Mr." by both George and Mark, even after they had graduated from their respective universities to become active in running the business.

They attribute this respect for elders to their parents, Red especially. There is conjecture that it comes from his religious upbringing and schooling, and not from an attempt at being formal. Red does not like being called "Red" by children even today.

Red and Ida would seldom disagree in front of the children. All the children report that their mother never told them to "wait until your father gets home." Ida may have thought it would have been an idle threat anyway because, in most cases, the children would have gone to bed by the time Red got home.

Sunday was always family day, and Red and Ida developed a Sunday routine. They were both early risers; but on Sunday, Ida was allowed to sleep late. Red would get up with the "kids" and prepare pancakes for breakfast. They all say that he was not a bad chef, and had few failures.

After breakfast, the four of them would head for the sawmill. The children would put their bicycles in the back of the pickup so they could ride them in the mill yard. In the office, they could use pencils and paper to scribble on, or to make pictures to take home to Ida. Red, in the meantime, would be talking to the manager of the operation, checking maintenance problems with millwrights, or checking other operations by telephone. He was good at combining family responsibilities with business.

As the children grew older, Red would fabricate such things as monkey bars in the machine shop for them. He built stilts for them to walk around on. Caroline remembers that she was once interested in becoming a potter. Red decided to make her a potter's wheel in the machine shop. She watched in fascination as the project neared completion.

Red was used to building things for a sawmill. He made everything "hell for stout", because mill machinery takes an awful beating. Caroline's potter's wheel was made from 1/2-inch steel plate. It had precision ball bearings and weighed over 300 pounds. They had a difficult time loading it aboard a pickup to haul it home, and a more difficult time unloading it without help.

She tried to use it so Red wouldn't feel bad, but it was a tough machine to master. She explained that it had a "kick wheel" that had to be continuously shoved with her foot. This kept the monster spinning, and the heavy wheel acted like a fly-wheel; once in motion, it was difficult to stop. Conventional wheels are powered by an electric motor, but hers required constant "kicking" to keep the speed up while the pot, or vase, was being formed. In a short time her foot was sore, and she also began to wear out her shoe.

Years later, I asked Red whatever happened to the device. He said with a twinkle, "I have it out at the ranch. There's a troublesome gully there that won't stabilize. I've got

it in the bottom of the ditch; I don't think it'll wash much more."

The children were not allowed to have friends at their house on Sunday. That was Red's day with them. They would do things together, and Ida would join them later in the day. They would throw camping gear in the back of their station wagon for a "camping trip" to places in Humboldt County. The trips were short; the destination could be a sandbar along a river, or a trip to the woods to check on a logging job, or to look at a patch of timber. Again, for Red it was partly business; but for the family it was fun to be with both parents. They still have good memories of those times.

Caroline and Mark remember camping below a "spring" and drinking the clear cold water that tumbled down to the river. They had been there for some time and had noticed a faint, strange smell that was hard to identify. After some time they began to search for the source, and found a decaying deer in the spring above their camp. Caroline came "awfully close to getting sick."

Vacations for the Emmersons were scarce. They began to ski together, but would seldom go to California resorts. By the time the children were almost grown, an airplane was available. Since Red had arranged his work schedule for the few days they could spend on the slopes, he was reluctant to change their plans if there was no snow at the selected destination. His work schedule was so full, there was no flexibility possible. As a result, Red would get on the telephone to find the nearest snow, and they would head to the airport to fly there.

All of the Emmerson children were expected to work. One of their first jobs was the pulling of mustard weeds from Curly's potato field in the Arcata bottoms. They did this while in grade school. By the time they got to high school, they were expected to have more meaningful employment.

Caroline once applied for summer work at the Arcata mill. Alan Smith informed her that help was not needed, so she began to search for employment. She finally landed a job at the Samoa Cookhouse waiting on tables. By that time, she had a driver's license but did not yet own an automobile. If Ida needed the car that day, she would take Caroline to work.

One day, Dick Smith and his wife Marcie went there for lunch to tease Caroline. When they drove up, there was Ida's Mercedes in the parking lot. They thought they might buy lunch for Ida, and visit with them both.

It turned out that Ida had other plans that day, and Caroline had driven her car to work. The Smiths teased Caroline unmercifully for a long time afterwards about being "the only kid that drove to work at the Cookhouse in a Mercedes."

George and Mark had cleanup jobs at the sawmill during their summer vacations. Dan Smith, Dick and Marcie's son, also worked there with Mark one summer. They worked nights and on weekends, shoveling out sawdust, slabs, bark and chunks. It was hard, dirty work.

One Fourth of July weekend, their parents had planned a vacation on a house boat on Shasta Lake. The two boys worried for several days whether they could get off work or not, and they badly wanted to go. After several discussions, they finally flipped a coin, with the understanding the loser would have to petition the manager, Gordon Amos, for the time off. Mark lost.

Gordon, at first, would not let them off. He lectured Mark about the necessity of having good work habits, and the need to have a clean mill before it started up after the holiday. After a stern discourse, Mark was told they could go ahead and take the time off, but they would have to do twice as much cleanup when they got back to make up for it.

While in high school, Mark was a pole vaulter and played on the football team. Red attended most of the games and the track meets. George suffered from an arthritic problem and was not able to participate in sports. Caroline, being attractive and vivacious, became a cheerleader.

All three children are a credit to themselves and to their parents. They grew to be heavily involved in the company, and to contribute to its success. Red and Ida are obviously proud of them.

A load of old-growth Ponderosa pine logs being unloaded from SPI log truck by Letrostacker at SPI's CV sawmill, 1990. Photo from SPI archives.

PART THREE

SIERRA PACIFIC INDUSTRIES

THE PRIVATE COMPANY

(1975-1982)

Stickered lumber on skids in SPI's Loyalton mill yard awaiting planing, prior to shipment.

Photo by author, 1990.

chapter twenty seven

THE NEW SPI

After reorganization of the company, the new Directors were Red and Curly Emmerson, Don Riewerts, Francis Mathews and Dick Smith. Net worth on January 1, 1975 was $8,300,000. The Bank of America loaned the new company $8,000,000 to finance the purchase of the outstanding public shares of stock. There were still 435 outside shareholders. The SPI office at Walnut Creek was closed, and Dick Smith and his family moved to Eureka.

The Gyrotex saga continued. In January 1975, it was sold to EMS Corp. for nothing down and a note-receivable valued at $1,750,000. EMS was organized by Earl Spiro, one of the owners of Gyrotex at the time of its purchase by SPI. The new corporation contained only minimum assets, since Spiro was trying to minimize his risks in owning it. As far as SPI was concerned, the deal was nothing more than a fire sale. Dick Smith remembers it as "one big headache."

Spiro had operated Gyrotex for SPI between 1972 and 1974. During that time, he was importing veneer (Luan) from the Philippines to the port at Jacksonville. The importer was Sarmiento International Inc., a Philippine company. Sarmiento owned a U. S. company as well.

Spiro, while working for SPI, agreed to pay the U. S. branch of Sarmiento a commission on the veneer being imported. It was alleged that he then made a deal with the parent company to reduce the price of the veneer by the amount of the commission. This, in effect, lowered the value of the veneer being imported and the import duty the government collected, since the duty was computed on the value of the veneer. He was also accused of inflating freight rates because duty was not charged on shipping costs, and of misgrading some of the veneer to reduce its reported value.

U. S. Customs sued SPI for over $10,000,000, charging all of the above. Spiro was charged personally on several criminal counts as well. SPI engaged a law firm in Chicago to handle the case; and Jon Lyons, SPI General Counsel, and Dick Smith made a number of trips east to look after the company's interests. Spiro engaged his own attorney to fight the criminal charges.

Before the case went to court, Customs agreed to allow Spiro to plead nolo contendere. He paid a fine and escaped a jail sentence. SPI went on to fight the case for a number of years, finally settling in the 1980s for approximately $1,000,000.

Spiro operated Gyrotex until sometime in 1976; however it was still a loser, and SPI had to guarantee a bank loan of $1,250,000 for Gyrotex to operate. It finally went bankrupt. SPI settled for approximately $1,000,000 to the bank, and got nothing for the receivables. The Gyrotex saga was over.

The Siskiyou Division was sold to Southwest Forest Industries on September 5, 1975. The price was over $6,300,000, plus the value of inventories. Red was especially glad to get rid of the operation, probably for a number of reasons. It was located at Happy Camp, a place that is quite inaccessible. The mill was, by his standards, inefficient; and the competition for timber, particularly from Oregon operators, was fierce. Lastly, it was John Crook's mill. As far as Red was concerned, it was good riddance to Happy Camp and Gyrotex.

The lumber market was turning down in 1975. It was a bad time for SPI, having prices for lumber decline while the company was trying to regain its footing after going private. The new management team had its work cut out for it if SPI was to succeed.

During the year 1975, 6,541 shares of outstanding public stock were purchased for $18 per share, and at year-end there were only 435 shareholders holding out.

As the year closed, total sales were $60,300,000, and total assets were valued at $42,700,000. Owned by SPI at that time were sawmills at Arcata, Redding, Susanville and Hayfork, and a millwork plant at Chico. That was all. The company was a streamlined version of its former self, and it was back in the lumber business where it belonged. The foundation was in place upon which to build for the future.

chapter twenty eight

GROWTH BEGINS ANEW

Red Emmerson had learned a lot during the debacle of the past few years. In his view, going public then private again, was indeed a debacle. He vowed nothing like that would ever happen again if he could help it.

By 1976, Curly was even more out of the business. He was frequently in the office at Arcata; but he was spending most of his time managing several ranches he owned, having lunch at the Anchor on South Broadway in Eureka, and visiting with the hundreds of friends he had made over the years. He had said a number of times that the company had outgrown him. He also believed that he was incapable of running a company the size of SPI, and that Red was "a lot smarter than he was." It was common knowledge that Red had been making the meaningful decisions for a long time.

Red possibly had never articulated his philosophy for promoting growth of his company, nor formally talked to anyone about it in any detail. Based on my observations of the process by which meaningful growth had occurred, it seemed to me that his philosophy evolved into something like this:

The new Sierra Pacific Industries was a survivor. The people still working there, after it had become private again, had learned a number of lessons along the way. Probably the first one was to stick to the type of business at which they excelled. In the case of SPI, that was wood manufacture.

The second lesson was to expand at a rate that can be sustained. Do not expand for the sake of expansion, but recognize that an acquisition ought to be paid for quickly, and, unless sold, **it must be operated**. Pick a geographic area for expansion where there is a strategic advantage for the company in doing so, such as in the area of timber supply.

The third lesson was to control debt so that such debt could be paid off without incurring an excessive interest load. Big interest payments can sap the vitality of a company; and an otherwise profitable operation can be made unprofitable by "biting off more than can be swallowed."

The fourth lesson was to confine growth to a level that can be staffed with competent personnel. This would involve a recognition that there are many **very** competent people who could never work for SPI. The judgment as to whether a person is competent or not rested principally with one man: Red himself. Management is not done by committee. Each manager reports to the chief executive.

Last, perhaps, was the recognition that partnerships produce complications. Sometimes they are necessary to procure financing; but, at some point, they will probably produce operational problems.

It is presumptuous of me to maintain that these points were considered by Red Emmer-

Old logger Gene Cornelius stands in front of old-growth Douglas fir logs awaiting shipment to SPI Arcata from SPI's Bear River tract, 1986.
Photo by author.

son and his team of managers as they talked about forging ahead. I believe, however, that such was done, perhaps subconsciously or inadvertently.

No matter; SPI began 1976 with the acquisition of the Rochlin properties in Humboldt County, consisting mainly of various plywood manufacturing facilities. Included was Rochlin Plywood Co. at Arcata, which was auctioned off. The land on which it sat was sold to George Schmidbauer. Fortuna Veneer was also auctioned off, and the land

sold to The Pacific Lumber Co. A veneer plant at Orleans was auctioned, and a veneer plant at Willow Creek was sold to James Kinsey.

Several tracts of old-growth timber were included in the Rochlin purchase. The largest was near the mouth of Bear River south of Ferndale. There also was a small parcel located east of Bridgeville. Total price of the acquisition was $10,275,000, and the deal closed on February 1, 1976.

On May 26, 1976, Francis "Moose" Mathews resigned from the Board of Directors. Moose had been associated with SPI for many years. As the company grew, legal matters became more and more complicated and time-consuming; and Moose Mathews's own business was suffering. Red and the company would still depend upon him for legal advice, but his duties on the board ceased.

The sawmill at Branstetter Lane was closed to be replaced by a new sawmill at Central Valley (CV). (SPI uses the name Redding and Central Valley interchangeably. When the name Redding is used to specify an operation, Central Valley is meant since SPI has no operations in Redding.) The move was made prior to the construction of an adequate office facility at CV.

The first time I visited the makeshift office across the street from the present office (1976), it was raining as hard as I have ever seen it in CV.

Jerry Gromacki was sitting at his desk with his raincoat on. He had scrounged up every container he could find to catch the drips that came through the ceiling. He had tin cans, wastebaskets, and even his tin hat placed at strategic locations. At one end, he had nailed some heavy black plastic sheeting a few inches from the ceiling so that all the leaks would converge in one "trough" as the plastic sagged under the weight of the water. Under the end of the trough, he had placed a garbage can to catch the torrent. The sound inside the office was deafening, with the roar of the rain on the roof and the sound of the plink-plunk of the drips in the various containers. It was a hilarious show to watch Gromacki trying to keep up with the water as each can neared its capacity. He was losing.

Sawmill complex in Central Valley as it appeared in 1987. Photo by Mark Fator.

At the time of the move to CV, there was only one government timber sale under contract for the Branstetter mill. The mill was still operating mostly on smaller logs when the new mill began production. The new one was designed as a "small log" mill, to continue in the tradition of the old one. It was constructed with a 36" ring debarker that would not allow the utilization of logs over 36" in diameter on the large end.

With this restriction, conflict was immediate and predictable. Nearly all of the SPI sawmills used all species of logs and all sizes from 8" to 10" on the **small** end. Arcata was an exception, using Douglas fir and not other species. The other managers, by the way, called Arcata "Mecca." Arcata did not have to contend with the problems associated with cutting multiple species, and it always made money. It was held up as an example for all

of them to copy. All of the remaining mills would saw whatever species they could get their hands on, with the possible exception of Incense cedar. SPI logging contractors were not usually required to sort logs in the woods.

With the restriction on log size at CV caused by the size of the debarking ring, too large a log simply could not be put into the mill. It would either get stuck in the ring or, if larger logs were recognized before loading onto the mill infeed, they had to be removed and loaded on trucks for shipment to another mill. In either event, it was a costly process.

Sorting of logs is a costly procedure especially in the woods. There, log landings are restricted in size; and depending upon the number of species and number of required sorts, a logger could have a landing full of logs and no logs to ship. A logger could not understand why he could not ship everything to the mill, where they could be sorted on a flat mill yard several acres in size, any way the mill manager wanted them.

Arguments abounded when the rules for sorting in the woods were published. Jerry Gromacki was in the middle of all of them. In addition, he was in the middle between Red and the loggers who worked for SPI when they delivered logs of the wrong size, either by mistake or on purpose. Jerry took the heat. Some log sellers refused to sell to the CV mill if they had to sort them. Jerry complained bitterly about that, too.

During the first part of the year, discussions began on another prospective acquisition. Frank Keene, of Bank of America, was the banker for SPI. Frank also was associated with DiGiorgio Corporation (DG) in a banking capacity and knew Robert DiGiorgio, their Chief Executive Officer, quite well. At the time, lumber markets were continuing to decline. The future did not look bright to most of those in the timber industry.

Frank had found that DiGiorgio was interested in divesting themselves of what they called their Feather River Division. He contacted Red Emmerson, who expressed interest in opening negotiations.

Bob McCracken was DiGiorgio's president. Red, with Dick Smith, met with DiGiorgio a number of times. One of the meetings took place in DiGiorgio's office in the Alcoa Building in San Francisco. For some now-forgotten reason, the four of them were to fly to Portland together. They headed for the Butler Aviation facility at the San Francisco airport in a DiGiorgio sedan. After parking, they boarded the airplane for the flight to Portland.

The meeting in Portland went quite well; Red was becoming enthusiastic about purchasing a position for buying timber from the Plumas and Tahoe National Forests. The Feather River Division would provide that position. The mills were old and obsolete in his eyes, but they could be modernized.

They flew back to San Francisco, discussing the transaction all the way. Upon landing, they hurried to the sedan, still talking vigorously, and climbed into the automobile. McCracken was driving.

He shifted into drive and pressed the accelerator. The engine roared, but nothing else

happened. All of them disembarked to discover that a thief had jacked up the car and stolen all four wheels. The negotiations just prior to the incident must have been particularly intense for all of them not to notice the wheels were missing.

On June 1, 1976, SPI purchased the Feather River Division for $11,719,610. Feather River also owned a few small parcels of timberland in Plumas County for which Larry Brown (from Ruth in Humboldt County) paid somewhat less than $2,000,000. He then traded the Plumas parcels for the Travis Ranch (also near Ruth) owned by R. H. Emmerson & Son. Brown operates the ranch today as the Flying Double A, a guest ranch.

The Camptonville sawmill was sold to Siller Bros., who owned or controlled a neighboring mill at Celestial Valley, just outside Camptonville. The Auburn office and plant were sold to Bohemia Inc., an Oregon forest products firm based in Eugene.

I came aboard with the purchase of DiGiorgio. Since I know from firsthand experience many of the details of the management of SPI from then on, this story may appear to emphasize the importance of that acquisition. Such is not intended. I simply know more of the details from my own knowledge instead of from research which, in some cases, may have produced sketchy information.

In September, SPI sold the old Johnson Soil Amendments property for $325,000. In December, a tender offer of $18 per share was made for the outstanding shares of public stock. At the time, there were 46,811 shares unaccounted for, and the stockholders were notified that the offer would expire on February 22, 1977. Also in December, the park and baseball diamond at Susanville were donated to the city.

At year-end, SPI reported total sales of $92,200,000, and assets valued at $76,000.000. The company was operating sawmills at Arcata, Hayfork, Redding (CV), Susanville, Loyalton, Sloat and Quincy, and a millwork plant at Chico.

chapter twenty nine

DIGRESSION

It is appropriate to leave the SPI story for a short time, to trace the history of several sawmills that became an important part of the company in 1976.

In 1957, five California lumber companies formed a corporation to manufacture plywood. They were Sacramento Box, Setzer Forest Products, High Sierra Pine Mills, Meadow Valley Lumber Co., and Feather River Lumber Co. They built a new plywood plant on Kusel Road in Oroville, California. Machinery installed there was mostly used, some of it quite old.

Sacramento Box had a sawmill at Woodleaf southeast of Oroville, and a tract of good timberland nearby. Setzer had mills at Elk Creek, on the west side of the Sacramento valley, and at Greenville in Plumas County. They also owned a large tract of timberland west of Elk Creek. High Sierra owned sawmills at Oroville and at Twain, and some timberland in Butte and Plumas Counties. Meadow Valley had a mill at Spanish Ranch near Quincy, one at Greenville, and a planing mill/dry kiln complex at Quincy. They owned some good timberland in Plumas County. Feather River operated mills at Loyalton, Sloat and Reno, but had very little timberland.

With the possible exception of Setzer's Elk Creek operation, none of them had enough timberland to sustain their operations for very long. In varying degrees they all depended upon Forest Service timber sales and outside log purchases for their raw materials.

They formed the Oroply venture to take advantage of what they thought was a way of utilizing their higher-grade logs to make plywood, and diversify their product line. Each of them owned 20% of the new company.

The plant got underway, but the peeler log supply became an immediate problem. None of the five wished to rob their sawmills of the high-grade logs; they each waited for their partners to supply logs to Oroply. They did not have a prior agreement among themselves to send logs to the new plant; nor did they want Oroply to bid on timber sales near their sawmills and run up the price for timber. Oroply was doomed to failure; it only lasted three years. The plant on Kusel Road would be purchased eventually by SPI and turned into a millwork plant.

Plumas County, for many years, was a lumber manufacturing center in the Sierras. In the early part of the century, a man named King had moved from the deep south to form Quincy Lumber Co. His mill sat on the site of what is now the shopping center in East Quincy. He brought a number of employees with him who formed the origin of much of the black population in Quincy.

Eventually a mill was established at Spanish Ranch, some seven miles west of Quincy. There was no railroad there, so a cable tramway was built from the mill over the ridge and down to Twain, where units of lumber could be loaded on rail cars. Full units were transported on the tramway. Bob Conradi, an old logger who worked in Plumas County for many years, remembers as a youngster riding on top of the bundles over the ridge. It was an exciting ride, especially when another unit was hooked up at the mill, and the cable would stop with his bundle high in the air.

The mill at Spanish Ranch was still running in 1957. By that time, it was called Meadow Valley Lumber Co. The company had abandoned the tramway long before, and trucked their lumber to Quincy where they had constructed dry kilns and a planing mill. They had built a short railroad spur from the main Western Pacific rail line across the valley to the complex in Quincy. It was officially called the Quincy Railroad. The mill that Meadow Valley owned at Greenville shipped its green lumber to Quincy by truck.

Lou Ohlson was an owner of the High Sierra Pine operations at Oroville and at Twain. By 1957, both mills were running at capacity. At the Oroville location was Las Plumas Lumber Co., a manufacturer of pre-cut homes. Ohlson and Bud Miller owned Las Plumas. The Dant family also was involved in these operations; and they handled the lumber sales for them under the name Dant and Warnock out of Menlo Park. Both of the sawmills would be closed by the late 1960s.

Ohlson's brother-in-law, Ken Metzker, owned the old Clover Valley Lumber Co. mill at Loyalton. He also had built a mill at Sloat and one at Reno: Tahoe Timber Co. of Nevada. By the late 1950s, the latter mill had been purchased from him by Bob Dant. It ran under his leadership until the late 1960s, when it was closed and auctioned off. Today there is an industrial park on the site where it stood along the Truckee River west of town.

High Sierra purchased Meadow Valley Lumber Co. in the 1960s and shut down the Spanish Ranch mill. They built a new sawmill at the site of the planing mill and dry kilns at Quincy. Thus, the truck-hauling of rough lumber from Spanish Ranch, something that had been difficult and expensive in the winter months, was eliminated. Jim Bloom managed both the new Quincy mill and the Twain mill

for High Sierra.

In the late 1960s, DiGiorgio Corp. entered the lumber business in California. When DiGiorgio purchased High Sierra Pine Mills, the mills at Greenville were long gone, and the Oroville mill had been closed. DiGiorgio chose not to operate the Twain mill. They took over the Quincy operations, but they did not purchase the timberlands. High Sierra sold the fee land to Soper Wheeler Co., who manages it today (1991) from Strawberry Valley.

DiGiorgio was a family-owned concern that had gone public. It was an old company based in San Francisco, and it had become a "conglomerate" during the diversification craze of the '60s and early '70s.

Originally a company that had concentrated its efforts in agriculture (grapes, peaches, pears), DiGiorgio had developed a sawmill for making box lumber in Klamath Falls, Oregon. They needed wooden boxes in which to ship their fruit. By 1976, that mill was getting old, but machinery inside had been kept pretty much up-to-date. It concentrated on cutting pine timber. A small log mill had been built at Chiloquin, Oregon, to better utilize the smaller logs that were developed near there.

Having been in the sawmill business for many years, the company decided to acquire the California operations described here. It was one way of diversifying

In a matter of weeks, DiGiorgio also purchased the two mills at Loyalton and Sloat owned by Ken Metzker. Metzker had rebuilt the Loyalton mill inside the old building; but the building itself still resembled an early 1900's mill, which it was. There were still tall smokestacks on the power house, where boilers produced steam for the mill and to run an electrical generator. Occasionally the plant actually sold power to the town of Loyalton.

The mill at Sloat had been built in the late 1950s and had burned shortly after. Metzker rebuilt it before DiGiorgio came along. Both of the owners ran the mill two shifts per day, and both claimed it was the best mill they owned. It was a double-cut band mill, very simple in concept, which took only a few men to run. There was no pony rig or resaw in the mill in the early years; and production was about 40,000 MBF per year on a

Log train of Clover Valley Lumber Co. (predecessor to SPI) in Sierra Valley heading for sawmill at Loyalton. Photo found in attic of Feather River Lumber Co. around 1971.

Date of photo unknown.

log-scale basis.

DiGiorgio had also purchased a sawmill at Camptonville, almost in the town itself, from J. R. Simplot, the potato king from Idaho. The mill cut about 36,000 MBF log scale, and existed on Forest Service timber and log purchases. Included in the purchase was a remanufacturing plant and a new office building at Auburn.

When DiGiorgio finally stopped their purchases in California, they owned four sawmills and the Auburn operation, all concentrated in the northern Sierra. They needed 160,000 to 170,000 MBF of logs annually to operate, and wood was becoming expensive.

To the old-timers in the timber industry in California the newcomers became known as "the farmers." They were never accepted as a part of the establishment, and they soon were having difficulty purchasing timber. The mills competed for Government timber sales from the Plumas, Lassen and Tahoe National Forests.

In charge of the operations for DiGiorgio was Coleman Greer, who had come from

DiGiorgio's operations in Oregon. The author was in charge of the forestry department, and Ron Voss was one of the senior foresters. The company ran a road construction side, but contracted all of their logging to local "gyppo" loggers.

Lumber markets were good when the mills were purchased by the farmers; but as the months wore on, timber was increasingly difficult to buy. There were a number of other mills in that region without their own timber supply, and they were competing for the same timber sales. One of the chief competitors was the mill at Susanville owned by SPI. The bidding wars were fierce, sometimes going into the evening hours after beginning at 2:00 p.m., which was the usual time for bidding to begin.

It was common at the time to bid huge sums on one of the several species in a sale offering. This was done by bidders who thought they knew more about cruising timber than the government foresters. The successful bidder paid for the timber as it was cut and scaled, based on the bid price that he had

Clover Valley Lumber Co. sawmill at Loyalton (later purchased by SPI from DiGiorgio), looking southeast up Smithneck Creek.

Photo found in attic of Feather River Lumber Co. around 1971. Date of photo unknown.

bid for each species. He would be the "apparent high bidder," but actually pay less then a competitor if his high bid was placed on a species that would cut out short.

I had always been fearful of the ability of cruisers to accurately estimate the volumes of the firs and Incense cedar, species which are prone to high defect. I knew from experience that defect was mostly a judgment call. In some cases, a species would represent less than 5% of the volume in a sale, and **all** of the individual trees were difficult to find for cruising purposes. If a mistake was made and a high bid was placed on a species that would cut out long, there would be dire consequences.

I had done some research of the records comparing the sold volumes to actual cut-out volumes on a number of timber sales on the Plumas and Tahoe Forests. The data indicated that Incense cedar consistently cut out

short in every case, not just the majority of cases.

The next sale to be sold after this bit of research was the Quartz Point sale on the Tahoe. The bidding was fierce, and went on well into the evening hours. DiGiorgio wanted the sale badly and competed with the rest. At the final bell, DiGiorgio was the winner. The bid for Incense Cedar was over $2400 per MBF; the other species were bid at minimum prices. I hated to go to work the next morning.

I took a lot of ribbing about bidding the record price for cedar up until that time. Weeks later, I was presented with one board foot of Cedar equipped with a picture hanger to hang on my wall. I still have it to remind me of the follies of the bidding wars.

The Quartz Point sale was not cut until a long time after the bidding. I was always fearful that the research on cedar bid prices might have missed something, or that DiGiorgio had purchased the first one on which the cedar would over-cut. By the time the sale was logged, some of the bidding details were hazy memories. I do remember, though, that the Incense cedar cut out very, very short.

During the mid '70s when the bidding was going crazy, lumber prices tumbled and stayed down. The industry was saddled with stumpage that had been bid to exorbitant levels. Such slumps in the past had weeded out the speculators, the under-financed, and those really not committed to a long-term operation. In some cases after the mid 1970s, the high bidders, even though adequately financed, were weeded out as well.

Some of the operators could not stand the down cycles for very long and they began leaving the industry. DiGiorgio was one of them. They had no stomach for the bidding battles while, at the same time, losing money on the operations. They began to look for a buyer. Being a conglomerate with many other divisions, they seemed to have no interest in modernizing their lumber-manufacturing facilities.

They were ready to leave the Sierras, and Red Emmerson was ready to help them depart.

Price list from Clover Valley Lumber Co. dated April 15, 1930.

Clover Valley Lumber Co.

Loyalton, California

Price List No. 140   Delivered Prices—Subject to Change Without Notice

CALIFORNIA WHITE PINE (TRADE NAME)	San Francisco Oakland	Los Angeles Salt Lake	Kansas City Omaha Dallas	Eastern Iowa	Chicago Milwaukee St. Louis	Detroit Toledo Cincinnati	Pittsburg Buffalo Toronto	New York Boston Philadelphia
NO. 1 AND 2 CLEARS	22c	39½c	59c	64½c	69c	82c	85½c	87c
4/4 x 6 & Wdr. Rough or S2S	72.00	76.00	80.25	81.50	82.50	85.25	86.00	86.50
5/4 " "	73.00	77.00	81.25	82.50	83.50	86.25	87.00	87.50
6/4 " "	71.25	75.25	79.50	80.75	81.75	84.50	85.25	85.75
8/4 " "	82.25	86.25	90.50	91.75	92.75	95.50	96.25	96.75
10/4 & 12/4 " "	113.25	117.25	121.50	122.75	123.75	126.50	127.25	127.75
16/4 " "	128.25	132.25	136.50	137.75	138.75	141.50	142.25	142.75
C. SELECT								
4/4 x 6 & Wdr. Rough or S2S	70.00	74.00	78.25	79.50	80.50	83.25	84.00	84.50
5/4 " "	70.25	74.25	78.50	79.75	80.75	83.50	84.25	84.75
6/4 " "	60.25	64.25	68.50	69.75	70.75	73.50	74.25	74.75
8/4 " "	73.25	77.25	81.50	82.75	83.75	86.50	87.25	87.75
10/4 & 12/4 " "	108.25	112.25	116.50	117.75	118.75	121.50	122.25	122.75
16/4 " "	123.25	127.25	131.50	132.75	133.75	136.50	137.25	137.75
D. SELECT								
4/4 x 6 & Wdr. Rough or S2S	53.50	58.00	63.75	65.00	67.00	69.75	70.50	71.00
5/4 " "	55.25	59.75	65.50	66.75	68.75	71.50	72.25	72.75
6/4 " "	43.75	48.75	54.00	55.25	57.25	60.00	60.75	61.25
8/4 " "	53.25	59.75	65.50	66.75	68.75	71.50	72.25	72.75
10/4 & 12/4 " "	86.25	90.75	96.50	97.75	98.75	101.50	102.25	102.75
16/4 " "	100.25	104.75	110.50	111.75	112.75	115.50	116.25	116.75

Specified Widths	4, 6, & 8"	List	13" & Wider	Add 20.00	
	3, 5, & 10"	Add 5.00	20" & Wider	Add 50.00	
	12"	Add 15.00	Drainboards 22&24"	Add 65.00	
	14 & 16"	Add 25.00	Resawing	Add 3.00	
	18"	Add 40.00	Resawing and S2S	Add 5.00	

Specified Lengths—8 to 16'—Add 2.00 to list
" " 18 & 20' Add 10.00 to list

JEFFREYI PINE .... Add $10.00 to above prices.

NO. 3 CLEAR								
4/4 x 6 & Wdr. Rough or S2S	37.25	41.75	47.50	48.75	49.75	52.50	53.25	53.75
5/4 " "	55.50	60.00	65.75	67.00	68.00	70.75	71.50	72.00
6/4 " "	55.00	59.50	65.25	66.50	67.50	70.25	71.00	71.50
8/4 " "	66.00	70.50	76.25	77.50	78.50	81.25	82.00	82.50
10/4 & 12/4 " "	104.00	108.50	114.25	115.50	116.50	119.25	120.00	120.50
16/4 " "	119.00	123.50	129.25	130.50	131.50	134.25	135.00	135.50
NO. 1 SHOP								
5/4 x 5 & Wdr. Rough or S2S	37.00	41.50	47.25	48.50	49.50	52.25	53.00	53.50
6/4 " "	39.00	43.50	49.25	50.50	51.50	54.25	55.00	55.50
8/4 " "	51.75	56.25	62.00	63.25	64.25	67.00	67.75	68.25
10/4 & 12/4 " "	86.25	90.75	96.50	97.75	98.75	101.50	101.75	102.25
16/4 " "	101.25	105.75	111.50	112.75	113.75	116.50	116.75	117.25
NO. 2 SHOP								
5/4 x 5 & Wdr. Rough or S2S	27.50	32.00	37.75	39.00	40.00	42.75	43.50	44.00
6/4 " "	25.50	30.00	35.75	37.00	38.00	40.75	41.50	42.00
8/4 " "	31.75	36.25	42.00	43.25	44.25	47.00	47.75	48.25
10/4 & 12/4 " "	46.25	50.75	56.50	57.75	58.75	61.50	62.25	62.75
16/4 " "	56.25	60.75	66.50	67.75	68.75	71.50	72.25	72.75
INCH SHOP								
4/4 x 6 & Wdr. Rough or S2S	29.00	33.50	39.25	40.50	41.50	44.75	45.50	46.00
NO. 3 SHOP								
5/4 x 5 & Wdr. Rough or S2S	24.25	28.25	32.50	33.75	34.75	37.50	38.25	38.75
6/4 " "	26.25	30.25	34.50	35.75	36.75	39.50	40.25	40.75
8/4 " "	25.25	29.25	33.50	34.75	35.75	38.50	39.25	39.75
10/4 & 12/4 " "	44.25	48.25	52.50	53.75	54.75	57.50	58.25	58.75
16/4 " "	54.25	58.25	62.50	63.75	64.75	67.50	68.25	68.75
PANEL STOCK								
1/2 x 6 and Wdr.—C. and Btr.—S2S	62.00	64.50	67.25	68.00	68.50	70.00	70.25	70.50
5/8 x 6 and Wdr.—C. and Btr.—S2S	73.00	76.50	80.00	80.75	81.50	83.50	84.00	84.50
MOULDINGS								
STANDARD 8000 SERIES PATTERNS								
$3.00 List and Over—(Discount)	40%	38½%	36½%	36%	35½%	34%	33½%	33½%
Under $3.00 List — (Discount)	45%	43½%	41½%	41%	40½%	39%	38½%	38½%

Clover Valley Lumber Co.
Loyalton, California

Price List No. 140   Delivered Prices—Subject to Change Without Notice

CALIFORNIA WHITE PINE
(TRADE NAME)

		San Francisco Oakland	Los Angeles Salt Lake	Kansas City Omaha Dallas	Eastern Iowa	Chicago Milwaukee St. Louis	Detroit Toledo Cincinnati	Pittsburg Buffalo Toronto	New York Boston Philadelphia
COMMONS		22c	39½c	59c	64½c	69c	82c	85½c	87c
1 x 4 to 1 x 12	No. 1 Common—S2S or S4S 13/16	49.50	53.00	57.50	58.50	59.50	62.00	62.75	63.00
1 x 4 & 1 x 6	No. 2 Common "	34.00	36.50	42.00	43.00	44.00	46.50	47.25	47.50
1 x 8 & 1 x 10	" "	32.00	34.50	40.00	41.00	42.00	44.50	45.25	45.50
1 x 12	" "	34.00	36.50	42.00	43.00	44.00	46.50	47.25	47.50
1 x 4 & 1 x 6	No. 3 Common "	25.00	28.50	33.00	34.00	35.00	37.50	38.25	38.50
1 x 8 & 1 x 10	" "	26.00	29.50	34.00	35.00	36.00	38.50	39.25	39.50
1 x 12	" "	25.00	28.50	33.00	34.00	35.00	37.50	38.25	38.50
1 x 4 & Wdr.—R/L	No. 4 Common—S2S	20.00	23.50	28.00	29.00	30.00	32.50	33.25	33.50
1 x 4 & Wdr.—R/L	No. 4 Common (Specified)	21.00	24.50	29.00	30.00	30.00	33.50	34.25	34.50
	Thick Common—5/4, 6/4, 8/4—Add $3.00								
11/16 x 4 to 12"	No. 2 Common—S1S	25.50	28.25	32.00	33.00	33.50	35.50	36.25	36.50
"	No. 3 " "	22.50	25.25	29.00	30.00	30.50	32.50	33.25	33.50
"	No. 4 " "	18.50	21.25	25.00	26.00	26.50	28.50	29.25	29.50
	For 23/32 H. or M. Add 1.50 to above prices.								
DIMENSION									
2 x 4 to 2 x 12"	No. 2 & Btr.—S1S1E 1-9/16 H/M	24.00	27.00	30.00	30.75	31.50	33.75	34.25	34.50
"	No. 3 Com. " "	17.00	20.00	23.00	23.75	24.50	26.75	27.25	27.50
	For all strictly No. 1 Dimension Add $1.50 to price of No. 2 & Btr.								

CALIFORNIA WHITE and RED FIR
SELECTS

4/4 x 6 & Wdr.—	C. & Btr.—S2S—13/16	52.00	55.00	58.50	59.50	60.50	62.75	63.25	63.50
6/4 "	" 1-13/32	50.00	53.00	56.50	57.50	58.50	60.75	61.25	61.50
8/4 "	" 1-25/32	57.00	60.00	63.50	64.50	65.50	67.75	68.25	68.50
COMMONS									
1 x 4 to 1 x 10	No. 3 Common & Btr. S2S 13/16"	26.00	29.00	32.50	33.50	34.50	36.75	37.25	37.50
1 x 12	No. 3 Common & Btr. S2S 13/16"	27.00	30.00	33.50	34.50	35.50	37.75	38.25	38.50
1 x 4 & Wdr. R/L	No. 4 Common S2S 13/16"	20.00	23.00	26.50	27.50	28.50	30.75	31.25	31.50
	Thick Common—5/4, 6/4, 8/4—Add $3.00								
11/16 x 4 to 12"	No. 3 & Btr.—S1S	21.50	24.25	27.50	28.25	29.00	31.25	31.75	32.00
"	No. 4 Common "	17.50	20.25	23.50	24.25	25.00	27.25	27.75	28.00
	For 23/32 H./M. Add 1.50 to above prices.								
DIMENSION									
2 x 4—2 x 8—2 x 12	No. 2 & Btr.—S1S1E—1-9/16	22.50	25.25	28.50	29.25	30.00	32.25	32.75	33.00
2 x 6—2 x 10	No. 2 " "	22.00	24.75	28.00	28.75	29.50	31.75	32.25	32.50
2 x 4 to 2 x 12	No. 3 Com " 1-9/16	17.00	19.75	23.00	23.75	24.50	26.75	27.25	27.50
	For all strictly No. 1 Dimension Add $1.50 to price of No. 2 & Btr.								
	For all Red Fir Dimension Add 1.00								
CEILING AND BASE									
⅝ x 5 & 6"—	C. & Btr.—Siding or Ceiling	34.00	36.75	40.00	40.75	41.50	43.75	44.25	44.50
⅝ x 5 & 8"	" Casing or Base	38.00	40.75	44.00	44.75	45.50	47.75	48.25	48.50

SPECIAL CHARGES		SPECIFIED LENGTHS	
Shiplap—Center Matched	No Charge	Common Boards 10 and 12'	Add 2.00
All Other Patterns	Add 2.00	" " 18 and 20'	Add 3.00
Rough Common & Dimension	Add 1.00	Dimension—8, 12, 14, 16'	Add .50
Resawing	Add 1.00	" 18'	Add 2.50
Ripping—Per Rip	Add 1.00	" 10 and 20'	Add 2.00

INCENSE CEDAR

4/4 x 6 & Wdr.	C. & Btr.—S2S	60.00	63.00	66.50	67.50	68.50	70.75	71.25	71.50
"	No. 3 Clear "	43.50	46.50	50.00	51.00	52.00	54.25	54.75	55.00
"	Shop "	33.50	36.50	40.00	41.00	42.00	44.25	44.75	45.00

LATH

4' No. 1 Pine Lath		5.30	6.10	6.95	7.20	7.35	7.90	8.00	8.10
4' No. 2 " "		4.10	4.85	5.70	5.95	6.10	6.65	6.75	6.85
32-Inch " "		2.35	2.80	3.30	3.45	3.60	3.95	4.00	4.05
4' No. 1 White Fir Lath		4.00	4.85	5.60	5.85	6.00	6.55	6.65	6.75

chapter thirty

FORESTRY CONSOLIDATION

Gary Shaffer, whose primary responsibility in 1976 was still raw material acquisition for the mill at Susanville, was also, unofficially, the head forester for SPI. Gary still lived in Susanville with his family and reported directly to the manager, Burr Coffelt.

Burr had become a sort of **super-manager** for all of SPI's mills, with the possible exception of the mill at Arcata. He had his own airplane and put in many appearances at Hayfork, Central Valley, Inyokern and the other facilities. He seemed to operate as a sounding board and confidant for Red Emmerson.

Upon the acquisition of DiGiorgio, the team of Coffelt-Shaffer was immersed in the day-to-day activities of the operations. At the same time, the accounting functions were being whipped into shape by Controller Dick Smith and Chief Accountant Ray Lowry.

There were several DiGiorgio foresters, Ron Voss, Pete Thill, Jim Marty, Jim Hamlin and the author, who were retained by SPI. All were in charge of supplying logs to the three remaining mills formerly owned by DiGiorgio.

By that time, the forestry staff included Otto Peters at Arcata, Jerry Gromacki at Central Valley, and Ken Bird at Hayfork. Jim McClure was a check scaler/forest technician at Susanville who worked under Shaffer.

These foresters operated independently where their "home" mills were concerned; but they worked as a team traveling to each other's mills to help out when and where needed, particularly in the area of timber cruising. Gary Shaffer was the leader of the team. SPI had always cruised all the timber in which they were interested, including U. S. Forest Service sales, even though payments were actually made for logs as they were scaled rather than on the cruise.

The "cruising parties" at the various locations were something to see. The DiGiorgio foresters were integrated into this process at an early date, and traveled to various forests to participate. They, of course, were not considered to be competent at cruising the way SPI did, since DiGiorgio had not cruised every timber sale in which they were interested. Occasional sparks were generated when good-natured banter was taken personally.

Gary Shaffer was a very competent field forester and very bright. He was also very aggressive and abrasive; and the "old" SPI foresters looked to Gary for guidance. Over the years, he had demonstrated his competence in cruising and buying timber. He continued as their leader. However, with the acquisition, there were two teams of SPI foresters: the old and the new.

The two teams had many good times together. A typical campaign to cruise a timber sale began at 5:30 or 6:00 in the morning, with breakfast at a restaurant near the property to be cruised. Lunches were ordered with breakfast, and the string of pickups headed for the woods as soon as the meal was finished. The forester in charge of the cruise, the cruise director, had laid out the cruising scheme previously, made strip assignments, and prepared maps and specifications. Steep ground was designated young men's ground and gentler slopes as old men's ground. Each forester worked alone.

At the end of the day, notes were compared, heads were tallied to see that no one had gotten lost, and the string of pickups returned to town in time for dinner. If there was a store on the way back to town, there was time for a beer to wash down the dust.

The evening festivities began as soon after dinner as possible. A few drinks, and tongues were loosened so that wild stories and reminiscences could begin. If any of the cruisers had fouled up that day, or any day in the past, he was not allowed to forget it. Stories were embellished over time, and a real camaraderie developed. Bedtime was as late as one could sit at the table telling stories and drinking.

The next morning was a repeat of the first, and the routine went on until the job was done. On a very large cruise of several days duration, the foresters would be dragging at the end. Especially interesting were those days when the weather was bad; and that seemed to be more the rule than the exception.

After two or three months of operating the DiGiorgio mills, additional changes were made in the forestry organization. The author was asked to move to Arcata which, at that time, was corporate headquarters.

Just prior to purchase by SPI, my wife Norma and I had bought a lot in the town of Graeagle. A contractor had agreed to build our dream house, and the contract was about to be signed when the impending purchase of DiGiorgio was announced. The building project went on hold. In a few weeks, I was asked if I would consider moving, and the hold became a cancellation.

Then the fun began. At each visit to Loyalton or Quincy, Red Emmerson would contact me and the conversation would go about like this:

"What do you think, Bud? Have you and your wife talked over the move to the coast?"

"Well, yes and no, I'm having trouble figuring out what I'll be doing over there. Is Otto Peters retiring?"

"Oh, no, old Otto has a lotta years left in him. We just need someone to coordinate the forestry activities for the company."

"I really like it here in the Sierra; if I don't go, do I still have a job here?"

"No question about it."

The next visit a few days later would be a repeat of the first with minor variations. When asked what coordinating forestry activities meant, Red would lapse into vague terms referring to reviewing timber sales and appraisals, making sure that SPI didn't miss any timber sales, and insuring that all the foresters did things the same way. I was afraid that this would involve an office job, and I would be in charge of nothing. There was never any discussion of a change in salary, and very little discussion concerning responsibilities, other than the generalities mentioned here.

Finally, at the fifth conversation (by actual count), I got the picture more clearly. Having by then gotten a better understanding of how Red operated, I became sure that I really had little choice, and that I had better accept the job or begin looking somewhere else for employment.

The fifth conversation took place immediately after lunch. Red, and Dick Smith, had invited me to lunch with them in Sierraville. Afterwards, we sat in the automobile to discuss my employment in Arcata. There still was no real job description given, but the magic words "salary increase" were said. That sold me. I learned, too, that Red's persistence meant that he was very serious in his desire to see me in Arcata.

The move was arranged, and on September 15, 1976, the corporate headquarters received a new resident. Ron Voss was left at Feather River as the head forester for that division.

The move might not have been made except for two considerations. Norma wanted to return to the coast after living many years inland; and I considered the job, while presenting many intangibles, to be a real challenge. I have never regretted the move, although my wife occasionally would complain about the long hours and the travel.

I left the Sierra with some sad feelings. I remember that those of us who had worked for DiGiorgio had a survivors' party several weeks after SPI took over. It was a fancy function held at Trader Dick's in Sparks. Everyone got dressed up and brought their wives. It was a bittersweet evening - a time to reflect upon those who were not retained by SPI, and a time to contemplate the future. For many of us, it was a time of uncertainty. We all drank a toast to those very good friends who were no longer our fellow employees.

Most employees take pride in their accomplishments. As time passes, they become quite proficient in their jobs, and they become comfortable with their ability to make good judgments. With the wrenching changes that occur during some acquisitions, many have difficulty adjusting to the new regime. It was no different for the old DiGiorgio people. It seemed that, in an instant, the employee went from one of the wisest to one of the dumbest. Immediately, his every decision was questioned and checked with someone else.

Morale was quite low for the first few months after the big event. Having gone through several acquisitions before, I knew what to expect. However, this one was worse than most. I vowed that if I ever was involved in a similar situation, and I was on the other side, I would attempt to integrate any new employees into the new organization as soon as possible, and try to make them feel wanted.

Soon after the takeover by SPI, I was too busy to reflect long on these kinds of problems.

SPI cruising party just prior to splitting up for day's work near Bradford Creek in Humboldt County, March 1983. From left: Tad Mason, Jim McClure (the Old Forester), Dan Tomascheski, Dave Nickel, Jay Webster.
Photo by Ron Hoover.

SPI office at Arcata. This photo was taken after the building was painted dark blue. It is the same building that was considered the "corporate office" as well as the office for the Arcata sawmill, until the late 1980s. Photo by author.

chapter thirty one

ARCATA CORPORATE OFFICE

By the mid 1970s, the Arcata office occupied a small frame building inside the front gate of the sawmill on Samoa Road. At that time, the sawmill was called the Emmerson Division of Sierra Pacific Industries to honor Curly. The office had been painted green, but the coast climate and ocean breezes had taken their toll. Paint was peeling and, in two locations, a newer section of wall was a different shade of green, repainted after a fork lift loaded with lumber had gouged holes in its sides. Since originally constructed, the office had been remodeled twice, always to add space.

The building housed office personnel for the Arcata sawmill, including sales and lumber shipping people for the division. Division Forester Otto Peters occupied a center office with no windows. Sam Witzel was the sales manager; Max Corning, the shipping foreman; and Alan Smith, the controller. Gordon Amos was the manager of the division, and he was responsible for all of the departments.

The "corporate staff" at the time consisted of Red Emmerson, Dick Smith (Controller), Bob Wall (Insurance Manager), Bud Tomascheski (Forest Manager), and Vic Beccaria (Transportation Manager). There were no "support" people for these managers, with the exception of Anna Nielsen, who was the full-time secretary for Dick Smith.

Anna kept Dick's files, did his typing, prompted him when he was forgetful, found his hat when he could not, and was involved with day-to-day banking reports and whatever else was required of a good secretary. In her spare time, she would type for the rest of us, but she did not have a great deal of spare time.

Many of us were envious of Dick Smith because he was the only one in the office with that kind of help. Everyone else had to find someone to type a letter, search files for items they had filed themselves only to forget where, and make their own appointments and travel arrangements. In many cases, it was necessary to plead for help in finding someone who might feel like lending a helping hand with some project.

In the corner office at the rear of the building resided Curly, the patriarch. He still came to the office every day when he was in town. R. H. Emmerson & Son was still a business entity, and Curly was consulted about the timberland the partnership owned, which consisted of some 20,000 acres, primarily in Humboldt County. Curly was still a rancher, and he spent most of his time dealing with cowboys and cows.

Curly's office consisted of a desk, a chair, a couch, a deer head, and a real cow pie that had been bronzed and made into a pen holder. He seemed to be prouder of the cow pie than anything else in his office, and it occupied a prominent place on his desk.

Presiding over Curly and his office, and

Alan Smith, Controller for Arcata Division, 1991. Photo taken several years after SPI switched to using computers. Photo by author.

occupying an adjacent office, was Audrey Griffith. Audrey had gone to work for Curly in June 1969, although she had known him since the early 1950s. Curly had the sawmill on Old Arcata Road and Audrey worked for Skelton Logging Co. Skelton was logging in the Bald Hills, east of Orick, and selling logs to Curly. Audrey, keeping track of logs and payments, became well acquainted with him.

Audrey had followed Curly when he moved his office to the Samoa location. She followed him again when he moved into the Lumbermen's Building on the square in downtown Arcata upon SPI's going public. As there were a number of other businesses in the building, Audrey worked part-time for R. H. Emmerson & Son, and part-time for A & E Redimix.

When SPI returned to being a private company, Curly and Audrey again moved, this time to the corner office with the cow pie. There she worked part-time for SPI instead of Redimix, kept the books for R. H. Emmerson & Son and Elk River Timber Co.

With the various businesses situated in the one building, is it any wonder that the office politics were a shambles? Office duties overlapped, and only a few individuals knew whether they were required to do tasks for someone in another department or not. Of course, there were several who would do anything for anyone as long as it was company business, but not everyone thought that way. It was fun to watch the action.

A newcomer had to learn very quickly where the power lay in such an office. It seemed evident that there were three women to be reckoned with: Audrey, Toots Gahart and Irene Batini.

Irene Batini had worked for Don Riewerts when he was an outside director for the company. Riewerts also had an office in the Lumbermen's Building and operated from there as a C.P.A.

Irene was an excellent typist, but was cool to just about everyone in the office except her boss, who seemed to be either Dick Smith or Alan Smith. None of the three women got along very well together; but they were competent, and turned out good work, usually on time.

I, as Forest Manager, soon began receiving mail that was addressed to the corporate office. Various pieces of mail would come to the office addressed to Director of Corporate Affairs, Environmental Planner, Manager of Real Estate, Forest Engineer, Computer Manager, and many people with similar titles. Since SPI had none of these, the mail would be deposited on the Forest Manager's desk, the newest guy in the office.

Soon, someone was snipping the titles from the envelopes and pasting them on my office door. The list got longer and longer. At one point a letter came addressed to Bud Tomascheski, President, and that one got top billing. As the list grew, Audrey began adding to it. She became quite friendly as she joked about a particularly inappropriate title that she taped to the door from time to time.

Since I always hung my jacket on the office door knob, she would often knock it off when taping titles to the door. She would always, with a stern glare, ask why the dummy who occupied that office never hung his jacket on a hanger so she would not have to stoop down and pick it up. The standard reply was that I had no hangers in my office.

One morning, there was a coat hanger hanging on the door knob, beautifully done up in blue and white crochet work. It was Audrey's handiwork; and the jacket was afterwards always hung on the hanger behind the door. The incident was the first indication I had that perhaps Audrey liked me, or at least could tolerate me.

The women in the office took turns baking birthday cakes when each person's birthday rolled around; there would be a cake in the lunchroom for the occasion. On my first birthday in Arcata, there was a kind of cake that I had never heard of before. It was called a pumpkin pie cake, made by Audrey, and it was very good. I made a fuss over it; and on each of my birthdays thereafter, there was a pumpkin pie cake in the lunchroom for me.

It soon became apparent that Audrey and Toots were the head women in the office, and were the individuals who were most likely to be helpful. Both of them were direct and forceful, knew their business, and were very firm in their judgments about people. It was always a shame that they never got along better together; but they seldom allowed their coolness towards each other show to the outside world.

By 1976, the lunchroom was no longer the lounge for after-work conviviality; but there were still a lot of stories being told of the good old days that were quite recently over. The lunchroom really was only a small room with a kitchen table, a refrigerator and a water cooler in it. At one side, there was a small closet with shelves that was always described as the liquor cabinet.

The stories of Curly hosting the "work sessions" after five o'clock in the lunchroom were legion. All of the old-timers, including Red himself, spoke lovingly of the old days in the lunchroom. If he suspected there might be an opportunity to get some free refreshments, Otto Peters used to show up at five o'clock, too. They remembered the meetings were invariably adjourned to someplace downtown like the Alibi, or Everett's Club, for additional cocktails and dinner.

Curly always kept a bottle of choice whiskey in his desk drawer in case a distinguished visitor might be thirsty. Otto soon found where the bottle was stashed and began to requisition some of it on a regular basis. There were occasions when the contents of the whole bottle disappeared; but Otto being a gentleman, always returned the empty to the same drawer. He could never understand why this infuriated Curly so much.

As the company grew, various changes occurred in personnel. Bob Wall left to pursue other interests, and John Godsey became the man in charge of personnel and insurance.

John was a very interesting character and a gentleman. He had many interests, including sports cars and Victorian houses. In fact, he purchased an old house in downtown Eureka and began to restore it. This turned out to be a monumental task, and he never did quite finish the job before moving on.

John read widely and had a prodigious memory. He was versed in many subjects; and any task that didn't fit exactly into someone's department fell to John to tackle. He seldom

Julie Hunter, who keeps log accounts for Arcata Division of SPI and manages the accounts for Elk River Timber Co., 1989. Photo by author.

complained of the role he played in the company even after he became editor of the company paper, which turned out to be a thankless job. The complaint was that it was never published on time.

In the late 1970s, another "John" joined the corporate office. This gentleman spelled his name Jon Lyons, and he was SPI's first "Corporate Attorney." The company had utilized the services of attorneys before, but always on a fee basis. Jon was the first one to be on the payroll.

Jon was quiet and low-key, and an excellent attorney. He had come from San Diego where he had worked for Wickes, a rather large forest products firm that was publicly owned. He projected an image that was completely opposite from the shrewd, hard-nosed type that corporate attorneys were supposed to be.

Red had trouble accepting this style from a company attorney. He was always worried that Jon was not tough enough, or perhaps did not have the bulldog tenacity to represent the company in the cold world of corporate law. He would never say this very loudly, nor did he complain to Jon himself about the perceived defect in Jon's personality. Jon, being perceptive, picked up on the problem and finally quit to go into business for himself in Eureka. He became one of the best attorneys in northern California specializing in workmen's compensation cases.

The two "Johns" became close friends. They were both in their early forties, and their families also became close friends. Both men were fun to be around, and their senses of humor relieved office tensions on many occasions.

Each Christmas, there was an office party that usually took place at noon just before the holiday. To John Godsey fell the task of being Santa Claus, it being another of those tasks that no one else wanted. He accepted the job graciously and, I suspected, secretly enjoyed it.

One year the party was held at lunch time at Jacoby's Storehouse in downtown Arcata. John donned his Santa Claus suit, which didn't fit at all, as John was tall and thin. His

Santa's beard was thin and wispy and his hat was too big. I accompanied Jon and John downtown to attend the party.

Walking along the street in Arcata, John drew a number of astonished stares in his ill-fitting costume. At one point he developed a dialogue with a rather attractive young lady whom we encountered. Jon and I had to remind him that he was the featured attraction at the office party in just a few minutes.

As we entered the elevator in Jacoby's Storehouse, John removed his hat and beard since it was uncomfortable; and at that moment, a young women walked in with a little boy about five years old. His eyes got very big as he saw Santa with no beard and with sparse black hair. John hurriedly donned the beard and hat and struck up a conversation with the young man. Even though he was a moth-eaten looking Santa, he managed to find out what the boy wanted for Christmas, and to promise him that he would get everything he wanted. The boy's mother tried to signal John to go easy, but John was having too much fun to tone the promises down at this point.

As we left the elevator, the young man's eyes followed John down the hall until he was out of sight. Since the rest of the SPI people had not yet arrived, the three of us repaired to the bar for a toddy. As we sat there, John again removed the offending beard and hat, and began to laugh and joke about his impersonation of the jolly old man.

Some sense warned me that we were under surveillance and, turning around, I noticed the little boy watching his idol from the doorway into the dining room. John quickly replaced the offending items and we spent the rest of the time visiting with a jolly old gentleman who laughed deeply and loudly and made a complete fool of himself before all of the other bar patrons that afternoon. I have often wondered how the young woman explained to her son why Santa Claus could spend an afternoon in a bar with his beard falling off, and that under his too-large hat he was dark-haired and balding.

The SPI corporate office was often compared to those of Louisiana Pacific, Simpson Timber Company or The Pacific Lumber Company. In reality, there was no comparison. SPI was becoming a very large lumber company being run like a Mom and Pop grocery store. Something had to give; there simply was too much for one man, Red, to keep track of. And there were not enough of the rest of us to take up the slack.

The company was about to begin its period of greatest expansion. The "corporate office" was extremely busy and understaffed for what was to come, but there would be two major additions to the staff when the office moved to Redding.

Jay Webster, front-end loader operator at SPI's Arcata Division, 1990. For a number of years, Jay worked for Otto Peters as a forest technician, cruising timber, buying logs and surveying property lines before returning to the log yard shortly after Otto retired.

chapter thirty two

MANAGEMENT PHILOSOPHY

Every organization develops a style of management or a style of operating which is unique. The procedures they use evolve over time; those that don't work are discarded if the company survives. Those that work are kept and are modified to fit current circumstances.

There have been volumes written by learned authors examining various management techniques and suggesting the good and the bad of each. Students in prestigious business schools learn how to run successful businesses, and what not to do if they wish to escape bankruptcy.

The founders of SPI probably have read few of the books and have not taken any courses in the art of being successful in business. By instinct, by careful observation of failing businesses, by sticking to some preconceived ideas and prejudices, by hard work, and by tremendous good luck, they have forged a very dynamic company that seems to have few limitations to growth and profitability.

After coming to work for SPI, I felt one of the first things that I had to do was to figure out what was expected of me. I had usually worked for small companies, and had enjoyed the close relationships and understanding that had developed there. I had known only one large company, DiGiorgio,

and had enjoyed the freedom management gave me to run the forestry division for them. I had also enjoyed access to funding that a large company afforded.

My introduction to Sierra Pacific's style was somewhat troubling. There was no readily perceived structure to the company. No one had a job description. I believe that if someone had asked for a job description then, he might have begun the down-hill slide to disfavor. Such disfavor might not be readily evident for a while, but eventually he might feel that he did not really fit into Sierra Pacific's scheme. SPI did not like titles or organizational charts.

Coupled with that problem was the fact that there seemed to be several persons to whom I reported. First, there was Red himself. I had no problem with this arrangement, because I knew he owned the company and his authority was absolute. It was more difficult to figure out where Burr Coffelt fit into the picture.

Burr, the super-manager, had a finger into everything. It was disconcerting to have him show up unannounced and ask, with what seemed arrogance, what you were doing. Since I did not think that I reported to him, I was somewhat reluctant to go into detail as to what I was doing. I also realized, though, that he wielded some power in the organization and it might be prudent to answer him.

After a few weeks of such questions, and my defensive answers to them, I felt it was time to meet the problem head on. Early one morning, I was confronted in the Redding office by Burr.

He walked up behind me and said, "Well, Tomascheski, what are you doing this morning?"

I felt the anger rising, "Burr, I'm not doing a goddamn thing. I usually goof off for a few hours in the morning. You might tell Red that."

He looked at me strangely, turned around, and left. He never asked me that question again. I was learning how the outfit operated.

Dick Smith was another man who I had difficulty figuring out. I knew early in my employment that he had a tremendous amount of influence in the company. I also knew that he was an accountant, and that every accountant with whom I had ever worked did not understand the forestry part of a business.

I learned that Dick did not understand forestry either; but he did have opinions on just about everything, and he readily voiced them. It took me a while to learn that some of the opinions he voiced were actually not **his**, they were Dick's interpretations of Red's opinions. On those occasions, he spoke as if he were Red, using Red's inflections and mannerisms as best he could. His interpretations were usually correct, too.

Over the months I grew to respect Dick Smith very much. He could irritate me no end, because he would argue about anything that struck his fancy. I also learned that if I needed to get information to Red, and felt uncomfortable discussing the subject with him directly, I only had to discuss it with Dick, and very soon Red would know about it. Dick was a direct pipeline to the Boss. That is a handy thing to have in any organization, particularly if it is a friendly pipeline.

As I learned the ropes, it became evident to me that my job consisted of whatever I wanted to tackle. Since there was no job description, and no formal organizational chart, I could do just about whatever I pleased in the area of forestry as long as I

did not cause too many irritations. The best way not to cause irritations was to put in long hours, project an image of knowing what I was doing, and make money for the company. It was also a good idea to get along well with those in management who counted.

To be a good manager at Sierra Pacific, it **was** necessary to know your business. This meant knowing it from the ground up, and that required experience. It was nearly impossible to be accepted as an "expert" with only schooling and limited experience. It was impossible to fake anything for very long.

To be a mill manager, it was necessary to start at an early age pulling green chain, or cleaning up in the mill. Then it was on to off-bearer, running a machine, grading lumber, and perhaps to the head-saw box. A similar sequence was necessary to be a forester for SPI. One usually began in the woods running property lines, cruising or marking timber. Then it was on to log scaling, buying logs and appraising timber. Eventually one had the responsibility for doing all of these things at a division.

There was always the feeling on the part of upper management that a manager could not ask his subordinates to do anything unless he had done those things himself. It was too easy for a subordinate to give the manager bad information and the manager, not knowing, could make a bad decision. If he had firsthand knowledge, the manager would not be subjected to bad information very many times.

SPI carried this philosophy further. A manager was expected to do the things that some considered beneath them. For example, every forester at SPI was expected to cruise timber and to be good at it. Division Timber Managers, as well as the Head Forester, were expected to show up when it was time to cruise timber, and they were expected to hold their own in the field.

The philosophy may also have been rooted in the feeling that it limited the number of people on the payroll. Every employee was a "doer," and there was no need to have managers on the payroll who only thought deeply but directed others to do the work. The trick was to find personnel who fit the mold and could be happy doing work that some considered beneath them. Red has bemoaned the fact countless times that **good** managers are almost impossible to find. This may be the reason.

By observing failing businesses in the timber industry, or those perceived to be inefficient, Red developed a perception that they fit a pattern. He thought they were "overloaded" with people, or employed a lot of people who were "meeting goers." He thought that having more than one representative at an important meeting was the height of stupidity. It was far better to have one representative there who could tell other employees what had occurred. That way, there was someone "minding the store" while the meeting was going on. Meetings that he perceived to be unimportant were not attended at all.

I tried to tell him on one occasion that to have someone go to an important meeting, then come back to tell others what was accomplished, was something like going to a burlesque show to watch the stripper. It was simple to describe what happened there, but there was something lost in the telling. Of course, the explanation fell on deaf ears.

Therefore, to be a valued employee, long hours were required and it was necessary to **know** the business. The long hours were very difficult for some spouses to accept, and some refused to accept it. The employees who were saddled with that problem suffered terribly and, in some cases, had to leave the company. Those employees who had families that accepted the unwritten rules were fortunate in one respect; they were paid very well. It was up to each family to weigh the good and the bad, and to judge what was most important to them. Red recognized this, and valued those spouses who made it possible for the employee to work for SPI.

It was difficult to find competent people who fit this scheme. There were many, very competent individuals who could not accommodate the other restrictions on their activities. On the other hand, there were some who could never figure out how to conduct themselves in the absence of firm direction with no structured organization to guide them. A good employee was an employee 24 hours a day, and a new one had a limited time in which to fit himself into the structure.

Having figured this all out as best I could, I felt it was up to me to see how I could make the Forestry Department work best with only a few talented people. It was difficult at first because of the two forestry crews SPI had - the old one with Shaffer at its head, and the new one that came with DiGiorgio. That problem was eventually solved when Gary left to form his own business.

To make the department work, I recognized that each forester was an individual, thus each was different. I thought I had to discern their capabilities and differences, strengthen their strengths, and de-emphasize their weaknesses, particularly those Red **thought** they had. On top of that, it was necessary to turn them loose so that they could do the things that had to be done in order to make money. Since there was a lot of overlapping of duties, and lines of communication ran both ways, it was possible to keep track of what was going on, but it took a lot of time and attention.

For example, since each individual was different, it was necessary to find those who could communicate well. Foresters are notorious for being poor at this. Most are introverts who love the woods and are uncomfortable around groups of people unless they are other foresters. In that case, the topic of conversation is always forestry, or some facet of it. All lumber people seem to be very narrow in their interests, and will invariably bore others to death talking business. Foresters are worse than most.

There were some SPI foresters who could write well and some who could speak well. They were in the minority, however. It was also a problem to assign speaking or writing roles to the gifted ones without getting them in trouble for not "minding the store." It was also difficult to find someone to do this on a subject with which he was not associated on a day-to-day basis. It usually took a certain amount of research on each problem before a person could intelligently address it, if he wasn't thoroughly acquainted with all of the circumstances surrounding it.

The same was true for other facets of forestry. Some had developed special skills and proficiency at cruising timber, working with computers, grading logs, negotiating with others, or working out problems with government agencies. Each was encouraged to concentrate on those things that he was good at. In many cases, this came naturally to them; and the only encouragement necessary was for other foresters within the company to call on them when there was a problem in their specialty.

Some persons could never fit within this unstructured existence no matter how hard they tried. It was always depressing to have to give up talented individuals who were judged to be lax, lazy or unintelligent. In many cases, they were counseled to find a better job in an outfit that would appreciate their talents more than SPI. In most cases, they did just that.

A special problem arose when there was a vacancy to fill. It seemed there were numerous individuals who were dying to go to work for SPI. It was another thing to sort them out, and to pick those who would have a chance of being successful within the company. Without a formal structure, it was also difficult to explain to outsiders how the system worked.

One good way to find a good individual was to remember those who worked for competing firms and who were miserable to get along with. There were several who were hired away from a competitor simply because they were difficult to negotiate with. It was usually easy to hire them away, especially if the offered position qualified for inclusion in the management-profit sharing plan. The new employee might find it difficult to work for the new employer, however.

It seemed to be the same in departments other than forestry. There it was probably a great deal more difficult, because in the earlier years the manufacturing parts of the company received a great deal more attention from upper management. I was never envious of mill managers who spent all day at their jobs, most of the night supervising repairs of a breakdown, and most of the weekends either running the mill or repairing it.

Once each month, each mill manager met to discuss their Division's operating statement openly with upper management. This was always a cause for concern, because the competition for profits was keen. Criticism was not always tactfully offered at such meetings, and managers dreaded them. They were usually held at one of the plants in the evening after the day shift, and included dinner at a nearby restaurant. The attendees did not get home until very late at night. The manager was expected to be at work by 6:00 a.m. the next day, or earlier if needed. It required a good man to handle such pressure.

It took me a while to figure out a part of the structure of SPI that is still difficult to describe. Each plant was a discrete operation with a Manager, Accountant and Forester. This was considered to be the management team for that Division. Sales were originally a part of this structure; but after they were centralized in Redding, they were not.

The Division Manager was responsible for the operation of his plant and its profitability. He was, in effect, the C.E.O. of that Division. The Forester and the Accountant reported to him. However, the Forester also reported to the Forest Manager (or chief forester), and the Accountant reported to the Controller. There was always opportunity for discord in such an arrangement.

It was necessary for the individuals in the latter two positions (Dick Smith and I) to gain the confidence of both the Division Manager and the Forester (or Accountant) as the case may be. Handled deftly and carefully, this turned out to be a very effective way to operate.

For instance, when the Manager called to criticize the work of the Forester, it was necessary to respond quickly and effectively. It was also necessary to get correct information from the Forester to make effective response. In many cases, it came down to arbitrating the dispute, or at least defending the action of one or the other. This made for some interesting conversations.

There was one facet of this arrangement

that has probably never been adequately described. By having each of these positions reporting to two people, it reduced the opportunity for the management team at the Division to do something stupid or illegal. It was another set of controls or balances that were, perhaps inadvertently, made a part of the organization. It took special kinds of people to make it work, and it took a lot of work to avoid problems.

With the emphasis the company placed on hiring "good" people and then paying them well, it was also necessary to recognize early when a mistake had been made. It seemed to me that many companies kept someone on the payroll simply because they hesitated to terminate someone who could not produce up to expectations. Of course, it is very difficult to identify the time when it is recognized that an employee is not "producing." It is even more difficult to determine what to do about it. It is up to the manager to determine those things, and it is up to him to solve the problem.

In retrospect, probably the single-most significant facet of Sierra Pacific management philosophy was the reliance on the C.E.O., himself. Red Emmerson managed by example. He was thoroughly committed to the success of the company. He was tireless in his pursuit of being the best, and no one could match him in the number of hours he worked. His day typically began before the day shift went to work. It ended long after dark, if not with a meeting, then with a visit to the night shift.

I once watched him walk through a sawmill. I was with another person at the time; I've now forgotten who it was. As we watched, nothing escaped his attention. He suggested to the man operating the edger that he edge a couple of boards differently. He stepped into the saw box and discussed the sawing of a log on the carriage. He criticized the grading of a couple of boards on the green chain.

As he passed one of the machines on the mill floor, I saw him stop and feel it at a number of places. He appeared to be caressing it, and he took a lot of time doing it. The fellow I was with asked me what he was doing. Having been a mechanic in the Navy during World War II, I knew exactly what he was doing. He was making certain that the bearings were running cool and that they had sufficient lubrication. It was evident that he loved that noisy, dirty equipment. Sawdust was in his blood. He transmitted that commitment to his employees.

Sierra Pacific has been successful in managing people, and it has been very successful in managing its plants. Even in the depths of the frequent recessions (or depressions) which occur in the timber industry, the plants were always kept modernized and efficient. Great quantities of money were spent on purchasing new equipment even in those times. When times got better, the company was always ready to produce its products as cheaply, or cheaper, than its competitors. Many times, when others were curtailing production, Sierra Pacific would go on overtime. By so doing, unit costs were reduced; and this may have had the effect of prompting others to curtail even more.

Management philosophy is always difficult to describe, especially when there is no manual that provides such information and the owners, perhaps, have not formally thought it out. The company philosophy might be better explained by the wording on a plaque I received from the foresters at a farewell get together. Neatly lettered and suitable for hanging were the words:

READY, FIRE, AIM

Cover photo from early SPI brochure in mid 1980s.

chapter thirty three

CONSOLIDATION & GROWTH

As the year 1977 progressed, the DiGiorgio mills were consolidated into the SPI organization. Gone were most of the accountants and office help. Each of the offices seemed to be deserted as modernization of the mills began.

The Sierra Pacific Holding Co. was formed, to which Red contributed all of his SPI stock. This amounted to 97.3% of all the stock of the company. The holding company was owned in its entirety by the Emmerson family, and it owned nothing but the stock in SPI. Then on June 30, 1977, each of the remaining public shareholders was notified that on July 11, 1977, Sierra Pacific Industries would be merged into the holding company. Upon the merger the public shareholders would be paid $18.75 per share for their stock.

That was done, and the Sierra Pacific Holding Company name was changed to Sierra Pacific Industries. The effect was to freeze out the public shareholders, and to vest 100% of the stock of SPI in the Emmerson family. There are still approximately 1700 shares of the old SPI stock outstanding and unaccounted for.

The corporate staff was split between Arcata and Central Valley, where a new building was constructed. The building was an attractive ranch-style edifice, set amidst a scattering of Digger pine across from the CV mill. It housed part of the corporate staff, the personnel for the mill, the accountants, and would eventually house the centralized sales staff. It boasted a maintenance man who kept the lawn mowed, fertilized and watered; something new for SPI. Up until 1977, no office even had a lawn.

Ray Lowry helped design the new office, overseeing its construction. He was a key person in the SPI management team. Ray was born in 1941, at Vallejo, where he also grew up. He attended Vallejo High School, after which he attended Chico State, then Brigham Young University where he earned a degree (BS) in Accounting. He came to work for SPI on October 1, 1971.

Dick Smith and Jack Hawley hired Ray during the time the Chico millwork plant was being constructed. Ray worked under Hawley, who was the Plant Manager, and was involved with the accounting and financing of the new plant. When Lassen Wood Products was purchased in Susanville, Ray would go there once a month to prepare the financial statement. He received a good basic knowledge of millwork accounting.

Ray Lowry was also involved in the public years of SPI. At the time SPI was having all the grief with Gyrotex, John Crook tried to sell Ray on moving to Chicago to take care of the accounting functions there. Ray turned him down, never regretting the decision.

When SPI occupied the Walnut Creek

New office at Central Valley housing corporate office, centralized sales staff and CV sawmill personnel.

Photo from company brochure, mid-1980s.

office, they purchased a Singer computer system which was being operated by one person. It was used mainly to handle the retail business of the Answerman stores. Ray was asked to go to Walnut Creek to offer his opinion on the system design. His report was "bad," stating they had purchased the wrong computer and the operator was unqualified.

At the end of 1974, Ray was asked to move to Susanville where he became the accountant for Eagle Lake Lumber Co. under Burr Coffelt. He then had to travel to Chico once a month to prepare the financial statement for Chico.

In many companies, there would be a full-time accountant at each one of the locations where people like Ray worked. In SPI, once a good employee was hired, his workload was increased until he could not take on additional work. The process was once described as "loading the wagon until the horse can't pull it anymore." Ray was one of those who, without complaint, took on additional duties when asked.

He remembers that on one of his early days at Eagle Lake he was asked by Coffelt to take care of the legal and financial requirements for a trapshoot facility to be built behind the log decks. The project got started, and a concrete slab was poured before Red found out about it. That was the end of the trapshooting club at Eagle Lake.

With the DiGiorgio purchase, Ray was asked to assist in the conversion to SPI accounting systems. He was part of the team that decided which of the DiGiorgio personnel would stay and who would not be retained. Ray was not popular around the new operations for a long time after such decisions were made. Only two DiGiorgio accounting people were retained: Karl Mundt who became the Division Accountant, and Jack Stanley who would assist him. Jack later took Ray's place at Susanville.

After the DiGiorgio mills began producing lumber for SPI, the manual accounting functions became an immediate problem. Ray was instrumental in convincing Dick Smith and Red that a computer was the only way to keep track of the expanded business. A contractor in Red Bluff was hired to do the accounting work on its IBM System 3. After DiGiorgio's computer system was scrapped, the manual method had lasted two months.

At the end of 1976, Ray was the only one in the company with sufficient computer experience to organize a system. Red, as well as Dick Smith, asked him to move to Redding, oversee the building of a central office, and set up the systems for a centralized sales staff. He spent most of the first months designing the office, working with the contractor, Steve Kiminski, and designing an invoicing system for the sales force.

The initial computer system was an IBM 3741 keypunch machine, a printer, and a modem hooked up to the Red Bluff contractor. The IBM System 34 was to come in 1981, with Fred Rich as Data Processing Manager. Before then, though, the office would be expanded in 1979, and again in 1982, to accommodate the forestry department and the millwork sales force moved from Chico.

Computers became an immediate source of irritation for Red and Dick Smith. People who had been denied access to the technology were hungry for the information it could provide. They began to find ways to get their data into the computer one way or another. Ray finally prepared a priority list; but people finagled any way they could to get their projects moved up the list.

Finally, computer requests came under scrutiny by Red himself. A process was set up under which Red, or Dick, had to approve each addition to the list of requests. Priorities were set; and many employees waited long months for their pet projects to work their way to the top of the list. Many of the requests were turned down cold. SPI was beginning to join the 20th century, but it was a rocky course.

Another significant acquisition was looming on the horizon as the year wore on. Publisher's Paper Co. indicated an interest in selling their California holdings. This included some 86,000 acres of timberland near Burney and their two sawmills located close by. Red had known of the possible sale for several weeks.

Two men who had been associated with DiGiorgio telephoned to promote the pur-

chase by SPI. The two, Bill Hardie and Rick McKannay, had formed a consulting and real estate business after leaving DiGiorgio. They met with SPI in August of 1977, and several times thereafter, to discuss facilitating the acquisition. A number of meetings with Publisher's occurred as August and September passed. Many were held in Oregon City, where Publisher's had their corporate office, and in Redding near SPI's office. SPI foresters began to check-cruise the timberlands.

The cruising presented some particular problems. About half of the ownership was located in the Big Bend-Curl Ridge areas northeast of Redding. That area had been surveyed originally by the Benson Syndicate which had become notorious for defrauding the government of large sums of money. They were convicted of faking the surveys, or of doing only a small portion of certain townships and faking the rest, and then turning in fraudulent billings.

A consulting firm (Procneau) from Albany, Oregon had recently cruised the properties for Publisher's. They had found a

Ray Lowry, the Corporate Controller, about the time he began working for SPI in 1971.
Photo from Ray Lowry.

minimal number of property corners when they did their field work, and had given up trying to find more of them. Since the properties were in a checkerboard pattern (from old railroad grant days), Procneau had taken the position that it was not necessary to search for more corners. They reasoned that if "good" corners were ever found, area lost from one section would be made up in the adjoining sections. They had obtained recent aerial photos of the area and had simply transferred the projected corners from Geological Survey maps onto the photos, then used the resulting locations for "approximate" corners.

SPI foresters were uncomfortable with the procedure. Most believed that before cruising started, it was mandatory to identify, without a doubt, where the property was. The country in question had been labeled, by some, the devil's triangle. It is very, very steep, covered with Tanoak brush and almost impossible to get around on foot. Many days were spent researching the Benson Syndicate work, and in searching for corners in the field.

It finally was decided that there was no choice but to agree with the Procneau decision to use map locations for the property corners. A scheme was devised for intensively cruising 10% of the sections, and of picking the sections at random. After several weeks of very hard work, bee stings, torn shirts, and scratched- up foresters, the check cruise was finished. The Procneau cruise was found to be a conservative estimate of the volumes of timber on the property. An appraisal was prepared using the cruise as a basis.

Then the acquisition was pursued with enthusiasm. Travel between Oregon City and Redding became a weekly occurrence; but negotiations ground to a halt as winter began.

Publisher's had an inflated estimate of the value of their assets. The two mills at Burney were located on the same property; one was a large log mill, the other utilized small logs. The large mill was old and obsolete; the small log mill was new and equipped with a quad-saw head-rig. Publisher's had not been successful in mak-

ing money at the location, but they had invested considerable sums in the new mill. They were very reluctant to sell and incur a loss. They announced that they would seek other buyers. Red was very disappointed.

As the year neared its end, Bison Robinson retired at Loyalton. Bison was in charge of logging road construction at the Feather River Division.

Bison and his wife, Lois, had grown up in Arkansas. They had come to California when most of the other refugees from the dust bowl had come west. Bison had gravitated to the logging business; and along with a partner, Bill Randrup, had formed R & R Logging Co. They were quite successful.

Their company logged for Ken Metzker when he owned the Loyalton and Sloat sawmills. By the time DiGiorgio came along, R & R had already grown to be a large logging concern, and the two partners decided to retire. They went out of business, and held an auction of their considerable inventory of equipment. Both became financially well-off.

Bison ran for the Board of Supervisors in Sierra County, won, and had been re-elected several times. He was an exceedingly smart man, a good politician, and affected the down-home manner of the "Arkie" country boy he was. He was also a hard worker. He could not stand the inactivity of being only a politician; so in the early 1970s he went back to work for DiGiorgio running the road side.

The road side was a company operation, thus a union outfit. Red did not like the prospect of having labor troubles, nor the "featherbedding" that he thought unions represented. He was constantly irritated when anything reminded him of company employees working in the woods where they were often out of sight of supervisory personnel.

Even though he could find nothing to indicate the construction operations were costing more than contract operations of a similar nature, Red kept suggesting that it be abandoned. Bison recognized his dislike for the road department, and decided to retire again. He did so on December 10, 1977. His wise counsel was sorely missed. The road side continued for several months afterwards, but its days were numbered.

As 1977 closed, SPI had sales of $122,000,000. Assets were valued at $82,000,000. There were 1,200 employees, seven sawmills operating, and a moulding plant at Chico. The mills produced 418,000 MBF lumber tally, and used 333,000 MBF of logs. The Publisher's deal seemed to be a dead issue.

As 1978 began, the company continued to modernize its sawmills. Forestry operations were also changing; as more wood was required, more staffing was needed.

At Quincy, Ron Hoover began employment on February 16, 1978. He was the first forester hired by the author as a Sierra Pacific forester, and he would become Ron Voss's "right arm" at Feather River.

Ron Hoover was born at Glendale in southern California. For six years he lived with his grandparents on a farm in Ohio, but moved back to the Los Angeles area where he began his education. He graduated from Van Nuys High in 1961.

After two years at L. A. Valley Junior College, he enrolled at Humboldt State where he graduated as a forester in 1966. Another year at graduate school at Humboldt State, four months in the National Guard, and Ron was ready to go to work for the Forest Service.

In August 1967, he went to Somes Bar on the Klamath National Forest, where he worked in timber sale layout, and all the other things young foresters do in the Forest Service. In March 1972, he began working at raw materials acquisition for Cal-Pacific Manufacturing Co. at Hoopa. From there he went to Southwest Forest Industries at Burnt Ranch. By that time, Ron had a good background in timber and log buying, particularly in the Douglas fir region of northern California.

Ron actually was recruited to take Otto Peter's place at Arcata, after Otto announced his retirement. However, his wife was tired of Humboldt County, so Ron asked about a job

Ron Hoover and Milford Bachman, a faller for Gott Logging Co. (the principal logger for SPI Arcata).
Photo from author's collection by David P. Bayles.

Tom Waddel and the author attending a "foresters' meeting" on the Klamath River, about 1977. Tom was an accomplished river guide as well as a timber cruiser.
Photo source unknown.

he had heard was open at Quincy. Instead of being the head forester at Arcata, he became Ron Voss's assistant at Quincy. He was an excellent addition to the staff.

Subsequently, Carl Jagodski took Otto Peters place as Timber Manager of the Arcata Division. Carl had worked for Bob Kleiner for a number of years, doing timber cruising and appraisal work. He was also well-acquainted with Humboldt County timber and was a hard worker. He began employment with SPI on March 15, 1978 in preparation for Otto Peters's retirement on June 9. Carl was to work only a year when he left to go back to Kleiner. Ron was then recruited for the Arcata job, which he finally accepted in 1979.

On April 1, 1978, Tom Waddel and Dan Tomascheski came to work as full-time cruisers for the company.

Up until that time, the foresters at the sawmills did their own cruising, with help from the others as needed. As the sawmills were modernized, each would require more wood and the cruising load became tremendous. Stumpage prices were rising with increased competition. It seemed wise to form a cruising crew that could, hopefully, become proficient in cruising the types of timber found at all the locations where the company had mills. It was a thankless job to cruise day after day with no respite, but Dan and Tom kept at it for many months.

Dan had been working at Fibreboard in Truckee when he heard about the job opening at SPI. He applied for the job. As the list of applicants grew, Red asked about the names on it, and discussed the prospects. He began to ask questions about Dan's qualifications. I was reluctant to get into discussions of the suitability of hiring such a close relative and told him so. Red finally took over the task, calling around to some of his contacts in the industry, and hired Dan himself.

Pete Thill, a survivor from DiGiorgio, left to go to work for Clover Logging Co. at Quincy. He began to "bird dog" small patches of farmer logs and do layout work for Clover's several logging sides. Clover deserves par-

Gyppo loggers Jim McCollum and Hale Charlton with Bill Banka, an SPI forester (left to right), late 1980s. Photo from author's collection by David P. Bayles.

ticular mention as one of the principal logging contractors for the company.

I became acquainted with Clover a number of years ago when the mill at Quincy was still Meadow Valley Lumber Co. At that time, Jim McCollum, the founder of Clover, was a small logger for the cedar mill at Quincy.

In the late 1960s, Glenbrook Lumber Co. (actually a logging concern) was the contract logger for Meadow Valley. I met Mead and Kershaw of Glenbrook when I began to manage the forestry affairs at Quincy.

Mead and Kershaw were high production-loggers, very aggressive and smart. It was difficult to keep track of what they were doing at all times; and they gave minimum attention to small timber sales and hard-to-log jobs.

Meadow Valley had just purchased a small salvage sale on Sockum Creek that was a tough logging job, with steep ground and small trees. It was late fall, and I was having difficulty negotiating what I thought was a

fair price for logging and hauling. Jim McCollum walked in unannounced and offered to do the job for less than I thought it was worth. He got the job.

I was pleasantly surprised by the contrast in dealing with McCollum and Glenbrook. The little Sockum Creek job went smoothly, and the logs were well manufactured. The Forest Service had no complaints; in fact, they were complimentary. Before winter came, the job was done. Jim McCollum had found a home.

From there, McCollum's company grew. He, his partner Hale Charlton, and their sons eventually formed several companies with different names but all owned by them. In addition to Clover there was J & K, Blue Sky, C & M and several others. Jim went on to be appointed by the Governor to the Board of Forestry. McCollum and Charlton owned one of the premier logging companies in the state which is still logging for SPI at a number of locations today.

Back in Humboldt County, Masonite at Ukiah decided to sell their Hoopa operations in early spring. This consisted of the old Humboldt Fir sawmill previously owned by Sam Arness. Masonite had shut down the mill in October 1977; but still had an office at Hoopa, a logging outfit, and two Forest Service timber sales on the Klamath Forest with 23,000 MBF of standing timber.

Escrow closed on April 1, 1978. An auction was held at Hoopa to sell the sawmill and logging machinery. The mill property was sold shortly thereafter. The price that Masonite had bid for the timber sales was so high that anyone who owned them would lose money. However, with the funds recovered from the sale of land and machinery subsidizing the timber sales, SPI was able to come out ahead.

In late spring or early summer of 1978, the Publisher's deal reopened. Publisher's had shopped the Burney properties to others in the industry, and had failed to generate enough interest to make a sale. At some point, they contacted Red to reopen talks. Red was quite enthusiastic, believing that if they had no takers, they would be easier to deal with this time around.

Several meetings took place; and then Hardie and McKannay came back into the picture. They believed that, since they had been involved in the negotiations the year before, the current talks were merely a follow-up to those a year earlier.

At one of the meetings between SPI and Publisher's in Oregon City, SPI learned that Hardie and McKannay were to be paid by Publisher's as well as SPI if the deal went together. Red became very suspicious of such an arrangement, believing it to be illegal and unethical for them to represent both the buyer and the seller. A dispute rapidly developed between them and SPI. By October, there was open warfare.

Even so, negotiations with Publisher's went swiftly considering the confusion and delays of the prior year. The cruising was already finished and, except for updating data to compensate for operations conducted since then, agreeing on price was the only problem to be solved. On October 4, 1978, an agreement was signed in Portland, with escrow to close on November 13, 1978.

Publisher's actually began "winding down" their operations on September 22, when about 100 workers were laid off. The mills ceased sawing logs; however operations to dry, surface and ship already manufactured lumber continued.

Newspapers of the day reported the sale had been made, noting that the Burney operation of Publisher's (owned by Times Mirror Co.) of Los Angeles received $36 million cash for two sawmills and approximately 69,000 acres of timberland. The mills employed 350 workers, and had been owned by Publisher's since 1968.

The large log mill was down for good. Red did not consider it to be worth the effort to modernize. Besides, there were large log mills at CV and at Susanville, owned by SPI, that would compete with it for logs and timber.

The small log mill was another matter. Red had spent some time watching it run while Publisher's owned it. In his opinion, it would never be a profitable operation in its current configuration, so he decided to completely rebuild the inside of the mill. Reconstruction was to begin at once.

There was a large inventory of both large and small logs at the Burney plants. SPI moved in a fleet of trucks and began to ship the large logs to CV, Susanville and Hayfork. To the idled workers from Burney, it was adding insult to injury, and stories began to appear in the papers critical of the new owners. Of course, the operations were unionized, and the workers felt threatened by SPI, whose mills were mostly nonunion.

The two mills remained closed all winter and into the spring while reconstruction of the small log mill continued. It finally opened in July 1979, essentially still a quad mill.

With the construction of the new CV office completed, the rest of the sales people were relocated there as the year progressed. Up until that time, lumber and millwork sales were handled by a sales manager at each sawmill, selling the products his operation produced. There were several reasons for the consolidation of the sales force at CV.

Some mills cut better lumber than others for a variety of reasons, and SPI mills were no different than most in that respect. Of course, some variation was expected because of the type of machinery at each mill and its relative age and maintenance. Also, the manager at each mill affected the quality of lumber cut, depending upon whether he concentrated on cutting for quantity or quality, and not both. Since salesmen ostensibly reported to the manager of that particular mill, they were subjected to pressures from him.

Additionally, timber from each area is different, and will produce lumber with differences in quality. Variation is probably greatest in Douglas fir because the species has such wide distribution. For example, Arcata produced the "best" Douglas fir, although some customers preferred that from Quincy. Trees in the vicinity of both mills produce fine-grained stock; preferences probably were due to past experience or habits. In the early years of CV, Douglas fir came from mostly "farmer logs," and lower elevation sites where the trees were short and knotty. CV lumber grades were, on the average, lower.

After considering the problems with decentralized sales, Red decided the situation might be improved by consolidation. While the salesmen at the various operations were actually competing with each other for sales, they were all working for SPI. It made sense to him to sell lumber from the mill that could produce it the most efficiently, and to employ top salespersons to sell it. He also thought it would be better to have the sales force located where it could receive closer scrutiny by him, and where specialists could be developed for a line of products instead of a mill's production.

Sam Witzel was put in charge of the sales force when it moved to CV. The salesmen from each division were moved into the CV office with him, where a large "bullpen" had been added to the east side of the new office. All of them were in one large room where they could converse among themselves, and where Sam was readily available for advice and direction.

As 1978 came to a close, SPI reported gross sales of $150,000,000, and assets at year-end were valued at $136,000,000. There were operating sawmills at Arcata, Central Valley, Hayfork, Loyalton, Sloat, Quincy and Susanville. The two at Burney were not yet operating at year-end, but the millwork plant at Chico was still operating to capacity.

The Publisher's purchase provided a significant land base for SPI in the Sierra. Besides the two sawmills at Burney and inventories of logs, the purchase consisted of the following:

Curl Ridge Tract	33,887 acres
Scott Tract	31,139 acres
Modoc Tract	1,200 acres
Plumas Tract	640 acres
Others	1,310 acres

Timber on above	334,000 MBF
Government contracts	52,000 MBF
Main Roads (capitalized)	49 miles

At the end of 1978, SPI finally had become the owner of a considerable amount of timberland. Considering the volume of logs the company required to run its sawmills, the acquisition was only a "drop in the bucket." However, to the SPI foresters, it was a first step, and in the right direction.

A portion of Publisher's tract on Curl Ridge looking down Chatterdown Creek. Note new road on ridge at center. Photo taken in 1980 as lands were being roaded by Clover Logging Co.

Photographer unknown.

chapter thirty four

"GOOD MORNING, SIERRA PACIFIC"

Every company must have an individual who sets the tone for the public's first impression of the organization. In most cases, that impression is gained from the first telephone call that one makes to it. In some companies, the first contact is made by a personal visit to an elegant office where an attractive young person greets visitors and answers the telephone. Such individuals are sometimes selected for their attractiveness, their tone of voice, and/or their quick responses to prying questions such as, "Is Mr. Emmerson in this morning?" The easiest way for a receptionist to get into difficulty is to reply in the affirmative to someone whom Mr. Emmerson does not wish to speak to at that particular moment.

As the individuals employed in those capacities gain experience and confidence, they become indispensable in managing the telephones, controlling access to those who wish to be inaccessible and, in many cases, managing the office politics. Quite often, all of these tasks are done at the same time while typing correspondence from the office typing pool.

The trick is to do all of the assigned tasks quickly and well while making the callers feel comfortable and special. One never knows when the one denied access today may become a special visitor tomorrow.

There are several individuals working for SPI today who do all of the above. In the timber industry in California, one of them is known as "Toots."

Toots came to the West when she was five years old. Her "Daddy" sent for her and her mother after fleeing Arkansas just after the Depression. She grew up in Humboldt County, living for a number of years at Klamath, a small community on the Klamath River.

Prior to coming to work for SPI, she worked for Simpson Timber Co. and her husband, until retiring recently, operated a log loader for them.

Toots does not fit the stereotype of the attractive young thing sitting in an elegant office greeting visitors. This does not mean to say that Toots is not attractive. She is definitely attractive, but she is a grandmother and not so young. She learned long ago how to handle people.

Toots's desk is just inside the front door at SPI's Arcata office. Due to lack of space, she had to greet all kinds of visitors, some important, some not so important, and some just looking for work. She frequently complained about various lumber truck drivers who hung over her desk to sign bills of lading, or other documents, when they came to pick up loads of lumber. In some cases, such drivers had driven all night, or perhaps for several nights, without benefit of shower or toothbrush. Toots did not take kindly to such closeness.

After she voiced objections to the famil-

Toots Gahart relaxing in her home in 1990.
Photo by Cecil Gahart.

iarities, Gordon Amos had windows installed in her office which could be opened. The old ones had been solid glass with no movable parts. The new windows helped for a time; but in the winter, cold drafts cooled her feet as she attended to the truckers' business. Finally, in desperation, she asked that signing of bills of lading be moved from her office to the shipping office in the rear of the building where odors of sawmill and log deck could somewhat mask the fragrance. Gordon reluctantly complied with her request.

Toots had a phenomenal memory for voices. If one were to call SPI, the conversation would go something like this.

"Good morning, Sierra Pacific".

"Good morning, this is Jerry Duffy, is Bud in?"

"Just a moment, I'll see if I can find him."

If Bud wished to talk with Jerry Duffy, the connection would be made promptly.

Of course the first "Good morning, Sierra Pacific" would be delivered with a lilting cadence - loud, but not raucous. It could be heard in the rear of the building and undoubtedly could be felt in Jerry's ear.

After a few calls from Mr. Duffy, a surprising thing would occur; on every call thereafter, even if Jerry would not announce himself by name, Toots would recognize the voice, and very soon would be on a first-name basis with him. At some point, she would know Jerry's kid's names, how they were doing in school, and whether his wife was feeling poorly or not.

Toots did not use this ability to recognize names indiscriminately, nor did she spend a lot of time visiting on the telephone. But she had a sixth sense for determining who might appreciate the informality and who might not. And instinctively she knew who wished to be addressed as "Mister." She also knew how to cut a wise-guy down to size, and was not bashful about using her talent to do so.

Toots became a fixture at SPI's Arcata office. As the upper management moved from the Arcata office to the office at Central Valley, Toots's job became less demanding. It was easier for her to keep track of the calls for Dick Smith, the Arcata Division personnel, or the author; and she had less typing to do.

As the company grew, and as more personnel were added to the CV office, the jobs that were similar to Toots's became more complicated. The communication systems were more sophisticated as well. Eventually the telephones had speakers, played music, and required a degree in computer science to understand the instruction manuals that came with them. The person at the switchboard did not have to hold the receiver; it was attached to the ear.

In the office where Toots worked, the resident staff was small enough so that she knew where everyone was at any given time. She even knew if someone was in the restrooms, since the doors to them were located near her desk and switchboard. It was very difficult to sneak out of that office and not reveal to Toots where you were going. If one forgot to tell her, she asked.

Such was not possible in the larger office at Central Valley. There, the person answering the telephone was far removed from some of the offices, and the telephone system had become far more complicated. It was possible to "page" someone over the intercom and to play the usual music to the waiting caller, even though he or she might not be in the mood for music, particularly **that** kind of music.

There were many irritations resulting from the effort to modernize the telephone system. In most cases, the irritations were caused by the inability of the users to learn the intricacies of the new procedures. People who were used to working in a sawmill, or in the woods, were wary of all the buttons and beeping noises that emanated from the new instruments. Instead of reading the manuals supplied with the system, they were used to hollering for Toots. Alas, Toots was not available.

At CV Sandy Anderson represented the new kind of Toots. Sandy, of course, was younger than Toots; but in her own fashion, she had a similar nature.

Sandy soon learned how to get the most out of the new system. She could sit at her switchboard, hour after hour, with a receiver plugged in her ear, fielding call after call, sometimes several at one time. With the mouthpiece a part of the receiver, she had both hands free to type a letter or a report for

Sandy Anderson at her desk and switchboard in CV office. Photo from Sandy Anderson.

someone in the office. When she answered the phone, she projected a very professional manner; but she did not have time to inquire into one's wife's illness.

As a result, a profound change occurred in the public image that was projected from the Sierra Pacific offices. In some ways, the company became a far more sophisticated member of the business establishment. It still could, however, return to its humble beginnings, especially when Red would attempt to use a speaker phone, and would succeed only in cutting the caller off without so much as a note of music. It was then that the office staff would learn what Red thought of the new telephones, the persons who purchased them, and the company that designed them.

There were numerous persons, over the years, who held jobs similar to those of Toots and Sandy, such as Lorraine Hilton at Anderson. One of the best, and very similar in nature to Toots, was Alice Bacon who, at different times, was at Loyalton, Sloat and Quincy. She finally became Alice Foote at CV. Some of them were only known by their first names, such as Eleanor at Susanville, and Maureen at Quincy. Many should have known their last names; but it is the nature of those in the lumber business to put on an air of informality, and last names sometimes are not important. Some, of course, have faulty memories, and last names can be easily overlooked by those so afflicted.

An example of this lack of memory, and of Toots's ability to set someone at ease, can be illustrated by the following incident that occurred shortly after I came to Arcata to work for SPI.

One day, my wife and I received an invitation in the mail to attend an event to celebrate the wedding anniversary of a Mr. and Mrs. Cecil Gahart. The event was to be held on a weekend at the Grange Hall in the little community of Requa, near the town of Klamath. No one at our house had ever heard of the Gaharts; and there was much conjecture as to who they might be, or if someone had gotten the wrong address on the envelope.

The next day, I thought of this puzzling invitation while in the presence of Toots and Vic Beccaria. Both had worked for SPI a lot longer than I.

"You two guys are old-timers at SPI; can you tell me who in hell are Mr. and Mrs. Gahart?" I began.

They both looked at me blankly, then at each other, then back at me.

Finally Toots said, "Why?"

"Because someone sent us an invitation to a wedding anniversary shindig at Requa, and I don't know who in the heck they are. Have you ever heard of them?" I asked.

There were some more blank looks and then Toots smiled and said, "One of 'em is me, but I didn't know anything about it. It must be a surprise."

As I hung my head trying to think of how to apologize and get out of this predicament with some fast talk, or some lame jokes, Toots started to laugh.

"Are **you** going to come?" she asked. "And are you sure of the date?"

"Well if it's you, I guess I better come so I can apologize to the whole family for screwing up your surprise party," I said, feeling that I needed a big hole to crawl into, or at least a mild heart attack to put me away for a while.

Toots was laughing and trying to make me feel comfortable again. She said, "Bud, you have just done me a bigger favor than you realize. Now I'll have time to get my hair done and get all gussied up. Maybe I can even get Cecil to put on a clean shirt."

So my wife and I went to the celebration, met all of the family, and helped Toots and Cecil observe the event. Toots was radiant, all gussied up, and with her every hair in place. Cecil had on a clean shirt. I asked if the party was still a surprise, and she told me that she had never acted more surprised than when everyone started showing up.

To this day, I believe the sponsors of the event think they really surprised Toots. I know better, and so does Toots, because every once in a while she will remind me of what a dunce I was.

chapter thirty five

SMALL LOGS & INFLATION

Ron Hoppe was assigned to the Central Valley sales force in January of 1979. In July, he became Sales Manager for all lumber sales, replacing Sam Witzel. The sales staff was expanding and becoming far more competent and specialized.

The sales staff eventually got too large for me to adequately describe each person's contribution to the success of the SPI sales organization. Their talents, backgrounds and personalities were many and varied. All of them were outgoing and noisy, as most salespersons are. They are a breed apart from the average forester or mill manager.

George Sharp was one of the early salesmen working for SPI. He began with the company in February 1975, before the CV mill was built. He sold lumber produced by the old mill on Branstetter Lane; and for a time, sold the lumber produced by Susanville and Loyalton.

George was a forester by education, graduating from Purdue in 1958 with a B. S. degree. He grew up in the midwest, attending schools in Indiana, and worked for the old Diamond Match Co. in Chico.

Another salesperson who began with SPI during the same era was Sally Renlund. She started as a receptionist in the Chico millwork office in 1972, learned all the "girl" jobs in that office, then became the shipping supervisor for the plant. She transferred to the Chico sales office; and then to the CV centralized sales office where she handles millwork sales. She is one of several women employed by SPI in both lumber and millwork sales.

During the first half of 1979, SPI's efforts were focused on the Burney area. Modification of the small log mill had begun, so it was not in production. The large log mill became only a shell, with the machinery removed and much of it sold. The SPI forestry staff was augmented with the Publisher's acquisition when two of their employees, Alan Jacobson and Bill Raibley, continued with SPI. Alan had been the Chief Forester at Burney, and Bill had assisted him in managing their timberlands. They were moved to the CV office.

A number of foresters from Publisher's were not retained. Many of them had left Burney by the time SPI took over, because they had known of the impending sale of the company for more than a year. It was best they had done so, for no one looked forward to telling any of them to look elsewhere for work. For the few who were left, it was a traumatic experience. The author agonized over the best way to deal with it, but found there was no easy way to tell an individual his employment was terminated.

Meanwhile, the union was not recognized as the bargaining agent for the new SPI employees. There was much grumbling and agitating; and a great deal of publicity given to the lack of employment in Burney with both mills shut down. The local papers, especially, were very critical of the way long-time Publisher's employees were treated. Nothing changed however; reconstruction went on at its usual frantic pace.

The small log mill was redesigned to permit the installation of a Far West Equipment overhead carriage ahead of the quad head-rig. The new equipment permitted the computerization of the mill. It was really an extensive reconstruction project, because much of the existing machinery was moved and new transfer chains installed.

The head-rig had four, movable band saws and three bent-knife chippers to square the log and saw it into as many as five boards in one pass. The system was developed by Applied Theory Associates, and included a Hewlett-Packard computer that scanned the log, positioned it for the carriage, and adjusted the saws and chippers for maximum recovery. The mill also included a twin re-saw, a shifting edger, a line bar resaw, and a sorter and lumber stacker system.

After the initial shakedown, the mill was able to saw over 1,200 logs per shift, using logs that averaged about 9.5" in diameter at the small end.

The mill was finally opened in July under its new Manager, Dave Allward, who also managed the CV operation. By that time, fresh logs were already being delivered from the SPI operations at Susanville and Central Valley. Since there were old logs in the yard that had to be used first, the log yard was a tangle of machinery, logs and people. Tempers were short. One of SPI's competitors said the log yard looked like a Chinese fire drill. He had arrived on the scene to determine why it took several hours to get log trucks unloaded. He departed with no suggestions on how to improve the efficiency of the operation. He thought SPI was a "Mickey Mouse outfit" for not hiring more people for the log yard, and not buying additional equipment.

A short time later, a new manager was hired so that Dave Allward could concentrate on the CV mill. Dwight O'Donnell, from Simonson Lumber Co. at Smith River, had

experience building their quad stud mill. After construction, he had assumed the position of production manager for both Simonson's large mill and the stud mill. He moved to Burney.

From the beginning, the mill did not make very much money for SPI. It was one of the first of its kind in California, although George Schmidbauer had built a similar mill in Eureka some time before. Schmidbauer sawed primarily Douglas Fir. Burney was trying to use all species from the Sierra, and the logs were from the upper portion of trees or from very small trees. They also got logs that no one else wanted. It became a dumping ground of sorts.

Red was particularly difficult during those times; but even he did not grasp the extent of the problem. In fact, he probably was a part of the problem.

I can remember, in particular, a trip to the woods that Alan Jacobson and I took with him to inspect the cleanup of some old Publisher's right-of-way logs left over from the previous summer. Clover Logging Co. was loading the logs that had been cut more than a year earlier. The bark was slipping from some of them, and they were beginning to deteriorate. Red was clicking his ballpoint pen and spitting.

We had driven up in Alan's three-quarter ton pickup which was equipped with a hook in the rear. As we drove up to a location from which the logs had recently been removed, we noticed a good-sized pile of loose bark that had fallen off during log handling. Red had spotted a log under the bark pile that he felt should have been loaded, so we got out to paw around in the debris. He asked for a choker, which was in the back of Alan's truck, and we hooked the log to the hook in the rear. I noticed a very short, small log off to the side of the road and asked, somewhat facetiously, if he wanted that one, too.

The two of us picked it up and tossed it into the back of the pickup. Off we went, towing one down the road, with the other in the bed of the truck, looking for the log loader. About a quarter of a mile farther, we found the crew loading a truck. They looked at us with amusement as we drove up with the two pecker poles; but the two logs were on the next load to Burney.

It took many months of trying to figure out what was wrong at Burney. Dennis Gomez, who eventually became the manager there, had much to do with the solution to the problem. Dennis did not come to SPI until early 1982, so the Burney operation struggled along until then without a great deal of success.

While the mill was having its problems, the woods operations were also struggling along. Publisher's had intended to haul all of the logs from their timberlands to Burney, so the access roads were pointed in that direction. Since SPI did not intend to run the large log mill, the destination of the large logs would be either CV or Susanville. The timber from the Curl Ridge tract northeast of Redding was quite close to CV; but access was nonexistent except through Big Bend and Round Mountain to Highway 299. Publisher's had not developed access to about two-thirds of the tract at all.

The winter months immediately after purchase were spent laying out roads at the lower elevations to utilize the county road (Salt Creek Road) from Interstate 5 to the McCloud River bridge. As the higher country opened up in the spring, construction began at the bottom and progressed northward.

The terrain in that area was extremely steep and broken necessitating ridge-top road locations, as much as possible, to minimize cutting of side slopes. Of course, that made costly cable logging mandatory, and increased haul costs due to adverse grades that had to be designed to come off the ridge-top main roads. There seemed to be little choice.

Construction on the main-line road went along quite well; but the first spur off to the east ran into trouble very soon. The spur was to access timber in Squaw Creek, a major tributary of the McCloud River.

Since the property was in a checkerboard ownership pattern, it was necessary to cross neighboring property to extend the roads into more SPI property. Adjoining lands belonged to the Forest Service; and SPI tried to locate

Alan Jacobson, his pickup (occasionally used for skidding small logs), and the author on North Fork Mountain, Publisher's tract, around 1980.
Photographer unknown.

roads to serve the Federal land as well as company land where desirable, or to cross Federal land as close to property corners as possible. Stern topographic features, in many cases, prevented that. In any event, it was necessary to obtain permits to cross Forest Service land, and consequently their approval could be withheld.

The spur into Squaw Creek had to pass through a tight notch in a limestone "dike," many of which were scattered throughout the tract. Upon applying for a permit to cross the rock, SPI was told that the limestone might be home to the rare Shasta salamander.

The critter was supposed to live in the cracks of the dikes, where it hid from the hot sun during the summer days, or sunned itself on top of the rocks in the winter. Foresters looked and looked for one of them to no avail. However, the Forest Service would not grant a permit unless a biologist searched the area and wrote a report describing his findings, and approving SPI's activities.

After weeks of delay, SPI found a biologist from U. C. Berkeley who would take on the formidable task of searching under rocks and in the cracks for the slimy little animal. A few more weeks of searching and finally, success! He found a salamander. Everone's heart sank.

He reported that he would have to take the little guy to the lab for analysis to make sure it really was a **Shasta** salamander. The test required centrifuging the animal to see if body fluids contained the correct kinds of DNA, or genes, or other identifying elements. Someone named the unlucky creature Sammy Salamander. He would become a symbol of all the crazy things that go wrong in the world of forestry at SPI.

After many more months of delay, SPI received the bad news. It was indeed a Shasta salamander. However, he was dead by centrifuge. More searches were conducted while the construction languished, but no more salamanders could be found in that particular dike. It made no difference to the Forest Service, since the limestone was obviously habitat for the rare critter. SPI foresters conversed many times with the Forest Service, and argued; but there was no movement in the government's position.

Finally, the biologist, with a stroke of ge-nius, suggested that the shaking of the rock by blasting and excavating would actually improve the habitat. The operation, by fracturing the smooth limestone, would produce cracks and crannies where Sammy could live if he ever wanted to. He wrote his report and the load was lifted from the Ranger's back, for he had a report from an expert. Construction resumed after delay of more than a year.

As a result of all the wasted time, the foresters of SPI fabricated a traveling trophy to be given annually to an individual in SPI management. To qualify for award, company operations would have to be delayed due to blunders made by the winner. The trophy was a wood plaque, suitable for hanging, with an enlarged picture of slimy Sammy taken before he died. The recipient was supposed to pass it on to an employee of his choice at the next annual management meeting.

Over the years it has been given to anyone who blunders, for any reason, even though no delays occur as a result. Ron Hoppe received it one year, and refused to give it to anyone else for three years. He thought it looked good on his office wall. It **was** a conversation piece.

Clover Logging Co. built many of the roads, and did most of the logging on Curl Ridge in the early years after purchase. They developed a skyline logging system, and a crew to match, for selectively logging some of the steepest slopes on the tract. They were instrumental in proving that it was not necessary, in every case, to clear-cut mixed-aged stands on steep ground even though cable logging was necessary. Some of the best examples of that type of logging is evident there today.

Gary Shaffer left SPI in 1979 to go into business for himself. He formed Almanor Forest Products to buy timber, and to log and sell logs. Eventually he was one of the founders of a small sawmill at New Bieber. Later, Jim McClure followed him to become Gary's forester-cruiser.

Joe Dillard replaced Gary at Susanville, beginning employment on June 1, 1979. Joe became a valued Timber Manager for SPI.

Joe was a native Californian, and attended high school at Martinez. He enrolled at Humboldt State in forestry and graduated in 1966, just in time for the Vietnam war. He signed up for the Marine Corps, and received his commission as a Second Lieutenant shortly thereafter. Joe served at Danang and was promoted to Captain while there.

In 1969, he went to work for Jim Niklos and Associates, a consulting firm in Carmichael. There he did cruising and appraisal work along with the myriad duties young foresters are assigned. In 1972, he went to Sonora to begin working for Fibreboard Corp. under Dick Pland.

Dick was one of the most astute foresters I have ever known, very knowledgeable and straightforward in his approach to problems. Joe learned a great deal from him. He was soon promoted to Fibreboard's Burney operations where he was their Chief Forester for Manager Glen Lorenz. Fibreboard by that time had been purchased by Louisiana Pacific.

Ron Voss and I had conceived the idea of trading logs with LP at Burney. We thought it might be possible to purchase their small logs for SPI's Burney mill and to sell larger logs to them. They seemed particularly interested in buying large logs; and we thought they might also take some Lodgepole pine logs that SPI had at Feather River.

We arranged a meeting at LP in Red Bluff. Up until that time, I was not well-acquainted with Joe Dillard, but he made an impression on both of us there.

There were several LP people attending the meeting, including Glen Lorenz, and Bud Fish from their Truckee operations. Every time we got close to agreement, Joe would press for a better deal for LP. He was a "royal pain" to Ron and me. We never did put a log trade together.

I remembered the way Joe conducted himself in that meeting, particularly the way he tenaciously stood up for his employer. When it was time to find a replacement for Gary Shaffer, I thought of Joe Dillard. It was not difficult to convince him to go to work for

SPI at Susanville, and I was glad he did.

With all of the sawmills operating, wood requirements were larger than any of the foresters could imagine. Prices being bid for stumpage continued to escalate. In March 1978, President Jimmy Carter had signed the bill that expanded Redwood National Park by some 48,000 acres. The expansion took from Arcata Redwood Co., Louisiana Pacific and Simpson Timber Co. some of their best timberlands. Arcata Redwood especially felt the bite.

The result was that all of them began to bid more heavily on Forest Service timber sales, especially those within hauling distance of Humboldt County. Those of us who depended to a great extent on those timber sales felt the pressure. Bidding became frantic; and the high-priced timber being placed under contract by many firms would be difficult to swallow in the years ahead.

There were similar pressures in other parts of the west, due not only to condemnation of private forests, but to pressures to set aside public lands and reduce the harvest of federal timber. SPI would match, dollar-for-dollar, the high bids at the auctions. The company was as crazy as the rest of the industry.

With the prices being bid for timber, Red became increasingly concerned that the foresters did not know what they were doing. While he did not say that directly to them, he asked me to pay particular attention to cruises and appraisals. The appraisals being turned in by the Timber Managers indicated that on nearly every forest where SPI was bidding, the winning bid for stumpage was more than the selling price of the lumber.

I talked with all of the foresters, particularly the cruisers, on many occasions about the problem. I could find nothing suspect in our methods. There was conjecture that the company had gotten too large, perhaps, and the sawmills were becoming inefficient. Salesmen and managers felt the scrutiny even more than usual.

In an effort to determine why we could

Joe Dillard (right) and his assistant, John Forno, 1989.   Photo from author's collection by David P. Bayles.

not seem to compete successfully with many of our neighbors, I sat down and began to fit some figures together. I looked back at logging and milling costs, the changes that had occurred in lumber selling prices, and the rate of inflation in the national economy. After finishing the research, it was evident that everyone was doing the same thing SPI was. We were all betting inflation would continue at the same rate, and that everything would work out in the long run.

The vast majority of those who own or manage timber companies are incurable optimists. Red is worse than most. He always believed that everything would work out alright, no matter how black the situation appeared to be at the moment. Additionally, he believed SPI was better than any other company, not only in terms of efficiency, but also because of the number of talented people who worked there.

He conversed almost daily with some of those he respected in the industry. They were all telling him the same thing he already knew. Timber was becoming more scarce,

principally because of withdrawals for perceived environmental reasons, and because the politicians were spending the country into enormous debt; inflation was rampant. Jimmy Carter was still in the White House.

SPI had no choice. It could stop bidding at the point where appraisals indicated break-even, or it could develop some kind of system for trying to predict a place to stop bidding to lessen the risk. Of course, the brave could do what Red had heard one of the competitors had done. He had given the forester bidding the sale instructions to "buy it, no matter what it cost." Red considered that foolhardy.

If SPI purchased no timber, it would soon run out of logs and the operations would be curtailed or closed very soon. If it bought timber, closing would be delayed, and there was a chance that something would bail everyone out. Since everyone in the industry was doing the same thing, no one could conceive that the whole industry would shut down together. SPI kept up with the rest.

It is amusing to look at a memo I prepared and sent to the Timber Managers for use in their appraisals. Dated Aug. 1, 1979, it reads as follows:

Data I have show the following:

1. Increase in lumber selling Prices:
1964 to 1970 ave. all species 5.26% / yr.
1970 to 1976 ave. all species 17.80% / yr.
1976 to 1979 ave. all species 22.93% / yr.

I suggest we use for time being 12% per year.

2. SPI manufacturing costs have increased from 6.7% per year at Hayfork to 12.3% at Eagle Lake. Emmerson Div. increase is 10.71%. Redding and Feather River data are not valid due to new construction.

I suggest we use:

Hayfork	*10%/yr.*
Redding	*10%/yr.*
Eagle Lake	*12%/yr.*
Feather River	*12%/yr.*
Emmerson	*10%/yr.*

3. By-product values are expected to increase. Suggest we use an ave. of 7% to start, and adjust later.

4. Logging costs have increased from 10-12% per year. With fuel costs and road oil costs increasing we should use 12-15% depending upon amount of oil required, especially on long hauls.

5. Yield tax adjustments are based on SBE harvest values. If stumpage values increase, harvest values increase. Suggest we use tax values at bid date and adjust upwards at same rate as lumber selling prices.

Signed
Bud T.
Inflation Fighting Dept.

The memo was discussed at length. Finally, I worked up a formula standardizing the timber appraisal forms that all the Timber Managers used. For us, it was quite sophisticated, working in such data as escalation formulas for each species, ineffective purchaser credit for building government roads on the timber sales, and the amount one or more species may have been short of the government cruise figures. It took up several, long pages and required many computations.

All the foresters called it the "inflation-fighting formula," somewhat derisively. In retrospect, it was a strange way to appraise timber.

Surprisingly, after instituting the system and using it for a short time, I was able to predict within a few dollars, on most sales, where the bidding was likely to stop. It was evident that the **real** competitors were using the same system, or a variation of it. Most of us would rue the day.

Jerry Gromacki worried about the price of wood that was being placed under contract, and who would be to blame when those logs would be delivered to "his sawmill" at some future date. We would kid each other about what would happen when that event occurred, and where we would find work after both of us got fired. As a result, I prepared an official appearing memorandum for him to display on his bulletin board. Jerry told me afterwards that Red did not appear amused by my attempt at humor.

By 1979, SPI finally had a forest large enough to manage. However, there was very little staff with which to do it, and no growth or inventory data that could be used to begin it. SPI did have a start and a few good people on board.

During the year, the timber division, under Alan Jacobson, had planted 158,000 trees, cleared 70 acres of brush for planting, logged over 11,000 MBF of fee timber, and constructed over 10 miles of main road. The resurvey of the townships on Curl Ridge began with the help of Griffith and Associates, a consulting engineering firm in Redding. About 80 property corners were targeted so that they could be aerially photographed in preparation for the final survey.

By year-end, Burney had run only six months. EMF Co. (the last of Gyrotex) went bankrupt, and $2,294,000 was written off. SPI was very big in terms of production, ranking tenth in the U. S. Gross sales were $168,000,000, and assets were valued at $135,000,000.

Lumber production was as follows:

Arcata	82,000	MBF
Burney (6 mo.)	15,000	
Hayfork	75,000	
Quincy	63,000	
Loyalton	63,000	
Redding (CV)	67,000	
Sloat	21,000	
Susanville	95,000	
Total	481,000	

The lumber market was beginning to weaken as winter approached. With the high-priced timber under contract, SPI was as worried as others, but was conceivably in better shape than some to weather what lay ahead.

September 27, 1979

TO WHOM IT MAY CONCERN:

This is to certify that Jerome Gromacki is not responsible for the high bids he submitted for the Rainbow and Zig Zag timber sales on the Shasta Trinity National Forest.

It is further stipulated that should he ever be criticized for the high price of logs hereafter delivered from those two sales, he is to specifically authorized to tell the criticizing party to "stuff it".

Signed this 27th day of September, 1979.

By J. Tomascheski

Sworn and subscribed to before me, Irene M. Batini, a notary public in and for the County of Humboldt, State of California, this 27th day of September 1979.

Irene M. Batini

IRENE M. BATINI
NOTARY PUBLIC
HUMBOLDT COUNTY, CALIFORNIA

Notarized memo to Jerry Gromacki from author absolving him of blame for purchasing high-priced logs for Redding Division during the artificial timber shortage in late 1970s and early 1980s.

chapter thirty six

HIGH PRICED TIMBER

The Burney mill continued to provide SPI with operating problems in 1980. Division Manager Dwight O'Donnell had experienced the difficulties associated with starting up and operating a remodeled sawmill. He had additional problems in turning a profit, since the price of logs continued to climb. Lumber prices continued to decline in the first part of 1980, then seemed to rally a bit. Even that did not help much; and no one, Red included, seemed to be able to make the mill run profitably (at least to the level that was required at SPI).

Red asked Bob Puett, Manager at Susanville, to replace O'Donnell, and Bob began to split his time between Susanville and Burney. Red had developed a great deal of confidence in Puett's ability in running a crew and a mill. Red was, however, spending much of his time with Puett at Burney.

Part of his time in January was spent in court, as well. On January 15, 1980, the Rick McKannay trial began in Redding. The dispute over whether SPI owed McKannay and Hardie a commission on the Publisher's purchase had boiled over. After SPI had offered to settle the dispute out of court for $100,000, McKannay sued for approximately $3,000,000.

Jon Lyons and Moose Mathews represented SPI. The author was privileged to watch Red Emmerson on the witness stand.

Red does not ordinarily show a great deal

of emotion except, on occasion, anger. Like many good executives, he uses anger to get his point across forcefully and without wasting time doing it. Only once have I seen him get carried away - when a customer complained that wood chips delivered to their pulp mill by SPI contained chunks of asphalt. He became highly incensed at the supervisor of the personnel who were loading trucks from the chip pile.

Moose put Red on the stand to describe how Red found out that McKannay was working for both SPI and Publisher's. As Red told his story, he spoke quietly. As he got into reliving the incident, the veins in his neck began to stand out, his face became red, and his eyes flashed. He finally banged his fist on the rail of the witness stand and said rather forcefully, "That's illegal, you can't do that!"

That evening at dinner, everyone teased Red about his performance on the stand. Moose called him "Richard Burton" for his skill as an actor. Red was insulted; he had not been acting, but he seemed pleased by the compliment.

The trial lasted until January 22. The judge finally ruled that SPI owed Hardie and McKannay $100,000, and SPI's tender offer to them was a fair one. Red considered it a victory, since both men had undoubtedly spent nearly that much in working on the acquisition, and their work had been useful to SPI.

A 1980 issue of the SPI newspaper, *BoardTalk*, announced wage increases for nonunion employees to take place on June 1, 1980. In the same issue, some production curtailments were announced. Some overtime was eliminated, and SPI sawmills were to go on a "week-to-week basis." There was no indication at press time that any specific mills had stopped production.

Soon the timber/log supply situation gained increased attention from management. SPI was still having considerable difficulty competing with others at the bidding table even though lumber prices were down. It appeared that a real "shake-out" was to begin in the timber industry in California and elsewhere.

I prepared a talk that I gave at a management meeting shortly thereafter. It was lengthy, but it summed up the problems facing not only SPI, but all those who depended on government timber. The text, dated Oct. 1980, follows:

So far in 1980 SPI has purchased some 453,000 MBF of timber. Of the total 325,000 MBF, or 73%, is government. Average delivered log cost of the government timber only is:

P.Pine	*$559/M*	*D.Fir*	*$289/M*
S.Pine	*922/M*	*I.Cedar*	*695/M*
W.Fir	*309/M*		

If the prices given here are re-allocated for differences in cruise estimates, and are compared to our present lumber selling prices (LSP), the figures look grim. We would need an LSP as follows to break even.

	LSP Needed to Break Even	*Present LSP*	*% Increase*
PP	*$607*	*$401*	*151*
SP	*665*	*420*	*158*
WF	*280*	*190*	*147*
DF	*382*	*293*	*131*
IC	*387*	*301*	*129*

On the timber sales we have purchased we have concentrated on buying particularly those that:

1. Have timber of good quality.
2. Are long term (most will expire 3-31-86).
3. Have several species locked in at base rates so they cannot escalate.
4. Have a "short" species that has been bid up.

As you can see we are betting on the "come" like everyone else. What happens if we do not get a strong housing market? We are committed to cutting these sales; in some cases starting in 1982. We can close our eyes and hope for the best, or we can try to do a little planning to soften the impact. We have several choices:

1. Go broke.
2. Continue to cut our lowest priced timber and save the higher ones till we have nothing but high priced logs left.
3. Meter in the higher priced logs as we go, taking one or two sales each year.
4. Cut some fee timber to go with the costly sales.

I suggest that we will probably use a combination of all of the above except No. 1. If we cut a few of the high priced sales we should cut those that have several species that can escalate and save those sales that have only one species that escalates.

Predicting the future is awfully hazardous. One thing is certain, it gets more difficult every day to operate. Some of you think the environmental pendulum is beginning to swing our way and that a new administration will solve some of our problems.

I don't see it that way. We are prevented from harvesting timber in "sensitive" areas, and it gets harder to sustain a viable timber program all the time. We are now being choked to death by Wild and Scenic Rivers, the California Wilderness Bill, Air Quality regulations, and on, and on, and on.

Lastly most of you think politics is a bunch of B.S. Most of us, including me, hate to get involved with it. You, however, need to recognize something:

If you work for SPI you are involved in politics and everything you do affects all of us politically. We are number one in purchasing public timber in California. Whether we like it or not we are becoming involved in supporting candidates who are business oriented. We are beginning to lobby; even Red is getting involved. Note his recent trip to visit Sen. Hayakawa.

A year ago we had under contract, or owned in fee, about 1.5 billion bd. ft. of timber. At that time the lumber market was good. The Burney mill had just begun to operate.

Here we are a year later and many things have occurred:

The market has gone to the dogs, but is hopefully recovering. Our mills have been modified to be more efficient and to use more wood. Also, there have been many changes in our industry.

Last year at this time I suggested that a shake-out (a separation of the men from the boys) was about to occur. I believe it is still going on. Consider what has happened over the past few years, just in our area.

MILL CLOSINGS:

Champion	McCloud
Publisher's	Burney
Cal-Pacific Hoopa	Orick
Masonite	Hoopa
LP	Alderpoint
	Myers Flat
	Greenville
Simpson	Mad River
S.W.F.	Salyer
Humboldt Fir	Hoopa

I believe the principal reason most of these closings have occurred is the shortage of timber and the high cost of wood. I also believe that more "shake-out" is likely to happen in the next couple of years. I would predict the most likely

candidates for serious wood supply problems are:

Essex	Quincy
LP	Burney
S.W.F.	Burnt Ranch
McNamara & Peepe	C. City
LP	Alderpoint
Beebe	Hyampom
Calendor	Alturas

I believe our single greatest concern has to be wood supply. We can have the most up-to-date facilities, the best sales organization, the most efficient trucking department, the shadiest legal advice, and the sharpest accountants, and be out of business because of an inadequate wood supply, or one that is too costly.

The outfits that will be here tomorrow are those that own timber that is competitively priced (whatever that is). Take a look at those companies we have trouble competing with, like Diamond, International Paper, Simpson, and Pacific Lumber. They own their own timber.

In the short run we are having trouble competing with Roseburg, LP, and Eel River, plus all those named above with wood supply problems.

I believe our job is to make sure we do not get in a position where we must buy a timber sale to run a mill next year or the year after. We must have enough timber so that we are buying three years out. Once our supply gets to a point where we are forced to buy for next year we are in serious trouble. That is where most of the companies named above are, and where Roseburg in California, and some of L.P's plants are also.

The talk went on for several more pages detailing cost problems, and appealing for SPI to begin managing its timberlands (some of which needed rehabilitation, having been purchased as logged-off land some years ago). A copy of the text was found during research for this history. It provided a feel for the concerns being voiced a decade or more ago, which are still prevalent today.

A few weeks after the meeting, Ronald Reagan was elected to the Presidency. Most good Republicans gave a sigh of relief, especially those in the timber industry. Most hoped the environmental movement would be slowed a little. It was not to be.

By year-end 1980, SPI had produced 478,856 MBF of lumber. The Burney mill was in full operation and had contributed over 53,000 MBF to the total. Total assets were valued at $149,780,000. Gross sales were nearly $165,000,000.

The numbers were not encouraging after the expansion of the previous years. Even worse times were ahead.

chapter thirty seven

THE SLIDE

On January 3, 1981, George Coulter became the manager of the Quincy and Sloat operations. With Red's approval, he soon began to make changes in the Feather River Division, culminating in the addition of a cogeneration plant at Quincy in 1983. The changes are discussed in a following chapter.

By 1981, the forestry staff consisted of several new employees and a number of old ones. At Arcata was Ron Hoover, Timber Manager, assisted by Jay Webster. Ken Bird was Timber Manager at Hayfork. Jerry Gromacki, Timber Manager at Redding, also was responsible for Burney, where Leroy Smith assisted him.

Smitty was an old SPI employee who had previously worked with Otto Peters at Arcata as a log buyer and forester. Later, Smitty moved to Quincy where he worked for Ron Voss, cruising timber sales and buying logs. He transferred to Burney on February 1, 1981.

Also on the forestry staff was Alan Jacobson, who was in charge of the Timber Department fee lands in Redding. He was assisted by Bruce Olsen, Engineer, and David Steele. Joe Smailes and Tad Mason had taken over the timber cruising duties. Ron Voss was the Timber Manager of the three mills at Feather River, with help from Dan Tomascheski and Tom Walz. Joe Dillard was Timber Manager at Susanville, with Jim McClure as his assistant.

Gromacki and Bird, the only two "old" SPI foresters, often grumbled about the size of the forestry staff as compared to the old one. They recognized that, since operations were continually changing, the company required more wood, thus more help. But the occasional gatherings of foresters that were being held were a far cry from the small, intimate meetings that used to occur. They missed the old days.

Ken Bird was beginning to complain about an old snowmobile injury he had suffered to his back while working for the Forest Service. He was to have three surgical procedures before he was finished with SPI; always, it seemed, to no avail.

Ken was also a Humboldt State forester from the 1964 class. He had been recruited by Gary Shaffer to go to Inyokern, but Ken turned the job down. At the time, he was working for the Forest Service at Quincy, doing timber sale preparation and administration. Three months later, SPI opened the sawmill at Hayfork and Ken accepted employment there. That was in January 1973.

He stayed at Hayfork all of the years he worked for SPI, gaining the confidence of Red Emmerson and Fritz Hagen, the Manager. He was an excellent forester and a good negotiator.

In 1983, after his third surgery, Ken requested duty where he would not be required to drive a pickup. The author met with him and his doctor at one point to discuss the problem. The doctor believed that, while there was some chance that he could be permanently injured by falling in the woods, or some other incident, Ken would know when he could not continue. The decision to remain a field forester was left up to Ken.

After further discussion with SPI management, Ken was offered training in either lumber sales or accounting. Having always been a field forester, he declined, and went into business with his old friend Gary Shaffer. SPI was sorry to see him go. Tom Walz would replace him.

Tom came from Minnesota where he obtained a degree in Forest Resource Management from the University of Minnesota. He worked for the U. S. Forest Service for a short time in Idaho, then went to Wisconsin where he bought hardwood logs for Webster Lumber Co. Webster closed its doors as the depression of the early 1980s deepened.

Tom came to California in June, 1980 looking for work. He appeared at the CV office, where he had heard SPI was interviewing foresters for a cruising position. He was one of the few foresters who showed up for the interview dressed in a business suit. He got the job, not because of his dress, but because he stood out from the crowd in manner and in the way he projected competence.

After cruising for a year, Tom transferred to Quincy to work with Ron Voss. In 1984, he would take the job at Hayfork as Timber Manager when Ken Bird resigned. Tom, his wife Cherryl, and their two little girls, would eventually settle in Weaverville - valued additions to the SPI family.

The industry began to suffer more and more as 1981 continued. Lumber prices began to decline again in the first quarter. While there was a little flurry of activity in White and Douglas firs at the beginning of the second quarter, it was all downhill from there.

The SPI paper, *BoardTalk*, carried a let-

ter from Red in the August 1981 issue. It read as follows:

Many people I have talked to while walking through our mills have voiced concern to me as to how the company is faring during these extremely poor times. Many mills have shut down for extended periods, some permanently, and everyone is concerned with their future prospects.

I believe that I can honestly answer these concerns by stating that, although current economic times are the worst in my memory, our Company remains very strong financially. Our strength is built upon the high quality people we employ throughout the Company.

To date, we have avoided major shutdowns and layoffs at all plants except Redding. The layoffs there are caused by a major remodeling project we have underway. It is our plan to continue to avoid layoffs or shutdowns, however these plans will be affected by market conditions.

I would suggest that all employees should be conservative in their financial plans and avoid taking on any new debts in the near future.

Even though SPI was experiencing serious problems, the sawmill at CV was undergoing a major revamping of the lumber sorting system and the log decking area. A new debarker was also being installed, enabling the mill to utilize larger logs.

The operation at CV was hard on managers. Jerry Gromacki used to be teased about the number of managers he would have to educate. At his last count, he thought there had been ten of them. He called it a revolving roster, where every SPI manager got a shot at the job at one time or another. There was Bob Anderson (no relation to Runar), Dave Allward, Carrol Lee, Fritz Hagen, Gordon Amos, Red Russel, Bob Gibson, Jack Davies and Darrel Dearman. There probably should be another name or two on the list.

It is not inferred that the men whose names appeared on the revolving list were incompetent. In fact, many of them went on to similar positions with SPI at other locations, and are still valued employees today. The problem may have been Red's doing.

Upon the move of the main office to CV, Red established an office in it. He then developed a new travel routine. While based at Arcata, he spent most of his time there, travelling to CV, Susanville, Hayfork, and the mills at Feather River as the spirit moved him. Occasionally, he spent a night at those locations, or even at Redding. The SPI air force, though, was based at Arcata.

After the move to CV, he and Ida bought a condominium in Redding and began to spend more time there than at Arcata. Since **his** office was at CV, he became intimately involved in the management of the mill there.

It used to be said that at Arcata Red was the manager and the forester, too. Many thought the "manager" was really only a superintendent and the "forester" was only a log buyer, since Red was in the mill on a daily basis and in the woods almost on a weekly basis. He always called the shots.

He began to operate the same way when he got to CV. Instead of every third or fourth day prowling the mill, Red was there every morning and nearly every afternoon. Often he was there at night, too. The early managers at CV, however, were not used to such close scrutiny of their operations.

Red can be very critical of what he perceives as operational deficiencies, even though they turn out to be minor. Some incidents that he considers major might seem small to outsiders. For example, I have seen stacks of used stickers (small wood strips used to separate layers of lumber in piles) on a manager's desk. They had been left there by Red who had found them scattered around the mill yard. He believed them to be perfectly good stickers which should have been recycled.

Of the CV managers named previously, only two seemed to be able to satisfy Red. Of course, Dearman is still there, so it may eventually be three.

Gordon Amos, coming from Arcata, knew how the system worked and could accommodate the inspections. Of course, Gordon was an excellent manager; but he did have the advantage of knowing what Red wanted because of his long association with him at Arcata.

In 1972, Gordon left Arcata to take over the ailing operation at Inyokern. He was gone only a year, then returned to his beloved Arcata sawmill. In March 1981, he was asked to manage the CV sawmill. He accepted reluctantly, only to return to Arcata in November of the same year. It seemed that whenever Red perceived a problem in a sawmill, he sent for Gordon.

Many times, Gordon was a very miserable person to get along with. Red knew that, and seemed to enjoy listening to the complaints others had about him. In most cases, Gordon was only looking after the best interests of the company as he saw them, and he was quite often right. Red, having become used to a manager like Gordon, was disappointed that all of them were not like him.

Jack Davies was the other manager at Redding who seemed to be able to satisfy Red. He was the opposite of Gordon Amos in his manners, and in his ability to get along with all kinds of people. He was the consummate politician.

Jack was born in Klamath Falls, Oregon in 1933. His father was a sawyer who moved to Yreka when the mill where he worked closed. Jack was 13. He went to schools in Yreka and Ft. Jones, but did not graduate from high school, and ended up in the Marines.

He made Corporal and was sent to Japan at the same time Red Emmerson was there. In later years, they learned that they both were at Camp Pendleton during the same time, but did not know each other. Jack married Jan Ragan on July 4, 1953, and was discharged from the service in 1955.

Jan and Jack had seven children, raising their family in northern California as Jack moved from place to place following the lumber business. He began pushing logs on the mill pond at Big Bend, east of Redding, then moved to the Ralph L. Smith Lumber Co. at Wildwood. Later he went to Ukiah to work for F. M. Crawford, and to Colorado for a short time, always leaving one outfit to take a better job at another. His first manager's job was at Potter Valley in 1965.

Jack Davies subsequently ran the Alderpoint operation for LP, and finally went into business for himself. He and Chet Richardson formed a partnership, named Preston Lumber Co., which they operated until the 1982 depression, when they went out of business. After that, Jack always wanted to return to owning a sawmill.

In 1983, Red, with Ron Stevens, interviewed Jack for the job of running the CV mill. He came to work in March, and turned the operation into one of the best mills SPI had. Ron especially liked the way Jack got along with the crew, and his knowledge of lumber. He was the "smoothest" operator most of the foresters had ever worked with. Jerry Gromacki thought he had found a manager who would be at Redding for as long as he wanted to stay.

It was not to be. In May 1988, Jack complained of being exceptionally tired all the time. He sought medical help, and, after many tests, was diagnosed as having liver cancer. He made a valiant fight, and was assigned a place on the list for a liver transplant.

It was too late. Jack passed away on January 6, 1989, leaving a vacuum in the SPI management group that was difficult to fill. Some of the Davies children are attempting to fill the gap. A son, Charles, works for SPI at Red Bluff, and Charles's wife is in the shipping department there. Bob Davies, another son, works for SPI in maintenance at Hayfork. One of Jan and Jack's sons-in-law works for the company at Anderson.

The loss of Jack Davies was a tragedy that affected SPI for a long time. Jack's second-in-command, Darrel Dearman, succeeded him, and the operation remained very much a success.

As 1981 progressed, manager problems were the least of the worries at SPI. Lumber prices continued their downward spiral. Except for those modernization projects in progress, all others that required significant capital investments were delayed or cancelled.

By the end of the year, all divisions had suffered reductions in hours and production except Arcata and Quincy. The company had produced 394,608 MBF of lumber, and gross sales were valued at $147,658,000. There was a pre-tax loss reported at year-end of over $13,000,000 - the first for SPI as a private company. Capital improvements for the year were just over $4,000,000.

Prime interest rates were at record levels at well over 20%. With such interest rates, the housing markets had quickly dried up. Timber under contract was also priced at record levels. The company tried to minimize the effects of such prices by harvesting over 10,800 MBF of its fee timber. It was not enough to have much effect on the bottom line.

chapter thirty eight

ROCK BOTTOM

The Burney mill was going through managers almost as fast as the Central Valley mill had; but in March 1982, Dennis Gomez came to Burney as its manager. Bob Puett went back to Susanville, but still kept a finger on what was going on at Burney.

Dennis grew up in Vancouver, Washington. He graduated from Lewis and Clark University and immediately went to work for LP. After nine years with them, he worked his way up to a management position, left LP, and went to work for Brand S in Portland. Red recruited him to run the Burney operation.

The mill at Burney had shut down in November of 1981 and had stayed down the month of December. It started up again in January; but by then the depression was upon the industry.

A part of the problem for Burney was the philosophy of trying to run it on "junk" logs. All of the divisions of SPI that shipped logs to Burney picked out the good logs first. The managers at the divisions did not want to send good logs to Burney unless they were high priced, since Burney had to buy the logs from them at cost.

By retaining the small logs, as well as the large, from low priced timber sales, the managers of the large log mills could keep down the average cost of the logs they sawed in their own facilities. Since there was keen competition between mills for profits, and the managers' performance was reviewed at the end of each month, pressure was upon them to use every means to show a profit at the end of the month. Some of them could devise strange schemes for doing so.

For example, Fritz Hagen at Hayfork decked his logs, not only by species, but by cost. At the time, each mill was charged for logs as they were used. Since logs were scaled by the government scaler on the mill deck, the cost of logs was computed based on his scale. Consequently, the cost varied due to price modification procedures in each government contract, adjusted to the time of scaling. Fritz kept track of where the costly logs were stored from **each** sale, since they were priced differently and prices were adjusted differently.

He also carefully watched the prices he was getting for his lumber. In the months when lumber prices for a particular species were good, he would select the higher priced logs to saw, and do the opposite when prices for lumber were less. That way he could consistently show paper profits each month, or at least minimize losses. Of course, everything would wash out at the end of the year when Dick Smith finished with his internal audit and reported **yearly** profits, or losses.

Red liked Fritz's method because he showed more months in the black than some of the other managers. He thought that Fritz was "on top of things" and knew how to manage his log yard. He wished some of the others would do the same.

Log deck at Burney, 1987. At the time, the deck included many of the larger "small logs" that Dennis Gomez had fought so hard to secure for "his" sawmill.   Photo by Mark Fator.

Fritz did not sell logs to Burney from his division because his mill was considered to be too far away from Burney. The example, though, is an illustration of some of the creative ways managers ran their divisions. The same sort of creativity took place when it came to delivering logs to Burney. The logs unwanted by reason of cost or quality were sent to Burney; those reasonably priced and/ or of good quality were kept at home.

It was evident to some, though, that one of the problems at Burney was that SPI was trying to run it as a small log mill, and it was **not** a small log mill. The author had spent a few months in Idaho where he had become acquainted with several small log mills that sawed logs of very small diameters, some as small as five inches. **Tha**t was a small log mill. Burney was different.

Burney could not efficiently handle logs of the sizes the mills in Idaho did. For one thing, the logs in Idaho were usually of one species - Lodgepole; the trees were small; and, in many cases, produced only one log. The overhead carriage at Burney made the very small logs difficult to hold; but, more importantly, mill production went down when small logs were used. Burney was simply a sawmill that could not use big logs.

Timber from the Sierras delivered to Burney consisted of four or five species, not one or two. Many of the logs were from the tops of larger trees, since the other divisions had kept the bigger logs from the lower portions of the trees. Such logs were heavily tapered. On top of that, the foresters managing fee land were glad to get rid of the little trees in thinnings. Burney was a good silvicultural tool with which to clean up the forest. A lot of really small wood was sent there as a result.

Red, himself, was involved in the dilemma. On one hand, he hated to waste any kind of a log (remember the logs loaded on Alan Jacobson's pickup); and he hated to see small logs cut in the large log mills. On the other hand, if a log had any clear wood or shop-type lumber in it, he did not want it cut in the quad mill at Burney. This was, of course, before there was a market at Burney for hog fuel for cogeneration plants, where very small logs could be chipped instead of sawn.

The manager at Burney took the heat, as well as the foresters and loggers involved in hauling logs to Burney. No one had a good answer for the problems the mill was having.

It took Dennis Gomez to put everything in perspective. Upon his arrival, he began trying to convince Red, and everyone else, that Burney was not a small log mill. He did not immediately try to modify the mill to cut the kinds of logs everyone thought should be sent there; he started trying to change the logs themselves.

For the first year, he tried to run it the way it was. There was a constant battle among Dennis, the foresters, the loggers and the mill managers who sent logs to him. Log lengths were a source of irritation, as were logs with sweep or crook, which Dennis considered to be mis-manufactured. He was constantly chewing on his forester, Smitty, to solve the log problems. On several occasions, he refused to unload loads of logs and sent them back to where they came from - either the woods, or the mill where they originated. The place was in an uproar.

He was having an effect though; the logs were getting better and bigger. Instead of **only** the small logs, Dennis was receiving logs more suited to his mill. He also got a new forester, Mike Bates.

Sawmill complex at Burney, 1987. Photo shows sawmill building at left center with lumber sorter extending to right. New kilns are at right center with white roofs. Adjacent to sawmill, near small pond, is the new cogeneration facility. Old Publisher's powerhouse with tall smokestacks is at lower left. Office is out of sight, attached to side of planer building to right of dry kilns.

Photo by Mark Fator.

Mike Bates came to work on June, 15, 1982. He was 33 years old, and had worked as a log scaler for four years for the Nor-Cal Bureau. After that, he worked as a timber cruiser for Arcata Redwood Company, then became their Timberland Acquisition Manager, and finally Manager of Log Purchase & Sales. He was a veteran, having interrupted his education to go to Vietnam. He finally received his B. S. in Forest Science from Humboldt State in June 1982.

Mike was enthusiastic and a talker. One did not have to be brilliant to converse with him; he carried the dialogue all by himself. He was an excellent forester, very energetic and a good log buyer. The rest of the SPI foresters enjoyed him immensely.

In the early going, he got along well with Dennis Gomez, and with Red. He would complain, though, that Dennis did not trust him to make decisions. Mike wanted more freedom to run the forestry program for the Burney mill.

Dennis was very difficult to work for. The author would get involved in most of the disputes involving logs, Mike, SPI managers, and loggers. It was constant conflict. In retrospect, Mike Bates was possibly the only SPI forester who could have worked for Dennis Gomez without blood being shed.

Dennis, though, was one of the most talented managers in SPI. He knew what made sawmills run well. Many people learned a great deal from Dennis, including Red and Mike Bates.

Dennis began to modify the sawmill shortly after Mike came to work. By so doing, he had it using more logs than ever before. By the time Dennis was through with Burney, he had added a Lundeen stacker and extended the bin sorter. A new Sherman gang was installed in 1983. The two planers were removed, and one good Stetson Ross planer was added. New kilns were built, so the mill had six 120', double-track, multi-zoned computerized kilns when he was finished.

Of course, Red was involved in all of the gyrations going on at Burney. His association with Dennis was rewarding for Red in many ways: he learned new applications for computers, and he learned how, if logs are properly manufactured, sawmills can be successful without using only high-grade logs.

There were other changes in management in 1982. Ron Stevens, who had been Manager of the Millwork Division, became the General Manager for all SPI facilities. Bob Puett, who had been managing the Loyalton Division, took on the Susanville operation again. He now had two large operations to take care of.

Fritz Hagen also took on two operations: Hayfork where he had been for some time, and the Redding Division (CV). Mike Schmidt, formerly Superintendent at Chico Millwork, was promoted to Manager of the whole Chico operation.

SPI was on reduced schedules most of the year. Arcata was down to 40 hours per week, from a normal 48 hours. Hayfork and CV were also down to 40 hours per week. Susanville was still on 9-hour shifts, but planing and shipping were on eight hours. Quincy and Loyalton were completely down; and Sloat was on a 40-hour-per week, one-shift basis. Burney, on the other hand, was running 9-hour shifts, and a night shift had been added to the planer. Dennis, even in bad times, had saved the operation from almost certain death.

As the depression in the industry deepened, I used to say that SPI responded by speeding up and working more hours. I know that is what happened for the first part of the 1981-82 collapse. At some point, however, lumber began to stack up in the mill yards.

Even when the sales staff cut prices, inventories continued to build. After several months of that, it was necessary to curtail production. SPI did it by reducing working hours to eight hours per shift at some locations, and shutting down those that were more costly to operate because of labor costs, or productivity, or both.

I was involved in many meetings and discussions about efficiencies, and the need to curtail expenses and staff. The depression of that period was certainly not fun. Red was a "bear" to get along with all during those times. The management staff understood. SPI was **his** company, but in some respects it was also ours. The pressure to formulate some program to stay alive was nearly unbearable. It must have been worse for him and the Emmerson family.

I had to be thankful that I had come to work for SPI. There were innumerable employees in the industry who considered themselves fortunate to be working at all. I was proud to have been a part of the effort to keep the operation going.

Later in the year, the Chico Division's millwork plants at Chico and Oroville recalled their laid-off employees and began hiring new ones. Since millwork plants purchase lumber at market price, their raw material costs were extremely low at the time. That helped them begin to operate at a decent level before the sawmills could do so.

At the end of 1982, the markets appeared to have reached bottom and were beginning to rise. SPI had sold over 424,000 MBF of lumber, and gross sales were a little over $136,000,000. All of the mills, except Quincy and Loyalton, had even increased production over the previous year. Total assets were valued at $118,277,000. The company had logged over 16,000 MBF of its fee timber. There still was a small pre-tax loss at year-end.

Of more importance, perhaps, was the fact that SPI was still alive, and had invested $2,912,000 in capital improvements for the year.

In September 1982, Raleigh H. (Curly) Emmerson died suddenly. It was just before Labor Day.

chapter thirty nine

CURLY'S LATER YEARS

As mentioned many times in this story, Curly's later years were not spent intimately involved with day-to-day company management. Even though he came to the office frequently, he spent many hours doing some of the things he liked to do: visiting with friends, telling stories and jokes, and drinking quite a bit. He was treated with love and respect. Old-time employees treated him with deference as well. He played the roll of patriarch, and he played it well.

It was a blessing that, when his time came, he went quite quickly. Curly's wife's sister had come to stay with them for the Labor Day weekend, and they had gone to Bergie's for dinner. Curly was wearing his new hearing aid, trying to get used to it, and making comments about the lack of intelligence exhibited by the manufacturer of the device. The three of them had a few drinks, then dinner. When the band began to play, Curly began to complain about how loud it was, and finally asked if they could go home early.

A little while later, he complained of not being able to sleep. He got up to sit in his favorite chair, and when he did not return to bed, Orvamae got up to find him feeling "just awful." She got him into their automobile for a desperate rush to the hospital. On the way, a policeman stopped them, determined the gravity of the situation, and escorted them the rest of the way. Two days later, Curly was

gone. If he had lived, Red says that he would have been a vegetable.

He left his wife Orvamae with cherished memories. She graciously responded to questions about their life together, and was frank and sensitive about the role she played in SPI.

Curly met Orvamae Oncken 22 years earlier in San Francisco. In 1962, they married and Orvamae was to devote the next 20 years of her life to him.

A long chapter in Curly Emmerson's life was interwoven with Orvamae's. After his separation and divorce from Myrtle Emmerson, Curly did not have anyone at home to confide in, or to share his problems and frustrations with. He was, of course, too busy to let that bother him, and he was accustomed to "running around."

Sometime in 1960, Curly had gone to San Francisco on business. Orvamae does not remember why he was there; she may never have known. She was at the Chancellor Hotel having a drink with a girlfriend when she noticed a distinguished gentleman across the room. Curly usually stayed at the Chancellor when in the city.

Ron Stevens remembers being in the city when he met Curly for the first time. The meeting took place in a bar, and Ron remem-

Curly with granddaughter Linda Billingsly (Margaret Emmerson's daughter) at ranch near Blue Lake, California, 1958.
Photo from Emily Thorpe collection.

bers Curly had a "striking looking woman" on his arm. He thinks it may have been Orvamae, although he is not sure. He does remember Curly was drinking vodka martinis with a beer "back." He ordered the same drink all evening, with no apparent effect. Ron was awed by the image this distinguished-looking man projected, particularly the way he could handle booze.

Orvamae Oncken had been raised in Sterling, Illinois, some 25 miles west of Chicago. Her grandparents had come from Germany. Her parents were farmers who raised six girls and one boy. After growing up, Orvamae found work in Chicago, but was saving her money to move to California where she thought she would have a better life. She had learned to dislike the noise, dirt and cold of the Chicago winters.

In the early 1950s, Orvamae had visited California by train. On board, she had met some "diplomats" who were connected with the United Nations located in San Francisco. She was impressed with the vitality of the city, particularly the U.N. complex which she visited.

By 1952, she had saved enough to make her move. On New Year's Eve 1953, she headed west. She found an apartment, a job, and wrote for her sister to join her, in that order. She worked for Pacific Gas and Electric, running a comptometer in the office. She loved the San Francisco of that era.

Shortly after the chance meeting at the Chancellor, Curly and Orvamae began to date. Curly made frequent business trips to the city, and he and Orvamae would have dinner together. They fell in love and were married in 1962.

The wedding took place in Redlands, California. Runar and Dorothy (Dot) Anderson were at the wedding, as were Red and Ida. The Andersons were invited to go on the honeymoon with Curly and Orvamae.

Dot was reluctant to go on anyone's honeymoon except her own; but Ida suggested it was "no big deal; they should go." Curly had a big Cadillac; and the four of them set out for the Mardi Gras in New Orleans. The trunk contained mostly the bride's trousseau with very little room left over for the rest of the luggage.

After several days at the Mardi Gras, they left for Chicago to visit Orvamae's family. Again, it was Curly who did all of the driving. Dot reports that Curly always had at least one martini with a beer-back for lunch all the way across the country, except in Texas.

One day they stopped in Texas for lunch, as well as to find some flowers for a funeral in California. Dot cannot recall how Curly found out that a friend had died back home. In any event, the town was dry; Curly could not find his noon libation.

He asked the florist in his inimitable drawl, "Where do you fine people find a drink in this fair town?"

"Well, sir, it's pretty hard to do. You almost have to join a club to do that, or go to a State liquor store," he said.

"Son, I don't usually drink a whole bottle for lunch, I just want to wet my whistle," Curly replied.

"I'll loan you my card for the club just down the street, if you'll bring it back," the man said.

"You've got a deal," Curly said. The four of them went to the private club for cocktails and lunch. The florist got his card back with a sizeable order for the funeral back home, and the entourage was on its way.

After a few days in cold and windy Chicago, the Andersons had enough of travelling. They flew back to Arcata to leave Curly and Orvamae to finish their honeymoon alone. Curly drove all the way home.

Immediately after the honeymoon, Orvamae moved to Arcata to the big house that Curly owned on the hill next to the Arcata City Park, and where Red and Ida would eventually raise their family.

Curly eventually built a new home on the lower end of Buttermilk Lane in Arcata. It looked out over a big green pasture to the south where they could see cows and horses. Orvamae says that "Curly was always interested in raising cows."

As the years went by, they bought a ranch in eastern Oregon, a big one, where she "spent half her life after that." She remembers

Curly Emmerson and Orvamae Oncken just after their wedding in 1962, and before the long drive to Chicago by way of New Orleans. Red is at right. Photo from Orvamae Emmerson.

**Curly the rancher
on one of
his favorite horses.**
Photo from
Orvamae Emmerson,
date unknown.

spending considerable time in Susanville with Curly while he took charge of the construction of the mill there. She also remembers that Curly did not like Redwood House ranch, the one that Red and Ida loved so much. She believes it was because of the long, one-lane road that had to be driven in order to get there. In Curly's later years, he did not like to drive, and she had to do much of it for him.

When they were home, every Saturday noon they could be found in the Anchor on South Broadway, which was Curly's favorite lunch location.

I had the privilege of attending one of those lunches, not on Saturday, but on a workday, and Orvamae was not there. Curly was in fine form.

Several of his cronies were sitting at the bar playing liar's dice. From curbside as I parked, I could hear the dice cup striking the bar. Curly's gruff voice could be heard joking

and laughing with everyone in the room.

I was called into the bar, and had to drink, rather quickly, two stiff ones at Curly's expense. I had come for lunch; but this was Curly Emmerson suggesting that I "have another one." How could an employee refuse? By the time lunch had been served at the bar, it was going on 2:30 p.m. I can remember the lunch was very good, but I cannot remember what I ate.

Francis Carrington, a good friend of Curly's, was an occasional participant at the Anchor lunches. He had first met Curly when he moved to Eureka in 1978. At that time, Curly had assisted him by recommending him for membership in the Ingomar Club, to which most influential Humboldt County men belonged. Curly was one of the early members.

Once, Francis asked Curly for advice regarding a real estate transaction in which he was involved. The sessions were not going well. Curly told him the next time he was in the middle of a meeting, when things were not going right, to just get up and leave.

Francis took his advice and did so. Sure enough, he was stopped before he got to the door, was asked to return, and the deal was put together in short order.

As Curly got older, he still drove quite rapidly. People remember on one occasion that Curly got pulled over for going too fast. The officer, Jim Vaissade, upon recognizing him, let him go with a stern lecture on the hazards of driving too fast, especially as one got older.

Later in the week, the same officer noticed Curly going down the freeway at about 35 miles per hour. There was a string of traffic whizzing by, underscoring how slowly Curly was going. Thinking Curly had imbibed too freely, Jim pulled him over.

Curly was incensed. As he rolled down his window he growled at the officer, "For Chrissakes, Jim, what's the matter now?"

"I'm sorry, Curly," he said, "There's a law about driving too slow, you know."

Curly looked at him in astonishment. "Son," he said, "make up your mind. You told me day before yesterday I was driving twice as fast as an old man should. I was doing 70 then; today I'm doing 35."

In later life, Curly acquired a special friend, Joe Nellist, a local real estate man. Joe sold Curly several ranches and houses over the years. There were questions raised on several occasions over the propriety of selling real estate to his best friend; but Curly enjoyed Joe Nellist immensely. He probably thought it was worth the cost to have Joe driving him all the way to his Oregon ranch several times a month. Joe would drink with Curly, especially at the Anchor luncheons, and they would go hunting together in proper season.

The first annual SPI management meeting the author attended was in Arcata at the end of 1976. The company had just acquired the Quincy Railroad. Curly and Orvamae were at the party at Sam Merryman's Beach House after the meeting, celebrating the end of a successful year.

After dinner, Curly was given several awards and gifts. He was named the President of the Quincy Railroad, taking his place

Curly and Orvamae Emmerson, Christmas 1975.
Photo from Orvamae Emmerson.

Curly tries out a porta-pottie given to him for use on hunting trips, 1979. He was known to shock people occasionally by pulling outlandish stunts. In this case, he is still wearing his underwear. Photo from Orvamae Emmerson.

Curly and fire truck donated to the Quincy Fire Department. Date and photographer unknown.
Photo from Red Emmerson collection.

alongside Huntington of the Southern Pacific, and Harriman of the Union Pacific. He received a toy train, a brakeman's lantern, an engineer's cap and bandanna, and assorted gifts of a similar nature. He wore the articles of clothing the rest of the evening, thoroughly enjoying himself. At the presentation, the entire room rose to give him a standing ovation.

In 1979, the Sierra Pacific Foundation was formed by Curly Emmerson.

Over the years, Curly had accumulated a substantial amount of SPI common stock. Much of it was purchased on the open market when SPI was a public company. In 1979, he sold all of his shares to the three Emmerson children, for nothing down and interest to be paid quarterly. The principal was to be paid over ten years.

The Foundation was formed as a 501 C(3) charitable organization, and approved by the Internal Revenue Service. Curly agreed to donate to the Foundation all of the interest he received from the younger Emmersons, and to contribute the balance of the principal at his death. This provided approximately $150,000 annually for the Foundation to disburse to qualified recipients.

Most of the funds were used to provide scholarships for dependent children of SPI employees, and for charitable contributions in local communities where SPI maintained plant facilities. Up to and including 1990, the Foundation had paid over $958,000 to charitable organizations, and almost $511,000 in scholarships. In 1990, 83 individual scholarships were given.

During the years the Foundation has been in existence, it has given many major grants. Some of them are noted below:

Humboldt State University	$65,200
Boy Scouts of America	56,600
Lions Club Eye Bank	20,000
Redwood United	36,300
Lassen High School	19,000
Hayfork High School	16,900
Shasta County YMCA	35,000
KIXE TV	33,200
Quincy Fire Department	17,000

The list goes on and on. Curly was very

proud of his ability to have done so much for the communities where the employees of SPI live. He was more proud of the children who received scholarships to universities, community colleges and trade schools.

Current officers of the Foundation are Ida Emmerson, President; Dick Smith, Vice-President; and Caroline Emmerson, Treasurer.

The Emmerson children remember their grandfather with respect and affection. They say that while he loved children very much, he was somewhat "stiff" when they were around him, attributing this to his strict training in early life. It was difficult for him to openly show emotion; but it was also impossible for him not to show affection for those he loved. They were sure Curly loved them very much.

I talked with many people while trying to gather the information for this history. Everyone spoke of Curly with high praise. I even began to ask some of them if they knew of anyone who did not like him. After thinking on the question for a while, everyone, with one exception, told me they could not think of a single person.

The exception told me he had heard once that Curly had a falling out with Jalmer Berg prior to the time they dissolved their partnership. There may be more; anyone in Curly's position in business would have stepped on a few toes, but I never found them. For a lifetime of work and play, Curly had friends galore.

With Curly's passing, an era closed for Sierra Pacific Industries. Indeed, an era was passing for the whole timber industry. Curly had been involved with the industry he loved for some 70 years. He left his mark on it in numerous ways. He worked hard and he played hard. There would never be another Raleigh Humes Emmerson.

Caroline Emmerson Dietz, Director, SPI Foundation.

Ida Emmerson, Director, SPI Foundation.
Photos from SPI archives.

Curly Emmerson as most employees knew him in later years. Photo probably taken when Curly joined the Ingomar Club in late 1960s or early 1970s. Photo from SPI archives.

PART FOUR

SIERRA PACIFIC INDUSTRIES

POST DEPRESSION ERA

(1983-1989)

Quincy sawmill complex, 1987.
Photo by Mark Fator.

chapter forty

RECOVERY

In the waning months of 1982, lumber prices seemed to steady, then rise in December. Most of the survivors were wary that the first rise was only a glitch and the market would decline again; after all it was December, the dead of winter.

The rise continued into the spring. The fear was unfounded; the recovery was real. It appeared that the Republican President had meant what he said when he had promised to slow down the rate of inflation. It also appeared to many that the timber industry had borne more than its fair share of the convulsions that resulted from Reagan's policies.

The problems for the industry were not over; they were only continuing. Some were the same old uncertainties of raw material supply, and confiscation of timberland under the guise of saving the environment. The latter was being revived with greater vigor than ever before. But one of the problems for the survivors was what to do with the timber under contract. SPI faced the new era with hope and, at least on Red's part, confidence.

Plans to modernize the DiGiorgio mills had been slowed by the economic conditions, but not stopped. As a result, when the economy recovered, the company was in a better position to take advantage of markets. The mills were in better shape than those belonging to many of the competitors. SPI decided to forge ahead to complete the rest of the modifications.

Back in 1976, Coleman Greer, DiGiorgio's Division Manager, had not been retained by SPI. Charlie Nordic, Superintendent of the Loyalton operation, was. Charlie was a soft-spoken man with very slow, deliberate manners. He was given the job of managing the Loyalton mill.

Charlie walked as if he was in low gear all the time; and to see him strolling across a very large mill yard, one had to wonder if he was ever going to reach the other side. This irritated Red almost immediately, but he said very little about it. It wasn't long, however, until there were other irritations - like unsuitable profits. His employment with SPI soon ended.

Bob Puett, the manager at Susanville, was intense and committed, the opposite of Charlie Nordic. He was a very large man, perhaps six-foot-four or -five and very broad. In fact, he had played football at Humboldt State from which he graduated. While attending school, he had lived in an apartment above Red and Ida s garage in Arcata, and worked at the Arcata sawmill to make ends meet.

Bob was appointed the manager of both the Susanville and Loyalton mills, and in a short time he moved to Loyalton with his family. He ran both mills efficiently and profitably, inspired confidence in his crew, and fit right in with the citizens of Sierra County and Loyalton.

Old powerhouse at Loyalton, long abandoned, 1989. New sawmill building visible at right. Photo by author.

Load of logs selected for the Loyalton Fourth of July parade in 1989. Photo by author.

By late 1980s, log deck at Loyalton contained many logs that were perfect for a mill like Burney, but distance to Burney was too great for an economic haul. Photo by author.

The Loyalton mill, built in the early 1900s, looked like the typical sawmill of that era, with several tall smokestacks on the powerhouse and a sagging old building for the sawmill. In the 1950s and 1960s, Ken Metzker had completely rebuilt the interior of the mill, but not the exterior. The waste burner had been eliminated, and a bark manufacturing facility had been added. Decorative bark of several sizes was produced primarily from Red fir. The mill pond was simply Smithneck Creek dammed up close to the mill to form a storage pond. The mill cut about 50,000 MBF per year on a log-scale basis.

The Sloat mill, under Metzker's ownership, had been run on two shifts, cutting pine and fir. Its production was about 40,000 MBF per year. It had burned once; and he rebuilt it prior to the sale of both Loyalton and Sloat to DiGiorgio, who continued to run both on two shifts.

Red decided early that the Loyalton mill, in its condition, would not be a profitable one to run. The decision was made to tear it down and build a new one from scratch. Bob Puett was to be in charge of the project.

This mill was perhaps the first sawmill that was designed and built from the ground up by SPI, using new materials and new machinery. Modernization began in 1983, and was completed in the summer of 1984. The new mill was an almost immediate success. It consisted of an 8' double-cut head rig, a 6' horizontal resaw, a 60" ring debarker, a double-arbor edger, two Ukiah board edgers, an Irvington trimmer, a 65-bin lumber sorter, and a Lundeen lumber stacker.

The log pond was eliminated by removing the dam in Smithneck Creek and diverting the creek around the log yard. The yard was eventually paved, and the logs were handled with front-end loaders and a shovel.

When the pond was drained, it was found to be the home for a number of large German Browns. This was supposed to be impossible since dissolved bark, wood and tannins were considered to be toxic to fish. No one had told the youngsters of Loyalton about the toxicity; they fished it anyway, with excellent results.

Meanwhile at Quincy, Al Novak was in charge. Al not only had responsibility for the mill there, but also the mill at Sloat. He, like so many SPI managers, did not depend upon subordinates for information about his operation; he was personally involved with running the whole thing. He was aware of what was going on in all departments. Al was a DiGiorgio man also, and lasted a relatively long time at Quincy; but he eventually gave way to the new-type Sierra Pacific manager.

Typically, the new breed was a younger man. It was getting to the point where a manager was not required to start out as a cleanup man in a mill at the age of 18 (although that was preferable), progress to the head sawyer job, and eventually become a shift foreman or superintendent. That was the old way.

The new kind of manager had to be people-oriented, know the technical aspects of lumber manufacture and, above all, be a politician who could determine what upper management wanted while producing profits. However, it was still necessary to put in long hours and to be "on top" of everything.

A man who fit this description was George Coulter. George had much in common with Dennis Gomez, the Burney manager. They were both young, aggressive, and very smart when it came to sawmills. Both could be abrasive to excess if they chose to. They would be the forerunners of the new managers for SPI.

George had actually replaced Bob Chase at Quincy. Chase had been an interim manager after Al Novak left, and was there only a short time.

George was a very young man. He had been born at St. Ignacious, Montana. He knew sawmills, and worked for Southwest Forest Industries before being hired by Sierra Pacific. When hired, he was working at Graceville, Florida, managing a hardwood mill and a small log mill, cutting Southern pine. He had been involved in the purchase of those mills by Southwest a short time before.

When George began at Quincy in 1981, the mill at Quincy included a 9' band, and a 7' band as head-rigs. There was a 6' horizontal resaw, two edgers (a four saw and a three saw), a 6" "combo" edger, a 10" gang edger, and a 5' line bar resaw.

Under his direction, the mill became very efficient and profitable. Production increased; and as profits increased, George became proficient at getting what he wanted in the way of new machinery or improvements to his facilities. Other mill managers in the SPI family were occasionally heard to grumble that George could get away with murder. He could order equipment before getting approval to do so. Up until that time, that was unheard of. For a long time, he lead a charmed life, and was able to get away with operating a division

Quincy sawmill, 1990. The building at left was built by Meadow Valley Lumber Co. in 1960s and still houses SPI's sawmill today. New lumber sorter extends to right behind shop building in foreground. Photo by author.

**George Coulter stands proudly in front of the
new cogeneration plant at Quincy, 1990.**
Photo by author.

**New blacktopped log yard at Quincy, 1989.
LeTourneau log stacker shown sorting logs.**
Photo by author.

in a manner the other managers envied.

During George's stay, the two gang edgers
were replaced with a 12" double-arbor gang. A
4-megawatt cogeneration plant was built in
1983 which was replaced with a 20-megawatt
plant in 1987. Seven 120' dry kilns were built,
and 18 acres of log and lumber yard were
paved. Production of lumber increased to approximately 90,000 MBF log scale. The operation became big-time.

It was interesting to watch the transformation of this facility from a typical sawmill
to a completely integrated lumber manufacturing complex. The buildings were painted,
the yard was cleaned up, and the mill gained
the appearance of a first-class operation. Logs
were handled and decked efficiently, on black
top, and the employees became proud of their
facility.

It is appropriate, perhaps, to look back at
some of the events which preceded the modernization of the SPI mill at Quincy. The
community had been a lumber town for many
years. A man named King had come to Quincy
from the south in the early part of the century. He had established a mill, known as
Quincy Lumber Co., on a flat area that is now
the shopping center at the eastern edge of
Quincy.

By the early 1950s, that mill was gone,
but others had taken its place. Some seven
miles west of town, at a place called Spanish
Ranch, Meadow Valley Lumber Co. owned a
mill that boasted company houses for the
workers. It had a small log pond, off-highway
roads to the woods and, at one time, a tramway that carried units of lumber over the
ridge to Twain, where there was a facility for
loading lumber on rail cars.

With the improvement of the road to
Bucks Lake, the tramway had been abandoned; and lumber was being transported by
truck to Quincy for drying, planing and loading onto rail. Another mill had been constructed at Twain where the tram had terminated.

There were two mills at Greenville, one at
Crescent Mills, one at Genesee, and a small
mill at Quincy cutting Incense cedar. Quincy
had become the hub of the lumber industry in

the Feather River Country.

The sawmill at Quincy that SPI took over from DiGiorgio was built in the mid 1960s. Of those mentioned here, it is the only one currently operating. It was built on the location of Meadow Valley's planing mill and car loading facility, and still occupies that site. Of course, the mill which is there now barely resembles the mill that DiGiorgio sold to SPI.

The sawmill at Sloat, meanwhile, had also been transformed under SPI's ownership. While DiGiorgio's, it had cut both pine and fir. Incense cedar usually had been sold to the other mill in Quincy, that was owned by Essex Lumber Co. Shortly after SPI's purchase, all cedar originating from the Susanville and Feather River operations was hauled to Sloat. This mill began cutting Incense cedar on a one-shift basis, and is still doing so.

Red Emmerson is a man who hates to sell logs. In his opinion, they are too difficult to acquire. Since he is in the sawmill business, it does not make sense to him to sell something that can be utilized in an SPI mill. He is far more interested in developing a mill that can most efficiently utilize the resources available.

This had not always been the case. When raw materials were readily available, the emphasis had been on production. In some cases, sawmill capacity had been increased with little thought given to where the logs were going to come from. For some reason, there always seemed to be enough logs to go around. Perhaps, in a small way, good foresters had something to do with it. It is probable though that the efficiency of the sawmill had more effect than the skills of the forester in acquiring logs. Since efficient sawmills operate with lower production costs, SPI could pay more for logs than its competitors.

In the case of the Sloat mill, there was another consideration. Cedar had always been a problem. The mills that used cedar did not always pay very much for logs, and cedar was a minor species. It was a species difficult to de-bark because of the stringy bark, and markets were limited. The mills that tried to cut it usually found that they ended up with a few "jags" of different lumber sizes that were

Some of the large logs decked separately at Quincy on hard-surfaced decking area, 1990. Because of their size, the logs are split (sawn) before they can be placed in sawmill.
Photo by author.

Mobile home made into Sloat sawmill office, 1990.
Photo by author.

Sloat sawmill complex, 1987. Photo by Mark Fator.

difficult to sell. To top it all off, lumber production was less when cutting cedar, because the logs were heavily tapered and highly defective.

Red decided that there was enough Incense cedar in the area to run one shift at the Sloat mill, supplemented with an occasional purchase of "outside" logs. Of course, that did not set well with the owners of the cedar mill at Quincy (by that time, Fred Ducchi), but the decision was made anyway. The mill was already set up to use cedar, as it had a Rosser Head debarker instead of a ring debarker which, in effect, ground off the bark instead of scraping it off.

The operation was successful from the beginning, but not up to Red's expectations. Pencil stock was cut for the Japanese market, but the supply of suitable logs was limited. The Feather River foresters spent a considerable amount of their time trying to buy cedar logs; and logs were hauled long distances to supply the mill. Some of them came from as far away as Hayfork. At one point, two shifts were tried, but that only succeeded in driving up the price of logs. The mill soon returned to one shift, and has remained moderately successful ever since.

Within ten years after purchase by SPI, the three sawmills in Plumas and Sierra Counties were cutting 200 to 220 MMBF on an annual basis. They had been upgraded to become efficient and competitive. They provided stable employment and high wages, and they contributed mightily to the tax base of the two counties.

During the time the Feather River mills were being revitalized, a full-time check scaler was hired to begin work in June 1983. He was Jerry Kingsbury, who had been the log scaler at the CV sawmill.

Jerry was the right person for a check scaling position, where politics is as important as technical knowledge. I must confess that I had doubts about his abilities on both counts when his name was first mentioned for the position. Jerry Gromacki was sold on Kingsbury, and I had learned to listen to what Jerry had to say. However, I was particularly concerned because of Kingsbury's age. He was a very young man to be a check scaler; but he got the job.

Most successful check scalers are older, with many years of experience. They are usually involved in disputes of many types, some of which take a great deal of diplomacy to resolve. Sometimes it takes a man with "whiskers" who, over the years, has developed respect in the scaling fraternity to prevail. I could not see how a man in his 30s could do the kind of a job that was necessary.

I should not have worried. In a very short time, Kingsbury was a recognized leader in resolving scaling problems and, most of all, he projected an image of total integrity. He travelled to all of the SPI sawmills, especially those where U.S. Forest Service scalers were employed. He became an arbitrator of disputes between SPI managers and the log scalers located at the divisions, most of whom worked for the scaling bureau.

In the middle of the depression, Fritz Hagen had left Hayfork to take over the CV operation. When Fritz left Hayfork in October 1982, George Coulter took over as interim manager for a short time. Tom Arlint then replaced George in January 1983.

Tom Arlint also was a young man, quite aggressive and intelligent, who tried to run the operation his own way. He was also a "new-type manager," but a little too new for SPI's tastes at the time. He lasted two years with SPI before Red became disenchanted with him. A few months after Tom arrived,

Matt Taborski, Manager of Sloat operation, 1990.
Photo by author.

Rosser head log debarker at Sloat sawmill, 1990. This debarker grinds bark from log instead of scraping it off. Photo by author.

Red Emmerson and Mr. Soga of Tokiwa Sango, a Japanese firm which purchases cedar pencil plank from SPI. 1987 photo from Red Emmerson.

Liz Hoaglen left the accounting job to Jim Macy, having found it difficult to accept the new manager's ways. She returned in 1986 after Tom Arlint left.

In 1983, during Arlint's tenure, a new horizontal resaw was installed in the mill, and construction of a new cogeneration plant began. A very large paving project was begun, which included the mill yard and a portion of the log deck area.

By the end of 1983, SPI had produced 556,445 MBF of lumber. Total assets were valued at over $146,000,000. Total sales for the year were $213,379,000. Over 15,000 MBF of fee timber had been logged. Capital expenditures for the year were nearly $8,000,000, of which $1,600,000 had been spent at Loyalton, over $2,000,000 at Quincy and Sloat, and some $630,000 in the Trucking Department for new trucks and shop facilities.

The company had survived the depression. All of the SPI sawmills were back to full production; and some new faces were to be found at the various operations. The old DiGiorgio mills were becoming a thing of the past. It remained to be seen how the high-priced timber under contract would be utilized by the new SPI.

chapter forty one

TIMBER PRICE RELIEF

Lumber prices remained relatively high through all of 1984. The recovery, once underway, seemed unstoppable. Red had returned to his old optimistic self, believing that SPI was on its way to even better times than before the depression.

Construction of the Loyalton sawmill was on schedule and was completed in August 1984. The facility was no longer an old wood mill building; it was a spanking-new steel building with steel catwalks overhead and steel underpinning for the mill floor. To those who were familiar with the old Loyalton mill, the new facility had the "smell of money" when first seen. It was bright and clean inside, and there was plenty of room for all of the brightly painted machinery. Many of the employees worked in relative quiet, in enclosed, dust-free cubicles, a far cry from the noisy work stations of yesteryear.

At Arcata, a new manager was appointed to take over from the retired Gordon Amos. The new man was Gordon's son, "Gordie," who had worked at various jobs at the Arcata mill.

Gordie was born in 1952, while his father was in Korea. After the war, when Gordon moved the family to Arcata to go to work for Red and Curly, Gordie came to Humboldt County. He attended schools at Dows Prairie for the first six years, then Rio Dell for his seventh and eighth grade. Gordie spent one year at Fortuna High School while Gordon worked for Eel River Sawmills, and three years at Eureka High School. Two years later, Gordie earned an A.A. degree in drafting from College of the Redwoods.

Gordie was an old-type manager, having learned his work ethic from his father. During summer vacations, he worked in the sawmill, cleaning up at first, then pulling on the green chain. He progressed through the various sawmill jobs as so many young men in timber country do. He became the handyman, and worked at that job for three years.

The term "handyman" is somewhat misleading to many people. In the timber industry, it denotes a very skilled individual who can do just about any job in the mill. Since a sawmill does not normally stop during a shift, there must be some way for individual workers to take a break to relieve themselves, to have a smoke, or just to relax for a few minutes. The handyman travels to each work station in turn, takes over each job, and allows the regular worker to take his break. The job is good training for a supervisory position.

In 1975, Gordie became the planer foreman, then took over quality control and the shipping department. He became an excellent lumberman, particularly expert in the manufacture of Douglas fir, and gradually assumed more and more responsibility. In later years, after Gordie became the manager at Arcata, Red would send him to many of the other SPI mills that cut Douglas fir to solve an occasional problem.

New Loyalton sawmill at left. The long, narrow building extending to the right from the sawmill is the lumber sorter. Dry kilns are at center and dry sheds at center right.
1987 photo by Mark Fator.

When Gordie took over at Arcata, a new dry shed was under construction, and a new planer was being installed. A new crane was purchased for the log yard, and a new resaw was installed in the mill. After the modernization, Arcata still looked like an old mill, but looks were deceiving. It was an exceptionally efficient operation, sporting up-to-date equipment inside an old building. It was still "Mecca."

Hayfork was in the midst of a major renovation also. The planing mill and dry kilns were moved to the sawmill site at the east side of town. This eliminated the split operation, and the need to haul green lumber through the middle of town to the kilns and planer. A new pony and a new edger were installed in the sawmill.

In 1984, the new 9-megawatt cogeneration plant was being built just east of the sawmill. It included a new wood-waste-fired boiler. When completed, the plant would pro-

duce enough electricity to provide the annual consumption for about 2,500 homes.

Since the CV sawmill had been renovated in 1981 and 1982, only minor changes were made there. Included was a new sawmill infeed and the paving of additional lumber storage areas.

About the same time, Susanville began the construction of a new 15-megawatt cogeneration facility. Improvements in the mill and kilns were also underway.

At Quincy, a new head rig set works, a dry sorting chain, a new edger, a boiler exhaust scrubber system, and a new lumber shed were finished. A new 4-megawatt power plant was also completed.

At Sloat, a new carriage setworks was installed, along with a new resaw. A planer and resaw had been finished a year earlier. The mill was still sawing Incense cedar.

The Millwork Division was not left out of the modernization program. At Oroville, a new Reclaim Department (to augment finger joint operations) was added to utilize trim ends from the sawmills located within economic hauling distance. Chico had added a new moulder and a new priming line, where products could have a coat of primer paint applied.

The largest project was at Richfield, just outside of Corning, California. On April 1, 1984, SPI had purchased some 20 acres of an existing plant site that included a small remanufacturing facility with dry sheds and shipping capabilities.

Construction got underway on a new millwork plant. The building was an impressive-looking affair of 168,000 square feet. It was of reinforced concrete; the trusses were a unique design made of pre-stressed concrete. There were no posts or pillars inside the huge building. It looked like a squat blimp hanger from the inside, or an indoor sports stadium. It was scheduled for completion in 1985, and would require approximately 250 new employees to run it.

In 1984, the SPI Foundation, in addition to its charitable contributions, awarded scholarships to 39 dependent children of employees. Curly Emmerson was well remembered by them and their families.

Of course, during the year, the good news was the continuation of the good lumber markets, and the extension of the modernization programs at SPI. The bad news was the expansion of the environmental battles, and the inescapable fact that most of the California industry had timber under contract priced so high it probably could never be used at a profit.

The two U.S. Senators from California, Alan Cranston and Pete Wilson, announced agreement on a 1.8 million-acre addition to federal Wilderness in California. If anything, environmentalism was stronger than ever. Instead of the battles being fought almost exclusively in the media, or in the political arena, they were increasingly found in the court system. This also contributed to the high prices still being bid for timber.

There was a difference to the bidding battles taking place in 1984, though. It appeared that all of those who had been betting on the come, had thrown away their "inflation fighting formulas," and they were bidding at a subdued rate. There would be an occasional timber sale attracting considerable interest that would go quite high, but the panic bidding seemed to be over.

Two new foresters joined SPI in 1984. Tom Nelson left the Forest Service on the Tahoe National Forest to help manage fee lands, and Bill Banka began working at Feather River Division.

Tom Nelson was born in Minnesota, where his father was a rural mail carrier. After growing up in North Branch and attending local schools, he went to Vietnam as a Marine Corporal. He was discharged from the Marine Corps in 1970.

Tom moved around quite often after returning from Vietnam. He attended five schools in five years, among them Humboldt State and the University of Minnesota. He graduated with a B.S in Forest Management in 1975 from the latter. From there, he went to work for the U.S. Forest Service in California, spending time at Forest Hill, Georgetown and Truckee. SPI found Tom on the Sierraville District of the Tahoe Forest, where he was the District Silviculturist.

Dan Tomascheski, Manager of the Timber Department at the time, and I, had an interesting experience in trying to hire Tom Nelson. The forestry department, after acquiring Publisher's, was seriously understaffed. Some of the foresters had sufficient experience in silviculture and planting to do an acceptable job of intensively managing the timberlands that SPI then owned. However, their efforts were concentrated on getting logs to the mills, not planning forests for the future.

Dan and I thought we needed someone with the right combination of experience and ambition to take on the task of managing SPI's silvicultural activities. We lobbied Red for several months to allow us to hire an additional person. Red was always reluctant to add anyone to the payroll. It was still the "load the wagon until it can't be pulled" syndrome. Finally, after many discussions, we got permission to hire Tom.

Just before he was to report for work, Red

changed his mind. We could not figure out what had happened; in fact, to this day I am not sure that I know what occurred. It is possible that Ron Stevens or Dick Smith made a chance remark about a new forester. It is probable, though, the problem stemmed from the label we had given the position. We had billed Tom as a silviculturist.

Red at that time hated specialists. The government was full of them, as were large companies. Both usually became top heavy and inefficient. Since we had said that Tom would concentrate on silviculture, to Red he was a specialist able to do only one thing. We were still short-handed.

It took several more weeks of intense lobbying to get him to change his mind. The next time, Tom was called just a **forester** who knew how to plan logging systems for maximum growth of the remaining stand, and to plant and tend baby trees. Dan and I gave a sigh when Tom was at last on the payroll.

Since being hired, Tom has remained one of SPI's top foresters, able to do just about anything for which a forester is needed. He seems to like steep ground better than flat ground, performs well with very little direction, and figured out long ago how SPI works.

The other forester hired in 1984, Bill Banka, came from New Jersey. He was born in 1954, in New Brunswick where his father was a CPA for a chemical company. Bill grew up there, attending local schools, until he enrolled at Rutgers University in 1972 to study forestry.

During the summer of 1975, Bill got a seasonal job marking timber for the U.S. Forest Service at Sierraville. He liked the eastern part of the Sierra Nevada and, upon graduation in 1976, returned to go to work for Fibreboard Corporation at Truckee. He worked there until July 1984, when he was hired to help Ron Voss.

While working at Truckee, Bill met and married Terri Moriwaki, a Cal Berkeley forester. They moved to Loyalton, where Bill concentrated on acquisition of raw materials for the Loyalton sawmill, and on learning from Ron Voss how SPI foresters operated. Bill Banka was to become an important

member of the management team for SPI.

SPI scheduled a management meeting during the summer of 1984 at Konocti on Clear Lake. At such meetings, each of the corporate heads gave short talks pertinent to their activities. All of the talks for the Konocti meeting indicated confidence was building for the sustained advances in the market; and there was enthusiasm for the future.

Directed at the management personnel, the author's talk included some predictions and some worries to be reckoned with. Excerpts follow:

I would like to be able to report that we have all kinds of cheap logs for you to cut. That is not the case, even though recently, we have been able to acquire our fair share at reasonable cost. However, we have one big problem: we buy high and sell low. We get too wood hungry, and when the market turns down we have a hell of a time catching it. We need to form the mental discipline to say no to log sellers sometimes, especially early in the season.

Next, our industry continues to change. Timber sale defaults are here - not in wholesale amounts - but they are here. SPI hasn't faced up to this problem yet; we haven't had to. The problem is close at Susanville, and will be close at Feather River next year. We must give this problem more attention than it has gotten so far.

There were several comments concerning fee land management, then the following:

I've been asked to look at the future for SPI. That's a pretty easy thing to do. All you have to do is listen to the experts - like economists, bankers, politicians - then, since they are all different, pick the forecast you like best. At the risk of sounding pompous, I'll tell you what I think.

I believe people in business, at least in the lumber business, are like a herd of sheep. We follow the lead of those who make the most noise. Opinions are formed based on what a sales manager, or a production manager, said over the phone this morning. If what they said is repeated often enough, it becomes gospel. We don't think for ourselves, nor do we (especially at SPI) do the research necessary to make intelligent business decisions. I think that is one reason we are in the fix we are in today. We went along with the crowd.

What are the opportunities for our future? I think there are many of them, but we had better plan ahead. I mean for 1987, '88, or even 1990. Since I'm approaching 60 I can afford to make some dumb predictions:

1. Investments in timberlands are timely. Buy when prices are down and acreage is available. That's now.

2. If we plan ahead we will make SPI grow and go. This will take understanding on the part of Red, Stevens, Hoppe, Dick Smith, George, and Mark, and everyone else on the management team. We need to listen to the key employees - the people in this room. Also, we need to separate the B.S. from the solid information in the conversations that take place everyday outside this company.

3. There is going to be timber sale contract relief, but not in the form we are thinking about now. I don't know what form it will take, but it is going to hurt. We had better start figuring how to cut some of the high priced sales without defaulting on them.

For weeks after the meeting, there was a lot of attention focused on operational problems. In the back of everyone's mind, though, was the nagging worry about high-priced stumpage.

Considerable controversy developed within the industry, in government circles, and among some members of the public concerning what to do about the timber contracts. The arguments were predictably based on where one stood philosophically, and whether one had any of the timber under contract.

SPI was in the thick of the arguments, because the company had purchased more

Gordie Amos, Manager at Arcata, with Ron Hoover, Timber Manager, 1990. Gordie, being a heavy cigarette smoker, must suffer the indignity of having signs posted on his office door by nonsmokers. Photo by author.

timber than any other firm in California. Since its production was greater than any other, it needed a good share of the wood available. That did not make much difference to those who competed with the company for timber. Many of them said they wished SPI would go broke.

Those within the industry, particularly those who had been outbid by SPI, argued that SPI had been stupid to bet on the come. They considered themselves to have been prudent bidders, showing restraint, even though they did not have enough timber to run for the foreseeable future. They lobbied hard to insure that SPI, and firms like it, would pay the price by being forced to cut and pay for the trees they had bought. The words "a contract is a contract" were used countless times. Of course, they were right.

The companies with high-priced timber argued they had been led down the wrong path by the government itself. It had been the government that had caused runaway inflation, and exorbitant interest rates that killed the housing market, while at the same time predicting a housing shortage as a result of the "baby boom," and setting more and more of the forest aside for other uses. It was also the government that, by reason of those policies, had encouraged the Canadians to usurp over 30% of the lumber sales in the U. S.

Many companies, instead of blaming the government, formulated an argument that

Hayfork office, a double-wide mobile home, 1990. Photo by author.

Sawmill infeed at Hayfork, 1990. Debarker is at left. "Surplus" debarked logs are stored on blacktop log yard. Photo by author.

used more logic. It gained many converts. The argument went like this:

Even though the companies had been stupid to bid the way they had, there were too many of them to just let them go bankrupt. While that would please many of the survivors, there was too much at stake to let it happen.

Schools and local governments depended on the revenues from the timber sales; and the revenues would dry up if the sales were defaulted. Most rural communities would experience wholesale unemployment if the mills in their towns went broke. Local businesses, and local governments, would suffer as a result. Timber owners who did not own manufacturing facilities would also be disadvantaged if there was not a viable industry in their areas. They needed some place to sell their wood.

The government was caught in the middle. They had tried to formulate some temporary relief measures by granting wholesale extensions to the contracts. This was done on several separate occasions. In some cases, the "diligent performance" clauses in the rules for extensions - wherein certain portions of the timber had to be removed, or portions of the required logging roads had to be built prior to extension - were waived. Two of the schemes were dubbed "Soft I and Soft II" shortly after they came out, in reference to the soft lumber markets.

These schemes were wishful thinking. They were designed to give the industry an extended time in which to swallow the timber, figuring that lumber markets would improve to such an extent that catastrophic losses would not be incurred. The markets had improved, but not enough to allow cutting of the timber; and there were no signs in the foreseeable future that prices would increase sufficiently to allow it to be cut. Even though current market prices were good, it would take **much** higher prices for any of the timber to be economically operable.

Finally, after much wrangling, the Federal Timber Contract Payment Modification Act was signed by the President on October 16, 1984. The legislation permitted a purchaser to be released from certain contractual obligations by returning to the government a volume of certain qualified timber sale contracts. The procedures were quite complicated, specifying which contracts qualified, which purchasers qualified, and limiting the volumes of timber that could be returned.

SPI qualified for the return of 200,000 MBF - the maximum. Firms in that category were required to pay $2,000,000 in cash ($10 per MBF) to the government. In addition, the remaining timber sales had to be included in a Multi-Sale Extension Plan (MSEP) at a later date, which was to specify strict performance requirements for each contract, but would give an extended period in which to cut the timber. Operations on some of the sales would have to be scheduled each year, but there was a procedure for obtaining extensions of up to five years on the rest.

The idea was to allow the high-priced timber to be worked in with cheaper logs over an extended time, thus producing a lower average log-cost. The government would realize some money from the returned timber (they still had the timber), the companies perhaps could stay in business, and local communities would not suffer as much as if their mill had departed. The government was supposed to re-advertise the returned sales so they could be resold by competitive bidding.

Intentions were good. The scheme did allow many companies to stay in business. For some, particularly some of the smaller ones, it was too little too late. The returned sales were not often put on the market promptly, so there was still an artificial timber shortage. On top of everything else, the spotted owl issue was gaining strength.

Many games were played with the MSEP and the pertinent regulations. SPI foresters were in the middle of most of them. For example, the regulations allowed SPI to buy out a maximum of 200,000 MBF. However, each company was permitted to specify the sales to be bought out, and the order in which they would be listed on the buyout application. **One** sale over the maximum was permitted to be included. The portion of volume in excess of 200,000 MBF could either be removed from that sale and paid for at the contract prices, or could be paid for at contract prices. In no event could more than the 200,000 MBF be

paid for at the required $10 per MBF.

SPI selected a very large sale to be the last one on the list. The White fir on that sale had been bid at over $2,000 per MBF, while some 7,000 MBF of other species were bid at minimum prices. SPI applied for authorization to log and pay for the other species at current contract rates, and to buy out of the White fir for $10 per MBF. The application was approved, and harvesting began. The net effect was for SPI to get rid of over 207,000 MBF of high-priced timber, and to log part of the cheaper timber from the sale.

Another game could be played to affect the return of high-priced timber sales. The game resulted in the use of two terms that came into vogue during that time, each referring to spotted owls. If owls were detected on an existing timber sale, the government, to protect the creature, was required to modify the contract by removing from the sale the cutting units in which the owl nested or foraged. Thus, if an owl was found on a high-priced sale, it became a "good owl" because the government took back the timber with no penalty. If, on the other hand, an owl was found on a cheap timber sale, the same thing occurred. This one was called a "bad owl."

Purchasers played as many games with owls as they could possibly muster. They looked for owls in their high-priced sales and brought them to the attention of the Forest Service. They prayed that no one would find owls on their cheap ones; and if they did, argued forcefully against returning the sale. It was sometimes difficult to remember the bad owls from the good owls; and it was always difficult to accept the premise that forestry had degenerated to playing political games in order for an industry to survive.

By the end of 1984, SPI had largely recovered from the depression. The company had produced over 568,000 MBF of lumber, and total assets had risen to $148,784,000. Total sales were valued at $218,300,000. Capital improvements for the year totaled $20,734,000 and included:

Loyalton	$3,299,000
Hayfork	8,335,000
Millwork	4,893,000

With the passage of the timber sale contract relief legislation and the submission of SPI's MSEP, there was again hope for the future. Even though SPI still had to cut the timber and pay for it, Red seemed vindicated again. He had known all along that something would come along to allow the company to survive.

chapter forty two

THE BIG FIVE

As time went on, four of SPI's key employees were eventually given officer status. The four, along with Red, were dubbed the Big Five by some of the employees of the company. I was fortunate to be one of them.

All of us were embarrassed by the label, but could do little about it. Eventually, there would be others added to the roster; but the original group consisted of Dick Smith, Ron Stevens, Ron Hoppe, Red and myself. Dick, of course, was already an officer.

The five of us began meeting periodically, perhaps as often as once a month, at one of the homes of those living in Redding. The group never met in Arcata; and since Dick Smith and I lived in Eureka, our wives were never honored with the presence of the Big Five. Red's condominium was the usual meeting place; and Ida would have prepared snacks for the meeting. The two Rons' homes were used on occasion, and their wives did the same. The wives may have resented the incursions into their routines; but in SPI, such events were to be expected. The evening usually concluded with a drink or two, and then dinner at a local restaurant.

The participants in the meetings were expected to speak their minds, and they usually did. For the early meetings, there was no written agenda; but that was modified as time went on. Ron Stevens, considered to be more of a **general** manager, was eventually the keeper of the agenda, and steered the discussions in the direction he thought best. Almost any subject was appropriate for discussion if it involved business.

The meetings afforded some uninterrupted time in which to discuss all manner of things. Telephone calls were kept to a minimum; and the four of us usually had Red's undivided attention for a considerable period of time. There was an opportunity to send up trial balloons on different subjects, and to observe the reactions of those in attendance. Red may have gained as much value from the discussions as anyone, since he was able to watch the rest of us argue from different perspectives, and judge for himself the effectiveness of the arguments.

The people who formed the group had come together from various backgrounds and from different parts of the country. It interested me that such a diverse group could get along so well together. Perhaps, I thought, they shared a few common traits that steered them to a company like SPI.

Ron Stevens had come from a sawmill family. He was born in 1931, in Burlington, Washington, where his father managed a sawmill. At an early age, he had become acquainted with the long hours, the jargon, the good times and, most of all, the bad times in the timber industry. He understood the meaning of work, and what it meant to be a lumberman.

By the time he graduated from high

school, his father had convinced him that a sawmill was not a good place to work. So Ron entered the University of Oregon to study business administration.

Sometime during his younger years, he had developed some allergies and they were affecting his ability to concentrate on his studies. He transferred to the University of Arizona where his health improved markedly. He eventually returned to Eugene, Oregon, where he graduated in 1953. During his school years, he found temporary work in the sawmills near Eugene. He also fell in love and was married in September of 1952.

After graduation, contrary to his father's advice, he went to work in a sawmill. The mill was at Marcola, east of Springfield, Oregon. He continued working there until the mill was sold to Willamette Industries, at which time he was laid off. He soon found work at another mill, continuing in the sawmill business - first at Milton Freewater, then in Portland, and finally at Eugene.

Ron learned quickly, and he progressed rapidly through various jobs in the mills. He was a shipping clerk, a shipping foreman, a lumber salesman and, at one point, he managed a sawmill making studs. In Eugene, he ran a remanufacturing plant, and bought lumber from "brush mills" which were scattered around Oregon at the time. They were the same type sawmills that Curly Emmerson had owned in his younger days.

The brush mills were inefficient; and as small patches of timber became more difficult to find at reasonable prices, the mills were phased out. By the late 1950s, they were nearly extinct; thus, in 1959, Ron accepted a job with Siskiyou Mills, owned by John Crook.

He was the Sales Manager for the mill at Happy Camp; although the sales office was at Yreka. During his first few months of employment, he met Red Emmerson when Red came to visit the operation.

In 1961, Siskiyou built a small, one-moulder millwork plant in Yreka. While John Crook was the principal owner, Ron also had an interest in it. It was the facility that burned in 1969.

By the time of the fire, the Emmersons and the Crooks had formed SPI and had bought out Ron Stevens's interest in the plant.

When the fire occurred, the loss was covered by insurance and the proceeds were used to purchase Lassen Moulding at Susanville. The Yreka plant was never rebuilt.

As time went on, Ron became a key employee of SPI. The principal stockholders found his knowledge and commitment to the company invaluable, and a long-term relationship was forged.

Meanwhile, Ron Hoppe was growing up a mid-westerner. He was born in 1936 in Lincoln, Nebraska; his parents were farmers. They lived near Dorchester, a town of only 630 persons.

In 1953, Ron graduated from high school, with no idea of what he wanted to do for the rest of his life. During his first summer after high school, however, he found work in a local lumber yard, unloading cement from rail cars. The sacks weighed 95 pounds and Ron weighed 135. The pay was good and the $140 per month was more money than he could spend, although he made a valiant effort to do so. With the taste of success, he decided to give college a try and enrolled at the University of Nebraska. He still did not know what he wanted to do for a career; but he looked forward to working in the summers when he could earn a little money to buy the things he thought he needed.

After a little experience at the lumber yard, he heard of a job opening at the Curtis Co., an old time "river mill." This company had mills all over the midwest, and they were into millwork in a big way. They bought Ponderosa pine lumber from various sources, probably having given up on Eastern White pine when it gave out in the Lake States, and manufactured it into door and window frames, mouldings and other products.

Ron Hoppe did a "little of everything" for Curtis. He was the janitor, tried clerking and a little accounting. He worked his way up to the city sales desk. There he met a customer from Clark Lumber Co., who hired him to do cost-estimating for producing windows and doors. His formal education was about over.

Sometime in 1956, Hoppe met a traveling lumber salesman named Roger Bowker from Midwest Lumber Co. Bowker asked Ron if he was interested in becoming a lumber salesman.

Ron thought for a moment, then asked, "What do **they** do?"

Bowker answered, "They travel around and call on lumber dealers, ask them what they want, and show them new products."

At that time, there was a lumber dealer in every small town, and the towns were about ten miles apart. Hoppe was making $250 a month, and thought he was doing just fine.

"Is the pay good?" Ron asked.

"We can start you out at $350 a month plus an expense account. You'll need transportation, so we'll furnish a new Oldsmobile for you to get around in," Bowker said.

That was all that was necessary; Ron Hoppe had found his calling. He worked for Midwest Lumber Co. for ten years, and in that time worked his way up to Sales Manager.

The company had an operation similar to a part of SPI's Richfield plant today. They bought lumber by the car-load, broke it up into lots of roughly one thousand board feet, palletized it, and sold the lots to the small-town lumber dealers.

In 1968, Hoppe made his first trip to the west. Since 1963, he had been buying lumber from western mills and, while doing so, had met Jack Hawley who was the General Manager for Diamond National at Chico. The tour of the west opened his eyes to the opportunities that might be available to a bright young man from the midwest. Near Oakridge, Oregon, he saw logging in the west for the first time. He was impressed with the stands of timber and the big donkeys that were yarding huge logs for the western mills.

Ron soon went to work for Diamond at Chico, but left after a short time to accept what he thought was a better job at Mouldings Inc. in Harrisburg, Oregon. Just then though, it was time for one of the periodic recessions; and soon he was trying to return to California. He had heard that Ron Stevens was looking for someone to be the Sales Manager at the millwork plant SPI had just purchased at Susanville. He had met Stevens before, but did not know him well. When he applied for the job, he was turned down.

At the time, neither Hoppe nor Stevens knew they were about to begin a long and productive relationship.

Jack Hawley, who had hired Ron Hoppe to work for Diamond, was hired by SPI to run the Lassen Moulding plant at Susanville. The plant was situated next to the Fruit Growers complex that was subsequently purchased by Sierra Pacific. Plans were to have Hawley build a millwork plant for SPI in the industrial park at the Chico airport. In 1971, construction at Chico began that took the rest of the year and most of 1972. The new plant began production in 1972.

The plant was "state of the art" for millwork plants in 1972. There was only one problem with it; it didn't work. It was nearly impossible to get adequate production through it. Ron Stevens, still running the operation at Happy Camp, was sent to Chico to find someone to manage the plant. After several months of looking for a manager, he gave up and stayed to try to run it himself.

In the meantime, Hoppe, in his search for work in California, had become reacquainted with Bob Ahrens who was also looking for work. Ahrens had worked for Diamond, and had also been "chased" by John Crook to go to work for him. The two had never made a deal. Ahrens and Hoppe decided to go into business together.

Each of them had managed to scrape together $5000 for the venture. For $100 a month, they rented an old barn "just up the road" from the Champion complex at Anderson, California (now owned by SPI) on old highway 99. The rent included the use of a forklift. They were in business.

They called their company "Coachmate." A man named Robert Vorhies built some of the machinery for the operation and was paid in stock. In a short time, they were making vinyl-wrapped mouldings and, after a year, they moved the plant to the Chico airport. Soon they found they were not adequately financed to compete successfully in the millwork business. They were unable to raise the capital to expand, or to buy the necessary machinery to remain competitive.

About the same time, John Crook was on his diversification kick. On behalf of SPI, he invited Ahrens and Hoppe to visit Crook's cabin at Lake Tahoe. There they met Red Emmerson and, after negotiating for a short time, a deal was struck. SPI took an option to

A.A. (Red) Emmerson

purchase Coachmate. The deal was for three years, and Ahrens and Hoppe were to run the plant.

With the two plants side by side at the Chico airport, it was natural that a close working relationship developed. With Stevens trying to run the Happy Camp and Chico operations for SPI, and the competent Hoppe and Ahrens running a plant next door at Chico, it soon became apparent to Hoppe that Stevens needed help. He volunteered to help run the SPI plant.

On March 30, 1970, Hoppe and Ahrens were each paid $123,000 for their shares in Coachmate. Vorhies's stock was purchased in August 1972, and SPI owned Coachmate 100%. Ron Hoppe became the Sales Manager for SPI's Millwork Division.

Bob Ahrens would go with John Crook to run the retail lumber yards when John Crook and Red Emmerson split up to return SPI to private status. Stevens and Hoppe continued on with SPI to work together as part of the management team.

The third member of the Big Five was Richard Leroy Smith. Red Emmerson has often called Dick "my brains." He was born in Portland, Oregon, on August 25, 1924, the youngest of three children. The family lived in Lents, a suburb of Portland. His father, a laborer, usually worked steadily for only nine or ten months each year, so family finances were a constant concern.

Dick was considerably younger than either his brother or his sister. His brother had managed to work his way through college in six years and had become a CPA. While Dick's father was advising him to go to trade school so he would amount to something, his brother was advising him to go to college.

Dick attended Franklin High School, taking a college prep course. It was 1941, and Dick was in his last year of school but attending only two hours per day while working in the shipyards in his spare time. He started there as a "burner," operating a cutting torch. The pay was good - 95 cents an hour - and he worked his way up to mechanic at $1.25 per hour.

In June 1942, Dick graduated from high school; but not having enough funds for college, he continued working in the shipyards.

From top left
Richard L. (Dick) Smith, Joseph (Bud) Tomascheski, Ron (Hoppe) Hoppe, Ron (Ron) Stevens,
All photos from SPI archives. (Nicknames in parenthesis).

Since there was a chance for college students to be deferred from the draft, he was saving diligently for college. By January 1943, he decided that he had better enroll at the University of Oregon at Eugene, or the draft would get him. By June of 1943, though, the draft was bearing down on college students, too.

Upon being drafted, it was possible at that time to have a choice of the branch of service in which to serve. Each branch had slightly different physical requirements, and Dick found that he qualified for service in the Navy. He was soon on his way to trade school; then served overseas as a Navy Radioman until the end of the war.

In April 1946, Dick got his discharge and, with the G.I. Bill, enrolled immediately at the University of Oregon. He went straight through summer school, and graduated in June 1948 with an accounting degree. He took his CPA examination and passed with little difficulty.

Dick soon found work as a CPA for I.D. Wood Co. making $200 per month - good money in his opinion. He was on his way to becoming a top-notch financial expert.

He met his soon-to-be-wife Marcie, and they were married in 1951. By then he was often travelling from the Portland office to audit firms in outlying areas. Children began arriving in the Smith household and, before he knew it, there soon were five of them. The Smiths decided that Dick's travel did not help Marcie in raising a big family.

One of Wood's clients was Pope & Talbot, a large forest products firm. While auditing their books, Dick met Jim Laier, one of their managers. Jim was later to leave Pope and Talbot to settle in Cloverdale, California, where Dick would spend two or three weeks every year doing accounting work for him. When I.D. Wood merged with Arthur Young & Co., Dick quit and went to work full-time for Jim Laier. The Smith family moved to Santa Rosa, where they stayed until 1970.

As mentioned earlier, Jim Laier and Henry Trione owned three sawmills located at Guallala, Cloverdale and Arcata. While in Arcata on one of his frequent business trips, Dick met Red Emmerson. By that time, Jim Laier was involved with the Humboldt

Flakeboard operation with Red. Red recognized in Dick a keen mind and a willingness to work.

In 1970, Laier and Trione sold their stock to Masonite Corp. Dick continued to work for Masonite, and stayed there until April 1971. Red then asked Dick to come to work as Controller for SPI, since he felt a change was needed in their accounting department. Dick was interviewed by Red, as well as John Crook. Crook noted that Dick was perhaps too old for their needs at the time. He was 47.

Somehow, Dick got the job; he was to work at Arcata. Since John Crook was Chairman of the Board of SPI, Dick theoretically worked for him. John advised him not to buy a house in Arcata, since he might not be there permanently. The Smiths leased a house in Eureka and, sure enough, they were transferred to Walnut Creek within nine months.

Dick worked in the corporate headquarters that Red grew to dislike so much. He stayed there until 1974 when he moved back to Arcata as Treasurer of the new SPI when it went private. He was to become the senior member of the Big Five.

I, like Hoppe, had grown up in the midwest, having been born in 1925 in Rockwell City, Iowa. My father was a fireman on the railroad. Both mother and father were farmers at heart; thus, when my father quit the railroad, they settled on a farm near Mason City. I attended first grade in a one-room school house situated on "the hard road" about three miles from home.

The Depression was fast approaching, and we were soon out of the farming business for good. My father got a job with the U.S. Postal Service and moved the family, now including a brother, to Des Moines. I lived there until World War II.

The Depression scared many people, including my father, into a frugal existence. While we were never starving, there was insistence on never wasting anything, including time. His frugality extended to transportation and, after 1933, he never owned an automobile until he retired in the late 1950s. I always thought that was carrying things a little too far.

I contributed to the family economic system by doing the things city boys do: mowing lawns, selling papers, working on an uncle's farm during summers, and pumping gas. At one point, my brother and I worked in the stockroom for a large department store - I in drugs and he in ladies' lingerie.

By January 1943, I was a senior in high school and afraid that the war would be over before I was old enough to be drafted. At 17, with parents' grudging permission, it was possible to enlist. Several of us did so, and I ended up in the Navy. We left the good life for a life of adventure.

I became a diesel mechanic (Motor Machinist Mate), and served in the South Pacific trying to repair landing craft engines. In January 1946, I was discharged and, like Dick Smith, had an opportunity to go to school. I wanted to be an architect.

After two years at Iowa State, in Ames, Iowa, I was convinced that I did not have the artistic ability required of an architect. I liked the math and engineering, but not the design courses. Forestry seemed about as far from architectural design as I could imagine, so the switch was made. I have never regretted it.

Having worked a couple of summers as a Forest Service lookout and firefighter in Idaho before graduation, I determined that government service was not to my liking. Upon graduating, I sought employment in the private sector. My first job was as road engineer for the old Fir Manufacturing Co. in Myrtle Creek, Oregon. There I soon became the company timber cruiser.

I met my wife Norma in Myrtle Creek; and like Dick Smith's family, the children began to arrive. Before we knew what caused it all, we had accumulated six.

After three years, we moved to Port Orford, Oregon, where I became Timber Buyer for Western States Plywood Co-op., then to Oroville, California, where I was hired as the Forester for Oroply, Corp.

While working for Oroply, I met Ken Metzker and his brother-in-law, Lou Ohlson. Together with Bob Dant, both of them were involved in a sawmill in Reno, Nevada. Bob was one of the Dants who came from a long line of lumber people in the northwest. Soon I was offered the job of Forester for the Reno operation; and I accepted the challenge of a new, better-paying position in a unique community. It was a good move for us.

In January 1961, I moved our family to Reno, and we spent 15 years there. By the time DiGiorgio Corp. purchased the sawmills at Loyalton, Sloat, Quincy and Camptonville, I was spending most of my time at Loyalton, since the mill at Reno had just about outlived its usefulness. I became the Chief Forester for DiGiorgio Corp. With the office in Loyalton, we continued to live in Reno, and I commuted some 40 miles to work each day.

I had learned that most successful lumber operations had, somehow, secured a stable timber/log supply. I felt very strongly that my responsibilities could not be met without a great deal of effort being put into that phase of the operation. While at DiGiorgio, we were aggressive purchasers of timber and, I believe, the timber under contract was what attracted Red to the DiGiorgio operations. That, and the fact that DiGiorgio occupied a strategic location with their four mills, made the purchase a good one for SPI.

The last member of the Big Five was Red Emmerson himself. Since this story is essentially Red's story, his background will not be discussed here. However, there does seem to be a similarity in the types of backgrounds from which all five people came.

The five all had humble beginnings. It is likely that without the G.I. Bill, the majority of them might not have attempted college. Each of them had the work ethic imbedded in them and, it appears to me, each loved what they were doing. They were committed to making their company a success. By so doing, they participated in that success.

Moreover, the four of us were fortunate in having Red find us. We learned from him. No matter how hard we tried, we could not out-think him, nor could we out-work him. He could shame an employee into extra effort merely by his example. He was the catalyst that made his company prosper and grow. The rest of us went along for the ride.

Dave Dun, with hangover, splitting wood at Redwood House, 1991. Photo by author.

chapter forty three

THE COUNSELORS

Nearly every company, no matter how small, needs legal advice at some time during its existence. SPI was no exception. As described earlier, Francis "Moose" Mathews was one of the first attorneys hired by Curly Emmerson. He gave legal advice concerning personal matters as well as business transactions.

Jon Lyons was also mentioned earlier as the first attorney employed directly by SPI. He gradually assumed all of the duties previously performed by Moose, although Moose continued to be involved with trial work.

When Jon quit to begin his own business, Red hired Ted Hannan, an attorney who had most recently worked in Hawaii. Ted was with SPI only a short time before he fell into disfavor with several of those on the SPI management team. He returned to private practice in Honolulu. He eventually brought suit against SPI for wrongful termination that was subsequently thrown out of court.

Dick Smith ever after would tease Red about hiring Ted, claiming that he was the one who did it, therefore **his** attorney. Actually, Dick had as much to do with Ted's going to work for SPI as anyone. At one time, most of the managers were quite pleased with him; and he was a good attorney.

Shortly after Ted Hannan left, Red hired Dave Dun, a local attorney who was working with Moose Mathews. Dave went on to be a valued associate, not only of Red, and Dick Smith, but of mine as well. He was a delightful individual to know and to work with. His story needs to be told in some detail.

When I asked Dave where he was born, he said, "In Seattle in 1949." When I asked him where he had grown up, his reply was typical, "I never did." He was always truthful.

His father, Henry, worked for Weyerhauser in their Real Estate Division; and Dave attended schools in the Seattle area. He tried selling soap (something called Royalite) for a company that developed a franchised sales system similar to Amway. Dave said he did not like selling "soap and junk," so he decided to go to law school. He earned a B.A. degree from the University of Washington in 1973, and J.D. degree in 1976 from the University of Puget Sound Law School.

He met Laura Kirsch, a registered nurse, at church while he was in school. She helped get Dave a job at University Hospital in Seattle where she worked. He became an orderly, drawing blood, and working as a lab technician. Laura and Dave were married in June 1971, after which she put Dave through law school. She reports that she "thought he was going to die before he ever earned a nickel as a lawyer."

Laura's father owned the Sun Valley Bulb Farm, a very large producer of bulbs and cut

Dave and Laura Dun on porch at Redwood House ranch, just before the evening's festivities began, and the day before chopping wood, 1991.
Photo by author.

flowers with operations in Humboldt County. The couple moved to Eureka when Dave, after passing the California Bar, went to work for Moose Mathews in August 1976. In June 1982, Dave entered private practice, forming Dun and Barnum, with Bill Barnum as partner.

Dave had become acquainted with the timber industry and its legal problems when he worked with Moose Mathews. He always thought that kind of legal work was more satisfying than divorces, child abandonment, and domestic violence disputes. In August 1985, he took a giant step in that direction by going to work for SPI as Corporate Attorney.

Dave became somewhat of a company character; and there were numerous stories told about him. He had a crazy sense of humor, could tell stories before a large audience that would do a professional comedian proud, and affected the manner of a simple-minded person on occasion.

I had met Dave when he worked for Moose Mathews; but I really did not know him well until he took Hannan's place in the Arcata office. He was somewhat taken aback when he discovered he did not have the support staff that he was accustomed to in a law firm. He had one person, Mary Moore, who looked after the filing, typing and organizing his office. Even though Mary was very competent, she did not take care of Dave the way he was accustomed. Dave had to make his own travel arrangements, and stand in line for the company airplane like the rest of us.

Shortly after Dave came to work, he was to attend a meeting of some kind in Portland, Oregon. I do not recall the subject of the meeting except to remember it had something to do with forestry or timber contracts. Dave made arrangements to fly commercially to Portland to attend the meeting. That evening, I received a telephone call around 8:00 p.m. at my home. It was Dave.

"Bud, do you know where I'm staying tonight?" he asked.

I drew a blank. "Dave, where are you?" I asked.

"I'm at the Portland airport," he replied.

"How did you get there? How come you're at Portland. Are you lost?" I asked.

"No, no, I'm supposed to go to a meeting

here first thing in the morning, and I couldn't make it with the early flight tomorrow. I came up the night before; but I don't know where I'm supposed to stay," he said.

"Who made your reservations," I inquired.

"I did," he replied. "Yesterday."

"You mean you've forgotten where your room is?" I asked, snickering.

"Yeah, usually my secretary gave me a list of where I was to stay, and a travel schedule; but now I don't have anybody to take care of me," he said.

"Hell, Dave, why did you call me? I have no idea where you are supposed to stay," I said. "Does Laura know? Why didn't you call her?"

"I didn't want to bother her," he replied. "Besides I'm staying at the same place where the meeting is that I'm supposed to go to. I thought you might know where that is."

"You mean you don't know where the meeting is?" I was beginning to wonder if we had the right attorney on the payroll. "Are you sure you're in the right city?"

Dave thought a minute. Then he said, "I think so. Yeah, I'm sure of it. Don't you remember, we talked about the meeting a week or so ago?"

Then a bell rang. I remembered he had talked about the need to attend that particular meeting. I remembered seeing the announcement that came in the mail.

"Dave, I think the meeting is at the Lloyd Center. Does that ring a bell?" I inquired.

"That's it! That's where I'm staying!" he yelled with relief. He hung up and was gone.

Dave Dun is one of those persons who loses track of time, and where he is, when he becomes involved in a project. He begins work before daylight, and stops well after dark. He is an excellent attorney; but his first several months on the job did not impress some of the SPI management with his disorganized work habits.

It turned out that Dave had no enthusiasm for details such as travel, lunch, sleep and things of that nature. When he zeroed in on a problem, he forgot everything else, including other problems that might need attention. At his former law office, someone

undoubtedly kept him pointed in the right direction. At SPI, he was on his own.

Soon there were many irritations developing over the work he was doing, or rather the work he was not doing. Dave would occasionally be in a panic because he had forgotten some task that needed doing. After a number of discussions with Red, and with Dick Smith, Dave returned to private practice. SPI did not fill the position of Corporate Attorney after Dave left.

That wasn't the end of Dave's story at SPI, though. After Dave returned to his practice, he seemed to have a revolving roster of associates. The firm was Dun & Barnum for awhile; then Dun, Barnum & Arkley; then Dun and Arkley; then Dun, Martinek & Ham; and finally Dun & Martinek. It was unclear whether Dave was hard to get along with, or whether he had forgotten who his partner was at the moment.

Dave began to carry around an appointment book that was almost as thick as a Bible. Many attorneys and business people carry them wherever they go, to remind them of appointments, things to do, things that have been done, etc. Perhaps the reminder book was what made Dave one of the best attorneys SPI could have hired; he carried the thing constantly.

One day, Dave misplaced his "daily organizer." He broke out in a cold sweat immediately and appeared to panic. He looked everywhere, even in the wastebasket. He lost his train of thought, and seemed to go into a trance. Luckily he found the book a few minutes later in his briefcase and, with a sigh of relief, was back in business.

With his new-found organizational skills, Dave Dun again became SPI's attorney. Even though he **is** SPI's Corporate Attorney, he never actually returned to the payroll. He takes care of all SPI legal matters, and those of the Emmerson family, all on a fee basis. He attends company meetings and has only a few outside clients. He has become an excellent trial lawyer; and his peers have recognized his legal briefs concerning timber law as authoritative and well-reasoned.

Dave has assumed a prominent place in the west coast timber industry. He is perceived as a spokesman for SPI. He has become expert in solving environmental problems, and is consulted by the timber associations to which SPI belongs. He has not lost his sense of humor, although it is sorely tried at times by the environmentalists.

chapter forty four

AIRPORT LIMOS

At each airport close to one of the saw-mills, SPI kept an automobile for use by those flying in for a visit. Many companies did the same for the convenience of their employees, and to save time and expense in securing ground transportation.

A few of them, SPI included, did not supply a first-class car for this purpose. Red modified the procedure a little more perhaps by providing one that was not likely to get stolen. Each looked so bad, it was difficult to tell whether it had come from a junkyard or not.

The one at the Quincy airport was typical. It was a Plymouth Duster of uncertain vintage. It could have been 1964 model but no one was ever very sure. At one time it was blue; but it had turned into a two-toned model - rust on top and faded blue on the bottom. It was a two-door sedan with a big engine and lots of power.

The headliner inside had ripped and come loose from the ceiling so that a sort of curtain hung down just to the rear of the front seat. This afforded the person in the back seat a certain amount of privacy; but it was difficult for the passenger to see to the front. The back of the front seat on the passenger side was defective, so without adjustment, the rider lay back at about a 45 degree angle. It may have been one of the first reclining-seat-back models in existence. To sit somewhat upright, the passenger had to insert the buckle of the seat

belt in the hinge for the seat back and lean back against it. That held the seat-back more upright. Of course, the seat belt was useless when used as a hinge stopper; but that was of little concern to the passengers.

The engine in the car was exceptionally dependable. Even in the coldest Plumas County dawn, with a few pumps of the accelerator pedal, the engine would catch with no trouble at all. Brakes were another matter. After a couple of brake relining jobs, it was discovered that there were no power brakes, or power steering for that matter, on this car. It drove like a truck, but it ran well. One only needed two strong arms to steer it and a strong leg to stop it.

It was fun to watch the expression on the faces of visiting bankers or dignitaries when Red chauffeured them to the mill in the limo. Invariably Red climbed into the driver's seat without any explanation whatsoever. He explained the adjustment of the seat-back without so much as an apology. The passengers had no choice but to follow instructions, and few made insulting comments regarding the mode of transportation.

In the Duster, Red chauffeured Ed Bond, SPI's Human Resource Manager, all the way to Loyalton one rainy day. There was a hole in the floor boards just below Ed's feet, and the water kept spraying up through the hole to wet Ed's trousers. Finally, Red told him if he wanted to "keep his balls dry, he should put his foot over the hole." Ed rode all the way to Loyalton with first one foot, then the other over the hole, keeping the Duster warm and comfy inside.

The car at Susanville was a Chevrolet of similar vintage. It was slightly more pleasing in appearance, but did not start as readily as the Duster at Quincy. I was "privileged" to occupy the back seat early one morning after the previous driver (probably Red himself) had left a couple of windows down.

It had snowed during the night and the temperature was in the 'teens. There were snowdrifts on both seats and on the dash board. In addition, the windows were frozen over, both **inside** and out. The defrosters did not operate very well and the heater even less so. Dick Smith elected to drive; the pilot occupied the other front seat; and I hurried to claim the back as I considered it to be safer, especially with Dick driving. I remembered that he had hit a bridge on Samoa Road, dented Alan Smith's car in the parking lot, and run into the office at Arcata on separate occasions.

It was impossible to see through the windshield, so the front windows had to remain down to enable the pilot and Dick to stick their heads out to see where the road was.

When we hit the highway and speeded up, a blizzard developed inside the limo from the snow drifts inside. The snow was cold and dry. Tears and running noses rapidly froze on the faces of the front seat occupants as we drove into town. I, in the back, hunkered down and congratulated myself for having the foresight to seize the rear seat. We made it, and appreciated the coffee pot warming on the counter.

This car seemed to have it in for Dick Smith. One winter day, some of us, including Red, attended a meeting in San Francisco. We flew by way of Susanville, where Dick was dropped off to attend to some accounting business. We were to pick him up on the way back to Arcata that evening.

It was well after dark when we arrived at the Susanville airport to find it socked in with fog. We could not land, and we knew that Dick

Smith awaited us in the Chevrolet on the ground. As we circled overhead, Red called him on the intercom and suggested that he drive the limo to Chester where we would be waiting for him. It seemed unfair to go off and leave him to spend the weekend in Susanville, it being Friday. We flew to the little airstrip at Chester, perhaps 20 miles away.

We sat in the airplane to observe the cocktail hour (with the exception of the pilot, of course). There was always a moderate supply of refreshments on board to take care of such emergencies. We depleted the inventory considerably while waiting for Dick. Without the engine running, we sat in the dark, sipping booze, and trying to stay warm.

After about 40 minutes, a shivering controller arrived. He had driven with the left window down since it would not roll up. Dick's little pork-pie hat was not much protection for his ears and bald head from the icy blast. Through chattering teeth, he cussed us all out, Red included, for sitting in relative luxury sipping cocktails while he drove through the Sierra winter in the middle of the night. It took more than one of Red's triple Crown Royals to mellow him out.

It was part of the pilots' duties to care for the airport equipment. The limos were considered to be connected to the airports, so the pilots were to keep them gassed and ready to roll. Passengers always hoped that the airplanes in which they flew were in better shape than the ground transportation that awaited them.

The limos at Redding at one time consisted of two vehicles, one of which had come from Arcata. Most residents of the coast learn that cars from that damp climate develop an odor that immediately identifies their origin. The odor intensifies if the car is closed up and is left in the Redding sun for any length of time.

The Arcata car had the musty smell, and actually grew a mushroom in the back seat. It was a pretty good-sized toadstool that popped up one day after a heavy rain in the Sacramento Valley. I was fortunate to be one of the first to recognize the phenomenon as I drove into town from the airport.

As I slowed for a turn in downtown Redding, a surge of water inundated the front floor boards and my feet. The surprise caused me to brake harder and, as I entered the right turn, the front door flew open. I narrowly escaped leaving the auto to complete the turn by itself. Pulling up at the curb, I found the "wells" where the back seat occupants put their feet had been completely filled with water from the rain the night before. There, in the middle of the back seat, was the mushroom.

The other car in Redding developed a problem while I was driving it to the office one day. It seemed to be a minor malfunction since one turn signal did not work. Upon arriving at the office, I stopped at the forklift shop and asked the mechanic there if he would take a look at the problem. I suspected that a new bulb was needed.

Sometime later, as I was about to leave, he informed me that he was just not able to fix the light. In fact, he had spent a considerable amount of time tracking the wiring through the system, and he still had not identified what was wrong. There was a slight problem, though. He told me when the turn signals were turned on, both headlights flashed on and off. I thought he was kidding me; but sure enough, not only did the headlights flash, but the tail-lights as well.

The limo at Hayfork was an Oldsmobile that had been driven by one of the managers at Publisher's in Burney. It was a powerful machine, full of gadgets, befitting the man of stature who used to drive it. It had also seen its best days.

One day quite recently, Jerry Gromacki had driven his pickup to Hayfork where it had promptly broken down. He decided to borrow the limo while his vehicle was being repaired. Several times, Jerry drove the limo back and forth from Hayfork to Redding where he lived.

After three days of this, Jerry's neighbor across the street could not bear the uncertainty any longer. That evening, he saw Jerry drive up in the beat-up Olds.

"What happened? Did you get fired?" he asked.

Jerry replied, "Nope, don't think so. Why?"

"You must have fallen on hard times by the looks of your car," he persisted.

Jerry said, "Pretty nice car, don't you think?"

The neighbor replied, "What're you going to do, restore it?"

These stories are typical of all of the stories associated with airport limos. They contributed to the Sierra Pacific folklore, and provided a subject that was fun to discuss over drinks and dinner on a number of occasions. The employees who had the privilege of driving them swore at them good-naturedly. The more bizarre the incident, the better the story. The incidents continue to occur to this day.

Plymouth Duster, the same airport limo described by author. This automobile became famous as the "best" limo SPI had at the Quincy airport. After so many stories were told about this machine, George Coulter, Quincy Division Manager, had it completely restored. The author insisted on having it photographed, believing it to be in the same condition as he remembered it. After Teri Banka did so, and sent him the pictures, he accused her of taking pictures of the wrong automobile.

chapter forty five

ETHNICITY

There were a lot of ethnic jokes that I heard while growing up. With a name like Tomasczewski, I drew Polish jokes like a lightning rod. My father told me that his grandfather had changed the spelling of the name to Tomascheski. Maybe he was getting tired of Polish jokes and thought the new spelling would disguise the fact that he was Polish.

People with names that are unpronounceable probably draw different kinds of attention. Perhaps that is why Polish people became the subject of jokes about their intelligence. When they tried to change the spelling of their names, and they still came out misspelled, it's no wonder. And the name was still unpronounceable anyway.

As I became acquainted with members of the SPI family, they seemed to save jokes for me to listen to the next time they saw me. Some I heard many times, with a little different twist now and again, but the same joke nevertheless.

One of the early jokes had to do with a Polish football team playing an Italian football team. The playing field was next to a railroad track, and the score was 0 to 0 in the fourth quarter. At about that time, a train went by and blew its whistle. The Italian team, believing it was quitting time, left the field. Ten minutes later, the Polish team scored a touchdown and thought they had won the game.

The joke was told by Bill Peterson, Supervisor of the Plumas National Forest, at a joint meeting with the timber industry in Quincy. I laughed as hard as anyone present; but after the laughter died away, I raised my hand.

Bill Peterson threw up his hands in mock horror when he acknowledged my presence. "I hope I didn't offend you, Bud," he said.

"Not at all, Bill," I said. "I thought you might like to know my mother was born in Italy though."

Bill never forgot the incident; and he would remind me of it nearly every time I saw him after that. He probably did think I was offended.

There were some strange coincidences that I noticed after a few years at SPI. It seemed that most of the accountants were Mormons, and most of the foresters had Polish names. At one time, there were two Tomascheskis, Bill Banka (both parents Polish), Carl Jagodski, Jerry Gromacki and his nephew, Steve Gromacki, Matt Taborski (not a forester), Jim Ostrowski, and I wondered about Joe Kosak. The Mormons that I knew about were Ray Lowry, Pat McEuen and Alan Smith, all accountants.

The standing joke at SPI was that Red always hired Mormons to look after the money. No one could ever figure out why he hired Polacks.

On one occasion, Gromacki, Jagodski and

I were riding in Jerry's pickup, telling each other the latest Polish jokes. We were coming off a steep grade near Castle Craigs north of Redding when Jerry remembered he was driving the same vehicle that lost a front wheel while he was headed down Highway 299. He immediately slowed to a crawl coming down the mountain.

"What's the matter, Jerry, are ya out of gas?" I asked.

"Naw, but I just happened to think. My front wheel fell off not very long ago. It'd be awful to go off over the side and end up in all that manzanita. What would everybody think, three Polacks in one pickup, deader'n mackerels?" he said.

At the time, Pope John Paul, the first Polish Pope, was head of the Catholic Church. The Polacks working for SPI used to boast that the Poles were taking over the world. There was enough proof to show anyone: the Church, one of the largest organizations in the world was headed by a man from Poland; and SPI, becoming one of the largest lumber firms in California, certainly had a head start on all of their competitors in the Polack department.

At one of the first annual meetings of the Big Five ever held with wives in attendance, the subject of Poles working for SPI was brought up. Immediately the Polish jokes began, most of them ribald and in poor taste for polite company. Since there were not many in attendance who were polite, the jokes went on for a considerable length of time. Of course, quite a few of those in attendance had been drinking.

At a lull in the joke telling, I piped up, "You people are just jealous. You know the Poles are taking over the world. You should all be ashamed of yourselves and go to confession."

Ron Stevens, at that time unmarried, but very much interested in the lady he was with, leaped into the breach. "What do you mean, go to confession?" he said. "I haven't done anything wrong."

"Ron," I said, "You and Ginger are living in sin. Unless I am mistaken, you are staying in the same room tonight."

"What's wrong with that?" he said, "Ginger doesn't mind."

"If you were Polish, you'd understand," I said.

Ron was insulted. "You mean, I have to get married to stay in the same room with Ginger?" he asked.

"Yep, that's the way it works," I replied. "You know. You can marry Ginger without a minister if you want to. It's between you and her; usually there are witnesses, and a formal ceremoney that takes place just to make it all legal and solemn."

"You're kidding," Red chimed in. "Can you marry them?"

"Me?" I said, "Hell no, it won't be legal."

"Who said anything about legal?" Marcie Smith said.

Ron Hoppe couldn't keep quiet. He jumped in with both feet, up to his eyeballs.

"There's no way you two can stay in the same room tonight unless you're married. I'll see if there is another room for Ginger." He left, returning in a few minutes. Naturally there wasn't; the place was full.

Red had the solution. "Bud, you seem to know all about this," he said. "You marry 'em."

"Red, I don't know how," I replied.

"Aren't you a Polack?" he asked. "Polacks can do anything. You said so yourself. Marry them."

"Yes, sir," I said.

I was hooked. I stood up, blessed the sinners, and made up a dumb ceremony in my mind. The words were ridiculous, designed to make the unlucky couple embarrassed (which they didn't appear to be). At the end, we toasted the newlyweds with a couple-dozen more drinks, and staggered off to bed. Ron and Ginger occupied the same room, but not as sinners.

The "Polish Pope" was born. In the cold light of day, I was thoroughly embarrassed by the whole incident. At every annual meeting thereafter, Red would get the microphone to ask if there were couples in attendance who were not married. I would have to get up before the group and offer to hear their confessions. I always hoped that I would not offend Ida, Red, Poles, Catholics, sinners, and my wife in that order.

Several years later, Cheryl Coulter presented me with ceremonial robes to wear for future festivities. They were bright red with a billed cap covered with crimson material that hung down in back. Two long wires that looked like insect antennae protruded from the headgear. The hat was about four sizes too small; but I had to stand up before the group to hear the sinners' confessions, and to marry those who were not too embarrassed to admit they needed it.

A few years later, I was to marry Ron Hoppe, too. None of the ceremonies ever took place when the participants were completely sober, and Hoppe's was no exception. There was a funny thing that all of the ceremonies had in common though - it seemed the marriages all lasted at least as long as I remained at SPI.

The Polish Pope in full dress, late 1980s.
Photo from author's collection.

Band saws in filing room from head-rigs are typical of those in many SPI sawmills.
Photo from SPI archives.

chapter forty six

THE MID '80S

It is difficult to separate the events that occurred in 1985-86 from each other. This 2-year period was a very significant time in the history of the company. During that interval, the company began to enjoy its greatest growth. Lumber prices were high and stable. It was to begin the longest stretch of good markets lumbermen could remember.

Inflation remained under control. After the economic contraction of 1981-82 subsided, the economy began expanding. The good Republicans who survived in the timber industry regained their confidence in the Reagan administration. Inflation **was** under control, employment **was** high, and people could afford to buy houses again. Times were good as the survivors worked their way through their high-priced timber sales.

Everything was not going right, though. The environmental battles escalated to the point where foresters spent as much time fighting as producing anything from the land. The lawyers became involved in most of the discussions of the day involving forestry.

Many of the larger companies in California began to doubt the wisdom of continuing in business in the state. They began to look closely at other options. Some began to leave or sell out.

In 1985, Champion International closed its doors at Anderson, California. Charles Hurwitz and Maxxam Corp. signed a definitive agreement for the acquisition of The Pacific Lumber Co. for $868,000,000, setting off the biggest environmental battle of the century. The result would be further contractions in the timber industry as other firms got caught in the fallout.

As a result, even though lumber prices were high, costs of production were becoming higher. The phenomenon affected all regions of the western United States. California, in particular, became a poor place for a firm in a basic industry like timber to be in business.

SPI ran counter to the flow. Perhaps it always had done so. When times were bad, it produced more wood by working more hours. When others were shutting down, SPI bought their assets. It modernized in the face of recession or depression, making substantial capital investments in its facilities. How could it do that? Was it better than those who were giving up? Was it different from Champion, or Kimberly-Clark, or International Paper, all of whom were gone?

There were differences, of course. SPI was better in some respects than most of the others. On the average, its people might have been more committed to working harder. Most of the operations **were** non-union. The great majority of its employees **did** have a sense of pride and accomplishment in their company's success.

Then, too, SPI was a private company. There was no need to ask for a meeting of the board of directors before an action was taken.

The owner called the shots whether the board met or not. The company could move fast when necessary, and often did.

For example, I remember a Saturday afternoon in 1977 when we learned that a tract of timberland was for sale. The tract was part of an estate sale to be confirmed in court the following Monday morning, just two days hence. I received the call from Red Emmerson late on Saturday.

On Sunday morning, Red, Bob and Bill Kleiner, Bob and Brian Graham (a couple of Kleiner's employees), Ron Hoover and Jay Webster (from SPI), and I headed for the timber off Fickle Hill, east of Arcata.

Francis Carrington dropped each of us at different locations as close to the perimeter of the parcel as we could get. We, including Red, measured trees on several random strips through the 2,400 acres of redwood timber before 3:00 p.m. that Sunday. By 5:00 p.m. we had developed an appraisal, handwritten on a yellow tablet. Early Monday morning, the tract was bid in court. SPI was the successful bidder.

Speed was only one of the advantages SPI had. There was probably no **one** ingredient that accounted for the company's success; it was undoubtedly a combination of several; but there was one principal reason SPI continued to gain strength.

The ingredient was optimism. The optimism was in Red himself. It was like a disease - incurable. Sometimes one could call it bullheaded optimism. In some cases it bordered on foolhardiness. He felt there was only one way to go - straight ahead, at full speed. Even when times were bad, he knew the bad times would end sometime. SPI would be in the best position to expand when the good times began. He had complete faith in the lumber business, in the U. S. economy, and in his company. In his whole experience, everything had worked out alright. What more proof was needed?

After a few years at SPI, I began to think he could be right. Everything he touched turned out well. Even if a project ran into difficulty, he spent little time worrying about it. He would stop and start over. For example, the pre-stressed concrete trusses for the plant at Richfield were incorrectly designed. While being erected, they began to show cracks when tilted upright. The defect was a major problem. Had they been installed, they could have failed with tragic consequences.

The trusses were redesigned. The old ones were broken up and hauled to Hayfork where they were placed as riprap along Hayfork Creek. The broken reinforced concrete stabilized the creek banks near the new cogen plant. It was undoubtedly the most expensive riprap ever devised. Red wasted no time looking back. There would be time for discussion of fault and liability later. It was full speed ahead, get rid of the debris, build the plant, get it into production, and get on with something else.

Another example of his optimism was his insistence that the high-priced timber under contract was really not an insurmountable problem. There would be relief of some kind; no one knew what kind. It bothered him that computations showed the costs were so bad that there would never be a possibility of cutting the timber for a profit; but it did not bother him enough to worry very long about it.

He would have scoffed at the idea that he relied on his schooling at the Academy, where he had learned that God would take care of him. To many, that it is the way it appeared; and the author used to tell him that someone was certainly looking after him.

As SPI submitted its Multi-Sale Extension Plan (MSEP) to the Forest Service, one wondered what would happen to SPI in the years 1990 and 1991. Those were the years when the MSEP showed the highest-priced sales would have to be cut. Two of the worst sales from a loss standpoint was one called Primrose on the Tahoe Forest, and one named Tamarack on the Plumas. The price for several of the species on both of them would result in substantial losses. Losses on Tamarack

New Anderson sawmill under construction in 1987. Sacramento River is in foreground. Large building at lower left is an old Champion building housing SPI planing facilities. Porta-Crane is being assembled in center of photo for handling logs. Photo by Mark Fator.

alone could be as much as $7,000,000.

What happened to the two sales? Insects attacked the pine on Primrose to such an extent that it became unusable. Pine was the species that carried the huge overbid. A fire on Tamarack burned many of the cutting units, reducing the losses there. It seemed, indeed, that Red had God in his hip pocket. In the final analysis, SPI cut all of the MSEP sales and didn't even burp.

In August 1985, SPI secured financing arrangements to begin construction of several wood-waste-fired electrical cogeneration facilities. They were to be located at Burney, Quincy and Susanville. Included in the projects was the blacktopping of log yards at Susanville, Loyalton, Quincy, Hayfork and Burney. The total cost of the projects was estimated at $30,634,000.

Of the total, $17,000,000 came from the issuance of California Pollution Control Fi-

nancing Authority's variable-rate-demand, pollution-control revenue bonds. The bonds were rated AAA and were tax-exempt, with interest set weekly. They were backed by Barclay's Bank of London.

Dennis Gomez, meanwhile, had brought the Burney sawmill to a prominent place in the SPI success story. Many visitors went through the plant to marvel at its speed and efficiency. Dennis was proud of the accomplishments of the crew "on the hill."

In September 1985, Dennis prepared a pro forma schedule for a sawmill similar to the Burney plant that might be situated in the Redding-Red Bluff corridor. Red had been discussing such a project for some time. Dennis's figures showed a profitable operation could be built that would require up to 135,000 MBF log scale per year.

The project received a lot of attention. There were numerous conversations with Red,

Ron Stevens, Jerry Gromacki, Mike Bates and others. The questions that had to be answered were: where do the logs come from, and what kind of logs should they be? Would another mill similar to Burney result in driving up the price of logs to a level where neither mill could make a profit? Where should the mill be located?

Stevens, Gromacki and Bates were initially against the concept. One had to agree with their assessment that a new mill at Anderson would compete with Burney. Mike and Jerry were already charged with supplying two mills (Burney and CV) from the surrounding mountains, so they had a good feel for the log market. They could not see where all the logs would come from.

Ron Stevens was initially always a pessimist when new projects were proposed. His nature was to be negative and extremely conservative in forecasting good times, usually playing good counterpoint to Red's optimism. He was always a good devil's advocate.

The author could sympathize with Gromacki and Bates but, after talking with other SPI foresters, could see that Anderson was a strategic location for log supply. Logs could be delivered there from places inaccessible to Burney due to haul distances. Logs could come from the Mendocino Forest and from the Feather River operations. Hayfork and Central Valley were very close to Anderson, so small logs would be separated from their supply and delivered to Anderson. The smaller logs taken from them would increase their efficiency, because all they had to saw then were the remaining big logs. The big question was: could SPI supply **all** the mills, not just a new small log mill?

Red solved that question. He decided to build the new mill and worry about log supply later. Stevens, Gromacki and Bates were the last holdouts, but they were overruled. As always, Stevens, once he got over his initial objections, got into the planning stages with enthusiasm. Of course, Red and Gomez were the catalysts who got the whole thing going. Dennis became thoroughly engrossed in the design and construction once it got underway.

On March 4, 1986, SPI bought the Champion manufacturing complex at Anderson, California. The site included 390 acres and many buildings, including an outdated sawmill and plywood plant. A large office building occupied a part of the property. SPI planned to auction the machinery and excess property.

In June 1986, the Hayfork sawmill broke several production records for its division. The mill produced 8,444 MBF lumber for the month, and the planing mill surfaced 10,151 MBF. In one day, Planer Foreman Don Babcock's crew produced over 434 MBF in one 9-hour shift. The six-man shipping crew shipped and invoiced 8,782 MBF of lumber for the month.

Burney, under Dennis Gomez, was also setting production records. In June of 1986, the Division kiln dried 8,300 MBF of lumber, the sawmill produced 12,869 MBF, the planing department produced 12,850 MBF, and the shipping department sent 13,762 MBF on its way. Red could not wait to begin work on a new mill similar to Burney's.

Perhaps Gomez was working his crew too hard, for the next month Local 2608 of the Lumber, Production and Industrial Workers Union, based in Anderson, requested an election at the Burney mill. The National Labor Relations Board authorized the election for July 10, 1986. Out of 114 votes, the union got 33, the company 81. The facility remained firmly non-union; but the number of votes for the union troubled Red Emmerson.

Construction of a new sawmill at Anderson began in August, 1986. The decision to build the facility was one of the best SPI ever made. The design of the mill was excellent. By the time it was completed a little over two years later, it was a source of pride and accomplishment for those at SPI.

Bob Ahrens came back to SPI in September 1986 as the new plant manager for the Oroville millwork plant. He was the same Ahrens who was Hoppe's partner at Coachmate, and who had stayed with the Answerman stores when John Crook and Red split up. The Millwork Division, including Oroville, Chico and Richfield, had over 600 employees when Ahrens came back to work.

The new Richfield plant was in production with 165 employees. Primary manufacture was being handled by two Portland Iron Works shadow-line ripsaws, ten high-speed cut-off saws, and three new finger-joint machines. Among the machines on the finish side were three resaws, four new moulders, two used moulders, three tenoners, and two autonailers in the window department.

The facility was still expanding with another ten high-speed cut-off saws, two more finger-joint machines, and two more moulders yet to come. When at full capacity, the plant would employ 290 persons.

The mill at Central Valley completed paving its log yard in the spring of 1986. Later in the year, a water treatment system for the boiler was completed, and a new Temposonic computerized setworks was installed on both the headrig and the pony. The inside of the sawmill was completely repainted an off-white color, and two new dry kilns were completed.

Meanwhile, the Forest Service planning process was in full swing in the mid-'80s. Most of the figures, some of them preliminary, showed there would be less timber placed on the market by the government. The planning program produced few final plans, even though large sums of money were spent on them. Many, including the author, doubted the plans would ever work. In the face of it all, SPI went ahead with expansion.

Earlier in 1986, a major flood hit the Sierras especially hard. The middle fork of the Feather River rose so high it put the mill at Sloat, located at the confluence of Long Valley Creek and the river, in a precarious position. Access to the mill was by log loader only, as Long Valley Creek flooded the road into the plant. Employees were ferried across the raging water by the log decking machine. The mill lost little time.

Access to Plumas County was severely limited when Highway 70 in the Feather River Canyon was washed out in several places, closing it for months.

Through a lease agreement, Susanville had acquired the operation of the 23-mile-long rail spur connecting the sawmill to the main line of the Western Pacific Railroad at

Wendel. It became the second SPI facility to have its own railroad, although SPI technically made it a subsidiary of the Quincy Railroad. The division purchased a 1950 GE locomotive from the Southern Pacific Railroad. The train made about three trips per week with engineer Earl Grooms and brakeman Earl Drake, longtime SPI employees, operating the equipment.

The flood did considerable damage to some of the fills and culverts along the spur line. Joe Dillard was recruited by Bob Puett to take care of some of the reconstruction. Foresters are supposed to know something about engineering, surveying and road construction. Joe was a logical choice.

The high water had damaged a trestle near the Susanville Forest Products mill east of Highway 395, the main north-south route from Reno to Oregon. The trestle was located a mile or so from the SPI mill.

The flood waters had left debris around the pilings of the trestle; and Joe decided the log loader from the mill could yard the material from around them. He also decided the best way to get the loader to the site was to drive it there along the railroad tracks. The loader straddled the tracks just right, and they started bumping over the ties on the way to the trestle.

Joe watched it depart, jumped into his pickup, and headed for the job. As the loader approached the Highway 395 crossing, the crossing gates came down, the bells rang, and the red lights blinked on and off, just as they were supposed to do. Traffic stopped to watch the strange locomotive go down the tracks.

On the loader went, across the flat desert for several hundred feet past the highway to the trestle. They went to work; Joe setting chokers in the bottom of the gully. The loader towed the logs away, or picked up the smaller chunks and logs and carried them out of the creek bed.

After 15 or 20 minutes, the loader operator noticed traffic backed up on the highway. He could see the cars stopped in a long string all the way over the hill to the south.

"Joe, there must be a hell of a wreck on the highway," he yelled, "Look at the traffic jam over there."

Joe climbed out of the creek and took a

Long Valley Creek at flood, March 1986. Sloat mill in background. Middle Fork of Feather River out of sight beyond buildings.
Photo from Ron Voss collection.

Log loader used to ferry workers to Sloat sawmill during flood in 1986.
Photo from Ron Voss collection.

look. As far as he could see in both directions, cars, trucks, motor homes, and every conceivable vehicle were sitting idle. They had been there for some time, for drivers and passengers were standing in little knots, or walking around on the pavement talking about the traffic delay. However, Joe could not see a wreck.

Then it hit him - the crossing gates were still down. SPI had traffic backed up for over two miles in both directions. The loader had triggered the gates to come down, but not to go back up. The driver had paid no attention and, over the noise of the loader, had not heard the crossing bell continue to clang.

Joe ran for his pickup and headed for the crossing. His mind was racing. He radioed the office to make a telephone call to the Highway Patrol to tell them of the problem. As he neared the crossing, he could see a knot of drivers looking up and down the tracks for signs of a train. Joe knew he was in trouble.

He took a quick look at the steel box housing the controls for the gates. Even if he could open it, he did not know what to look for inside. No matter; it was secured with a big shiny padlock. He tested the gates; they were made of wood, but they were sturdy-looking affairs. He thought there might be a way to dismantle them without tearing them up. No such luck.

Joe Dillard is not a very big man, but he looks tough and wiry. At one time, he had been a bartender at the Keg in Arcata, where he also acted as bouncer when an occasional football player got too rowdy. In his younger years, he had tried bull riding on the rodeo circuit with some success.

The gates became a challenge to him. He got under one of them and lifted. It was heavy; but with a little extra effort, he got it high enough for a car to drive under. Immediately the first car took off; it had been there for 20 minutes or so by that time. The drivers behind ran for their vehicles, and one of the strings started to move.

Joe stood there like Samson holding the gate. He began to sweat. The heavy gate was biting into his shoulders; but the traffic would not pause long enough to allow him to let it down to rest. Joe began to yell for someone to stop the traffic.

Finally, his partner got the string stopped long enough for Joe to let the gate down. They decided their only chance was to get into the control box.

They had brought a toolbox with them in case they had loader troubles, and they quickly found a hacksaw. Joe went to work on the lock. After several more minutes of sweating, he had it cut in two. Inside was a mass of wires and a series of electrical relays. He could see one of them that looked like a solenoid jumping up and down in time to the clang-clang of the bell.

He grabbed a stick and shoved it between the contacts. Merciful silence descended on the scene; even the flashing red lights stopped. But the gates were still down.

About that time the Highway Patrol officer got to the scene to unsnarl the mess. With his help, they managed to find a couple of pieces of wood stout enough to prop the gates open, enabling traffic to move again. The officer waved the vehicles on while he lectured Joe about the problems he caused. Joe was to receive one more lecture before the incident was over.

The Western Pacific signal system evidently triggers an alert if there is something amiss with a traffic control device along the way. Joe shortly received a couple of visitors from the railroad. They wanted to know what caused all the commotion.

Joe patiently told his story, apologizing for the trouble SPI had caused. After he finished, the Western Pacific official told him of the charges to be filed against him. They included destroying company property, jeopardizing the safety of the public, and the most serious crime of all - it was a federal offense to sabotage a railroad crossing device.

Red became involved, explaining that Joe should not be prosecuted for several reasons, the most important being that SPI was a large customer of the Western Pacific.

Joe, however, would have to buy a new padlock. That was bad enough. But his worst punishment was listening to his fellow foresters tell and retell the story, and having

them embellish it with all kinds of details that were only partly correct. The **true** story is the one told here.

Some time later, Joe was presented with a foot-long section of model railroad track, fixed up to resemble his infamous crossing. It was complete with signal lights and gates, suitable for display in his office.

While Dillard was working as a section hand, the Forest Service declared the Northern spotted owl a "sensitive" species, in response to considerable pressure. Each owl was granted some 1,100 acres of old-growth forest in which to live and breed. The immediate effect on SPI was to eliminate 18,000 MBF of timber for Susanville, 6,000 MBF for Hayfork, and 16,000 MBF for CV. All of the affected timber was in timber sales already under contract.

I heard a talk given by irrepressible Anna Sparks, a Humboldt County Supervisor, to some of her constituents at Willow Creek shortly after the owl decision. At one point, Anna, somewhat wistfully, said, "I wish someone would give me 1,100 acres in which to breed." Of course, her remarks brought down the house.

With the pressures on the public timber supply more evident every day, SPI actively began to pursue the acquisition of timberland. In the summer of 1986, SPI bought some 2,000 acres of Trinity County timberland from Agnew Timber Products of Brookings, Oregon. Over 35,000 MBF of old-growth timber was growing on the parcel.

In the summer of 1986, SPI held its annual management meeting at Sun River, Oregon. I was again on the stump, giving the same talk as always. I was getting more strident each year, but could not stop.

The talk at Sun River went like this:

I have been giving this same talk since 1976. It's not because I like the subject that much, nor that it's easy to just revise last year's, I have to do it because I have a spot on the program. The points I always make are these:

Engine for Quincy Railroad, 1989.
Photo by author.

1. *Timber is scarce (artificially) and getting scarcer.*

2. *If you want to stay in business, get involved politically because "they" are taking our supply away.*

3. *Don't worry - we'll get our share because we are SPI.*

Let's look at last year. Here's how your sawmills were supplied with logs:

Redding (CV)	67,332 MBF	24.9% Public
Burney	61,938	45.0%
Hayfork	49,839	96.7%
Quincy	68,987	82.0%
Sloat	8,353	26.0%
Susanville	71,708	74.0%
Loyalton	55,632	86.0%
Arcata	61,834	34.3%
Total	445,616	61.4%

As our volume requirements go up, the government volumes sold go down. Last year, on the forests on which we work, the Forest Service sold 72,000 MBF less than they did the year before. You can see the future for timber sales does not look good.

You ask, why do we keep getting bigger while the timber base keeps shrinking? Are we nuts?

Let's look at recent occurrences:

*California has two things going on now, (1) fewer operators, and (2) conversion to a young-growth economy in some places. We are **not** getting competition from Diamond, Arcata Redwood, Simpson, Champion, International Paper, and to a lesser extent from LP, Schmidbauer, Collins, Eel River and a few more. I'm not sure why.*

The second point (young-growth) - we are buying young-growth logs from Champion, Fruit Growers, Santa Fe Pacific, Collins Pine, Beaty and Associates and others.

So far these two circumstances have taken up the slack for SPI's increased need for logs. This is no long-term solution.

***All** of you have to get going on the timber supply thing. Red has given full support and has been personally involved more than you realize. George Coulter at Quincy has done a great job in Plumas and Sierra Counties. The foresters have done well, especially Bruce Olsen, Ron Voss, Bill Banka, Tom Walz, Ron Hoover, and Dan Tomascheski. But where are the rest of you? I never hear from Dick Smith, Bob Puett, Gordie Amos, Jack Davies and others. Don't you people care?*

There's a group of us in every community in which we operate, trying to gain support from merchants, business people, and community leaders. It is nearly impossible to get them steamed up if they never see anyone but a forester trying to get their support. If you think you can't do it, or don't have time, take a lesson from George Coulter. I heard him give a short speech a few weeks ago that he was positive he could not make. He did a hell of a job and those efforts are far more impressive than listening to a polished politician. If you can't talk, at least do some personal arm twisting. Get going, we haven't got much time.

Now for the opportunities:

We must convert or prepare our mills for "small logs." We are o.k. at Burney and will be with the new facility planned for Anderson. As time goes on, we need to do the same thing in the Feather River country and on the Coast.

One thing that is encouraging is that we are planning the Anderson mill to fit the log supply, rather than the other way around. Normally, we would build a mill, then try to find logs that fit the mill. And Gordie, at Arcata, you will have to recognize that a sawmill can do just fine on something besides a #3 peeler over 30" in diameter. It just takes a little work.

The other opportunity lies with getting our timberland in a productive state. Red has committed a lot of money to this effort. Some of you don't like the results. We produce highly defective logs and

small logs that are hard to utilize. My advice is to look ahead, past your monthly statement. We are planning your future, and the progress is good. We are rehabilitating land that was abused by others in the past. We are releasing young trees and thinning others where appropriate.

The last opportunity is in timberland acquisition. We are one of the few California companies involved in acquisition, and not divestiture. We have recently purchased:

Tooby	*1,154 acres*
Kerr Ranch	*6,498 acres*
Agnew	*2,007 acres*

We are currently working on others. I hope we can continue to purchase timberland.

Finally, I am happy to report that the timber sales we were so concerned about because of price are mainly gone. We bought off 207 million board feet and the good owls took some more. We have a few sales to swallow at Feather River. Susanville is eating their way out, and so is Hayfork. Burney and CV are home free, and Arcata has only one sale to worry about. Company-wide, the problem of exorbitantly priced timber is largely behind us.

The rest of the meeting was upbeat, full of optimism for the future. Many, however, expressed worries for the timber supply problems ahead. The Polish Pope had to marry only two couples that evening.

The Quincy operation was in the middle of extensive remodeling. The power plant was undergoing reconstruction, and new computerized dry kilns were in operation. Three more were scheduled to come into production before the end of 1986.

Arcata began shipping 1" and 5/4" Selects to the Richfield remanufacturing plant in 1986. Under Gordie Amos, the mill also broke some production records, shipping almost 12,000 MBF of finished lumber in one month.

Over the Labor Day weekend, Arcata also installed a new computerized setworks on the headrig. As usual, no production was lost since the work was done in time to permit the mill to start up as scheduled after the three-day holiday. Dave Koskinen, an electronics specialist and an SPI employee, directed the installation. Red now accepted specialists as a necessary part of modernization, something that would have been impossible a few short years before.

The Millwork Division was doing well. The new plant at Richfield had been in production for a year. The plant had installed four new finger-joint machines. The new moulders, purchased from a German manufacturer, were setting records and producing excellent stock. Four of them were purchased for the Chico millwork plant.

In September 1986, SPI began looking at another acquisition. Paul Bunyan Lumber Co., with a sawmill and small cogen plant at Anderson, decided to sell out. The principal owner was Kenneth Walker, one of the last of an old lumber family still in the business. He asked for bid proposals.

The SPI foresters did their usual cruising job, descending on the timber tracts in force. The largest of the parcels adjoined Viola just above Shingletown. It supported considerable old-growth timber on high-site land. Some of the other tracts were scattered around Susanville and northeast of Burney, where timber growth was slower.

It was timberland well worth acquiring. Red got deeply involved with Tony Zanze at the Bank of America, and received a commitment for the necessary funding from them. He then opened a dialogue with Mr. Walker.

Ken Walker did not care for Red and SPI. Something had occurred during the time SPI was acquiring the Fruit Growers Supply Co. in Susanville that turned him off. Evidently John Crook and Red had denied him access over a rail spur which they had acquired with the purchase of Fruit Growers, a spur that Paul Bunyan had used for many years. Many lumbermen have long memories; Ken Walker was no exception.

Red, in his usual style, attempted to negotiate the purchase. At several points in his conversations with Ken Walker, he thought he had a deal. At the eleventh hour, everything fell apart, and Roseburg Lumber Co. was the successful bidder at a little over $100,000,000. Red was hurt and frustrated by the whole transaction. He felt SPI could have paid more than that for it; but he was trying to buy it for less.

The summaries for 1985 and 1986 showed operations mushrooming. By the end of 1985, lumber production for the year was 628,266 MBF. Gross sales were $242,572,000. Total assets were valued at $186,230,000. The company logged almost 23,000 MBF of fee timber.

By the end of 1986, lumber production had risen to 722,148,000 MBF. Gross sales were $298,000,000. Total assets were valued at $211,434,000. SPI had logged over 24,000 MBF of fee timber.

The cogeneration plants at Hayfork and Susanville were in operation, generating over $4,000,000 in income. Millwork sales were almost 30% of total sales. Capital improvements for 1986 were $30,655,858 which included:

Anderson sawmill	$ 2,815,000
Quincy & Sloat	10,706,000
Burney	10,500,000
Susanville	1,302,000

SPI had become quite large in the generation of electricity. The cogen operations are treated separately and are a story in themselves.

chapter forty seven

COGEN & THEN SOME

In January 1987, the Internal Revenue Service (IRS) finally settled with SPI on the status of income taxes for the years 1973 to 1982. Up until then, all of the ten years' returns were "open," meaning that the amounts paid were disputed by the IRS.

Each year, Dick Smith met with the IRS and argued forcefully that the numbers he reported were correct. IRS auditors spent days in the Arcata office, poring over the books, looking for mistakes, or Dick's faulty interpretations of the regulations. Dick Smith could be a formidable adversary when he made up his mind. He won more than he lost.

On some occasions, Don Riewerts got involved in the discussions, particularly in the earlier years. When the two of them got their heads together, I felt sorry for the IRS auditors. Even the IRS agents, who would arbitrate some of the disputes at their level, had a tough time with Smith and Riewerts.

I got involved in many of the timber valuation questions, particularly the computations for capital gains taxes. I hated the time of the year when the valuation process began. The research and computations took hours of tedious work. I could never understand how accountants could enjoy doing that kind of work hour after hour; nor could I understand how their minds worked to allow them to sit there indefinitely with one hand pounding on a calculator. I guessed their triumphs came when they won one against the IRS.

Dick celebrated when the last year's returns were settled. From the time I met him, his goal was to settle the cases. He always said he could not retire as long as there were "open years" with the IRS. No matter how hard he tried, he kept falling behind. Even if he settled one case, another would take its place at year-end. When it was all finally finished, he did seem ready to kick back and relax a little.

Also in January 1987, SPI bid on several parcels of timberland in Mendocino County owned by Collins Pine Co. Collins had owned the properties for many years, and some of the property still supported old-growth redwood and Douglas fir timber.

Since SPI did not saw redwood, it contacted Arcata Redwood for market prices for redwood logs. After considerable discussion, a joint bid was submitted for the properties.

SPI foresters and Jim Brown, Chief Forester for Arcata Redwood, discussed many times the problems associated with the purchase. Environmentalists were as thick as trees in Mendocino County. Many of them, the flower children of the 1960s, had moved there after leaving Berkeley and the Bay Area. By 1987, they were grown and far more sophisticated in their attacks on the country's institutions and systems.

Jim and the author were worried about the problems to be inherited by the successful bidders. One of the trees on the property had a name - a sure sign of trouble. It was called Big Red. These concerns were stated many times to Red, and to Burnett Henry, Arcata's President; to no avail, the joint bid was submitted on the properties anyway.

Perhaps the appraisals were conservative, or the concerns expressed to Red and Burnett Henry resulted in a conservative bid. In any event, Eel River Sawmills bought the timberland. Both forestry staffs gave sighs of relief.

Today, in 1991, Eel River is still trying to harvest some of the timber bought from Collins. They have been to court several times. They have had their harvest plans rejected by the state, and their loggers' equipment has been sabotaged. The problems for them never seem to end.

By the middle of the '80s, cogeneration had been a big part of SPI for quite a while. With the involvement of Ray Lowry, Dave Allward, and later Phil Heckenberg, the business flourished. The latter two, in turn, each bore the title of "Energy Czar" for the company.

Ray had become involved in the early years of cogen when, in 1978, the government passed a law called the "Public Utility Regulatory Policies Act" (PURPA). It was signed into law by Jimmy Carter.

The act was in response to the Kuwait oil embargo of 1973 when the price of a barrel of oil rose from $3 to $17 in one month. In 1978, there were other oil supply problems causing long lines at the gas pumps in America. The result was PURPA.

Under it, utilities were instructed to buy electricity from qualified facilities at avoided costs, that is, the amounts they would avoid paying by not burning their oil-fired, or natural gas plants. Ray immediately thought of the old generator at Susanville that produced electricity for the mill. He arranged for SPI to begin selling the surplus to PG&E.

Dave Allward was reassigned to cogen. He was placed in charge of improving the power plant at Susanville, and of building a plant at

Quincy. Ray Lowry was heavily involved also, dealing with PG&E and negotiating contracts for the sale of power.

In November 1983, Phil Heckenberg came to take over as Energy Czar. He was a Forest Products' graduate of Iowa State University, class of 1968. One of his first tasks was to take over the construction of the plant in Hayfork.

Phil explained the term "cogen" is derived from the process by which some of the steam originally produced for power generation is also used in the lumber manufacturing operation. In a normal steam-powered generating plant, the steam, after leaving the turbine, must be condensed before it can be recirculated to the boiler.

In a **real** cogen plant the steam, after leaving the turbine, is used for equipment operation, kiln drying, space heating, etc. before it is returned to the boiler. It can be diverted to these uses from several different stages in the turbine, depending on the pressure of the steam desired. The energy that normally would be used in the condensing process is reduced considerably as a result.

SPI's early plants were not **real** cogen plants in that sense. While the steam produced in them was used for both processes, it was not recirculated from the turbine to the other uses; it went directly there. The newer plants, like those later built at Burney and Quincy, were true cogen facilities. While not technically cogen plants, the older plants, under the language in PURPA, qualified as such.

Many of the old sawmills used to have their own electric generators. The old mill at Loyalton had one that was built in the early 1900s. The Susanville mill also boasted one that was built when it was owned by Fruit Growers Supply Co. The public utilities would not purchase the power developed by the sawmills at the time they were built, although in emergencies the mills would often supply their communities with power. The Quincy mill kept Quincy in electricity for several days during the 1986 flood.

With the passage of PURPA, the production of power opened new opportunities for

Sawmill complex at Susanville, 1987. Sawmill is at center, crane shed is round-roofed building in foreground. Old powerhouse is visible at upper right.

Photo by Mark Fator.

SPI. A market opened up for the by-products of lumber manufacture - bark, sawdust, slabs and edgings.

In the old days, such by-products were burned in tepee burners. Every mill had one. If not, the material formed a huge pile that usually caught fire. Even mills with burners developed big piles of ashes and clinkers that were difficult to dispose of. The pile usually included debris from the log decking area, mostly bark that had fallen off logs during handling.

Pulp mill needs for wood chips made the chipping of slabs and edgings possible, resulting in the demise of the tepee burner. But chips for pulp had to be free of bark, dirt and rocks, so there was still a pile of debris at most mills that grew in size each year. The one at Quincy in the early 1970s was named Mt. Novak in honor of the manager there. From the top of it, you could see the airport a couple of miles away.

Cogen gave an added dimension to the operators who had them. Red was one of the first to recognize their value. He got into the business very early and pursued it with vigor. He saw that the pulp mills would have competition for their purchase of wood chips, as the technology developed. He also could see that fuel could be made from the material the pulp mills would not take. Prices for both should stabilize.

These circumstances permitted the paving of log decking areas where bark and woody debris could be scooped up for the making of hog fuel. Such fuel had to be relatively free of rocks and dirt so it could go through the hog, where steel knives ground it up. Very dirty fuel would affect the operation of the boiler, as well as ruin the hog, so the paving of mill yards and cogen plant construction went hand in hand.

As mentioned earlier, Hayfork had a very old boiler located at the old planer site west of

Abandoned powerhouse at Loyalton, 1989.
Photo by author.

New cogen plant at Burney, 1987.
Photo by Mark Fator.

New cogen plant at Loyalton, 1989.
Photo by author.

town that provided steam for the kilns. In February 1984, SPI had begun the construction of a new cogen plant at Hayfork.

Atlantic Gulf Co. put up the boiler and piping. A contractor, Dale Rich, erected the fuel-handling structures and did most of the steel work. The new plant was essentially a "turnkey" facility when finished. It went on-line in December 1984.

By that time, the whole operation had been moved to the sawmill site east of town. The new cogen plant consisted of a new Zurn boiler, producing 110,000 pounds of steam per hour. It was connected to a Westinghouse 7.5-megawatt turbine generator. A separate small 1-megawatt back-pressure turbine produced low-pressure steam for the new dry kilns, while simultaneously producing electricity.

At about the same time (late 1984), Susanville began to build a new cogen facility. It came on-line in December 1986.

Construction of the new cogen facility at Burney began in April 1986. Consisting of a Riley boiler producing 200,000 pounds per-hour of steam, and a General Electric turbine, it went on-line in November of that year. It produced over 20 megawatts of electricity. Fuel came both from Burney and the mill at Central Valley.

Construction of a new cogen plant at Quincy got underway in early 1986 to replace the 3-megawatt plant built in 1983. Prior to that time, two boilers were required to run the Quincy complex: a small Kipper boiler for the dry kilns, and a larger Keeler boiler for the Allis Chalmers turbine generator. The new plant would be nearly identical to the one at Burney, producing 20 megawatts of power. It began to produce electricity in 1987.

The company went on to build one additional cogen plant at Loyalton. The story there is somewhat different, since the power was to be purchased by Sierra Pacific Power Co. (a Nevada public utility and no relation to SPI). Construction was to begin in June 1988. The plant would be nearly identical to those at Burney and Quincy, that is, 20-megawatt.

At that project, Phil Heckenberg and Ray Lowry became involved in a "dog fight from day one." During the permit process for the facility, local environmentalists appealed at several stages, expressing concerns about deterioration of air quality. Delay followed delay. At one stage, the Environmental Protection Agency stopped construction. Sierra Pacific Power Co. was actually better to deal with than PG&E, according to those in SPI who negotiated the agreements for the sale of electricity. It was not the Nevada utility's fault the delays in construction occurred.

Finally, in November 1989, the Loyalton plant began producing electricity. SPI was a substantial producer of elecricity by then, generating over 80 megawatts at the five locations.

The numerous construction projects spawned another important part of the company - its construction department. A large crew was needed for construction of the facility at Susanville, and a long-time employee, Bob Cummings, was recruited to manage the crew there. While most of the Hayfork cogen plant was built under contract, SPI employees did some of the work there, also.

Bob Stricklan, one of the original contractors at Hayfork, took over much of the work after Cummings left the company to go to Alaska. Stricklan's son, Bob Jr., who had worked for his father, later became an SPI employee. He ran SPI's fabricating shop at Anderson in one of the old Champion buildings, where many of the components of some of the projects were made. The crew did considerable work for the new Anderson sawmill and the Loyalton cogen from that location.

As SPI's construction projects continued to grow, the construction crew got quite large. It would become an important part of the expansions of the sawmill and millwork plants for the next several years.

The Anderson sawmill began producing lumber in August 1987. It was designed to produce 130,000 MBF per year, and to employ 110 persons. Dennis Gomez was very proud of the role he played in bringing the mill to production. Mark Emmerson, Red and Ida's youngest son, became the new manager for the Anderson Division, and Red was visibly proud of the appointment of Mark to the position.

A 265-ton P&H log crane towered over the Anderson mill yard. It added a very distinctive landmark to the Anderson skyline. The crane ran on two rails. The two legs were 175' apart,

and 105' high. The bridge on top spanned 300', enough to deck some 30,000 MBF of logs underneath.

The mill itself sported a 24' twin-band headrig, with an end-dogging overhead carriage. The mill was completely computerized. An "optimizing edger" was located behind the headrig. A horizontal resaw received the larger cuts from the headrig, and the center cant from it went to a double-arbor edger. The operation, from the log crane through the mill, to the lumber stacker, was "state of the art" from start to finish.

Dave Koskinen designed and programmed the sophisticated computer systems for the new mill. The computer scans each log before it is positioned for dogging by the overhead carriage. The hydraulic pistons that hold the log in position can be adjusted within 1/1000th of an inch by the computer to maximize the quantity and quality of the lumber to be cut from it.

Bruce Olsen was promoted to the position of Timber Manager for the new division under Mark Emmerson. He moved from Quincy where he had been Ron Voss's assistant, and went to work at Anderson in March 1987.

Bruce was born in southern California in 1948. He graduated from Crescenta Valley High in 1966 and went to Glendale College. After service in the Navy, working on the surveying crew for the City of Glendale, and attending Chico State, he received his degree in Biology in 1973. He spent two summers with the Forest Service on the Shasta Trinity Forest during school, then went to the Oregon Department of Forestry at Tillamook, Oregon.

SPI, after acquiring Publisher's, learned of Bruce Olsen when searching for a surveyor-engineer for the Curl Ridge surveying project. By that time, Bruce had gone to work for a surveyor in Tillamook, where he heard about SPI's job opening. He came to SPI in August 1979, worked for the Timber Department for over three years, then went to Quincy to help Ron Voss.

California was in the early years of what was to turn out to be an extended drought.

Turbine and generator at Burney cogen plant, 1987. Photo by Mark Fator.

There had been periods of drought before, resulting in reduced water for agriculture and fears that those in southern California would migrate northward; but the dry years, beginning in 1986, were different.

Trees, stressed by the lack of water, began to die. This had occurred before, but these were in unprecedented numbers. The Tahoe basin was especially hit hard. Salvage of the dead trees was delayed as environmentalists appealed timber sales for various reasons, most of which made little sense to anyone except to them.

Then on August 30, 1987, a series of dry lightning storms struck northern California. Fires were started in every National Forest, burning out of control for days. Fire crews came from far and wide to try to control them. To no avail; California was on fire.

More than 1,000 lightning strikes were recorded on the Shasta-Trinity National Forest that Sunday. Within minutes the southwest part of the forest was burning. Logging crews were called to help the Federal and State agencies fight the fires.

Red McKenzie, who was the "main" logger at Hayfork, was working on the Yolla Bolla Ranger District when the lightning storm struck. Thirty-six of the strikes were on that District. Red did not wait for instructions; he shut down the logging, gathered the crew and his equipment, and headed for the nearest fire. By the end of the next day, they had fought eight of the fires to a standstill, having worked all night. None of the fires covered more than 16 acres.

By September 3rd, several fires on the Hayfork District began burning together, threatening the town of Hayfork. McKenzie's crews, meanwhile, had gone to the Hyampom area, west of Hayfork, to tackle a number of fires burning there. They headed back to the Tule Creek drainage southwest of Hayfork, again without waiting for instructions from the Feds. They began to build fireline.

Red and his wife Judy are special people. They knew their livelihood depended upon the forest surrounding the Hayfork valley. More than that, they loved the beauty of the country. It was **their** country, their home, that was threatened. They could not sit idly by while the whole country burned up.

In a short time, McKenzie's crew had scratched out a line on the ridges around the Tule Creek watershed. By that time, they had been without sleep for days. Judy manned the radio system, keeping track of what was going on, ordering fuel, supplies and lunches and hauling them to the crews. Then controversy erupted.

The Forest Service had assumed command of all the fires burning on the Hayfork District. While the local Ranger, Dave Wickwire, was initially in charge of the fires on his District, he had been relegated to a minor role when the "Incident Commander" assumed control.

The government had set up an organization similar to a military operation to handle catastrophes. As always, they spent days, and millions of dollars, readying their forces for the day when they would be needed. Labor Day 1987 was one of the days.

They took over the Hayfork fairgrounds, set up "ready-rooms," dormitories, latrines, intelligence equipment, kitchens and all of the support systems armies usually require. Crews from all over the United States began to arrive. There were hotshot fire fighters from Arizona and veteran crews from Idaho. Even workers from Alabama showed up to plan their assault.

The Commander was a competent individual from the Boise Fire Center. His map room would do a General proud. He was ready to call in air strikes from the Redding airport. One problem, though, he could not find the fire.

An atmospheric inversion moved in, damping the spread of the fire. That was a blessing. But the smoke from the smoldering fires would not lift. People coughed their way to work in the morning. Air power was useless, and the new equipment used aerial photography to find, and map, where the fires were. The Commander was reluctant to send crews to the field without knowing where the fires were, worrying that they might become trapped if the inversion lifted and the fire blew up. He should have asked Red McKenzie

where the fire was, he knew; or Dave Wickwire, who had to stay in his Ranger Station while his District burned up.

I arrived at the Hayfork sawmill with several SPI foresters. We decided to assume some responsibility for saving the town, and the sawmill, if the need arose. Logging equipment from SPI loggers at CV and Arcata were put on stand-by. The Hayfork mill shut down, and 40 of the crew volunteered to help McKenzie on the lines at Tule Creek just outside of town.

Jerry Gromacki assumed responsibility for Bill Schmitt's crews and equipment. Schmitt was CV's main logger. Bruce Olsen and Ron Hoover headed to the woods to scout where the fires were the hottest. Tom Walz and Dan Brummer were very familiar with the Hayfork District, having worked there for several years. They did the same, and reported the fires were easy to find. Tom Nelson, Dan Tomascheski, Jim Ostrowski, Steve Gromacki and Bill Bailey, from SPI's Timber Division, came to Hayfork to work on the lines. Gary Blanc, controller for the division, spent hours on the fire lines. Jim McCollum of J & K Logging and his son, Keith, had much of their logging equipment and crews committed to the fires.

At one point, I attempted to volunteer the intelligence the SPI people had gathered to the command center. I had driven some of the roads to find fires burning alongside them. Relations became strained as the information we had was rebuffed or ignored. Soon SPI foresters were not welcome at the fairgrounds. The information was accurate; but it did not fit the planning that had gone into the Incident Command system.

A problem surfaced involving the protection of homes and other structures that had been built in rural type subdivisions scattered around the forest. The agencies committed the majority of their equipment and manpower to saving the threatened structures. Wide firelines were built and backfires set, sometimes several miles distant, to fireproof those areas. The locals claimed there was more of the forest burned on purpose than there was accidentally.

New cogen plant at Quincy, 1989.
Photo by author.

As the weather moderated, air power became available. Finally, ground crews were released to fight the larger fires. Many of the fires had grown together by that time; and after several weeks, many parts of the fires were still unmanned. They were left to burn themselves out in the rocks.

McKenzie and his crew became a symbol for all the SPI employees and the townsfolk at Hayfork. He had, indeed, saved the Tule Creek drainage. It was an island of green in a blackened forest. The rest of the forest was not so lucky.

When it was over, the Shasta-Trinity had lost over 230,000 MBF of timber, most of it on the Hayfork District. Most of the fires were still burning inside the firelines, and would do so until the winter rains began. McKenzie and his crew got very little rest. Before the smoke cleared, they were hauling burned logs to the mill.

A day after the crews were released to go back to their normal work schedule, I overheard a conversation on the SPI radio system. A load of logs heading for the mill had caught fire and was burning briskly in the wind caused by the movement of the truck. Salvage had begun so quickly after the burns that some of the logs were still smoldering when loaded aboard trucks. That could have been a disaster, had the log smoldered long enough without detection and been placed in the mill's log deck.

Several days later, SPI shut down the Hayfork mill for several hours between the day and night shifts to honor those who did so much to save as much of the forest as they could. Red and Judy McKenzie were singled out for their contributions to the effort and their dedication during the catastrophe. At the fairgrounds, where the Incident Commander had set up shop, Red and Judy were presented with special T-shirts. Emblazoned on the front were red flames with the words **McKenzie's Hotshots** above and below. One of the T-shirts was presented to each of the SPI employees who had volunteered for duty with Red and Judy.

The Hayfork District would never be the same again. Since much of the wood for the Hayfork mill came from this District, and significant amounts for CV and Anderson too, SPI became intimately involved with the salvage of the burned timber.

Some of the fires had burned portions of several areas that were un-roaded. Environmentalists wanted those areas to remain un-roaded, claiming they were suitable for wilderness. When the Forest Service proposed removing some of the dead timber, they objected. All kinds of subterfuges were used to stop the salvage. Delay followed delay, until the Forest Service prepared lengthy and detailed environmental impact statements (EIS) instead of the shorter environmental assessments (EA). That did not work either; those were appealed. Meanwhile, the trees rotted on the stump.

One of the timber sales involved over 50,000 MBF of timber. After listening to the comments from Sierra Club, Wilderness Society, Audubon Society, Northcoast Environmental Center, and a local environmental leader Joe Bower, the Forest Service reduced the volume of timber in the offering to 18,000 MBF. The rest would be left to rot.

SPI bid on the timber sale; and after being the successful bidder, prepared to log it. More appeals were filed. Shortly after the sale, an injunction was filed in court to stop the harvest. The Forest Service was sued, but SPI filed a brief as an affected party. Years of litigation would follow. The timber, in 1991, still stands on the hillsides making homes for insects, worms, and birds, instead of people.

I became thoroughly discouraged with our court system and government procedures during the litigation. Being naive, I thought that judges were independent thinkers, who carefully listened to arguments and made up their minds based on the law and the rights of the litigants. I learned that is not necessarily so.

Judge Karlton sits on the bench in Sacramento District Court. As the "head judge," he assigns the cases to one of several fellow judges. He keeps for himself the cases he wishes to hear. SPI's case came before him.

Environmental lawyers know the judge to be sympathetic to their views and try to get their cases tried before him. He will pick the cases that are important to him. I was told by several attorneys that Karlton was a member of the Sierra Club in earlier times, and did research for their attorneys. I was also told that his decisions in environmental cases were predictable and that, early in a trial, he always seemed to be on the opposite side of the one where he truly was.

On the first day of the trial, I sat in the courtroom, listening to the judge telling the Wilderness Society attorneys about the defects in their filings. He was quite blunt and lectured them at length.

When it was time for the Forest Service to present its case, he was polite and sympathetic to the Forest Service attorneys. He was quite complimentary to Dave Dun, SPI's attorney, too. I was encouraged. After the session was over, I was warned that that was the usual performance from the judge.

The assessment was correct. After weeks of briefings, Judge Karlton rendered his decision. In it, he castigated the Forest Service for

Completely computerized, twin-band head rig installed in new Anderson sawmill.
Photo from SPI archives.

not preparing a plan for the South Fork of the Trinity River, detailing how it would be managed. He described in convoluted legal reasoning why he made the decision, citing the Wild and Scenic Rivers Act, and the differences of the sections of rivers designated under state procedures and federal procedures. It appeared to me that he had made up his mind long ago, and was reaching hard for law to justify the way he felt.

The dead timber to be salvaged was a long way from the river that Judge Karlton was worried about. I suggested to our attorneys that we offer to take the judge on a trip to see for himself what the area looked like.

"No deal," they said, "Judges don't do that except on TV. The system doesn't work that way. He makes his judgments based on the testimony presented in his court."

The judge was more inclined to believe

P. & H. 256-ton Porta-Crane for decking logs and feeding the Anderson sawmill.
Photo from SPI archives.

the testimony of those he thought had no economic interest in the case. Since SPI would suffer economic harm if the timber was not available, testimony from its experts was tainted in the court's eyes. To me, that was another reason the system was defective. In a free enterprise system, I thought a person who had an economic interest had a right to speak to protect his interests, and that such testimony was accepted on a par with those who do not have a **perceived** economic interest. I learned otherwise.

I also learned that environmentalists **do** have an economic interest in the cases they bring to court, even though they are perceived as not. Their attorneys, club officers and staff persons are not all volunteers. They get paid only if the pot is kept boiling. Many of them live on grant money from government and private sources. The issues about which they argue must be kept in the public eye for them to succeed in procuring funds.

The attorneys had been right all along; the outcome was predictable. The judge stopped the sale.

More appeals followed, this time on the part of the Forest Service and SPI. Time was not on SPI's side, however, as the timber continued to deteriorate. I retired before the last appeal was filed, thoroughly disillusioned with the system.

Going back to mid-year of 1987, a set of circumstances began that would have profound effects on SPI. The largest timberland acquisition in its history would get underway. The story of that purchase will be described later.

By the end of 1987, SPI had produced 796,948 MBF of lumber, of which over 9,000 MBF had come from the new Anderson sawmill. Sales amounted to $371,793,000. Total assets were valued at $247,986,000. There were four cogen plants operating, bringing in over $13,000,000 for the year. Capital improvements were valued at $23,662,000, of which Anderson took $11,653,000.

The plants and support facilities were in place at year-end, so that emphasis could be placed on the acquisition of timber and timberland. Red's timing again was impeccable.

chapter forty eight

THE SANTA FE I

Before the turn of this century, the Southern Pacific Railroad had received alternate square miles of land for 24 miles on each side of its proposed rail line. Many people today think the grant was a gift of public land - their land - and a big giveaway. People of that day wondered what the railroad would do with so many miles of worthless land on which they would have to pay taxes.

Even the "gift" was not without strings attached. Among them, the railroad would have to transport the government's goods in time of national emergency at reduced rates. Of course, they also had to construct and run a railroad.

The grants **were** a way to get a portion of the huge public domain into private hands. Over the years, much of the land received by the railroads was actually sold off; but in California, the Southern Pacific kept a considerable part of the whole. They formed the Southern Pacific Land Company to manage the land.

When I first came to California in 1957, I got to know their people in the San Francisco head office and at Grass Valley, one of their district offices. In a short time, I considered District Forester Leon Sanford and his assistant, Chuck Carter, to be close friends of mine.

Southern Pacific sold timber from their timberlands, putting the offerings up for bid.

Their style of management was to harvest trees very conservatively, mostly in partial cuts, and utilizing tractor logging even on ground that was quite steep.

When I worked for Tahoe Timber Co. in Reno, Nevada, we bought timber from them. Foresters on their small staff marked the trees to be cut. As their sale program got larger, they were unable to keep up with the amount of work, so they contracted timber marking and cruising to outside consultants.

Ron Voss and I took on some of the work, thinking it would save us from cruising the sales in which we were interested. Southern Pacific paid Tahoe Timber Co. 35 cents per MBF for marking and cruising the timber. The company then purchased most of the sales that we marked.

During that time, we became well-acquainted with their Chief Forester, Kermit Cuff, and the head of the land company, Louis Frandsen. Frandsen would visit Reno occasionally to meet with our manager, Vic Clark, and to have a couple of Gibsons with lunch, while discussing their timber program.

Sometime in the 1970s, Southern Pacific Land Co. moved their main office to Redding. They became the Santa Fe Pacific Timber Co. upon the merger of the Santa Fe and the Southern Pacific. Vice President Bill Herbert managed the timber company with the aid of a very competent staff. Bob Muir became the Chief Forester. Under their leadership, the staff expanded to include some new foresters who were thoroughly versed in forestry computer applications.

They developed a sophisticated Geographic Information System (GIS), and began to intensively manage their timberlands. They were offering in excess of 200,000 MBF of timber for sale every year; and SPI was the largest single purchaser of their timber, averaging over 60% of the total. By that time, Leon Sanford had retired, and Chuck Carter had moved to Redding.

Several district offices had been established years ago by the old Southern Pacific. In addition to the one at Grass Valley, there were offices at Mt. Shasta, Weaverville, and a small one at Redding. A staff of foresters and support personnel were at each.

On June 30, 1987, the Santa Fe Southern Pacific Corp., parent of the timber company, announced the Santa Fe Pacific Timber Co. was for sale. Also for sale was the Santa Fe Transportation Co., three pipe lines, and Bankers Leasing and Financial Corp.

The timberlands, about 522,000 acres, were located in nine northern California counties:

Trinity	162,300 acres
Placer	17,500
Shasta	92,000
Butte	6,900
Siskiyou	166,500
El Dorado	5,000
Nevada	48,000
Plumas	1,600
Sierra	21,000

The Santa Fe hoped to have a buyer before "the end of the year." Robert Slocum of the American Forest Council, an industry trade association, was quoted as saying, "Right now it's probably going to be difficult to move." He noted there were already eight million acres of the timber industry's 68.8 million acres in the U. S. for sale.

Mark Rogers, a Prudential-Bache Securities Vice President, noted that "nobody pops into mind" as a potential buyer. He also said, "There's been a lot of timber for sale in the west for several years and it's still for sale."

An immediate gag order was placed on all Santa Fe employees, while a prospectus and other information describing the sale procedures were prepared. If no one was interested in the purchase, as the media was reporting, there were strange goings-on at SPI.

Even though SPI was in the midst of large construction program requiring substantial sums of money, Red immediately began to discuss ways of financing the purchase of Santa Fe. One of his first calls was to Tony Zanze, at the Bank of America (B of A).

By that time, Tony was a Vice President and Manager of the Forest Products Group. He had known Red and Curly Emmerson since 1972 when he had worked under Frank Keene in the Forest Products Group. He did not know at the time that he would take over Frank's job in July 1977, and go on to become an important part of the SPI expansion.

Tony grew up in Sacramento, attending local schools through high school. He received a B.S. in History from the University of San Francisco in 1952. After a stint in Germany in the Army, he came back to California and went to work at the B of A.

Late in 1961, Tony went to Washington, D.C., where the Bank had opened an office. Tony went to night school there, studying economics and business. In September 1965, he was transferred back to San Francisco, where he was assigned to the office of Rudy Peterson, the B of A President. He was to spend the next four years in that position.

One of Tony's first assignments was to research and recommend ways to keep good young people working for the Bank. He became a trouble-shooter for the President, where he attracted the attention of Frank Keene. He joined Frank's group in September 1970.

When the call from Red came, Tony knew of the impending sale of the Santa Fe. In fact, he and Red had discussed the possible sale before the Santa Fe publicly announced it. It was different after the announcement, though - the discussions became very serious.

The impending sale became **the** topic of

discussion among the foresters at SPI, too. Upper management became involved in daily conversations about whether SPI could handle such an acquisition or not. Red questioned the author repeatedly, expecting responses, even though no one had sufficient information with which to give intelligent answers.

A typical conversation would go like this:

"The Santa Fe has over 520,000 acres. Is that pretty good timberland, Bud?" he would ask.

"Some of it is excellent timberland, especially around Weaverville," I would reply.

The next question would be, "How much do you think you could log from the property?"

"You mean in one year, or forever?" I'd ask.

"Both," he'd say.

"Well the Santa Fe is cutting over 200 million every year. They seem to know what they're doing. Since I don't know their inventory, growth rates, or anything else, that's probably a pretty good place to start," I'd reply.

He would whip out an envelope and a ballpoint pen, do some quick calculations on the back of the envelope, then say with a far-away look, "I think we can handle it. What do you think?"

"Hell, Red, I don't know. Where are you going to get that kind of money? And one of the key questions is are you willing to sell logs like they do?"

"I hate to sell logs; you know that. Why would we want to sell them?"

"Some of their timber is on the Klamath River, close to Happy Camp. That's a long ways from CV. Some of it is way down there, southwest of Lake Tahoe, too. Besides we have commitments for next year, like a few sales on our MSEP."

By that time, Red's eyes would have glazed over. He had tuned me out. He was scheming and worrying about who might be able to outbid SPI when the bid date came. I was wondering what sawmill he would want to buy next, or which one he would want to modify so it would cut more logs. I was also wondering how to cruise 520,000 acres in a few weeks.

Soon the Santa Fe announced they would put on a "show and tell" for the prospective purchasers. Those who were selected would receive the same type of information, and would be permitted to question selected members of the Santa Fe staff. Maps, inventory figures, personnel resumes, and similar information would be provided.

Dan Tomascheski and I discussed getting a jump on the competition. We felt that Roseburg Forest Products, our neighbors in Anderson and Weed, would be hot after the Santa Fe. They were financially strong and very competent. We worried more about them than any of the others. For one thing, they might not sell logs the same way the Santa Fe did. In that event, SPI would be deprived of the 120,000 MBF, or more, that it purchased annually from the Santa Fe.

Dan and I requisitioned the helicopter. Red presented no problem this time. He was eager to see us get started on assessing the worth of the timberlands. Since there were no sawmills to go with the timberland, he did not have to worry about what to do with them. While that was an advantage, I felt he might feel a little left out, not having the stimulus of criticizing a competitor's operations, and planning how they might fit into SPI's operations.

Dan and I had obtained maps on which we were able to put the Santa Fe ownership. Since their "official" maps were not yet available, we did the best we could with the information we had, which was considerable. We took off with the maps to see what we could find.

The timberlands had been managed for many years. They were easy to spot from the air. The alternate sections, in most cases, belonged to the Forest Service. Santa Fe, until quite recently, believed in tractor logging. Other owners, including the Forest Service, had begun cable logging several years before the Santa Fe began to do so.

Tractor logging requires many more miles of road than does cable logging; the roads are usually placed down-slope from the unit to be logged. Tractors skid logs downhill quite efficiently, but not uphill. Cable machines are better yarding logs uphill to avoid hang-ups when logs roll sideways and get hooked on stumps or other obstructions. For cable logging, the roads are usually built on ridges, spur ridges, or at least up-slope from the cutting units.

After several hours in the air, Dan and I could readily pick out the Santa Fe sections. It was even quite simple to pick out where the property corners lay on each parcel.

After the first day of flying, we discussed a systematic method of looking at the ownership to assess whether we should spend additional time and money to cruise it. We designed a one-page form that could be filled out while flying each section. It had a place to designate the parcel by section, broad timber type and major species, percent roaded, percent old growth vs. young growth, estimated volume of merchantable timber on the section, and a place for remarks.

We began using a three-man crew in the helicopter. One on each side in the back seat, Tom Nelson and Dan, would do the assessment, using the maps, and speaking into the intercom to the man in the front, who would fill out the form. As the man in the front seat, I would write and help navigate, telling the pilot where to turn, and pointing out topographic features to help guide him.

We began again to fly the areas. The job was mind-boggling; 520,000 acres covers a tremendous area. For several days, we flew in squares, identifying each corner of a parcel, flying down each property line, then back to the beginning. We three foresters became tired and peevish, glad to see darkness descending each evening. The data began to mount.

At the same time, I called several SPI foresters and asked them to inspect several well-roaded Santa Fe sections from the ground. I asked them to provide the same information on each section we were gathering from the air. I did not tell them what we were going to do with it.

Initially, we were quite discouraged with what we found. We started on some scattered parcels close to Redding, then went up the Sacramento River canyon to the Klamath River area. There is a great deal of brush, rocks and low-site ground in some of those areas. It would be difficult to grow successive crops of trees on some of them.

Red was eager for information. He could not wait to question us about what we were finding. We told him it wasn't looking good. After the first few days, he was becoming discouraged, too. But he was still worried that a competitor would cut SPI out of a significant volume of logs every year.

Then we got to the Weaverville District. Our discouragement changed to delight. There we found timberland that any forester would be proud to manage. There was a lot of steep, rocky ground, too, but there were acres and acres of high-site forest land. Much of it was well-stocked with young timber and there were still old-growth trees standing in areas that had been treated under a "high risk" logging system. The trees that were not expected to live very much longer had been removed.

From there, we went to the McCloud "flats" east and southeast of Mt. Shasta. It was the same story: well-managed timberlands were growing substantial volumes of wood. There were many acres of well-tended plantations. While the alternate Forest Service sections supported some old growth, some of it was dying or being attacked by insects. The Santa Fe properties appeared as though someone was caring for them. I gained a lot of respect for their foresters after those initial inspections.

After compiling the information gathered from the air, we compared the results to that obtained from the ground by Tom Walz, Ron Voss and the others. The estimates of merchantable volumes of timber matched well. We were in business.

With the news that the timberlands looked good and supported large amounts of merchantable timber, Red regained his enthusiasm. He and Ida, some time before, had become close friends with Santa Fe's Bill Herbert and his wife, Marjorie. Red began to pester Bill for information. He asked me to do the same with the friends I knew in the Santa Fe.

Bill Herbert was courteous and friendly, and so were the others. But they were professional people who played by the rules laid down for them. We found out very little that was not already known, or was not available to everyone. Even though they were speaking with a prospective purchaser for whom they might work one day, they did not break the rules.

Finally, we attended the show-and-tell session held in the Santa Fe office at Redding. Salomon Brothers had been hired by the Santa Fe to advise them during the sale process. They were there to assure the public that "due diligence" was being observed by Santa Fe management. They attended all of the meetings to make sure their recommendations were observed. Many of the reports carried captions evidencing their approval.

Bill Herbert ran the show, having given speaking parts to a number of those on his staff. Their computer system was exhibited with pride; they had invested well over $1,000,000 in it. The programs had been largely designed by Stu Smith, Art Stackhouse, Tom Engstrom and Dean Angelides of their staff. A thick book displayed their timber inventories; another showed qualifications and experience of all the employees. And there were maps, maps, maps. There were charts generated by their computer showing age classes of the timber, growth rates, percentage of species, all by districts and by region. There was so much information presented it was impossible to digest it all.

We later learned the wealth of information, visual aids, and lengthy reports were similar to those regularly prepared for Bill Herbert to take back to Chicago for Santa Fe management meetings. Since the emphasis for the Santa Fe was not on timber, but on running a transportation system, Mr. Herbert had to convince railroad people what he needed from time to time. The displays must have impressed the Chicago office.

The SPI foresters expressed envy of the Santa Fe foresters with all the tools at their disposal. We had waited in line to get our timber cruise computations on the company computer. The Santa Fe foresters had a computer work station on their desks, with a staff of foresters who were computer experts setting up the programs. One good feature of the show-and-tell - Red had to sit still long enough to watch and listen to the features of such a system. It would have taken us perhaps ten years to get him to see the wisdom of using

such advanced systems for SPI's own work.

With the exhibition behind us, we designed a cruise for the entire ownership. Tom Nelson was particularly helpful in designing it, as was Dan Tomascheski. Gary Blanc, a corporate accountant from the Redding office, became expert in getting the data put together and in running pro forma statements after it was all over.

Field work consisted of a cluster of three circular plots placed diagonally through the center of each section, with the middle plot placed on the center. Using the data given to us by the Santa Fe, we concentrated our work on those management units that contained the most timber volume, thus the most value. We gave assignments to each SPI forester and went to work.

Western Timber Services, Kleiner's company, helped with the field work. They cruised a major portion of the Tahoe District, and helped finish up on the Weaverville District.

I received the usual "old man's ground" assignment on the McCloud flats. With the timber-type maps from the Santa Fe, it was easy to find the approximate location of the center of each section by scaling off the distance from a bend in a road, or a creek crossing, etc. My first section was flat, much of it being a plantation of trees about head high. There were a few "stringers" of young timber of merchantable size. It appeared that I had, indeed, gotten old man's ground.

The second section was nearly as easy, but difficult to get to. It required a long hike to get to the starting point. It was still great going.

The third one was a different story. It was only about a quarter of a mile from a road to the edge of the section, but from there it was all downhill. It was a substantial hill, but the problem was brush. It was head high, and mostly tanoak. After a quarter-mile of that, the brush turned into a Knobcone pine thicket. For the rest of the day, I thrashed around in Knobcone, sometimes finding a tree large enough to measure, but most of the time trying to keep my shirt and pants from being torn to ribbons. Part of the day was spent on hands and knees. Foresters do not pace well on hands and knees.

After finishing, I had to go uphill through the same vegetation. The whole section was the same. I was sure the old man's ground graciously assigned to me was the worst section the Santa Fe owned. I hoped someday it would become a plantation of young trees. Perhaps then, while standing up, I could visit it to see what the ground looked like.

By the time the fires on the Labor Day weekend were out of control, the Santa Fe cruising project was nearly finished, and we were in the midst of doing the computations for the appraisal. Gary Blanc was spending most of his time running through different scenarios, showing what would occur if lumber prices moved either up or down, and pro-

jecting how SPI might amortize various, suggested purchase prices.

We kept track of the locations of the fires in relation to Santa Fe's land. There were only a few lightning strikes on them, and their foresters and loggers attacked them early. Jim Nile, their Government Affairs Manager, named their timberland "the asbestos forest." They lost very little.

Red was in daily huddles with Dick Smith and personnel from the B of A. After the initial shock wore off, Ron Stevens accepted the prospect of SPI taking on more debt. He told me many times that he had never seen "the Old Man" so enthusiastic about an impending acquisition. He just hoped someone would "tone him down a little," meaning me. There probably was no use trying.

chapter forty nine

THE SANTA FE II

When the cruise of the 520,000 acres was finished and all the figures were in, we adjusted the merchantable volumes downward for timber that would probably never be harvested for various reasons. The Santa Fe owned timber in streamside zones, in recreation areas, alongside mountain lakes, and on mountain tops. There were acres and acres of granite ridges with small patches of trees scattered among the crags, especially north of Donner Summit. The volume of merchantable timber was almost four billion board feet.

Red was asking the same questions as before. Now, though, we had hard data with which to answer them. The numbers were so large, he needed a bigger envelope to scratch out various options with his ballpoint pen.

I kept telling Red I thought that, while the total volume of timber was important, it really did not make much difference whether there was three, four or five billion feet out there. If SPI were allowed to manage the property correctly, it could produce a lot of timber forever. That certainly was enough time in which to pay for it. The growth, again if managed correctly, would at least pay part of the interest. The key was not to cut the growing stock, but to harvest the amount that would help repay the debt. There was certainly enough inventory to do that.

The B of A became an important member of the team pursuing the acquisition. Tony Zanze had become acquainted with Rob Krebs, President of the Santa Fe, the parent of the Santa Fe Pacific Timber Co. On May 1, 1987, prior to the public announcement of the impending sale, he arranged a meeting in Chicago with Krebs, a Santa Fe Vice-President Fred Schulte, and Red Emmerson.

Red and Ida flew to Chicago. Tony, Red, Rob Krebs and Fred Schulte met in the morning to discuss the pending sale, after which Ida joined Tony and Red for lunch. The purpose of the meeting was for Krebs and Schulte to meet the owner of SPI, and to give them the flavor of the family operation it was.

Tony reports that Ida "definitely was a member of the SPI team." She always did a "good job of entertaining Red's business associates." Tony says also, "Red sold SPI to Rob Krebs and Fred Schulte."

Tony Zanze did his best to convince them that SPI could finance the acquisition, and could probably pay more for it than any other prospective purchaser. He knew that was dangerous ground, because it was not wise to raise Krebs's expectations too high, then have his hopes dashed if Red decided to offer less than Krebs expected. But it was important for the Santa Fe to know that the B of A stood squarely behind Red and SPI.

Tony backed SPI at the B of A, too. He took the position with the Board of Directors that Red Emmerson was merely buying his inventory of raw materials for the nine sawmills he owned. It was not a leveraged buyout

Red and Ida on rare vacation in 1987. Photo from Ida Emmerson collection.
Photographer unknown.

(LBO) similar to those that were occurring at the time. Instead of selling off many of the assets to pay for the acquisition, SPI was going to utilize the wood in its own operations. Of course, the net worth of the company, the commitment of the Emmersons and, most of all, their long history of paying off debts early did a lot to "sell" the company.

Later, Tony announced to Red that the Bank would guarantee him up to $500,000,000 if he needed it. He cautioned him not to try to "low ball" his bid as he had done on the Paul Bunyan bid earlier. If he truly wanted to purchase the Santa Fe, he would have to figure out what he could pay for it and go with that number. With the pressures to reduce government timber sales, it was important for SPI to be the top bidder if the company wanted to proceed at its current level of production.

Red must have been proud and a little uneasy about having a half-billion dollars available to him. This was the same person who had arrived in California in 1948, with no money and a 1937 yellow convertible. It was also the same person who had fried hamburgers in his room to earn a little extra money, and had been expelled from the Academy just before he was to graduate from high school.

He had survived all of the negative things that had happened to him. He had adapted to the risk-taking that was required for success in the lumber business; but this was different. He was thinking in terms of hundreds of millions of dollars. He could easily adapt to that, too; it was the paying-back part that concerned him. He could compute the interest he would owe by the minute, instead of by the year or by the month.

Tony Zanze says the commitment was the largest, single real estate transaction in terms of acreage the B of A had ever financed. The only real estate transaction that was larger in value was the sale of the B of A building itself in San Francisco.

A short time later, Black Monday hit. The stock market took an historic plunge. Tony Zanze nearly had a heart attack. The B of A was on the hook for $500,000,000, and he could not back out.

Tony, meanwhile, went to work to lay off

as much of the debt as he felt was wise. The reason was not Black Monday; this is the way most large transactions are structured. He was like a bookie spreading his bets around to reduce the risk. By invitation, he asked ten other banks if they were interested in participating in the transaction. He picked the invitees. There was no problem with them. Tony says he did not have to "sell the deal at all." The banks were eager to join the B of A and SPI in the proposed venture.

The rate of interest was set at the B of A "reference rate," plus a small fraction of one percent. From that time on, the rate the other banks charged was set, and B of A would receive a small annual fee for putting the consortium together and for managing the transaction.

The participating banks were:

Bank of America
Irving Trust Co.
Barclay's Bank
North Carolina National Bank
Chase Manhattan Bank
Rainier National Bank
Bank of California
Seattle-First National Bank
First National Bank of Chicago
Societe Generale
Canadian Imperial Bank of Commerce

I attended several meetings with B of A people. Without Gary Blanc and his computerized pro formas, SPI might still be trying to convince the lenders of the wisdom of the purchase. Gary travelled several times to San Francisco to work jointly with Tony Zanze and John Cullison of the B of A, setting up various projections for each year's future operations. They exhibited cash flow and profits or losses, depending upon various levels of lumber market prices. His forecasts were used as the basis for many of the presentations made to the B of A, and to the other banks' representatives.

At one point in the process, SPI arranged a field trip to exhibit many of its operations to the selected banks' representatives. After presentations by Red, Dick Smith, Gary Blanc, Dan Tomascheski and myself, we loaded up a bus and headed for the Anderson sawmill, the millwork plant at Richfield, and finally the Burney sawmill and cogen plant.

The purpose was to sell the company to the bankers. It was not difficult to do. The operations were new and clean. The SPI personnel were intelligent and dedicated to the company. I felt fortunate to be associated with all of them. It was a far cry from the way I perceived the SPI organization when I still worked for DiGiorgio. I also thought I perceived something else.

It seemed to me it would be easy to mislead many of the bankers who were on the bus with us. They were all very intelligent people, far more sophisticated and polished than most of the SPI people. They lived in an entirely different world than we did. Theirs was a world of finance, numbers and big money. It was foreign to me.

On the other hand, they knew very little of our business. Tony Zanze and his Forest Products Group were knowledgeable, but most of the rest were not. With very little effort, we could have sold the group on some wild schemes, especially with Gary Blanc and his computer. Perhaps I underestimated their capabilities, or overestimated our own, but I thought I could see how banks get into deep trouble when they lend huge sums of money to some sharp borrowers. It also appeared to me that the group was sold more on the Emmersons' and SPI's track record than they were on the operations.

When it was all over, the various banks were aboard; but we still had the bidding process to go through. Red was very confident at that point that SPI would be successful. I was not so sure. There were rumors going around that some Japanese companies were in the running for the Santa Fe. John Walker at Simpson Timber Co. had been quoted in the media as saying that "no one was going to steal the Santa Fe." The biggest worry, though, was Roseburg.

Jerry Duffy, Roseburg's Resource Manager, and I were good friends. Jerry is a gregarious and lively individual, with a wife, Maxine, to match. They are fun to be around, both being involved in numerous civic activities. Jerry and I would discuss mutual problems quite frequently, particularly those involving the Timber Association of California

Field foresters Jon Miller, Bob Amsbury, Mike Bates, Dan Tomascheski, in old-growth Red fir on SPI's Mt. Shasta District.
Photo from author's collection by David P. Bayles.

(TAC), for which we both were Directors.

With the impending sale of the Santa Fe, we became wary of each other. We would converse freely, but each of us was probing the other for information. I enjoyed the jousting with Jerry, and I think he enjoyed himself, too. Neither of us got much information from the other that was meaningful. Some of it, probably, was quite misleading.

Jerry would call me, or I would call him. After the pleasantries of discussing weather, the market, cussing the Forest Service, or other standard openings, the real subject of the call would come out.

I would start by saying, "How's your cruise on Santa Fe coming, Jerry?"

"Pretty good, Bud, how's yours?"

"Good, where ya working?"

"I don't know where the crew is today. I've been doing some other things for Kenneth. Where are you guys at?"

"We're just finishing up at McCloud. Pretty crappy timber up there. It sure isn't worth much. What do you think of it?"

"Yeah, I agree. Pretty flat ground, though. Logging costs should be low."

"The Santa Fe is a big property. It will probably take more money than we can come up with. I wish we were as well off as Roseburg," I would reply.

Jerry probably knew I was lying about the McCloud timber being poor timber. He knew the ground was flat at McCloud, so I had not found out if they had cruised it or not. He also knew where his men were working, and he did not want me to know where they were.

I hoped I had planted a seed in his mind that we might put a low value on it, though. If I could, somehow, indicate that we would "lowball" our bid, such as we had with Bunyan, Roseburg might not bid quite so high.

Through it all was the nagging thought that Red **had** lowballed the Bunyan bid a year ago. I knew that Tony Zanze was lobbying Red to figure out what the property was worth to SPI, and **if he wanted it**, to go after it without worrying about exceeding the next lower bid by a substantial amount. I had to agree.

Red used to lecture me about "leaving money on the table" on a sealed bid timber sale. He would explain how Otto Peters used to be proud of missing buying a sale by only 10 or 20 cents per MBF. On the other hand, Otto would worry about buying one for 20 dollars per MBF over the next bidder. Red always said he would rather have the sale than to miss it by a few cents.

He was not really comfortable with leaving a large sum on the table, though. On the occasions when that occurred, he would complain that perhaps we did not know what we were doing. Red wanted it both ways. I would have to remind him of the Otto Peters story occasionally.

Red, meanwhile, was involved in some intense personal diplomacy. Fred Schulte appeared to like Red, so Red invited him to come to Eureka for some salmon fishing with the Emmersons. Schulte was a fisherman, and Red had learned from Tony Zanze that he would like to try the waters off northern California. The trip was arranged, and Red picked Fred and his wife up in San Francisco for the trip to Eureka.

They toured the Redwood parks north of Eureka, then returned to spend the night in town. The next day they went salmon fishing. The fishing was outstanding. On one occasion, there were five lines out and five fish on at the same time. The Schultes enjoyed their northcoast sojourn very much.

Schulte was like the rest of the Santa Fe people. He was not about to break the rules laid down by those in charge of the sale. Since the Santa Fe was owned by a public company, the employees, particularly the officers and directors, were vulnerable if they did not protect the stockholders' interests. If the Santa Fe sold for less than expected, there could have been claims made by stockholders that management's duties were not discharged with "due diligence." I was to hear that term many times during 1987.

The rest of us at SPI worried that Krebs was using the opportunity to lobby Red for a higher price than we thought appropriate. We knew Red as an aggressive purchaser of timber and timberland. Sometimes he paid too

Tom Walz with increment borer checking tree growth on young-growth trees on SPI timberland, 1989.
Photo from author's collection by David P. Bayles.

Jim Ostrowski on SPI Mt. Shasta District, 1989.
Photo from author's collection by David P. Bayles.

much, though he was prone to try to make too good a deal sometimes, and foul up the whole transaction in negotiations. We hoped Krebs wasn't telling Red about some prospective purchasers who were not there, or of some that were there and how aggressively he thought they were pursuing the purchase.

Finally, the bid date came. The bid SPI submitted was $460,000,000 and that was that. From then on, no amount of agonizing over the bid price would do any good. The agonizing part was to await the outcome.

On October 13, 1987, the *Record Search-light*, Redding's daily paper, reported that "last Monday, Sierra Pacific Industries was to purchase the Santa Fe Pacific Timber Co." The story referred to a joint announcement made by the two companies on October 12th.

On October 15, 1987, Weaverville's weekly, the *Trinity Journal*, described the sale of the Santa Fe. SPI was "buying 522,000 acres from Santa Fe by the end of the year." The story went on to note data from the 1986 annual report of Santa Fe as follows:

    1986 operating income $17,000,000
    1985 operating income   12,800,000
    1984 operating income   12,100,000

In 1986 the company had sold 200,000 MBF of timber which was under the volume sold in 1985. There were 63 permanent employees, and 33 seasonal employees.

On November 4, 5 and 6, 1987, Dan Tomascheski and I began to interview the Santa Fe foresters. We flew to each of the three Districts outside Redding to spend some time with each of them at those locations. It was a traumatic and difficult process. I remembered the takeover of DiGiorgio and the hard feelings that were left over for a long-time afterwards.

Even though it was just prior to the year-end holidays, I felt it would be necessary to tell all of them the good news, or the bad news, as soon as we knew what it was. At the time, we did not know how many of the Santa Fe people we would need, so we told each of them that fact, and that we could not hire all of them. We promised to contact them again as soon as we knew. It was not an easy task.

At first, Red wanted to close down all of the Santa Fe district offices. He thought it would be better to have all of the timberlands managed from Redding, where he could have easier access to the managers. Since there was not enough room in the CV office for the additional staff, it was decided to refurbish the old Champion office at Anderson and move all of the foresters there.

Dan and I impressed on Red that it would be inefficient to have all of the forestry staff at Anderson. Driving time to the woods would take up most of a forester's day unless he had an airplane at his disposal. Finally, Red agreed to a reorganization plan.

We decided to establish field offices at Mt. Shasta, Weaverville, Grass Valley and Redding. A District Manager would be in charge of each office. He was to have three foresters to help him. There would be no support staff at those locations, only a computer terminal, a fax and a telephone answering machine.

We decided to move the Santa Fe computer system to the Anderson office. In addition to those manning that system, there would be inventory, accounting and office staff housed there. Correspondence for the districts would be prepared at Anderson, sent over either the fax or to the terminals at the districts for printing, then mailed from each district. It was a rather cumbersome system; but it satisfied Red that duplicate support staff would not be necessary at each field location.

On December 17, 1987, the Weaverville paper ran a story that SPI had toured each Santa Fe office on Monday the 14th. Ed Bond, Dan Tomascheski and the author had talked to all of the Santa Fe people again. The paper noted that SPI was to retain 17 permanent and 2 seasonal Santa Fe employees. The paper quoted George Belden, Weaverville District Manager for the Santa Fe, as saying, "The Weaverville District had 14 permanent and 6 seasonal employees. Only three were to be retained by SPI: Bill Blackwell, Bryan West and Art Tenneson."

On the same day, the *Record Searchlight* announced that 42 Santa Fe employees would lose their jobs.

George Belden was one of those not hired; he went on to open a consulting office in Weaverville. Several of the Santa Fe inventory and computer managers decided to open an office of their own in Redding. They called their new business "Vestra," and they specialized in Geographic Information Systems, the new technology of the times.

For SPI, the hard decisions had been made. Whether they were the correct ones remained to be seen. There were still hard feelings evident. Some claimed that SPI had not hired the higher-paid employees, only the lower-echelon "troops." Some of the newspapers carried stories critical of the "meat axe" approach just before the Christmas season. George Belden was one of the few who handled the situation with tact and understanding.

We had taken the position that whether a person was permanent or seasonal with Santa Fe made no difference. We were looking for **field** foresters, not managers as required by the Santa Fe. Their former pay scale was not a part of the equation at all; their commitment to work was. We also needed those who, in our judgment, would fit into the SPI team with as little trouble as possible. Those who had worked for Santa Fe for a long time might not accept the unstructured routines of a private company like SPI.

After the reorganization, Tom Walz moved from Hayfork, where he was Timber Manager, to take over the Weaverville District. Tom Nelson managed an expanded Redding District based in Anderson, and Tim Feller, one of the Santa Fe foresters at Grass Valley, was promoted to manage that district. Jim Ostrowski, formerly working with Tom Nelson at Redding, became the new District Manager at Mt. Shasta.

Tim Feller was born in 1954 in Minnesota, one of four children. His parents moved to the Redding area where his father worked in constructing the tunnels for the Trinity dam west of Redding.

The family lived next door to Paul Caster, a consulting forester, who became quite influential with Tim and his two brothers. They would all eventually work as foresters. Tim went to work for Paul when he was 14, and worked for him during summer vacations from then on.

After obtaining an A.A. degree in Forestry from Shasta College, Tim entered Humboldt State where he graduated with a B.S. in Forest Products in 1977. After working again for Paul Caster for a year, he went to work for the Southern Pacific Land Co. in 1978. Dan and I were favorably impressed with the knowledge of forestry Tim exhibited when we interviewed him for the position at Grass Valley.

The other District Manager, Jim Ostrowski, was another employee stolen from a neighboring company because he was a little miserable to get along with. When I first met him, he was working for Champion out of their Eureka office. We had scheduled a meeting to try to arrange joint maintenance for the Roddiscraft Road being used by a number of the companies hauling logs in Humboldt County.

Of all of those present at the meeting, Ostrowski was the only one who had carefully inspected and documented the maintenance problems evident to him on the road. He stated his opinions forcefully and at length. He would not back down, nor would he shut up. He mostly got his way in the final agreement; Champion was well represented. I remembered him when we needed more help.

Jim was born in 1957, and grew up in the Bay Area. In 1980, he graduated from Humboldt State with a B. S. in Forest Management. From 1977 until 1983, he worked for Champion seasonally before he graduated, and permanently afterwards. He was a logging engineer when I became acquainted with him.

He came to SPI in 1983, working out of SPI's Redding office, writing timber harvest plans, designing roads (particularly at Curl Ridge), and running tree planting crews. Jim took care of the Humboldt County lands owned by R. H. Emmerson & Son and SPI all by himself. He certainly was not afraid of work.

As the end of the year approached, the Santa Fe acquisition was still not completed. While Santa Fe tried to hurry the process along, Red was in no hurry to consummate the purchase. On the day SPI would take over, money would change hands, and the interest clock would start to run.

He did not have to worry about dragging his feet. The sheer size of the acquisition made the research of public records and transfer of all of the deeds so complicated that the title company needed additional time in which to complete their work. The agreements had been signed, though. Red could relax, as much as he ever could, knowing SPI owned the timberland. He could look forward to the transfer of title early in 1988.

Tim Feller and Chauncey on the Grass Valley District of SPI timberlands, 1989.
Photo from author's collection by David P. Bayles.

chapter fifty

EXPENSE ACCOUNTS

With the Sante Fe acquisition, SPI had come a long way, much of it during my short tenure with the company. It was fun to reflect how the organization had changed over the years. Some of the changes were quite significant, some only colorful. The handling of employee expense accounts was indicative of the kind of company it was.

Most companies the size of SPI publish memos giving their employees guidance on the types of travel and lodging arrangements that are appropriate for their status within the company. Some have company credit cards that can be used only for specified purposes, and then require the employee to turn in a report of its use periodically. SPI issued very few company credit cards.

In the matter of an employee's expense account, the first hint that something could be amiss usually came by way of a discrete inquiry from Dick Smith about a certain item appearing on the expense report. In most cases, the expenditure that Dick questioned would be perfectly legitimate; but the conversation gave him an opportunity to tell the employee about "Joe Blo who had incurred Red's wrath because he stayed at the Red Lion instead of Motel 6 down the street." A sensitive person might catch on immediately that he had stayed at the wrong place.

Red himself frequently stayed in places that were not always top of the line. As long as it was clean, had a good bed and was close to work, he could see no reason for spending $100 to rent a bed for five hours when $27.50, or less, would accomplish the same thing. He would look with disdain upon those executives in other companies who flew first class and stayed at the "Ritz." Most of them, of course, worked for publicly-owned companies and they were used to using stockholders' money for such things. To Red, that was living a little "high on the hog" and was a sign of decadence.

At one point, Sierra Pacific hired an attorney. He was somewhat enamored of his importance and of the station in life that he had attained. He considered his mode of travel, the places where he stayed, and the restaurants where he ate to be symbols of his status as an attorney. He was actually an excellent attorney, but he had difficulty in figuring out the company that had hired him.

On my frequent trips to Redding, I had begun staying at a modest motel that had a restaurant (called Lulu's) adjoining it. The food there was not the best to be found in Redding, but it was adequate for breakfast or for dinner, if one was in a hurry to get to bed. Since I stayed there often, the other foresters would do so also when business brought them to the valley.

Our new attorney began staying at the Red Lion and could not understand why I did not do the same, especially when we had business to attend to together. I attempted to explain the way we operated, and to suggest that Lulu's really wasn't so bad. He was hard to convince.

One morning, he consented to meet me and two of our foresters for breakfast at Lulu's, prior to leaving for the woods to inspect one of our timber sales where we were experiencing a legal problem. Before ordering, he carefully inspected his fork, knife and spoon for signs of water spots. He fogged each with his breath and wiped them with his napkin. He ordered a stack of hotcakes with the remark that it was pretty hard to ruin hotcakes unless the cook was an imbecile. Several of the others, including I, ordered the same.

When the food arrived, he carefully inspected both sides of each cake muttering all the while. He called the waitress back to return one cake to the chef to be replaced with one more to his liking. The rest of us buttered up, applied the syrup and settled down to eat.

When we were about half-finished, the replacement came back. By that time, he had two cold pancakes with a hot one on top. He methodically applied the butter and syrup and took one bite, chewing while the rest of us were finishing our breakfasts and remarking how good they were. He launched immediately into a graphic description of the texture, temperature, taste and weight of the offending cakes. He complained about the thinness of the syrup, the ancestry of the cook, and the cleanliness of the floor.

None of us said anything, we just headed for the door, to be followed soon by the counselor. We had an unhappy attorney who would be starved by noon.

I found that by telling new foresters stories about such things it was easy to alert them to some of the idiosyncracies and foibles of their company and its management. I would tell them of going to San Francisco with Red, and of having lunch not at the St. Francis, but at McDonald's in the financial district. I would relate the story of Red flying to Washington, D.C. in steerage, and of his not even staying there overnight, but returning in time to visit the sawmill when the morning shift began at 7:00 a.m. And I would tell them of Ida's lunches that she had prepared so that they could be eaten on the airplane without wasting time by stopping for lunch on the way to an important meeting. They were excellent lunches, too.

I heard a story about a trip to Japan, made by Red with Ron Hoppe, to discuss lumber sales with customers there. Ron's wife was a travel agent, and one of her "perks" was the privelege of flying first class. She made the travel arrangements for both of them, assigning her seat to her husband. Red, meanwhile, bought an economy seat in the rear of the plane, perhaps hearing that it was safer in the rear in case of a crash. In any event, he rode in back while Hoppe enjoyed the comforts of wide seats and free drinks. They did arrive in Japan at almost the same time, Ron a little ahead.

As customs of this kind became second nature for the employees in the company, there was a certain culture that developed. The employees became proud of their ability to operate with no frills, and to take pride in those abilities. Some of us would brag about this, and at one point I was accused by an "outside" attorney of being a reverse snob. Actually, he said that all Sierra Pacific people were reverse snobs.

He would come to work at 10:00 a.m. every day and he drove a Jaguar. He owned a sail boat, flew first class, and stayed at the best hotels. Of course, the cost of such things were added to each client's bill. He resented the fact that SPI people would make fun of those who thought as he did. He was, incidentally, a hard-working attorney who worked into the late evening hours at his office.

Red never complained of such habits; he just did not believe that such operating procedures could ever result in a successful business. Pretense was not in his vocabulary; and it took more than a title or impeccable taste to make an impression on him.

For a long time, SPI had very few titled officers. There was Red as President, Dick Smith as Controller, and a few Directors. When Dick Smith, Ron Stevens, Ron Hoppe and the author became V.P.s, our duties did not change, nor did our salaries. The move was made more for outside appearances than for anything else. Of course, members of the Emmerson family were officers, but they were also owners of the company. The four of us took a lot of good-natured ribbing about our new status, and new business cards were ordered for us.

Soon after the promotion, I received a large box of business cards and the following correspondence:

                                        3/31/86

Dear Bud,

Enclosed are your new business cards. No longer will you be mistaken for one of the homeless. These cards will bring you opportunities enjoyed by a very select group of SPI employees:

1. Your pickup, once it reaches 150,000 miles, will have priority over the sawmill maintenance welding truck for tune-ups.

2. Unrestricted use of corporate assets (shovels and picks).

3. Additional perquisites too numerous to mention.

> *Congratulations*
> *Mark Emmerson,*
> *Director of Corporate*
> *Employee Recognition and Titles*

I replied in similar vein:

                                        4/4/86

Mr. Mark Emmerson
Director of Corporate
Employee Recognition and Titles

Thank you for the supply of business cards and the reminder of how my new status results in added perks and privileges. I shall carry them with me and pass them out with pride. When the supply is depleted may I order more through you? If possible, on the next order, I would prefer a deeper shade of blue with the logo actually embossed on the card.

Also, please be advised that I shall, in view of my new status, begin to conduct myself with new dignity and bearing. I shall begin to fly first class, seek lodging at Red Lion Motor Inns and Hyatt Regencies (not Motel 6), and to hire cabs (rather than take the bus), when travelling from airports to the many meetings I shall be attending. I shall also begin to order martinis for lunch (instead of beer) and rare prime rib sandwiches (rather than Polish sausage).

If you should desire to reach me on Friday afternoons please call (707) 833-3686 and ask for V.P. That is the Baywood Country Club and I can be paged at the bar or occasionally in the sauna.

Please also inquire how I may apply for membership in the Ingomar Club and the Pacific Union Club and whether there are special organizations that cater to Polish executives like me.

> *Sincerely, J. Tomascheski*
> *V.P. Timber Resources*

P.S. Are polyester suits and wide ties ever going to make a comeback?

I am still awaiting a reply.

King Air 400 in Portland, Oregon, on date of delivery. Pilot Bob Congdon, Red Emmerson, Dick Smith, Don Riewerts and Bud Tomascheski. Photographer unknown.

chapter fifty one

THE AIR FORCE

The SPI air force was an important division of the company, gaining great importance as SPI's growth reached its peak. Over the years, many funny stories were told in which the airplanes, their pilots, and the people who rode in them played a part.

Going back to the days of the stud mill at Weitchpec, one of the first airplanes that the Emmersons had was a Super Cub. Many old pilots loved this machine since it was small and slow, but had a big engine. It was more like flying a kite than an airplane. Two people could be fairly comfortable in it if they didn't mind the noise, and sitting in tandem. It would fly into tight places with very little trouble and still take off. There probably was no better airplane for looking at timber unless it was a helicopter. It could be throttled back so that it just barely moved along, the whole side could be opened up, and one could lean out in the wind and look straight down at the terrain below. Red used to fly this machine himself, often to the stud mill at Weitchpec.

The next airplane was a Piper Apache which was purchased in 1958. It was a used machine, but in good shape. Gil Moore was hired to fly it. At first, Gil was a part-time pilot working out of Murray Field. He was paid by the hour for ferrying Red and the others around. The Apache was owned only a year or two, and was followed by a used Cessna 310. Gil Moore quit soon after that ship was acquired and George Nixon took his place.

Curly, of course, always refused to fly. Red would have to drag him into an airplane, and then it would have to be a momentous event that would get him there.

For the era, the 310 was a good airplane for the Emmersons, that is, fast and dependable. It was a twin with tricycle landing gear. Red remembers finally getting Curly into this airplane. He settled in the rear seat, having climbed in before Red. Red got in the front seat and tried to slam the door on his side of the plane, but it would not stay shut. After two or three tries, he looked behind him to see what was preventing the door from closing. Curly had his hand in the door, holding on for dear life with his eyes shut. His knuckles were skinned raw, but he had not noticed. He was ready to die.

In 1963, R. H. Emmerson & Son bought a Cessna 320, in effect, a souped-up 310. It was also a good airplane for the short flights and some of the rather primitive air strips that it was required to utilize. George Nixon left in 1964 and was replaced by Bob Congdon. Congdon was from Eureka, and had been a pilot for Les Pierce. A Cessna 411 was purchased in 1964.

During the years that SPI was public, John Crook also had a 411. In addition, there was a famous airplane that was acquired for use by the officers and directors - a Lockheed Lodestar that at one time had been owned by

Governor George Wallace of Alabama fame. It was well-appointed with a bar, couches and all of the necessities of the good life. It carried a co-pilot, as well as a pilot; the co-pilot doubled as a mechanic. The belly of the aircraft was half-filled with engine spare parts, since the engines were obsolete and parts were hard to find.

Dick Smith remembers flying into Inyokern in the Lodestar with only the two pilots for company. The next morning turned out to be one of those howling windstorms that often occur there; and no one noticed that a small airplane of some kind had parked in a spot not normally used for parking. As they headed down the taxiway, there was an awful noise and Dick looked out his window to see the small plane, now ground up in little pieces by the propeller, being blown against the fence by the hurricane. Dick had never seen an airplane disappear like that.

In 1971, the first of the Mitsubishi MU-2s was bought. This machine was a pressurized turboprop with plenty of power. It could utilize short fields and fly in all kinds of weather. Red bought the machine himself, and rented it to the company when it was needed. Bob Congdon was as proud of the airplane as if it were new, even though it had over 100 hours on it when acquired.

Bob was a different sort from the usual corporate pilot who inhabit the world today. He should have been an Alaskan bush pilot, since he was resourceful and very skilled at driving an airplane in any kind of weather and to any destination. He usually had dirty fingernails from just having worked on an airplane, or on his automobile. He seldom wore a tie or jacket, and he was considered by the ladies to be a handsome man; he was tall and thin. His overnight kit was a battered suitcase with a broken handle; his car, a battered brown subcompact of uncertain vintage.

Sometime in 1976, an additional airplane, a Cessna 210, was purchased from Don Riewerts. It was a good machine, but limited to mostly daytime flights or for passengers of lesser stature. This is not to say that Red himself did not use it; but it was slower than the MU-2 and did not carry as many passengers.

I have previously recounted my first experience with the MU-2; however, the first flight in the 210 was even more memorable.

Congdon had picked me up at Quincy on a bright, shiny day for a trip to Arcata. As we approached the coast, it was obvious that there was a fog problem, and an instrument approach was necessary. Since we intended to land at Murray Field rather than Arcata where there was adequate instrumentation for I F R conditions, there were added complications. The usual procedure was to use the Arcata approach, come out of the fog just before touchdown, and then request clearance to fly under the overcast to Murray. When we got close enough to begin the descent to Arcata, the field was closed.

Bob knew how to approach Murray Field by coming under the fog bank at the head of Freshwater Creek. There it was usually clear enough to sneak under the fog and to fly down the creek just above the tree tops. If the pilot knew the country, there really was no danger in the procedure, as long as the ground and trees were in sight.

We attempted the short cut to Murray, only to find the fog was too low. Each time we attempted to get under it, the sight distance would deteriorate to the point where it was nonexistent. After a couple of tries, Congdon decided that this would never work.

It should be mentioned that I was perfectly at ease flying with Bob Congdon. For some reason, he projected an air of total competence to me; I could not say the same for some other pilots with whom I have flown. As we climbed up through the fog on our last failed try, I thought we would head back to Redding. Not so; Congdon wanted to get home.

We flew in bright sun over the south bay. He had done this a number of times and, as we saw the smoke from the pulp mills boiling up through the overcast, he knew exactly where he was. We began the descent over the bay near King Salmon. As we came down through the fog, I wondered whether I had been correct in my assessment of his competence.

After an eternity of seeing nothing but white fog, we spotted the water a few feet below. We were right in the ship channel with

Ron Voss with Cessna 310 at Cedar City, Utah, about 1985. Photo by author.

the marker buoys visible on either side of our path. Seagulls on pilings at window height flapped off as we roared between them. As we approached the Samoa bridge, the top of the arches was obscured by the fog. No matter; we hopped over the top and came down on the other side to land at Murray a few minutes later. Bob thought nothing of it; but I had seen a master flier at work.

The 210 was a different matter. It always seemed to have a problem with the landing gear, which was supposed to be retractable. Most of the time it was; but occasionally it would not come down when it was time to land. There was a hand lever between the front seats that enabled one or the other of those in the airplane to pump the gear down. Sitting next to Bob, I usually fell heir to the task. I cranked the gear down on that airplane four times in my career. I was a lot more afraid of the airplane than I was of the pilot.

The 210 finally cracked up with Dick

Smith aboard after it tried to take off from the airport at Beckwourth. A baffle of some sort had become dislodged in its exhaust system and plugged up one of the exhaust pipes, rendering it incapable of climbing over the surrounding hills. The pilot was not Congdon, but a young man who had been hired for the trip. It wasn't his fault, but the airplane just would not fly. They almost made it back to the airport, but not quite. They landed with the landing gear half-down in a field across from the airport. No one was hurt, but Dick had Curly's phobia about airplanes for a long time afterwards. Dick reported that he had the door open as the plane hit the ground, and was out in a flash, hitting the ground running. It must have been a sight to see Dick taking off across the field in his accountant's uniform. The plane was a total wreck.

There are a number of good flying stories that have been circulated within SPI. I was a participant in one that could have been a disaster.

Red Emmerson, Pilot John Refsnider and Mark Emmerson on timber inspection trip in 1989.
Photo by author.

Moose Mathews and I had business in Quincy, and Red had a meeting to attend in Reno. It was a sunny summer day and Congdon was the pilot. Since there was enough room in the MU-2, our three wives were invited to go along to shop. Moose and I were dropped off at Quincy, and Red was delivered to Reno. We were to be picked up later that afternoon.

At the appointed hour, Moose and I were at the Quincy airport. The runway was being reconstructed and lengthened, so the portion available for use was quite short. The drop-off of Moose and I went as planned, but the pickup was another matter.

I was in a phone booth with my back to the runway when I heard the roar of the MU-2 on its approach. I never looked up, but a very loud splintering crash got my attention. I spun around to see splinters flying through the air, and the MU-2 accelerating away with the wheels down. One of them dangled at a strange angle.

I yelled to Moose, "What in hell happened? What's the splinters from? What's the matter with the wheels?"

"The son of a bitch hit a truck," he hollered excitedly.

There was no sign of a truck that I could see. I thought he had flipped his wig. I ran out to the highway, looked both ways; there was no truck. Then I saw it coming back up the highway. It had turned around and was out of sight for a moment. It was a small truck with a shattered wooden rack on the back. The wheel of the airplane had snagged the top two boards of the rack as Congdon made a low approach over the highway because of the shortened runway. The driver was white and shaken but not hurt. The truck was fine, except for the sideboards that were in little splinters all over the vicinity.

As Congdon flew by for us to see the damage, it was obvious that there would be a difficult landing ahead for those aboard. I could imagine the panic felt by the wives, while Red was probably cussing out the truck driver, pilot and anyone else who came to mind. Moose and I were terribly concerned that there was a disaster in the making.

We had not known that Red and the rest had been unloaded at Chester just a few miles away. Bob Congdon had taken a look at the load of merchandise the ladies had purchased in Reno, and thought it would be better to lighten up to come to Quincy to pick up Moose and me, then fly back to Chester to get the rest. He relayed that information to us on the ground via intercom and decided to head to Redding where there was foam, a long runway, and expert assistance in case it was needed.

We finally arranged to get home in a Cessna 210. It was pretty tight quarters with all of us piled in that little airplane. Meanwhile, Congdon landed the Mitsubishi on two wheels, one of them the nose wheel. I later talked to a pilot at Redding who told me he would fly with Congdon to hell and back after witnessing the landing he made on the damaged wheel. Though the wheel was cocked at such an angle that it could not roll, it left a rubber mark on the concrete as straight as an arrow.

After the 210 made its unscheduled stop in the field with Dick Smith abroad, another Cessna 310 was purchased. The air force then consisted of the MU-2 and the 310. Both were good airplanes, but there was only one pilot. A pilot from Arcata Flying Service usually was hired to fly the smaller plane when it was needed.

In 1977, the MU-2 was sold, and a Beech King Air 200 was purchased. This aircraft was a demonstrator but was in new condition. It was fast, comfortable, and very much suited to the kind of flying SPI needed. It could use short strips, and still fly high and fast in all kinds of weather if it was necessary. The author was along on the maiden voyage when it was picked up in Portland.

Congdon left shortly after to begin an odyssey, sailing in his catamaran down the California coast through the Panama Canal and through the Caribbean. He and his wife ended up in Florida after a couple of years. Today, he is back in Eureka flying for Federal Express.

Rick Mansfield came to take Congdon's place. He looks more the part of the corporate pilot, young and blonde. He also is a very accomplished flier, instilling confidence in his passengers. However, he seems to have a slight problem of finding a second pilot with whom he can get along.

Shortly after Rick came to work, the 310 was replaced by the second MU-2, this time a shortened version that would carry only five passengers comfortably. A Bell Jet Ranger helicopter was acquired to provide access to not only sawmill locations, but to the expanding land base the company acquired as time went on. It became a valuable tool for the foresters to use on occasion.

With the acquisition of the helicopter, it was found necessary to obtain the services of a second pilot. Rick Greggore (Rick #2) came aboard to perform double duty as a fixed-wing pilot, also. He stayed long enough to become familiar with SPI; but found it difficult to get along with Rick #1 who was the "chief pilot." He left to fly helicopters for the California Highway Patrol.

The Flight Department, as it came to be known, was moved to Redding in the early 1980s, where a new hangar was eventually built at the Redding municipal airport. All three aircraft are housed there today. Greggore was replaced by Mike Pennington, who was also a helicopter pilot. He also flew airplanes, and did much of the maintenance work on all three machines. When he left, John Refsnider, then a pilot for LP, came to take his place. The author retired before having the opportunity to become familiar with John.

Most SPI foresters became quite familiar with the helicopter pilots. Of the three, Rick Greggore was the most enjoyable to be around, although they were all very nice people and excellent craftsmen. Rick loved the woods as much as a forester does. If the trip included landing for closer inspection, he wanted to go along for the hike in the woods. Since he was in good physical shape, he would grab his sack lunch and tag along. For some, he was a challenge to keep up with.

The SPI air force became a professional outfit. The only thing about it that was puzzling was the way airplanes were dispatched.

Red Emmerson was the dispatcher. He wanted to keep intimate track of who was

Rick Mansfield, Chief Pilot, working on airplane "tug" in SPI hanger at Redding airport, 1989.
Photo by author.

flying, when and where. He would arrange his schedule to make full and efficient use of the machines.

In many ways that made a lot of sense, but I, for one, was uncomfortable when he altered his schedule to fit mine. In most cases, however, it was the other way around. It was difficult to match my schedule with the airplanes' schedules. As I grew older, I would try to arrange my time so that I would drive my pickup instead of relying on the air force. This caused a lot of wasted motion, since most of the driving distances were three to six hours long. I put up with it, but it was always an irritation.

Red was a good dispatcher most of the time. I remember one instance where he was to pick me up in Redding on his way to Arcata from Quincy or Burney. He evidently had a lot on his mind that day, because I saw the plane overfly Redding on its way to the coast. It never even waggled its wings as it went by. It left me high and dry to spend another night in Redding. I guessed Red had something on his mind besides my travel schedule.

chapter fifty two

TRANSPORTATION DEPARTMENT

From the time the company began to expand, SPI had need for a great number of trucks, all kinds of trucks: not only pickup trucks, but log trucks, lumber trucks, and just plain trucks. It took personnel to drive them and managers to look after them.

Vic Beccaria was the manager of the truck fleet at Arcata in the 1970s. Vic was also responsible for a fleet of log trucks at Susanville; but he spent very little time there since he had competent help from George Lemmel who was the local truck boss. At the time, Hayfork also had a fleet of log trucks, and Vic travelled to Hayfork a couple of times each month.

Vic was a good friend of Curly's, and became one of his drinking buddies. He also spent quite a few lunch hours at the Anchor when he was in town. Red and Ida became quite friendly with Vic and his wife Pat. Vic, being a good story teller with a keen sense of humor, made the Beccarias fun to be with. After several years of drinking with Curly, and a stint in the drunk tank at Eureka after a party, Vic quit "cold turkey." No one ever saw him take another drink, and many admired him for his fortitude in abstaining.

Vic had developed a good crew of log truck drivers. Even though it was a company-owned outfit, which usually indicated an inefficient operation, Red put up with it, possibly for two reasons: it was non-union, and it seemed to make money. As time went on, the Transportation Division was expanded to include lumber trucks, and log truck fleets at additional locations.

The log trucks were employed for a number of reasons, not the least of which was to control costs. Since it was quite difficult to know true costs of an operation without access to the books, owning the truck fleets was a way of learning what it cost logging contractors to haul logs from each logging job. SPI retained the option of placing one or more trucks on each job to determine driving time, loading time, and the scale that could be hauled on each load. Thus, when it came time to dicker with outside hauling contractors, SPI had firsthand information concerning costs.

After the purchase of DiGiorgio, a fleet of log trucks was placed at Quincy. Actually "Mecca" got a new fleet of trucks, and the old ones were sent to Quincy. After that development, Vic began to spend considerably more time on the road. He drove a fancy pickup that in reality was an automobile, what the manufacturer called an El Camino. It had a powerful engine, a CB radio, and eventually a company radio hooked up to the foresters' radio system.

When radio call numbers were assigned, Vic was given the number 99. At the time, the TV show Get Smart was popular and the lead role was a secret agent who had a radio in his shoe. He was a harebrained individual who had the call number 99. Vic was certainly not harebrained; but the foresters always snick-

Truck fleet at Susanville, 1989.
Photo by author.

ered about the private joke on Vic when they heard him on the radio say "This is 99." Vic may never have known about the joke played on him.

Vic did not take to the extra travel, and used to complain about spending all the time on the road. He was looking forward to early retirement, and talked about buying a dump truck, just to have something to do with his time.

When Vic departed from SPI, Larry Maciel took his place as Truck Manager. Larry had been one of the log truck drivers assigned to Quincy when the used fleet departed from Mecca. Larry was more easygoing than Vic, and seemed to be able to get along better with the logging contractors who got company trucks assigned to their jobs. Under his leadership, additional fleets were assigned to CV and Loyalton. Several lumber trucks were added to the transportation operations at each location; but log trucks always made up the bulk of the rolling stock.

While Larry's department manages the company lumber trucks today, they come under the control of SPI's George Rogers, who manages their scheduling from the CV office. George does not schedule the logging trucks though; Larry does that.

After SPI set up the centralized sales force at CV, the hauling of lumber became a big-time operation. Lumber hauling is entirely different than a log-truck operation, where the trucks are normally home every night. Lumber is hauled by all kinds of different trucks, many of which are on their way back to where they are based. In such cases, they are looking for a back-haul and, if they can arrange for a load of lumber that needs delivery close to where they are going, they are glad to pick it up on the way. This affords a certain amount of efficiency in hauling operations, and saves money.

A formal traffic department was set up adjacent to the sales department in the CV office. George Rogers, formerly a lumber salesman at Loyalton, later in centralized sales at CV, became the Director of the Transportation Department. He held the post of Manager of By-Products for SPI at the same time.

George had been hired by Sam Witzel in 1978. He was right at home at Loyalton, having been raised just up the road a few miles at Susanville. George had attended Shasta College for an A.A. in Business, then graduated from Chico State with a degree in Social Sciences. In the summers, his son Steve worked on SPI's surveying crew while he attended college.

When millwork operations were expanded to CV, Richfield and Oroville, additional responsibilities for the transportation of the products fell to the traffic department. As a result, SPI became the largest shipper of lumber on the Southern Pacific Railroad, and truck shipments increased. Incoming lumber to the millwork plants was also handled by the department.

The volume of shipments is difficult to visualize. In a day's time, it is equivalent to about 230 truckloads of lumber that are handled by George Rogers and his crew of four people. SPI routes approximately 9,000 rail cars annually, spending over $5,500,000 each year on rail shipments. Such volumes result in a competitive advantage for SPI by reason of a reduced freight rate for its products. This translates to additional revenue added to the bottom line.

While Red did not like to have SPI build logging roads, he accepted the need to have company trucks. Perhaps he was more comfortable with the department because it was run as a profit center, and he could look at the monthly statements to see how it was doing. Of course, the monthly statements were required to show the department running in the black.

SPI logs on Cheek Logging Co. truck heading for CV sawmill 1984. Photo from SPI archives.

chapter fifty three

PICKUP TRUCKS

There are probably a number of things that Red Emmerson does not like, but one of the things he dislikes the most is pickups. He probably does not dislike the pickup itself, nor is it probable that he dislikes **a pickup**, he dislikes **pickups** in the plural.

At first, I thought that the reason he seemed to be so hung up on pickups was because when he saw them parked near the office, it indicated that the driver was not doing anything constructive. Since foresters always drove pickups, it showed that the forester wasn't in the woods; he was in the office. A forester's place was in the woods.

Red could judge the efficiency of a company by the number of pickups that were parked outside the office at any given time. He seemed to be able to count the number of foresters a company had on their payroll by counting the number of pickups. Any number greater than one indicated an inefficient outfit.

Eventually, some of the SPI foresters got in the habit of gathering up their office work early in the morning, climbing in their pickups, and driving somewhere out of sight to answer letters or write a timber appraisal. There developed within the organization a certain mystique about the use of these vehicles and many good stories are told to this day about the effects the trucks had on Red.

My first experience with this problem began the day I came to work for SPI. The pickup I had been driving while working for DiGiorgio had been driven many miles, and a new one had been ordered for me. Since it had not been delivered, the order was cancelled when SPI took over.

After hiring me, Red assured me that he would take care of this problem by ordering a vehicle from his old friend Mo Olson at Sacchi Chevrolet in Arcata. The presumption was that he could make a better deal there. I suspect that he bought the truck right off the lot because, when I first saw it, it had big wheels and fat tires. It was what is known as a "step-side" with a very small box, and little running boards with the spare mounted in one of them. This one was two-wheel drive, not four. It was the kind of truck youngsters liked to squirrel around town in.

I accepted the pickup with thanks since it ran well and it smelled good. It was a racy-looking thing, and actually turned into one of the best trucks I ever drove. Youngsters would pull up beside me at stop signs and race their engines. It was a temptation not to accept the challenge. For a two-wheel drive machine, it got around in the woods wonderfully well.

One day, I passed a sheriff in Sierra Valley. I had noticed that I usually passed a lot of cars, even though I was not exceeding the speed limit, and passing a sheriff seemed a natural enough thing for me to do. In a moment, the siren was on, red lights were flashing, and I was talking to the deputy alongside the highway. He claimed that I had zoomed by him at a rate far in excess of the legal limit.

I tried some fast talk, explaining that my speedometer must be off, and asked him to check it for me. He agreed. So I drove down the highway at a legal 65 (without cheating) with him clocking me from the rear. After a mile or so, I pulled over. He got out of his vehicle shaking his head.

"Sir," he said, "You were doing a steady 79. That's against the law."

"Officer, you've cleared up a mystery for me," I said, "I couldn't figure out why the traffic had seemed to slow down after I got this truck that Red Emmerson bought me. Now I know; the damn speedometer is screwed up."

The deputy smiled at the mention of Red's name. "He probably had the thing ordered that way so you would get to work faster; but you had better get it fixed." He jumped in his car and was off.

It turned out that a little reduction gear had not been replaced in the transmission, or had been replaced with the wrong one when Red had the fat tires replaced. It was a simple repair to make; but it illustrated to me the reputation Red already had made in Sierra County.

Red had the idea that pickups should last forever. He explained to me a dozen or more times that logging roads by then were "pretty good roads;" in fact, many of them were paved. Thus a truck should last, rather than 120,000 miles, perhaps double that. He was also fond of telling me that there were forklifts within the company that were over 20 years old, and a 5-year-old pickup was practically new.

Vic Beccaria had logging trucks in his department that had "way over one million miles" on them. This became a topic of conversation whenever Red got into a forester's pickup. The standard conversation on the way to the woods would go like this:

"How many miles have you got on this pickup, Bud?"

"Red, it's getting along in years; it just turned over 129,000."

"It sure rides good; nice and tight, I notice."

"Yeah, it's been a good truck, but it's starting to cost us money; it's dinging us to death with little things now, like a brake job, and a new battery last week. We'll have to replace it pretty soon."

"You know, Vic has a couple of trucks with one-and-a-quarter-million miles on them. It's too bad our foresters don't take care of their trucks like that."

This was a no-win situation, because the logical retort to that line of reasoning was to begin to defend the forester, to explain the difference between a pickup and a logging truck (or a forklift), and to keep him in good humor for the trip to the woods. It was evident that all three could not be done at the same time. The best strategy was to change the subject.

Within the foresters' circle, stories abound about SPI pickups. One of them involves Jerry Gromacki with whom I was cruising timber one day. Jerry would usually comment on how "tight" his pickup was, even though it had more miles on it than any other. He had already heard Red's "tight" description many times.

As we were going along on a logging road, the front-end began to shake. I, at one time, owned a 1931 Chevrolet that shimmied terribly just like his truck. It would do it at about 45 miles per hour, but it would stop shaking at about 50.

I told Jerry about my old '31, and suggested that the next time the shimmy started to "just speed up" and perhaps the thing would stop. Naturally, it began again, and this time on a fairly straight stretch of rough logging road. As we both hung on, Jerry to the steering wheel and I to the dash board, I yelled to Jerry:

"Stomp on her, Jerry." Down the hill we went and I thought sure the thing would stop shaking. "Faster."

Jerry never let up; he had guts. The steering wheel was nearly impossible to hang onto. We were now up to about 50 (it seemed like 90 to me), and all of a sudden the cab was filled with fine dust. There was so much of it, and it was so fine, that we could not see where we were headed.

"Jesus," Jerry yelled, "What's that?"

He got us stopped, and we got out of the truck coughing and gagging. Looking the situation over, we discovered that Jerry had collected many miles of fine logging road dust in the headliner of the cab on his truck. The lining was the kind with small holes punched in it that allowed dust to collect behind it. The violent shaking had dislodged about ten pounds of the stuff which showered down on our heads. We gave up on the idea of trying to drive through the shimmy in that truck.

The incident could have resulted in a disaster, but it didn't, it only resulted in another pickup story. The pickup that shimmied was the same truck that had lost a front wheel.

Gromacki had left his pickup parked along the road where he had met some other SPI foresters to begin the day cruising timber. After a hard day in the brush, he was delivered to his vehicle so he could return to Redding. He got to Highway 44 in good shape, crested Eskimo Hill and started down the other side at a good clip.

All of a sudden, there was a big jolt and screaming metal. The right-front wheel took off ahead of him down the highway, bouncing several times before careening into the ditch several hundred feet down the road. Jerry slammed on the brakes and got the truck stopped upright on the shoulder of the highway.

He climbed shakily out of the cab, made the sign of the cross, and looked the situation over. There were skid marks on the pavement, some beat-up brush where the wheel had taken off through the ditch, but not much evidence of damage to the truck. Being Polish, and a forester, he had been in worse predicaments than this.

Jerry retrieved the wheel - a job in itself. He could find no evidence that there was anything wrong with the wheel, bearing or the axle. The only thing he could figure out was that someone had recognized his truck alongside the road and didn't like Polish foresters. What to do?

Jerry got the jack and lifted the low corner of the truck, removed one lug nut from each of the three good wheels, one from the spare, and got the machine on four wheels again. He drove sedately to town, the brakes seeming to need a little extra effort to apply.

The next day he drove to the forklift shop to explain his problem to another Jerry who ran the shop. They removed the wheel, looked it over, and then inspected the disc brakes. The disc had been flattened on the bottom when Jerry had applied the brakes, and the pavement had ground off the lower edge of it.

"We'll have to replace the disc," forklift Jerry said.

"Is that all that's wrong with it?" forester Jerry asked.

Forklift Jerry replied, "We wouldn't even have to do that if some dumb Polack would have slowed down slow, instead of jamming on the brakes. Next time your wheel comes off, don't panic."

Forester Jerry went on his way, muttering to himself. Later, he told me he thought forklift Jerry had made an unreasonable request of him.

As the company grew, it was necessary to acquire more and more pickup trucks. Foresters came with them, and foresters wore out their trucks. It became a sore subject with me when a forester began to ask for a new truck, because it was up to me to arrange for the purchase of these vehicles; and Red was always there with the forklift story or the logging truck story for me to respond to. I would just as soon have taken a salary reduction as to try to purchase new trucks. And I suspect, that is exactly what Red had in mind when he went into his act regarding pickups.

The fat-tired pickup which was bought in 1976 lasted until 1983. By that time, there really was not much mechanically wrong with it, but the Humboldt County climate had eaten away some sheet metal here and there. I never complained about the truck because it really was a good-running machine. Also, it looked so bad that the other foresters would take one look at it and feel sorry for me. Then they would not ask me to intercede for them to get a new truck. We finally donated it to the Boy Scouts so that they could haul gear to their camp on Elk River.

It has been said many times that a field forester is happy if he has a dog in the back of a good pickup. The machine is his home, his office, and I suspect his security blanket, especially in bad weather. I believe that to be largely true. It is really a tool of the forester's trade; and it should be a good one.

When Curly passed on, Ron Hoover got Curly's old pickup to drive. It was a good truck, but Curly had run into many posts, rocks, curbs and other obstacles. It had several patches on it where Orvamae had taken it to the body repair shop every so often to have it fixed. It also had Curly's personalized license plate on it; **MR RHE**. Orvamae had **MRS RHE** on her Cadillac, so Ron took some ribbing about liking older women.

Ron likes gadgets and fancy vehicles. After he had it for a few months, he got new license plates, and made a deal with a logger's mechanic to fix it up. When they were finished with it, the truck had new paint, fancy tool boxes in the back, clamps to hold shovels, jacks and spare tire, a bed liner, and hooks to tie things down with. It was the same old truck, but it looked like a new one.

Red was impressed with how Ron took care of his vehicles. There were no dents on them; they were kept washed and shined; and the inside was always kept clean. Ron had discovered one of Red's idiosyncrasies; and he made the most of it.

Most foresters take pride in their tools, and a good forester will keep his truck in good order, and clean. Red would complain bitterly if he saw a forester's pickup with the cab full of garbage, like gum wrappers, soft drink cans, etc., or all bent up. In that respect, I had to agree with him.

With the purchase of the Santa Fe, numerous vehicles were acquired. They were stored in one of the large buildings leftover from Champion's days at Anderson. Soon everyone who thought they needed a different machine was beseeching Dan Tomascheski, or me, for permission to trade. With the trades, the average age of the vehicle inventory was rising. Some of the inventory looked as if it had come from a junk yard.

The trading soon had to stop, since Red became suspicious of the deterioration in the value of the stash of trucks. Strict orders were issued that he, or Mark Emmerson, would have to approve the distribution of them. That slowed the process some; but eventually, the residual trucks were sold off to various persons.

The Santa Fe always bought pickup trucks painted a light blue. When SPI foresters took them over, there was a big fleet of light blue vehicles on the road. I could not keep track of who was driving which truck, and would notice all light blue trucks as they passed me on the highway. Some of the drivers would wave at me, but I failed to recognize who they were. It got so bad that I made it a habit of waving at all trucks painted the same blue. There probably are a lot of people driving blue pickups who wonder who the friendly guy was who kept waving at them.

Occasionally, a Timber Manager would get a new truck when his was almost ready to trade in, or junk. This might happen if his Division Manager prevailed in talking Red into a new one for him, after I had given up in campaigning for one. I was always thankful that a manager would have the initiative to run interference for his forester when it came time to buy him a new truck.

One snowy winter day, George Coulter went to bat for Ron Voss to get a new truck. Red and I were together that day in Quincy, having been dropped off by the company airplane. It was to come back for us after it delivered someone somewhere else. As the weather deteriorated, it was evident the airplane could not return to Quincy to pick us up, so Red made arrangement for it to land in Susanville, where the airport was in a more favorable spot when visibility got bad.

George Coulter offered to loan Red his pickup to get to Susanville, and have someone else return it later. In the meantime, unknown to me, he made the pitch for Ron's new pickup.

As we started for Susanville, I could see something was bothering Red. He was somewhat preoccupied and muttering to himself. As we got a couple blocks from the mill, he launched into his usual pickup story, comparing them to forklifts and logging trucks.

After about 20 minutes of driving too fast in the snow, he said, "George says Voss needs a new truck."

"When did he say that?" I asked with surprise.

"Just now," he replied. "They must think they need a new truck every year. What's the matter with the one he's got?"

I knew the drive to Susanville was not going to be fun. I could picture Coulter, chortling to himself, knowing that I was cooped up with an unhappy Emmerson for the long, long drive to Susanville. I would take the heat while he sat in Quincy, congratulating himself on his good timing. I also knew why he was so eager to loan Red his pickup and get rid of him for the rest of the day.

At Hayfork, Dan Brummer inherited a maroon truck that had been largely worn out by Joe Dillard at Susanville. It wasn't quite up to SPI standard for disposal; so Dan, needing one a little better than the one he drove, accepted Joe's old vehicle. It began to give him trouble at once, and always seemed to be in the shop.

One snowy day, Dan was driving on an icy logging road when the truck began to slide toward the outside edge of the road. He could not control the slide; it appeared to him it was going over the edge. Thinking quickly, he opened the door and rolled out onto the road. The truck continued over the side; rolled over a couple of times; threw everything out of the back, including a "four wheeler" he had borrowed from Quincy, and came to rest several hundred feet down the slope. It was in bad shape.

When I heard about the accident, I called Dan.

"Did you get hurt?" I asked.

"Naw, never got a scratch," he said.

"How bad is the truck?" I replied.

"Bad," he said.

I persisted, "How bad?"

"It won't run; the cab is squashed; I can't open the doors; but the four wheeler is only dented a little," he said.

"What are you driving?" I asked.

"The airport car. It's pretty hard to take it to the woods, though. But it's a better running machine than my truck was. Shall I keep it?" he wanted to know.

"Hell, Dan, you can't drive a car. Let me see what we can find. For cripes sake, don't spread it around that you might get a new truck out of the deal, though. Everyone that needs a new one will get the idea that they can get one by wrecking theirs," I said.

I found an old truck for Dan to drive out of the inventory at Anderson. He drove it for a while until we got a new one for him in the spring. Every time an SPI forester talked to him after that, they expressed admiration for his resourcefulness in getting a new truck.

Dan Brummer and his pickup after being fished out of the brush a few days after accident.
Photographer unknown.

Another truck incident involving pickups, that really has nothing to do with their condition, comes to mind. The foresters at Mt. Shasta were laying out a harvest plan near the small town of Etna. Several mornings in a row they roared through the little community on their way to work. On the third or fourth day, they were stopped by a policeman and given a ticket for speeding.

I received a call from Jim Ostrowski about the incident. He wanted to know if there was a company policy about paying the fine. I told Jim if they were breaking the law, they would have to take care of the problem themselves.

A few days later, I mentioned the story to Red, thinking he might hear of it from some other source. He listened carefully, then said, "Were they going to work, or going home?"

"It was early in the morning, about 6:45 a.m. They were going to work," I said.

All he said was, "Pay the fine."

In the last years of my employment, it became somewhat easier to get new vehicles. It still was not easy, but Red probably had more important things on his mind. Too, it seemed to me, he was mellowing as he got older.

With the larger number of trucks the company had on the road, it was surprising there were not more accidents such as Dan had at Hayfork, or as a result of speeding to or from work. Even though there were few wrecks, it was still necessary to replace more each year as they wore out. Upon retirement, I became eternally grateful that I did not have to campaign for several new pickups each year instead of one or two as I did so many times in the past.

chapter fifty four

EMMERSON FAMILY REVISITED

The three Emmerson children, George, Caroline and Mark, all graduated from college. They were all good students from the beginning, surpassing their father in that category.

George went to Humboldt State for one semester to study forestry, transferred to Oregon State to major in business, and graduated in 1978. While he majored in business, his course work emphasized accounting; but he obtained enough college credit to have a minor in forestry. During summer vacations, he worked at the SPI mill at Arcata.

After graduation, George and "Butch" Mathews, Moose and Minette's son, went on a European tour. George grew a beard, and began to look like the typical young traveler abroad. He and Butch had always been good friends; and they both thought it would be a good idea to get the traveling bug out of their systems before going to work.

Red did not take kindly to George gallivanting all over the globe while there was so much work to do at home. When he received a picture from George, he especially did not like the whiskers. He could not understand how George could waste so much time doing nothing productive. Moose, on the other hand, encouraged the two young men to see the world before settling into the world of business.

Finally, George came home and went to work for SPI. Early on, he worked for Otto

Peters doing tree stocking surveys on cut-over land as required by the California Division of Forestry. In the fall of 1978, he began to cruise timber with Dan Tomascheski on the cruising crew. He did not seem to be overly fond of cruising timber for a living. He also was uncomfortable, thinking he was getting favorable treatment from Dan because he was an Emmerson.

In a short time, George went to Loyalton where he worked with Reggie Macro, the saw filer. They installed 10" single-arbor gang saws at Loyalton, where George became acquainted with the saw filing trade. While at Loyalton, he lived in the old Loyalton hotel in a room over the bar. He could look down through cracks in the floor and see who was making all the noise while he was trying to sleep.

Early in 1979, he began to work in quality control with Forrest Orr. They traveled to various SPI mills, measuring lumber thickness, grades, moisture content, and generally checking the quality of each mill's output.

In June 1979, escrow closed on the purchase of a millwork plant in Oroville owned by Down River International. The plant was in the same building that was formerly the Oroply plywood plant where I had worked upon arriving in California in 1957. It had been converted to a millwork plant a few years before.

Ron Stevens recruited George to go to

work at Oroville. Ron thought a great deal of the young man, took him under his wing, gave him a hard time when he fouled up, and ran interference for him with his father on occasion. George learned well and quickly; found his calling; and in a short time, he was managing the plant.

Sometime in 1981, he met a young lady who lived in Chico. Her name was Susan Wells. A tall, attractive blonde, Sue was a registered nurse. She and George lived together for a time in Chico. They remember Curly and Orvamae came to visit them on one occasion, and Curly told George he had better marry Sue before she got away from him.

George took his advice, marrying Sue on "September 15 of some year in the early 1980s." George does not remember the year exactly; but he remembered that Caroline was getting married the next week after he first met Sue. Meeting Sue was more important to him than the date of the wedding.

George and Sue Emmerson produced, in rapid order, four sons: Garret in 1984, Collin in 1986, Vaughn in 1987 and Dain in 1990. They are handsome boys, active, and into everything. George spends as much time as he can with the boys, remembering the good times when he was growing up with his brother and sister in Arcata. "Family" is very important to him.

I asked George to explain to a "dumb forester" the differences in terms used by those in the millwork division when they describe the type of operations covered by the term "millwork." As nearly as I can remember, these were his rough definitions:

"Reman plant" is a catch-all term applied to all kinds of remanufacturing plants. The lumber that is purchased for them is cut up into some other product. Technically they trim, rip and cut pieces to length for different products.

A "cut up" plant takes lumber and cuts it up to make some product for someone else. It could be one grade of lumber that is purchased, cut into lumber to produce different grades of lumber, then sold as raw material, or shipped as a raw material, to a plant that makes another product out of it.

A moulding plant takes lumber and runs it to a pattern (moulding). Some of the common products produced are 16' long baseboard mouldings, door trim, window trim, etc.

A millwork plant manufactures parts of some product, such as door jambs, window parts, blanks for toys, and cabinet components. The production is sold as a finished product, to be further manufactured, or to another company for assembly.

When Bob Puett retired in 1987, George and Susan moved to Susanville to manage the operation. It was hard for George to take over a sawmill after several years in the millwork business. He also was one of the "new" managers, young and aggressive; but he was inexperienced in the management of a sawmill.

At Susanville, he inherited a crew that had been there for a long time, and that had developed allegiance to Puett over the years. George was the new kid, and the son of the owner. Of course, by that time he was part-owner, too. He was facing the same pressures his father, as a very young man, had faced when he was the "push" at the Arcata sawmill.

Some of the personnel did not like the new order. When George took over, the market also began to decline, and that always made things tough for a new manager. For a while, Red was somewhat displeased with the way things were going at Susanville. Ron Stevens tried to encourage both father and son to be patient.

George persevered in running the operation his way. He transferred some of the old supervisors to new jobs; and some left SPI. Only a few of Puett's men occupy the same position they did before. It appears that he is "over the hump," although there are still some of the old-timers on the crew who believe it was a better operation under Puett.

Caroline followed George to Corvallis, where she also graduated in business. She liked school, got excellent grades, and got straight A's in her last semester.

In 1981, prior to graduating, she married Robert Wade Dietz, who was studying Earth

Sciences at the University and coaching youngsters to play soccer on the side. Bob intended to be a teacher and coach after graduation.

After they were married, the young couple stayed in Portland about six months, then purchased a liquor store in Chico. They built up the business, operating it from 1983 to 1988, then sold it. While in Chico, they had two sons: Adam born in 1984, and Alex in 1986.

They had contemplated selling their business for about a year prior to actually doing so. With Robin Arkley II, a Eureka attorney, they founded a business that purchases properties from failed Savings & Loan companies. Until recently, most of their activities were in Alaska, and they lived in Anchorage for several years.

The new business has prospered and is expanding into the "lower forty-eight." In August 1991, the family moved to New Mexico where they have business interests. From there they can travel more easily to the southeast where they also have interests, and back to Alaska on occasion.

Mark, Red and George Emmerson at Anderson sawmill in 1988. George is measuring the length of fish that got away.
Photo from SPI archives.

Mark went to the University of California at Davis for two years, then to U. C. Berkeley, where he graduated in 1982. His degree was in business, with emphasis on accounting. He also got excellent grades in school.

While in school, he met a beautiful young lady, Marissa Dykes. Marissa is small, dark, and very much like Ida Emmerson in appearance. She and Mark were married on August 30, 1986.

For the first six weeks after graduation, Mark went to South America to see the country. After George's tour of Europe, Mark also thought it would be a good idea to take a little time off from work; but he was afraid Red would be doubly upset if both sons took an extended vacation, so his was shorter. He returned to go to work for Arthur Anderson & Co., a CPA firm, where he stayed two years.

In February 1985, Mark went to Burney where he was the Division Accountant, working with Dennis Gomez. He learned a great deal from Dennis, particularly about sawmills like the one at Burney. When SPI

**Red and Ida Emmerson
at the Ingomar Club
about 1987.**
Photo from Ida Emmerson.

bought Champion and began to build the new mill at Anderson, Mark transferred to Anderson. He became its first manager, watched the construction, and was there when the first log was sawn on September 30, 1987.

After about a year-and-a-half at Anderson, Mark took over some of the corporate accounting duties that Dick Smith was relinquishing. He is now based in the CV office, down the hall from Red, Jon Gartman and Ron Stevens.

On April 30, 1990, a son, David, was born to Marissa and Mark. They kept the string of Emmerson grandsons intact at seven, with no granddaughters. Red is very proud of his seven young men. It seems that he enjoys them more than he did his own three children, which is typical of most grandparents.

I asked the young Emmersons what they thought of the future of SPI. They all expressed concern for the regulatory climate that has evolved in California, and of their worries that they may not be permitted to manage their timberland for the production of raw materials for their sawmills. However, they believe that the company's affairs are in order for an orderly transition of ownership as Red and Ida become older and less active in the business. None of them can visualize the company without the "old lion" in the office down the hall.

They believe that George is the one who is production-oriented, with Mark leaning toward finance. They are glad to see Jon Gartman on-board to help with tax matters. None of them believe that Dick Smith will ever be replaced, that his varied duties will be split up among several people: Mark, Jon Gartman, Ray Lowry, and Alan Bell, a recently hired accountant.

I asked Mark on one occasion, if he remembered anything funny about his father. He never called him "my dad," it was always "my father."

He said, "Yeah, he got madder'n hell if I stole his socks."

"What do ya mean, stole his socks," I said with surprise.

Mark replied, "I could borrow anything he owned - shirts, sweaters, jackets, anything - except his socks. I'd hear him yelling at the top of his voice early in the morning, 'Where in hell are my socks? Who stole my goddam socks?' I used to take them just to hear him holler."

I couldn't help cracking up visualizing Red Emmerson, standing in his underwear, yelling for his socks before he went to work early in the morning.

The two sons, Mark and George, believe their father has changed considerably since they were children. They recognize, too, that they are older, and that they have much more in common with him now than they did when they were growing up. He seems to talk to them a lot more now, and to confide in them. Caroline marvels at how much he seems to like being with his grandsons.

Everyone I talked to about Red Emmerson in recent years mentions the change they see in him. There is no doubt that he has aged and matured. To me, one recent incident seems to have aged him more than any other.

In the fall of 1988, Ida was diagnosed as having cancer. Shortly after a mammogram was performed, she underwent surgery and chemotherapy at the hospital in Redding. The post-operative treatment made her extremely ill, and it was touch-and-go for a while. She lost weight and much of her hair, but not her spirit. Ida is one of the toughest persons I have ever known.

During the time that Ida was engaged in the fight of her life, Red aged considerably. His once-red hair was already turning color; but after several months of worry, his hair was noticeably whiter. There were new wrinkles around his eyes and mouth. Ida survived, it seemed to some, by shear willpower.

I called her several times when she was well enough to visit. I hated to bother her, for I was sure she must have been burdened with wellwishers from all over California. She always spoke graciously, with a very positive attitude. With her iron will, I was sure if

Red and Ida's retreat at Redwood House ranch near Bridgeville, California, 1990.
Photo by author.

anyone would beat the "big C," Ida would.

Soon she was up and around, and appeared in public in her new wig. She looked the same as I remembered her, though a little thinner, perhaps. Her spirit, at least publicly, was as positive as ever. She told me she was going to beat this thing that had her cornered.

After a few months, I saw her without the wig. Her hair had grown back, and she looked very stylish. I commented on how good she looked.

"Well, what did you expect, Bud?" she said. "I feel pretty good; and we're too busy for me to mope around being sick."

With her new, shortened hair-style, I said, "Ida, you really look sexy. You should have fixed your hair like that a long time ago."

She looked at me as if she thought I was crazy. I thought I might have insulted her. Then she smiled and said, "You're crazy."

Her reaction was typical for Ida. What she didn't know was that I really thought she was sexy. She is getting along fine several years after surgery, appears to be her old self, and is busier than before with seven grandsons to entertain on occasion.

Red and Ida have a big, new house to look after - one they built just east of Anderson, midway between the sawmill and the airport. They designed the structure so that each of their three children would have a small apartment to themselves when they came to

Red on early morning wood-cutting expedition, 1991. Photo by author.

visit. They have sold their Arcata house, and have taken an apartment in Arcata where they can stay when they visit the coast and the ranch they love in Humboldt County.

Anyone who works as hard and as long as Red and Ida Emmerson requires some form of relaxation from time to time. Neither of them play golf, or tennis, or games of a similar nature. They really do not have time for such pursuits, figuring that activities of that kind take time away from productive occupations.

Since both of them are gregarious individuals, Red and Ida have numerous friends. They like to entertain; and most of their gatherings are enjoyable, but quite informal. Ida is an accomplished chef, so an invitation to dinner at their home is cause for pleasant anticipation. Invariably, at such gatherings, Red is the bartender. He is never stingy with the booze; and the latter part of an evening can become rather loud and boisterous.

However, their favorite form of relaxation is spending a weekend at their ranch not far from Bridgeville. Usually, when they are in Humboldt County, they can be found there from late on Saturday afternoon until Sunday afternoon. There is no telephone, nor electrical service, although they have installed a small generator for lighting. Water is piped into the house from a spring on the hill above the buildings.

The place is a working ranch. A full-time ranch hand looks after the place; and Red pitches in as a full-time cowboy on occasion. He enjoys the activity and hard work as much as anyone.

Red is in good physical shape and, except when at the ranch, arises early every morning to run two to three miles. At the ranch, when not tending to business, he chops wood for exercise. Those who are invited to visit the place are expected to join in.

A typical invitation begins with a call from Ida. She will usually call late in the week to invite two couples to spend Saturday night there. If arrival time on Saturday is early enough, Red may take the visitors on a tour of the place. He drives the old logging roads, using binoculars to inspect an occasional cow or calf. He checks the water holes and fences and, particularly, the young Douglas firs that have restocked the timbered portion of the property. He often measures the terminal leader on a tree, especially if it looks to be over three feet long. Many of them are.

Before dinner, Red serves drinks. Ida is busy in the kitchen and, since the floor plan is open, she can participate easily from behind the stove. Her meals are outstanding.

After dinner, Red serves more refreshments. Conversation usually touches on the business and business acquaintances. The atmosphere is warm and friendly; and often there are stories told of the old days. By 10:00 or 11:00 p.m., the party is winding down; and each guest is given a flashlight in case they must use the facilities during the night.

The next morning, rain or shine, is woodcutting time. Those who wish to participate (all the male members are expected to), embark in pickups with chain saws, splitting-malls and wedges, for a short drive to the woods. Red selects a few scrub oak trees to fall, and takes over that part of the operation. For many, the first whine of his saw usually results in a squeamish growl of the stomach from the night before.

After the tree is down and bucked to length, the splitting begins. Red does most of the work, attacking the blocks as if they were members of the Sierra Club, or Earth First. He works up a sweat quickly, and keeps at it until all the pickups are full. Then it's back to the house for brunch. By that time, most of the participants have cured their hangovers, especially if it is a cold, rainy morning.

The weekend is over in early afternoon; and each couple departs with a load of wood for the coming winter. The visits are enjoyable, and reveal a charming, unpretentious couple relaxing at home.

I once received a telephone call from Dave Galitz, of Pacific Lumber Co., about Red's woodcutting. Red's ranch adjoined some of Pacific Lumber's timberland.

Dave began by asking, "Bud, do you have any influence with your boss?"

I replied, "Dave, maybe a little, but not a hell of a lot. What's up?"

"Someone's been cutting wood on our property next to Red's ranch," he said. "I don't know if it's Red or not, but we think he may

The Emmersons at Emily Thorpe's 85th birthday celebration in Portland, Oregon. From left, Marissa and Mark, Sue, Emily, George, Caroline Dietz, Red, and Ida.
Photo from Ida Emmerson collection.
Photographer presumed to be Bob Dietz.

know something about it. Would you ask him to stop if it's him?"

"Is the wood gone?" I asked. "And how big a deal is it?"

"Oh, hey, no big deal at all," replied Dave. "The wood's all cut and split alongside the road. We don't allow wood cutting on our property because of liability problems: and some of our employees want to know if Red Emmerson can cut wood why can't they?"

Later, I talked to Red about the problem, asking, "Red, have you trespassed on PL's property to cut wood?"

He looked blankly at me for a moment, then replied, "I don't think so. Why? Did someone catch me?"

"Yeah," I said. "I got a phone call from Dave Galitz. They're madder'n hell. Someone cut a whole bunch of wood and hauled it off. They think it's you."

"Oh, Christ," said Red. "I just cut a tree that was across the road. It wasn't a big deal; and most of the wood is still there. I'll load it up and deliver it to them if they want. I thought I'd save them doing it themselves. Besides I didn't know for sure where the property lines were."

As a result, at the next forester's meeting, Red was presented with an award for being a premier firewood thief. He received a certificate commemorating the event to hang on his wall. It is prominently displayed in the cabin at the ranch.

All of the Emmersons are deeply involved with SPI. Both Mark and George eventually became members of the Big Five, making the group outgrow its label. After they joined, it was with a warm feeling that I watched them begin to interact with the senior members of the group.

At first, they were tentative; but George was the first to begin to disagree with their father. George is people-oriented, much like his father, while Mark is more hard-nosed, also like his father. George, I believe, has a greater feeling for the livelihood of SPI employees than even his father does, although some of the personnel at Susanville may doubt that. Mark attempts to stick to business.

I believe the Emmersons have provided for the future of SPI and its continued success as best they can. It is certain that the new generation is smart, hard-working in the Emmerson tradition, and committed to the company their ancestors worked so hard to create.

The Emmerson family in December, 1989. From left, Marissa and Mark, Ida and Red, George with Garret, Collin (standing), Sue with Vaughn, Caroline and Bob Dietz with Adam and Alex.

chapter fifty five

BIG FIVE II

As time went on, there were substitutions or additions made to the roster of the Big Five. As that occurred, it was no longer labeled with that nickname. One of the first to be added to the group was a tall, distinctive-looking man named Ed Bond.

Ed was born in Honolulu. His father was an Englishman who was the Chief Game Warden for the state of Hawaii. His mother was from Hawaii, and the mixture of genes in Ed contributed to his distinctive bearing. He was very tall and handsome, with black hair, and a decidedly oriental cast to his face.

Ed had graduated from high school in Honolulu and had received a football scholarship to the University of Idaho, where he played end and studied psychology. He returned to Hawaii to graduate from the University of Hawaii in 1960 with a degree in psychology.

In 1961, he went to work for a building materials supply company later purchased by U. S. Plywood Corporation. The firm was to merge with Champion Building Products. By 1966, Ed had quit U. S. Plywood and was representing the Hawaiian Employers Council, a group with about 600 member companies. He advised the members in their relations with unions representing their employees.

In 1974, Ed Bond accepted a position with the Timber Operators Council (TOC), active in representing wood products manufacturers in the western U. S., where he became acquainted with Red Emmerson and Ron Stevens. He attracted their attention when SPI sought advice relating to potential labor problems upon the acquisition of the union sawmills owned by DiGiorgio. He proved to be an effective negotiator and advisor.

In 1984, Ed was enticed away from TOC to become the man in charge of personnel for SPI. He joined the Big Five and, in addition to his duties as Manager of Personnel, became editor of the company newspaper, *BoardTalk*. He was also charged with advising those in management how to respond to the press. Much as John Godsey had before him, Ed inherited the jobs that no one wanted, or for which few were qualified. He is an effective communicator, and a valuable addition to the management group.

Other additions to the Big Five included George and Mark Emmerson. As each of them graduated from college, and after they obtained meaningful experience in the family business, they were added to the Big Five. They contributed significantly to the discussions that occurred during the meetings, and offered good advice from their younger perspectives. Their father paid close attention to their points of view.

It gave some of us old-timers in the Big Five a good feeling to see that the company would be left in good hands with the younger generation coming on. We felt that the future was, indeed, being planned for.

The last man to join the Big Five was my son, Dan. Prior to my retirement in February of 1990, I had given considerable thought to the future of the Forestry Department when it was time for me to leave. There seemed to me to be two employees who might serve in my place, and perhaps be more effective than I.

One of these was Ron Voss, who had worked with me since his graduation from Iowa State University in 1961. The other was Dan.

Dan was our first-born, and arrived in 1952 in Canyonville, Oregon. As we moved from job to job, he attended schools in Oroville, California, and then Reno, Nevada.

His first year of college was spent at Oregon State in Corvallis. He wanted to be an anthropologist. With little sunshine and no night life, Corvallis was in sharp contrast to Reno; so Dan's last three years were spent at the University of Nevada in Reno where he graduated in anthropology in June 1974.

From the time he was capable of getting around in the woods, he seemed to enjoy working with me, marking and cruising timber, laying out roads, and surveying property lines. As he got older, he secured summertime work doing the same kinds of things near Truckee, California, where he worked for an old friend, Bud Fish, Fibreboard's Resource Manager.

He went to work for Fibreboard's road crew after graduation and, finally, in November 1975, decided that he would go back to school. He enrolled at Berkeley to study forestry. Having been gifted with the capacity for retaining just about everything that he read, and being a voracious reader, he soon found that he could be a forester without the effort of four or five years as an undergradu-

ate. He completed the course work for a Masters in Forestry at the University of California in June 1977.

He went back to work for Fibreboard, this time as a forester.

In early 1978, SPI began to look for a timber cruising crew to help with the acquisition of timber and timberland. Dan applied for the job of cruiser.

Being uncomfortable with this development, I sought advice from Red. He told me that it was unfair to penalize a person just because he might be related to someone in the company, and that he would take over and interview Dan himself. That he did; and Dan met Red in Redding. He was hired and went to work on March 1, 1978.

In February 1979, he went to Quincy where he became Ron Voss's assistant. Dan gained valuable experience working for Ron, especially in the negotiating process where Ron excels.

When SPI acquired the Santa Fe timberlands and reorganized the forestry functions in 1982, Dan left the Quincy area to return to Anderson where he assumed the duties of Timberlands Manager for SPI.

As my retirement approached, it was necessary to give Red the opportunity to choose the person who would replace me. I felt that both Ron Voss and Dan could do the job. Consequently, I arranged for Ron Voss to move to Anderson where he would work side-by-side with Dan - Ron looking after the forestry activities at each of the divisions, and Dan looking after the fee lands. The arrangement continued for a year or two prior to 1989.

In the first part of 1989, upon my announcing that I wished to slow down, Red selected Dan to take my place as Manager of the Forestry Department for the company. On February 1, 1990, Dan became a member of the Big Five and was subsequently made a Vice-President of SPI. His number-one assistant is Ron Voss.

From top left
George Emmerson, Mark Emmerson, Dan Tomascheski, **Ed Bond**
(All photos from SPI archives)

Looking south down North Fork of Squaw Creek from SPI's Curl Ridge in 1980. Note this is mostly "young man's ground" - with sparse timber and heavy brush on very steep slopes.

Photo by Alan Jacobson.

chapter fifty six

EMPLOYEE COMPENSATION

Red Emmerson has always been concerned with paying **all** employees well and treating them fairly. He worries that those working in the manufacturing facilities, or others being paid an hourly wage, may feel that their remuneration is not up to par with those employees on a monthly salary. Since, to a great extent, he identifies with the "working man," he tries to walk a fine line between the two groups, recognizing the different contributions to success that each of them makes.

I remember a management meeting attended only by those labeled "the management group" in SPI. The persons in the group are essentially heads of departments or divisions. They were listening to reports by the original Big Five. Afterwards, there were discussions led by several members of the group, both sawmill managers and department leaders.

At one point in the discussion, Red broke in to make a point for everyone to hear. The discussion had centered on the need for certain programs that might require additional staffing; and he was concerned that SPI would become top-heavy with more management-type persons.

In his usual way, he got directly to the point. He began by saying, "I don't see why we need more people on the payroll. A lot of companies get top-heavy with managers. We don't need unproductive people on our payroll like John Godsey or some of you other guys."

There was a moment of silence while everyone digested that bit of information. John sat there with a shocked look on his face. Ever afterwards, he would occasionally be reminded of how unproductive he was. Red thought a moment about what he had said, then explained what he meant. He had simply used the wrong word; he had meant those employees not in production, that is, non-production-type people. He was making his point, however. Production people were necessary; some managers may not be necessary.

At SPI, the employees not represented by a union are usually paid as much or more than those who are. Red seemed to believe that the unions represent union employees; therefore their compensation package is arrived at through negotiating and is subject to dictates of the labor market. Since unions usually represent workers in an industry, not just in a company, the resulting wage structure is set at a level competitive for the whole industry. If union employees wish to pay union dues to obtain such representation, that is their right.

Red is inclined to be concerned with the compensation paid to non-union employees as well. In general, he seems to feel they are more oriented toward being "company" employees, whereas union employees belong to the union; but neither group should be treated differently. He values all of them.

He also goes to great lengths to keep a lid on perquisites for salaried employees. It appears that he not only believes it to make good economic sense to do so, but it is unfair to other employees if they are treated differently. That may be part of the reason SPI management does not travel first class, nor stay at high-priced hotels when on company business.

At the end of each year, SPI contributes to a retirement fund for all of the employees. The plan is funded, and is managed to insure growth and security of the principal. Upon retirement, the employee can elect several options for payment, suitable to his or her needs. Workers are fully vested in the plan after seven years of employment.

Red and Curly decided soon after they formed R. H. Emmerson & Son that it would be good business to pay certain key employees a share of the company's profits, if there were any. They set up a plan to do so. Some of the first employees who participated in such a plan were Luther Stienhauser at Hayfork, Burr Coffelt at Susanville, and Sam Witzel at Arcata.

As I began to talk to people while collecting information for this story, several of them offered early recollections of the beginning of the scheme. Several of them, including Red himself, claimed they had conceived the idea of how to structure the plan. It is possible that, like all good ideas, it was discussed among several of Red's early associates; and the final plan contained several elements of the discussions. In any event, the few people who qualified were compensated according to a sliding scale, depending on the amount of the profits. The more the company made, the greater the percentage each person received.

This simple concept was in place in the early years, prior to the company going public. At that juncture (1969), it was decided that a publicly held company could not continue with the compensation package as then structured. Therefore, during the years the company was public, certain key people were eligible to participate in a stock option plan.

The current plan was put in place in 1975, when the company again became private. Since then, there have been only minor modifications to it. At the end of each year, a portion of pre-tax profits are set aside to be divided among qualified employees. At that time, a part of each person's share, usually 50%, is paid in cash to cover the employee's tax liability due on the total amount. The company then issues an interest-bearing note to the employee for the portion retained by SPI, in effect borrowing from the employee. Notes are secured by a first mortgage, recorded in the appropriate county, on certain of the company's real property assets.

The amounts retained by the company can be collected by the employee upon reaching the age of 59, or upon retirement. Since the income taxes have been paid each year, the employee receives a lump sum payment at the end of his employment. The total sum, except for that portion that is accrued interest, is not subject to further tax. The plan was amended over the years to make minor adjustments to comply with the tax laws, and to insure adequate security for the amounts loaned to the company.

At its inception in 1975, the number of participating employees numbered 19. By 1989, there were 60 people in it. Of those, only eight were from the original group in 1975. The eight are indeed key people to SPI. They are Dick Smith, Ron Stevens, Ron Hoppe, Ray Lowry, George Sharp, Alan Smith, Deke Fairchild, and Jerry Gromacki (the only original forester). Otto Peters was one of the first of the latter group to retire; and there have been several who have followed since then.

Red is very proud of the success of the company, and the people who made it so. He wished to compensate them well, and to ensure they would stay in the employment of SPI. He has always said that he demands great dedication to the company during an employee's working years. When those years are over, he wants their retirement years to be relatively free of economic hardship. Unless there are unforseen catastrophes, he has certainly succeeded in doing that.

Perhaps there is no greater tribute to Red Emmerson and his family than the esteem the great majority of SPI employees hold for them. The employees know that Red values their labor and participation very highly. He values the clean-up man (the occupation where he and his sons began their sawmill careers), as well as the person in the saw box, or the head of one of SPI's divisions. Most of the employees are proud of their company.

chapter fifty seven

NUMBER ONE

The Santa Fe acquisition was completed on February 29, 1988. The leap year date was not significant; it took that long to get all the deeds and agreements in order. Sierra Pacific Industries, with the final stroke of the pen, became the largest timberland owner in California. Since it was already the largest in terms of lumber production, there was no doubt the company was a continuing force in the western timber industry. The SPI foresters knew the sawmills gobbled up a lot of logs.

The table on the following page shows the growth of the company in terms of log usage from 1982, the depression year, through 1988.

In 1988, with the Anderson sawmill approaching full production and Burney operating up to its capability, the three large log mills, Hayfork, Susanville and CV began to use more wood.

In May, another old landmark was eliminated as the four tall smoke stacks on the old Susanville power house were dismantled. They had withstood wind and weather since the early 1920s. The new powerhouse and cogen plant made them obsolete.

By 1988, the Construction Division had expanded to include some 25 welders, electricians, machinists, computer technicians and fabricators. Greg Waalkes was the manager of the department. Bob Stricklan, Jr. was still shop supervisor, and Dave Koskinen was handling all of the computer technology for the company. The shop was in the midst of fabricating a new 72-bin sorter for the Hayfork sawmill. They were also at work on the Loyalton cogen facility.

I was beginning to think very seriously of retiring from the constant battles with the environmentalists and the regulators, with whom it was necessary to contend in order to do business in California. While I enjoyed the hard work and camaraderie associated with managing the forestry operations, it was becoming evident to me that my time was growing short. Perhaps, I thought, a younger person could do a better job than I, one who might even look forward to the daily fights that came with the turf.

The corporate office had moved lock, stock and barrel to Central Valley long ago. George and Mark Emmerson were very active in their Divisions; and Jon Gartman was now aboard. Jon was becoming an important player in the upper management of SPI.

Jon Gartman was born in 1950 in Vancouver, Washington. He had grown up and graduated from high school there. By 1974, he had a B.S. in Business from Portland State University. In 1975, Jon received his M.B.A. from Golden Gate University in San Francisco.

Like many young men with business

Sierra Pacific Industries
Volumes of Logs Used In Millions of Board Feet (MMBF)

	1982	1983	1984	1985	1986	1987	1988	Total
Arcata	62.9	69.3	70.3	68.5	72.2	74.9	76.4	494.5
CV	41.7	58.7	63.8	68.6	74.6	73.5	75.0	455.9
Burney	43.2	45.8	51.9	65.0	71.3	75.3	76.9	429.4
Quincy	17.2	53.4	65.9	70.8	84.7	92.3	94.1	478.4
Loyalton	15.1	48.1	38.7	59.5	63.5	66.5	67.8	359.2
Susanville	72.0	76.9	69.9	71.9	73.0	85.1	86.8	535.6
Sloat	10.6	12.2	10.6	11.7	12.5	12.1	12.3	82.0
Hayfork	49.6	53.9	54.7	50.3	70.3	73.7	75.2	427.7
Anderson	0	0	0	0	0	21.0	49.0	70.0
Total	312.3	418.3	425.8	466.3	522.1	574.4	613.5	3332.7

educations, Jon went to work for Price Waterhouse, an accounting firm that audited the books for many forest products firms. He was transferred from the San Francisco office of Price Waterhouse to the New York office in 1978. In 1980, he left New York to become Tax Manager for Weyerhauser Timber Company in Portland, Oregon; but returned to Price Waterhouse as Senior Tax Manager in 1984.

By 1987, Jon had joined Cavenham Forest Industries as Tax Manager. This proved to be a unique experience, for he was exposed to Sir James Goldsmith, the English financier and arbitrager. Sir James was the power behind the purchase of Diamond International, a firm owning a considerable acreage of timberland east of Chico and Red Bluff in California. Jon's education in tax matters continued with them.

By 1988, Dick Smith was considering the possibility that he might someday have to retire. He was 64 years old, and contemplating a life of travel and leisure. There were many conversations that took place among the Big Five, speculating how the company would get along without Dick and his expertise.

It was finally decided that one man could not occupy the place that Dick would someday vacate. In fact, it was felt that it would not be

desirable to entrust to one person the responsibilities that Dick had. It would be better to find a man who could specialize in tax matters, and have someone else responsible for fiscal matters. At the time, taxes were a full-time job in themselves. Jon Gartman was the man chosen primarily for his tax expertise. He came to work for SPI in 1988.

In 1988, the company was in full production, and forging ahead at full speed; but for me, there was something missing.

My wife Norma and I still lived in Eureka, as did Dick and Marcie Smith. Dick and I were the only two "corporate" people left on the coast. Since both of us were in our 60s, it did not make much sense for us to sell our homes and move to the Redding area for a few short years. Consequently, both of us were spending most nights away from home. Norma and I took a small apartment in Redding to lessen the time spent driving Highway 299 in a pickup truck. That helped somewhat; but at age 63, even apartment living becomes tiresome after a short time.

Red was still the air force dispatcher. While he had mellowed significantly, he still made me feel uncomfortable when asking permission to use one of the aircraft. I felt that I could have often used an airplane effectively, even though that mode of transportation was expensive; but I was reluctant to ask. The combination of circumstances made me think I was, indeed, too old to enjoy going to work each day.

In a long career, my duties had always included providing raw materials for one or more manufacturing facilities owned by my employers. With SPI, that task was always quite easy, for the company could always pay more for its logs than any competitor. Thus, instead of persuasion or guile, it only took a sharp pencil and a check to purchase virtually any timber (or logs) we wanted. However, I had always had a goal of securing an assured **long-term** timber supply for an employer. That one had always escaped me.

With the acquisition of the Santa Fe, that goal was nearly attainable; and that gave me a great deal of satisfaction. I thought, too, that if I could find a competent replacement, I could leave with a clear conscience, knowing the resource part of the company was in good hands.

The process of selecting a replacement was left to Red. After Ron Voss was asked to move to Anderson, Red chose Dan Tomascheski as related earlier.

When first asked to move, Ron was reluctant to leave Quincy. After so many years in Plumas County, he and his wife Carol had acquired many friends. They had built a beautiful house just outside of town; Quincy was home. It took several conversations to impress on Ron that his promotion was important. I remembered Red's vagueness when he tried to get me to move to Arcata. Thankfully, I did not have to be vague. SPI needed Ron in Redding.

Ron Voss occupied a special place in my career. I first met him when he came as a summer employee in the summer of 1961. At the time, he was studying forestry at Iowa State University, where I had graduated.

I had contacted an old professor for help in finding a young forester who could help cruise timber, buy logs, and do general forestry work. I specified someone who would work hard, was intelligent, was not a "smart alec," and would be dependable. He told me he had just the man for the job.

I was on the log pond at the mill in Reno when Ron showed up to go to work. I took one

Jon Gartman. Photo from Jon Gartman.

look at him and thought the professor somehow had misunderstood my specifications.

Ron is blond, and always appears to be younger, by a substantial amount, than he actually is. When he appeared on the log pond that first day, he had a butch haircut. He walked a little pigeon-toed, somehow appearing a little disjointed. I thought at first he was a local youngster, perhaps 14 years old, looking for me for some reason.

It was too late to turn back. Ron was a long way from his home in Cass County, Iowa, where he was born in 1939. He had graduated from Atlantic High School in 1957. Atlantic is a typical, small midwest town. Ron was good in school and a good baseball player; and his parents ran the local post office.

When Ron came to Nevada, my wife and I found him a room in Sparks, and Ron went to work. I soon found the old professor knew exactly what he was talking about. Ron was a hard worker. He got along with everyone he met, he was smart, and he was a good forester. We began a long relationship.

The next year, he came back to Reno to go to work. By that time, he had graduated, and married Carol, his high school sweetheart, who was also blond. Ron was ready to set the world on fire. We again found him a place to live at an apartment building in Reno called the Flophouse. It was quite a comfortable place, not in any way the kind of a place its name suggests. The young couple fit right in.

Ron and Carol produced two beautiful, blond daughters: Robin and Kristin. It was natural for us to remain close to their family; and we eventually became friends with Ron's and Carol's parents when they came west to visit the young people.

In 1967, Ron approached me with a strange request: he wanted to try working for the Forest Service. I was somewhat shocked, as we both used to converse about the lack of opportunities there for "good" people.

Ron began the conversation, "Bud, I think I had better try government service before I'm too old. I've been here almost six years. Think you can get along without me?"

I said, "Ron, I think you're nuts; but if you have to do it, I guess we can find someone to fill in after you. Do you have any idea when or where you'll go?"

"There's a job open in Colorado. I know a guy who works there. I'd like to try it and see if it will work out. If I don't try it now, I'll never know. I'll leave in about three weeks," he said.

So Ron left for Colorado. We never did find a person to adequately replace him, although we tried several young foresters. Then in the early spring of 1970, I received a telephone call from Ron. He started the conversation with a rather direct request.

"Have you got a job for me in California?" he asked.

"Ron, what happened? Did you get fired?" I asked.

"Naw, nothing like that," he said, "The country here is great; the people are nice; but the most challenging thing I have to do is to find which page in the Forest Service Manual I have to read in order for me to solve a problem the government way."

A few weeks later, on May 1, 1970, Ron, Carol and family moved to Quincy where Ron was to be in charge of the logging, road building and log buying for the sawmill there. I was greatly relieved that his experiment in being a government forester was behind him.

Ron went through a traumatic time with the rest of us when SPI bought DiGiorgio. He endured another when George Coulter took over as Manager of the Quincy and Sloat operations of SPI.

George, being young and aggressive, believed he had to immediately make a direct and lasting impression on everyone in his organization. He came on strong, criticizing their performance, and shaking up the whole crew. Ron was caught up in the process; and I began to receive numerous telephone calls from him, requesting advice on how to handle the new manager.

We soon determined that while George was smart and worked hard, he did not know very much about forestry, logging or getting along with people. He was an excellent lumberman, but he had a lot to learn. One of the best places to learn what he lacked was by listening to Ron Voss. Many times, I would counsel Ron to persevere and not give up. Meanwhile, I was working on George.

I would start out by kidding with Coulter, "How's things going in the forestry business there, George? Have you got them all straightened out yet?"

"The logs here are terrible," he would reply, "They don't know anything about logs. They don't know nothing."

"Calm down and tell me what's wrong," I would say.

After a long conversation in which George would cover most of his fears and problems, he would have cooled down so that he could be more objective. I soon found out that he was under enormous pressure from Red and Stevens to run a tight organization, and that his operation was a big one for him to get acquainted with. I would tell him I'd help by talking to Ron, and that I would come to Quincy to talk to him.

After a number of visits, large numbers of telephone calls, several conversations with Red and Stevens, and a few months under his belt, George was beginning to change his story. He and Ron were becoming good friends. Ron Voss, in his low-key way, had won George over.

When the conflict was about over, I paid George a visit. I began by asking him the old question, "How's the forestry department, George?"

"Just great, we've got the best bunch in the company here," he said.

"Didn't I tell you to listen to the guy across the hall?" I asked. "He'll make you look good."

George was somewhat sheepish, "Yeah, you were right," he said. "I overheard him yesterday in his office over there. He was negotiating with Loren McElroy over a logging job. Do you know he argued with him for over 40 minutes? And they were only a nickel a thousand apart. I couldn't hardly stand it. I would have got impatient and give him the nickel after a few minutes. Do you know what five cents a thousand amounts to on twenty million feet of logging?"

After that George became very supportive. He ran a good division, and Ron made a difference. Since Ron had several foresters working for him, we used to send young ones there for seasoning and instructions. They all came away from the internship better foresters, and better employees for SPI.

Most people outside the company do not

Ron Voss, early 1980s, wearing an "award" received from his fellow foresters. Ron's habit of falling asleep in a pickup truck put his head and neck at risk from banging around. The "safety hat" permitted him to fasten his head to the ceiling of the truck and thereby prevent injury and reduce the banging noise. Photo by author.

Ron Voss, 1989. Photo by author.

understand the kind of a person Ron Voss is. He is very quiet, unassuming, and does little in the way of public speaking. But he leaves his mark wherever he goes. He, indeed, makes his superiors look good.

In February 1988, Ron and Carol Voss attended a party in Quincy where Ron was the guest of honor. The Rock House at the Quincy fairgrounds was the site of his "roast." All of the local loggers, the same ones with whom he had negotiated logging prices so fiercely, came to say goodbye before he left for Anderson. Cowboy hat askew, he was forced to sit in a saddle on a sawhorse that had a wooden horsehead at the front, to listen to the roast. At a predetermined time, a local belly dancer came to kiss him farewell. I believe the loggers sincerely hated to see him leave. I know the Manager of the Quincy operation, George Coulter, did. Bill Banka, one of Ron's assistants, was promoted to take his place.

For the first year after becoming a large land-owning company, SPI continued modernizing its plants as usual. It was evident that SPI never stops modernizing. No sooner is a facility completed than it is remodeled, or expanded.

The company also was paying down its debt on the Santa Fe purchase, ahead of schedule as usual. The original loan agreement required the first installment to be paid six months after close of escrow. SPI essentially began paying each installment in advance, so that by the end of the first year the company was ahead of its payment schedule by one year.

As a result, the loan agreement was renogotiated, and the rate of interest charged by the banks was lowered. Red wished to be ahead of his commitments, not only to preserve his track record, but to weather any period of slow markets. It was fortunate that he did so, for the industry was in for some trying times in the early 1990s.

In 1988, a new millwork plant was installed in one of the old Champion buildings at Anderson. The building was completely refurbished, patched and painted. New machinery was installed, and the operation began production.

Bill Banka, 1990. Photo by Teri Banka.

As the year wound down and the Christmas season approached, I agonized about telling Red that I intended to retire. I knew that he depended upon me, not only to manage the resource operations of the company, but to provide a sounding board for his ideas relating to forestry matters. He had grown comfortable with what I did.

Finally, just before Christmas, I told him. He did not seem surprised; in fact, he seemed to welcome the change. I was somewhat taken aback.

I said, "Red, I'm getting too old for all the things going on in this business. It's not fun anymore. I think Norma and I need to slow down and do a few more things before it's too late."

"Like what?" he asked.

"Well, I don't play golf - never had time to learn. I used to fish once in a while, about 30 years ago. If I get addicted to that, my wife will divorce me. Maybe we'd like to travel a bit. And I think I might like to try to write a book sometime," I replied. "Besides I'm getting unsteady on my feet in the woods. I fall down a lot more than I used to. Maybe I'll just grow flowers."

He looked at me quizzically, "When?"

"Sometime in 1989. Whatever you're comfortable with. I'll stay as long as you want me to. I feel good about having everything pretty well in place, so the company won't need me anymore; and I'll stay the whole year if you want," I said.

He studied me a moment. Then he said, "Bud, I understand where you're coming from. We'll have to make a few changes, but I think that won't be too hard. Let me think about it a little."

The die was cast.

By year-end, the company had produced 921,962 MBF of lumber. Total sales were $452,586,917. SPI had logged 246,500 MBF of fee timber. Less than 200,000 MBF had come from the Santa Fe lands. Even though SPI had to honor some of the agreements made by the Santa Fe to sell logs, the company had actually reduced the harvest from the new acquisition.

At year-end, total assets were valued at $677,855,246. Capital improvements were valued at $10,566,673: $4,519,117 at Loyalton, and $1,160,733 at Anderson. The Anderson sawmill in its first year of operation under Mark Emmerson had contributed over $6,000,000 in income.

In 1988, SPI sold over $8,000,000 in solid-waste revenue bonds, part of which was used to finance the Loyalton cogen facility.

Bare root stock being planted on SPI timberlands in 1990. This is one of approximately 2 million seedlings planted that year by SPI.   Photo from SPI archives.

chapter fifty eight

Owls & Slowdown

In early January 1989, Red approached me several times about who would take over my duties. As usual, each conversation was a carbon copy of the last one. The discussions centered on Ron Voss and Dan Tomascheski. Each one beginning with a question from Red.

"Red, either one of those guys could do what I do," I replied each time to his questioning. "Ron has more experience than Dan and will do an excellent job. The only weakness he may have is his reluctance to speak publicly."

"We've got enough politicians already. We need someone who is a good businessman in that job," he said.

"Ron is great at that," I replied, "He's probably the best negotiator we've got."

"How about Dan?"

"Red, you'll have to make up your own mind about him. I can't say very much about him for obvious reasons. I know he's smart and can talk pretty well. He's awfully young, too. You'll have to make that decision yourself."

The same conversation would occur a few days later. Finally, at the end of January, he came into my office in Arcata again.

"I've made up my mind what to do," he said. "I think Dan can pull it off. I'm worried that he'll spend too much time at meetings, and there won't be anyone minding the store, though."

"If that's the case, you'd better tell him straight out what you think," I said, "When are you going to make the change?"

"I thought about February first," he said.

"You mean next week?" I asked.

"There's no use screwing around once your mind is made up, is there?" he asked. "I thought we'd put you on reduced salary and you can wind down for the next few months."

"That'll be fine," I said. And that was that.

I had thought I would remain at full employment for several months, giving him plenty of time to figure out what to do. Red, in his inimitable way, had made the decision and gone on to something else. I wondered if I had made a mistake. It was too late to worry about it.

The slow-down did not amount to much at first. I was still gone from the coast most of the time. The telephone rang incessantly. The environmental battles were getting hotter and more complicated all the time. I was working just as hard and getting paid half as much. It really wasn't what I had in mind when I announced to Red that I was thinking about retiring.

No matter, there were things to do. We were preparing countless timber harvest plans (THPs) for the Santa Fe, Publisher's, and SPI's other lands. The appeals on Forest Service timber sales were coming thick and fast. The spotted owl was possibly going to be declared a "threatened and endangered" species.

In 1989, SPI not only worried about its problems with the environmental movement, but began to do something about it. It was becoming increasingly evident that the movement was attracting big money. While environmentalists had been politically prominent for many years, the number of members of each group making up the membership was always published for politicians to see; the budgets of each group were seldom discussed.

Ron Arnold, author of *The Ecology Wars*, and a former member of the Sierra Club, described two types of environmentalists. He labeled them "big E" and "little e." The former, **E**nvironmentalists, were those similar to members of the Sierra Club, The Wilderness Society, and the Environmental Defense Fund. They were the activists who wanted everything to be saved from the activities of man, no matter what the cost. The latter, **e**nvironmentalists, were all the rest of us who were concerned about the environment.

Inside the Environmental Groups, a book by Bill Gifford, listed some 25 environmental groups with a combined membership of nearly 6,000,000 persons, and a staff of almost 4,000. The combined annual budget for all 25 was nearly $545,000,000. The National Wildlife Federation alone boasted a yearly budget of over $87,000,000; the Sierra Club, over $35,000,000.

With massive funding of that caliber, it was easy to see how the Environmentalists were such a force. It was also easy to see why they had a vested interest in maintaining membership and obtaining funding.

Many of the groups manufactured causes that they then promoted. A frequently used ploy was to claim something they wished to "save" was unique in some way.

For example, before being declared endangered, the Northern spotted owl was listed a "sensitive species" according to U.S. Forest Service regulations, after much pressure was brought to bear on the agency. As such, when found, it had to be protected. In addition, elaborate plans were made to protect its habitat.

On one occasion, an owl was detected close to a timber sale that had been purchased by SPI on the Tahoe National Forest. Opera-tions could not begin pending further analysis by biologists. Discussions began between the company and the Forest Service to find a solution acceptable to both parties. By eliminating some cutting units near the owl's home and substituting timber elsewhere, the problem could have been easily solved.

The local Sierra Club intervened in the process. This particular owl was the individual that had been found **farthest east** of any on the Tahoe. It therefore needed special attention. I suggested, at one point in the discussion, that we should pay particular attention to the owl that was **closest** to the geographical center of the forest, or **highest** in elevation, or **farthest** from the forest supervisor's home. That made about as much sense to me as trying to claim the uniquiness of an individual bird that happened to settle in that part of the forest. If it had set up housekeeping a little farther east, it would have been the farthest **west** on the Toiyabe National Forest.

Another common technique was to give a label to something that was to be "saved." The Pacific Lumber Co. (PL) owned some old-growth redwood. It was no different than any other old-growth redwood they owned except for two features: it was a fairly large block and it had a name given to it by the **E**nvironmentalists. It was "The Headwaters Forest." Every time PL submitted a timber harvest plan for a portion of "The Headwaters Forest," it was appealed by the big **E**s.

The spotted owl was supposed to require old-growth forests in which to live and breed. By 1989, the land base left over for timber management was becoming so small and fragmented that the industry was faced with a major reduction in available raw materials. In California, the industry decided to do something about it. They would survey their lands, seeking the owl, and note the kinds of habitat in which it lived. It seemed to most of us that no one had looked for owls anywhere but in old-growth forests where there were roads close by.

SPI was one of the principal supporters of the proposal to begin the survey. Wildlife biologists were hired to standardize the procedures and to instruct those doing the field work. They would also monitor the progress of the work, inspect the data, and ratify the results.

Spotted owls are nocturnal creatures. The search for them is conducted at night using a "formal" protocol prescribed by biologists. A recording of their calls is played at prescribed intervals over a loudspeaker, and their answering calls noted by compass bearing and estimated distance from the loudspeaker. The location of the loudspeaker is marked on the ground so that a biologist can "mouse" the owl in the daylight to determine age, sex, number of young (if any), and other data.

Most owls will accept a mouse held out to them. They become quite tame after repeated feedings and will take a mouse from one's hand. Some of them will follow a pickup that they associate with feeding time, alight near it, and wait for the driver to give them a mouse. SPI needed a lot of mice, and began to purchase them wherever they could find them.

The lunchroom of the SPI forestry office became a mouse nursery. The owl's meals were being fattened there for all to see. Though Red did not complain bitterly about mice in the lunchroom, he must have thought that the lumber business was certainly changing. It appeared to be going to the mice instead of to the dogs. Curly would have cussed the bureaucrats and headed for the ranch to talk to his horses, or retired to the Anchor for lunch.

And owls? The SPI foresters found them wherever they looked. In countless locations, they were in **young**-growth of **every** species. There were more of them in Humboldt County than elsewhere, but they were all over the map. One particular pair was on SPI land in the Sacramento River canyon very close to the I-5 freeway. That one appeared on TV. If the Northern spotted owl was sensitive or threatened in California, it certainly didn't know it.

I became aware of a local owl when I received a call from Bill Kleiner who had prepared a timber harvest plan for a client in Humboldt County. The location of the proposed logging site was quite close to my home near Elk River.

When I answered the phone, Bill said, "When are you going to move?"

I asked, "Why; do I have to?"

"Yeah, you're going to have to abandon your place. The owl is taking over," he said.

"Bill, what are ya smoking?"

He said, "Bud, no kidding, there's a pair of owls with young practically in your back yard. They're on the THP I filed on the property just up the road from where you're at. You're in their habitat."

There is a gully that begins very close to the back of the lot we own, and it is covered with young-growth redwood and spruce. A short distance away, in this timber type, the owls were contented, raising their young, and listening to the sounds of radios, dogs barking, and traffic on adjacent roads and byways. Bill was telling me that the owl counted; people did not.

The U. S. Fish and Wildlife Service (F&WS) had scheduled several hearings for the purpose of collecting new data concerning the owl. While only a few short years ago they had determined that the creature was not endangered, they were prevailed upon to reopen the case to receive additional data. They announced they would not accept economic data, only biological data.

One of the hearings was scheduled for Redding in August 1989. By the time the hearing date arrived, much of the industry's data was ready for preliminary publication. Steve Self, a wildlife biologist from the Timber Association of California (TAC), participated in the studies, coordinating the efforts of many of the industry participants. He compiled much of the data, and prepared the report for submission to the F&WS. It was an excellent presentation.

Just prior to the hearing, a rally was held adjacent to the Redding convention center where the meeting was to be conducted. Over 5,000 people showed up to exhibit support for the embattled industry. Yellow ribbons and yellow flags were evident, as well as innumerable jackets, shirts and hats - all yellow. The meeting hall was jammed with people wearing yellow. Many of SPI's employees were there, having arrived from as far away as Quincy and Loyalton. The SPI helicopter flew overhead with the media aboard to get a good view of the demonstrators.

While the show made the industry participants feel good, the effects were predictable. The owl would be listed as "threatened and endangered." There was beginning to be a difference, though. The employees of the timber industry were finally getting a different slant on what was going on. Of more importance was the effect on Red and others in SPI's upper management. They were also becoming alarmed.

The next day, August 18, 1989, I was honored at a "Slow Down Hoedown" in the same Rock House in Quincy where Ron Voss had his roast. It was a large affair attended by some real old-timers of the industry whom I had not seen for many years. Bill Dennison, TAC's President, was the Master of Ceremonies. Many nice things were said about me, many of which were exaggerated. If I had known that all of those people thought so much of me, I would not have retired. The best part of the festivities was that the drinks were on the house.

Meanwhile, operations of the company were going on as usual. Logging was in full swing. The continuing drought in California, becoming the longest on record, was affecting timber stands all over the state, particularly in the Sierra. The Tahoe Basin was especially hard hit. Salvage timber sales were the rule rather than the exception.

The Loyalton cogen plant began producing electricity as the year-end approached. For 1989, almost $8,000,000 had been spent at Loyalton on capital improvements. When the plant came on-line, it joined four other SPI plants in production.

As the year closed, lumber production peaked at 940,259 MBF. Total sales were $503,102,000, and total assets were valued at $715,423,000.

I felt good about my slow-down year. On February 1, 1990, I retired for good. When I left, Sierra Pacific Industries had the following operating Divisions:

Arcata - Sawmill
Susanville - Sawmill and Cogen Plant
Hayfork - Sawmill and Cogen Plant
Redding (CV) - Sawmill
Loyalton - Sawmill and Cogen Plant
Quincy - Sawmill and Cogen Plant
Sloat - Sawmill
Anderson - Sawmill and Millwork Plant

Chico - Millwork Plant
Oroville - Millwork Plant
Richfield - Millwork Plant and Central
    Distribution Center
Central Valley - Lumber and Millwork
    Sales, and Export Sales
Quincy Railroad - Railroad at Quincy and
    at Susanville
Transportation - Log and lumber trucks
    at Arcata, Redding, Susanville,
    Quincy and Loyalton
Timber - Main office at Anderson -
    District offices at Mt. Shasta,
    Weaverville, Grass Valley
    and Anderson
Health Benefits and Workmen's
    Compensation - Anderson

There were two computer systems with all of the necessary managers and support personnel: one at CV, the other at the Timber Division at Anderson.

SPI, with Red's blessing, to some extent had modified the intensive forest management prescriptions the Santa Fe had undertaken. The SPI district foresters began to decrease the total harvest, and also the amount which was "clear-cut."

As a result, the number of trees planted also declined because there was less bare ground requiring planting. A new inventory system was begun to serve as a basis for determining growth, mortality, and the amount of land which needed rehabilitation.

Scott Warner, one of SPI's foresters, prepared a summary showing the activity on fee lands since 1984, when the Santa Fe still owned some of the timberland:

Year	Planting # trees (millions)	Acres	Pre-commercial Thinning Acres
1984	2,828	5,864	1,187
1985	2,595	5,410	24
1986	2,614	5,862	124
1987	3,111	5,686	211
1988	2,119	4,573	0
1989	1,318	2,802	932
1990	1,980	3,700	1,194
1991	1,738	3,278	1,780

Dick Smith prepared a simple table showing the growth of SPI from the time it had been formed until the end of 1989. It shows in brief statistics what Red Emmerson and the people at SPI had accomplished in a short 22 years.

SPI GROWTH

Total Sales and Assets by Year
($ in thousands)

Year	Sales	Property Plants Equip.	Timber	Total Assets
1968	25,372	5,038	116	16,656
1969	38,114	11,619	1,305	26,461
1970	33,345	12,227	0	28,245
1971	58,344	10,541	0	33,964
1972	84,397	13,186	272	46,131
1973	123,343	15,145	3,634	61,864
1974	71,867	9,214	3,132	42,781
1975	60,272	7,089	6,654	38,205
1976	92,282	13,305	15,975	76,167
1977	122,287	14,839	18,752	82,062
1978	150,430	21,314	51,528	135,823
1979	168,038	25,398	52,969	134,745
1980	164,891	25,470	55,445	147,790
1981	147,658	25,261	53,838	133,659
1982	136,185	23,523	50,695	118,277
1983	213,379	26,694	47,159	146,669
1984	218,300	41,829	38,895	148,784
1985	242,572	68,297	37,305	186,230
1986	298,070	80,882	37,773	211,433
1987	371,784	88,143	35,008	247,986
1988	452,587	93,393	464,857	677,855
1989	503,102	89,662	493,661	715,423

(Total assets column includes cash, inventory, receivables)

Sierra Pacific Industries
GOVERNMENT TIMBER
UNDER CONTRACT
At End of Each Year
(Millions BF)

Year	BF
1978	885
1979	966
1980	1033
1981	1016
1982	1132
1983	1075
1984	1142
1985	885
1986	774
1987	784
1988	702
1989	681

The growth of the company was not the whole story, however. Perhaps it is appropriate to dwell on the growth because that is a positive thing to do. Pride is a human trait; and there were hundreds of people involved in the growth of the company who can take pride in it. But there is a short table I prepared to go along with Dick's table. It illustrates the dire straights that companies like SPI, to a great extent dependent upon government timber, find themselves.

As the months go by, the sale of government timber continues to decline. There seems no end in sight to the insatiable appetites of the Environmentalists for still more productive land to be set aside for their use and enjoyment. It is with trepidation I look forward to the problems on the horizon.

On the other hand, I was satisfied with the role I had played in the growth of Sierra Pacific Industries. I had been very fortunate that Red Emmerson had come along and purchased my services along with some junk sawmills in the Feather River country. Had he not moved me to Arcata, I would have missed all the fun.

chapter fifty nine

The Associations

A company like SPI would find it difficult to make its way in the timber industry, and in corporate America, without being a part of the establishment. In the early days, when Curly Emmerson was beginning his career as a lumberman, there was no need, nor did he desire, to be a part of a sophisticated, industrial society. He entered the timber industry to make a living the best way he knew how. However, as his company prospered and grew, he had no choice but to claim his rightful place in the industrial society. He became a leader in it.

Curly was not a "joiner." He could not see the wisdom of joining anything that was not required to make his business successful. His son, Red, felt the same way, perhaps learning the prejudice from his father. Neither of them could see any reason to join Rotary, the Elks Club, the Lions Club, or similar organizations. They did join the Ingomar Club in Eureka; probably because it afforded a place to meet businessmen like themselves, and a place to entertain important guests on occasion. Curly may have liked the bar there.

As time went on, there were some organizations that Red, particularly, accepted as a necessary part of doing business. One was the Timber Operators Council (TOC); the other was Western Timber Association. Both were instrumental in making SPI a successful organization. There were some smaller trade associations which SPI belonged to, but the two mentioned above were the principal ones.

As stated earlier, TOC was valued as an advisor in the area of labor relations. If SPI had not been involved with union labor at several of its sawmills, it is doubtful that the company would have belonged to TOC. It was fortunate that they **did** join TOC, since the membership resulted in the hiring of Ed Bond.

There are several reasons why it is appropriate to comment on the timber associations at greater length. First, and least important, is that I know more about them than the others, having been involved with them from the time I moved to California as a young forester. Of more importance, what happened to the timber associations in the western U.S., is mirrored in what happened to SPI. SPI is, in effect, a microcosm of the whole western timber industry, at least that portion that has enjoyed a certain amount of success. SPI's history is unavoidably interwoven with the history of the associations.

In particular, there are two individuals who were involved with industry associations and who affected, to some extent, the success of SPI. One is George Craig; the other is Bill Dennison, who succeeded him as the executive in charge of **the** timber association in California. Personnel of SPI, including Red himself, were directly involved in the formation, support and success of such trade associations.

A brief history of this relationship begins with George Craig, who became quite famous in the timber industry. George wielded a great deal of influence, particularly as he worked to modify government regulations affecting the members of the timber association he directed.

George was born in 1916, in Santa Clara, California, to modest means. His father was a machinist. He attended schools, through high school, in Oakland. In 1934, he enrolled at U. C. Berkeley to study Forestry, lasted six months, and had to quit to go to work because he was broke. However, he met his future wife Vi while at U.C.B.

George finally graduated in 1939, hitch-hiked to Lakeview, Oregon, and got a job in the woods with American Box Co. He began as a knot bumper on the landing, progressed through choker setting and the second loader job, finally attaining the exalted job of landing log scaler.

When the job shut down in the winter, George returned to California where he got a job on the docks in San Francisco. As spring approached, he and Vi decided to get married (they had been seeing each other for six years). They had $125, a 1928 Chrysler that one of George's relatives had given them, and a job in Oregon to return to. The Chrysler made it to Oregon in two days without a breakdown; and George piled lumber for 11 1/2 hours the next day.

From there, he progressed through various jobs in the woods and in the mill. Vi kept books in the logging camp when summers came; and George, in the winter, tallied lumber in the planing mill, did other work around the sawmill, and finally became a dry kiln operator. He eventually went to work for Manson Byrne, who owned a company that installed kilns. George was the kiln operator. One of his first jobs was at a mill in Algoma, north of Klamath Falls.

As World War II approached, George learned to be a welder and worked at the shipyards in San Francisco. He attempted to join the Army, figuring his forestry training might help him find a spot in the procurement or production of wood products the Army might need. That did not materialize; so he joined the Navy in November 1942. He was commissioned an Ensign after initial training that included schools in Arizona, Tennessee, Rhode Island, and several other states. At one time, he was the Assistant Chaplain, a job that would stand him in good stead when he took over a timber association in later years.

George Craig eventually became a naval intelligence officer, serving in the South Pacific. He was connected with naval aviation at several stateside posts, and finally served on the small carrier Kadashan Bay which survived a Kamikaze hit in the battle of Lingayen Gulf. George came back to the States in 1944, and returned to civilian life in 1946.

Soon he began his forestry career in earnest. At the time, the California State Senate met every two years rather than every year. In the off years, Manual Fritz, George's mentor at U.C.B., did research for the influential Forestry Committee of the Senate. Fritz compiled reports that were used as a basis for legislation that affected the timber industry. George went to work for the Committee as Forest Investigator. He continued a career in State service, at one time working for Swede Nelson when he was the State Forester. George left State service in 1947.

George did not work for a government agency long enough to become spoiled in his work habits. In rapid succession, he edited the *Redwood Forest Handbook*, put together by Swede Wallen for the Forest Service, then wrote a similar book for the pine region. He went to work for the Western Pine Association (forerunner to the Western Wood Products Association) as a Forest Engineer. While "good to work for," they did not pay very well, and George and Vi had three children to take care of.

Earlier, George had written an article about a new log loader he had seen while working in the woods. He submitted the piece, along with pictures he had taken, to the *Timberman*, a trade magazine. He contacted them to see if they would take his material, since they paid 4 1/2 cents per word for the edited article, and/or $100 per month. Eventually, he became a permanent employee of the *Timberman* at $1200 per month, working his way up to Associate Editor.

In 1957, George Craig was ready for a

change. A trade association in California was looking for a chief executive to take over from Pat Thompson, a retired Forest Service Regional Forester, who worked only about ten months per year as its director. George took over as Secretary Manager for the Western Lumber Manufacturers Association (WLMA). Elected to the original Board of Directors were Pat Ivory, Robert Grimmett, Charlie Gray, George Duff, Lawrence McLellan, Bruce Elmore and A.T. Matthews. Membership dues were 4 1/2 cents per MBF of production, and the annual budget was $18,000.

WLMA was formed in 1952 because the members felt they were not being represented by Western Pine Association (WPA), or the California Forest Protective Association (CFPA). CFPA, formed in 1909, concentrated on representing those companies that owned substantial amounts of timberland. Its interests were focused on fire control, reforestation, and taxation of forest properties. To some operators in California, WPA had become a service organization helping members with lumber grading, log scaling, statistical analysis and lumber promotion at the expense of advising the members, particularly those dependent on public timber, on how to control the cost of dealing with the government.

When George Craig began as Secretary Manager of WLMA in 1957, he dealt primarily with contractual issues unique to the Forest Service timber sale contract. The construction of access roads was a costly process, and companies were losing money on that part of their operations. Each new wrinkle the Forest Service inserted in the timber sale contract resulted in more costly operations for the members; and George went to bat in their interest. In many cases, he was instrumental in revising the language of such contracts, actually writing the clauses himself.

Stumpage costs, compared to present costs, were quite low, reflecting the availability of timber from the government. The costs were to rise dramatically as the availability decreased due to withdrawals of land from timber production. George was at the forefront of the early battles to maintain a resource base for the production of timber. Also, as the California yield tax came into existence, WLMA took up that matter when the tax was

**George A. Craig in front of
State Capitol building, 1989.**
Photo from author's collection by David P. Bayles.

applied to the purchasers of government timber.

Among the various associations, battles for "turf" would continue for many years after the formation of WLMA. In Oregon and Washington, a number of timber associations were formed by "small" business firms that thought their interests were not receiving proper emphasis in the organizations to which they belonged. As a result, the timber industry became badly fragmented in those states, and a number of smaller timber associations were formed.

Perhaps one of George's greatest accomplishments was to keep both small and large businesses relatively happy as members of WLMA. Since the views of each were so widely divergent in timber supply matters, WLMA had to take a "no position" position when it came to issues that would favor one or the other. He was one of the few who could pull that off through his diplomacy, good sense, and hard work.

As the years passed, WLMA had to direct a greater part of its efforts to timber supply matters, although contractual matters still occupied a great deal of attention. At a 1969 Sierra Cascade Logging Conference in Fresno, a young man gave a talk on road construction problems. He impressed George Craig with his knowledge of road construction, and the way he handled himself before an audience. The man was Bill Dennison.

Bill was born in Thermalito, near Oroville, California, in 1934. At the time, his parents were living in West Branch, a logging camp near Butte Meadows, where his father worked for Diamond Match Co. laying railroad ties. His father was later to become a cat skinner and dozer operator, constructing logging roads for the company.

In 1943, Bill's parents divorced; and Bill moved to Meadow Valley where his father worked for Cal Cole, the Logging Superintendent for Meadow Valley Lumber Co. After his father's suicide in 1949, Bill went to live with Plez and Mary Virden. Plez also worked in the woods for Cal Cole; and Bill lived with them for three years until he finished high school. When the Virdens moved to Woodleaf

to work for Sacramento Box Co., Bill got a job driving cat for Plez in the summers. He spent the last two years of high school at Oroville, where he met his future wife, Pat. They would be married in 1954.

Bill Dennison has said many times that becoming a very young cat skinner was the one thing that gave him confidence after the trauma of the divorce and suicide. He was a very young man in a tough job, but he was able to handle it quite well. He would follow his logging trade while attending Lassen Junior College in Susanville, where he received an A. A. in Vocational Forestry.

In 1954, Bill went back to Diamond, by that time it was called Diamond Gardner, where he worked on the surveying crew. The next year, a job came open in the forestry department, and Bill applied for the job. Guy Hall, one of Diamond's foresters, told Bill that he was not qualified since he did not have a degree in forestry. Guy encouraged him to go back to school.

After talking the situation over with Pat, Bill applied for the forestry program at U. C. Berkeley. Of his 63 credits from Lassen J. C., U. C. accepted only 11. It was back to school to catch up. It wasn't until 1955 that Bill could finally find classes available at Chico State, and where Pat could work all through his school years to pay the bills.

Finally, in 1957, Bill Dennison was accepted at Berkeley, from which he graduated in 1959. Then it was back to Diamond where he was hired as a surveyor, doing nearly the same type work he had done before. In a few months, Bill was promoted to Chief Surveyor. The company, at the time, was making large investments in constructing a permanent road system on its extensive timberlands. At one point, they asked Bill if he was interested in becoming a foreman for the road side. Bill thought long and hard on that development; he did not need an education for a foreman's job. He finally accepted the job for the experience it afforded. By that time, he and Pat had two daughters. He was the road construction foreman when he met George Craig in Fresno.

By 1970, WLMA was looking for someone

Bill Dennison in his TAC office, 1989.
Photo from author's collection by David P. Bayles.

to work on road construction and government timber sale problems. George Craig remembered the young man from the Fresno meeting, contacted him, and made the Dennisons an offer they could not refuse. Bill, by then Timber Manager, was in charge of all road construction and the purchase of Forest Service timber sales. He was making $10,250 per year. George offered them $15,000. Bill says that things for him had been good at Diamond, but the uncertainties were beginning to mount. Diamond was in the habit of shaking up their work force periodically, firing some good people; or so Bill thought. He wondered what was wrong with him - he should have been good enough to be fired, too. He and Pat decided to accept the offer, not only because of the uncertainties at Diamond and better pay at WLMA, but because of his desire to work with George Craig.

When they looked for housing in the Bay Area (the office was in the Monadnock Building in San Francisco), they were aghast at the prices. While they had a good home in Red Bluff, for which they paid $17,000, the

most reasonably-priced home they could find in nearby Pleasanton was priced at $32,000. They ended up, with George's blessing, working out of their home in Red Bluff. That was only a temporary convenience, for they were finally required to give up the Red Bluff residence after seven years. They again looked at a house in Pleasanton; but now the same home was priced at $120,000. They settled for a condominium in Oakland. The Dennisons were grateful to George for permitting them to raise their girls in Red Bluff.

Bill Dennison has related many times that he developed the greatest respect for his mentor, George Craig. He also gained a similar respect for Vi Craig, who soon began to suggest that Bill would be a good replacement for George when he retired. George passed on to Bill his work ethic, which involves no less commitment than does Red Emmerson's. All three of them are cut from the same cloth, albeit from different places on the bolt. Long working hours mean very little to any of them.

George has a mind that is coldly methodical. He can "crunch numbers" for hours;

in fact, he seems to enjoy it. When at work on a project, his mind is entirely focused on it and he will leave no detail unconsidered. When used as an expert in the courtroom, his data and testimony are formidable. He is a good man to have on your side.

Bill says that George set some limits on his work when Bill first came to work at WLMA. For the first year, he would not let Bill send out memos or correspondence without his approval. He told Bill it had taken him several years to earn credibility, and Bill could destroy it in a very short time. Bill understood and respected that. The information sent from the WLMA office was always correct. In fact, the Forest Service would look for the memos mailed to them for the "correct" slant on Forest Service news.

George told Bill that, at the top of his list, was the old motto, "Treat others as you would like to be treated." George followed it to the letter with one exception. Bill says he had no use for stupidity; so those whom he felt were stupid, he treated with a certain amount of sarcasm. Perhaps he felt that if they thought he were stupid, they would treat him with contempt, therefore he would be consistent in his treatment of others.

I remember a meeting at South Lake Tahoe, sometime in the mid-1960s, concerning timber harvesting in the Tahoe basin. The reason for the meeting escapes me; but I vividly remember a pompous individual who made a long presentation, and George violently disagreed with him. George sat next to me muttering under his breath; rather loudly, too.

Finally, when the speaker finished and asked for questions, George raised his hand. Upon being recognized, he asked, "Don't you feel stupid in taking the position that all of the activities that are to take place in the Tahoe Basin are governed by a host of agencies, like the Forest Service, the Tahoe Regional Planning Agency, the ...." and on, and on. George used up a good five minutes attacking every one of the points the speaker had made.

I watched the speaker squirm and try to interrupt George's speech. When he was finished, the speaker, with a smirk, said from the stage, "Mr. Craig, that was the longest question I have ever heard. You have talked so long, about so many things, that I can't even remember your question."

George replied with a smile, "My question was, don't you feel stupid?" The audience roared with laughter.

The two men, George Craig and Bill Dennison, made WLMA the premier timber association in the west. The staff included Jack Keene, Dick Reed and Wes Higbie, a young attorney, who would go on to become a prominent attorney in San Francisco specializing in timber matters. Their work was just beginning in the 1970s.

In 1972, WLMA became Western Timber Association (WTA). George Craig and the members believed the new name would better reflect the goal of the association, which had become increasingly involved with timber supply, rather than with the costs related to lumber manufacture.

George was beginning to think about retiring, although few of the association's members knew how serious he was about it. He was becoming increasingly concerned about the problems facing the industry, and the lack of movement toward an enlightened public timber supply policy. In 1980, George got very serious about retiring, and announced he would do so on February 1. His replacement was Bill Dennison.

George went on to be a member of the Reagan Presidential Transition Team in 1980, and began a very active life as a consulting forester in California. He continues in that role today.

Bill took over; and one of his first official acts was to suggest the dues for WTA be increased from 12 cents to 15 cents per MBF. He was concerned he would begin on a sour note by suggesting such action; but he noted the association would be broke in six months if income was not increased. George had treated WTA's money as if it were his own; and Bill continued in that tradition. Although he was forced to ask for a dues increase, it was the first increase in several years.

George Craig had always resisted moving the WTA office from San Francisco, believing that it was necessary to have ready access to the Regional Office (RO) of the Forest Service. Since most of the association's business was involved with the RO, he was correct in keeping the office there. However, soon after Bill Dennison took over the reins, it was evident that the RO was losing control of the National Forests in California. Increasingly, the Forest Supervisors were calling their own shots, quite often due to pressures from the Environmentalists.

At the same time, the environmental battles were being fought in the courts in ever-increasing numbers. Appeals and law suits were holding up timber sales - not only those in the planning stages, but those that were already under contract. At the same time, the Forest Service was caught up in the planning processes that were beginning to take most of the staff's time, time that could be spent on productive work like preparing timber sales. It was not only staff time that was being wasted, a good percentage of the Forest Service budget, heretofore devoted to the preparation of timber sales, was being used up in the planning process. The availability of public timber in California, as in much of the west, was going from bad to worse.

Bill resisted moving the office to Sacramento; after all, George Craig had instilled in Bill the need for WTA to have a presence in San Francisco. The majority of the Board of Directors, however, decided it would be best to move. It was 1984.

In retrospect, Bill believes the decision to move was a good one. The RO had indeed lost control. Also, it was cheaper to operate away from the Bay Area, and it was easier to attract good people to Sacramento where the cost of living was lower. One side effect, not originally apparent, was the ease of access to the WTA office for more of the members.

Early in Bill's career as leader of the association, timber sale contract relief became top priority; and the months during which relief was discussed were very traumatic for the association, and for Bill Dennison.

Bill had always thought it was necessary to have a big majority on any side of an issue before the association could take a position. This was usually achieved by leadership, by lobbying the members, and by being "right." George and Bill were both adept at bringing, first the Board of Directors, then the membership, to a logical conclusion on an issue that each of them had reached long before. They were usually right in their judgments as to which side of an issue the association should support. Timber sale contract relief was different.

As described earlier, the timber sale buyout process was extremely controversial among the members. WTA, therefore, took a "neutral" position, similar to that taken with the small business vs. large business questions that arose from time to time. Bill always was disappointed that WTA could not take a lead role, one way or another, in the controversy. He thought an association's executive should lead, and the association's members should be able to reach consensus on an issue as important as contract relief.

With the passage of contract relief regulations, it wasn't long before it became apparent that those operators harvesting private timber, as well as those harvesting public timber, were facing many common problems. The members of CFPA, primarily involved in private timber matters, and members of WTA, concerned with government matters, discovered they had more in common than they had differences. The timber supply for both was being adversely affected by regulations, and by the increase in appeals and litigation. After many long discussions among leaders of the two associations, it was decided the two organizations should merge.

The merger took several years to accomplish. There were a number of reasons that the merger was approved by both organizations - one being the effectiveness of the man in charge, Bill Dennison. It was also believed that one statewide organization speaking on forestry matters would be far more effective than two that offered divergent views.

On April 4, 1988, after months of discussion and lobbying each other, the members of the two associations approved the merger. It would take several months to accomplish the feat, but the process was in motion. The new organization would go by the name Timber Association of California (TAC).

George Craig had been against combining the two groups from the beginning. I talked with him a number of times during the merger discussions; and he was adamant that the interests of the two groups (public/private) were too divergent. He remembered that WLMA was formed because of that fact, and believed the chances for the success of the new group were practically nil. As a result of the differences of opinion, relations between Bill Dennison and George Craig became strained, perhaps because George believed Bill had betrayed him. That bothered Bill immensely, and still does today.

Presently, there is another issue which threatens to divide TAC. In 1990, several initiatives appeared on the California state ballot that would have adversely affected the timber industry. Had they passed, the chance for survival of many of the timber firms in California would have been slight. TAC was in the forefront of the fight to defeat them.

The Environmentalist-sponsored initiatives were poorly written, and would have shut down much of the timber industry in California had they passed. At issue were bans on clear cutting, stringent limitations on the harvesting of "old-growth," restrictions on harvesting timber that had not reached its culmination of mean-annual-incremental-growth, and a goal of restricting cutting annually to an amount that could be grown annually.

Many of the terms used in the language of the initiatives sounded good to the public. However, the industry had serious problems with many of the definitions used in them, especially those for old-growth, sustained yield, and clear-cutting.

The timber industry was fortunate that the initiatives were defeated at the polls. However, the defeat was by a very narrow margin, and it was evident that the battle was not over. While some in the industry thought they had scored a victory, others believed it was only a matter of time before another attack would be mounted.

The latter group believed the onerous parts of the failed initiatives would eventually become law, either passed by the legislature, or by way of the initiative process at the next election.

As a result, certain segments of the industry have been attempting to negotiate with influential Environmentalists to bury the hatchet. They feel it may be possible to agree upon certain increasingly restrictive forest practices, with the understanding that legislation would be introduced which would contain the elements of the agreement. Of course, there is a substantial minority of TAC members who do not believe it possible to negotiate with the Environmentalists at all, and they are very vocal. The membership is badly split. Perhaps George Craig will see his prediction, that the WTA/CFPA merger was a mistake, come true.

Most of the battles over the initiatives, and all of the negotiations with the Environmentalist have taken place after my retirement from SPI. As a result, I have requested that Dan Tomascheski provide an explanation of the process as he saw it. Since he was a participant in the negotiations, he has first-hand knowledge of the process, and can better explain the results. This explanation will follow in the Epilogue.

From the very beginning of my employment in California in 1957, I have been involved with all of the associations mentioned here. In 1958, I began serving on a committee of the old WLMA. As time went on, I served on a number of committees, including the California Industry Timber Sale Contract Committee (commonly called the "C" Clause Committee), the Audit Committee, and the Road Committee. After initial election to the Board of Directors, it seemed to me that I was on the Board for years on end. At one time, I was the Vice-President, and finally the President of the organization.

The reason for the explanation of my involvement is not to boast of the offices held, but to indicate my belief that a member of the timber industry in California cannot go it alone. Any firm attempting to do business in this state needs all the help it can get. In some parts of the state, many people consider any firm cutting trees to be the enemy, and education of the "public" has been sorely lacking. I felt that the only opportunity I would ever have for influencing the business climate in California, and promoting the acceptance of harvesting trees, was through joining those organizations that helped the businesses that employed me. Thus, I became a staunch supporter of those mentioned here.

To belong to such organizations takes money, sometimes in huge amounts. To me, it did not seem wise to contribute money, then let others determine how the funds were to be spent. I believed it was necessary to become involved, not only in looking after my employer's money, but after his interests as well. As a result, I spent a great deal of time discussing timber association affairs.

Red, in the early years of my employment for SPI, kept tight rein on my association activities. I continued involvement anyway; and after a certain amount of resistance, he finally grudgingly permitted me to participate. However, he never really accepted the necessity for doing so.

As the pressures on timber supply mounted, he began to become personally involved. In the late 1970s, it was rare that he would even attend an annual membership meeting. If he did, it would be for only a few hours or minutes, most of which was spent on the telephone "minding the store." As time went on, he became more and more interested in fighting for SPI's interests. He became heavily involved in the merger of WTA and CFPA.

As the battles began over the California initiatives, he not only became heavily involved, he became a leader. By that time, SPI was the number one lumber producer in the state. He used to say that he would "rather keep a low profile," and let others brag about their exalted status. He would rather they be the "lightning rods" that attracted the bolts hurled by an uninformed public. He was content to just make lumber.

Logo for California Forestry Association (CFA), formerly Timber Association of California (TAC).

chapter sixty

R*ED*

After SPI acquired the Santa Fe, a great deal of public interest was kindled about the ownership of SPI. Even though Red did not wish to stand out, he had no choice. Since he was the head of the family that owned it (he effectively **was** the owner) he was perceived to be the leader. He had to accept the mantle of leadership.

It was a lonely spot for him to be in. After my retirement, I was permitted to keep my old office at the Arcata sawmill, and I would frequently see him early on Saturday or Monday mornings. He would be in Arcata for his routine weekend visits to the coast; and I would see him when I showed up to sort through the junk mail accumulated on my old desk. He would want to visit about the role he was playing in the negotiating game with the **E**nvironmentalists. He was deeply concerned that he was too far out in front of the rest of the industry.

The thought often occurred to me that he was just not comfortable playing the role of a leader in public. He kept looking behind to see if anyone was following him. Leadership is a lonely profession. Some people with big egos relish the role; not Red. He believes he is just an ordinary man who loves the lumber business.

Which brings me to a point in the story of SPI and Red Emmerson. What kind of a person is he, this owner of SPI? Does one ever get to know him very well? Is he a real person,

with feelings and fears like any other person? Is he a genius? Is he reclusive, as some of the media people describe him? Or is he a man, such as the one that Knute Rockne described, who puts his pants on one leg at a time, just like everyone else?

Such questions are very difficult to answer. Perhaps a trained psychologist would judge him to be the opposite of the way I see him. Perhaps other close associates would see him differently than I do.

To me, Red is a very complicated individual. He fancies himself to be just an ordinary man who relates to the "working man" better than to the "upper crust." This is not necessarily so. While he comes from a working-class background, enjoys the people who make their living with their hands, and relates to them well, he is very effective in a corporate boardroom. In fact, he seems to feel superior to those who exhibit all the trappings of power in such surroundings.

Red fancies himself to be "people oriented;" and I must agree that he certainly appears to be. Once a person gains his confidence, there are only a few things that can shake that confidence. Among them are to stop working to capacity (or beyond), to use the company's money unwisely, or to develop an image of superiority. These things he cannot stand.

Some employees have fallen into his disfavor because of something that was said about them by someone whose judgment Red trusts. For example, a forester can have many years of yeoman service behind him, during which Red will have been very supportive of his activities. A few weeks later, after a Division Manager makes some critical remarks about him, Red begins to worry about the forester's performance. After that, he questions his decisions at every turn and, if confidence is not restored promptly, the forester may be on the way to demotion or termination.

Even though Red's confidence might eventually be restored in such an individual, the situation is very devastating for the employee to cope with, not knowing what has gone wrong. The tendency to believe ill of an individual on flimsy evidence is perhaps the most serious criticism I have of Red's behavior towards people.

Red, at times, may underestimate the intelligence of people whom he does not care for. Such people are usually those in the business world who do not give the appearance of working very hard. They may be golfing on Friday afternoons when he thinks they should be working, or having a martini lunch when they should be in their office. He may think such performance indicates they are mentally defective, otherwise they would be working.

To my mind, another trait which contributes to Red being a complicated individual is his ability to be generous and frugal at the same time. He is extremely generous in the way he treats valued employees, personal friends and family. No one knows how many peoples' lives have been touched with his generosity, since he never mentions these incidents. In fact, he is embarrassed if they are found out.

On the other hand, he is very frugal with expenditures in the conduct of SPI's business, insisting that every cent be accounted for. An individual who does not pay attention to this frugality is in for immediate criticism. For instance, I remember a forester who, prior to his old pickup being put up for sale, did not substitute worn-out tires for the good ones on it. I heard about that incident for months afterwards.

Red is a very friendly individual, warm and responsive. He is accessible to just about everyone who can track him down. He relates especially well with small groups of early-risers who develop the same routine for breakfast as he does. Many of them are truck drivers, construction workers, shopkeepers, and the like who have breakfast around 5:30 or 6:00 a.m. He loves their company, and banters with them and the restaurant help. They seem to love him.

At the opposite end of the spectrum, he can be cold, blunt, and calculating to those he perceives have crossed him. A long-time friend can feel his wrath when the friendship is over. He severs the relationship with finality. At such times, I have felt sorry for the recipient of his displeasure.

In the final analysis, Red is indeed complicated; an enigma, perhaps. At one time, he had the reputation of being untrustworthy, and people who dealt with him worried about being "taken to the cleaners." I found that misunderstandings developed because such persons did not bring up those points that could be subject to interpretation. One had to discuss every point in an agreement, especially verbal agreements, and not assume something that had not been discussed. Red seems to consider it a weakness, and a game, if he can best someone in a deal through a person's lack of attention to such details.

On the other hand, particularly in later years, he developed the reputation for integrity that Curly instilled in him. Perhaps, in the early years, Red could not afford to "give anything away," as he would often put it. Then, there was too much against him, and he was going to be a successful business man one way or another. Later, he matured, and learned that in the area of human relations, Curly's ways were best.

When Red's involvement with SPI is over, very likely not until his death, he will be remembered as a warm human being who touched many lives for the better. He should go down in history as one of the old lions who left the world a better place than when he came into it. It will be interesting to see what happens to the company Curly founded, and Red nurtured to its present prominence.

The third generation, George, Caroline, and Mark have become committed to the success of the company. SPI is in good hands.

I suspect problems of controversy and family dissension are a couple of generations away. It remains to be seen if the three children can instill in their offspring the same commitment to SPI that their father instilled in them.

Plastic wrapped lumber being readied for shipment from SPI Millwork Division 1987.
Photo from SPI archives.

PART FIVE

EPILOGUE

BY DAN TOMASCHESKI
VICE-PRESIDENT RESOURCES
SIERRA PACIFIC INDUSTRIES

Dan Tomascheski cruising timber on Mt. Shasta District of SPI.
Photo from author's collection by David P. Bayles.

1990 AND *BEYOND*

Bud is right; the business is neither as fun nor as simple as it once was. Since he left SPI only a few months ago, circumstances have changed tremendously. On some days, simple survival looks like a reasonable goal. The industry and its people are changing in response to outside pressures; not all of it for the better. Even so, I can still find much satisfaction in playing the game, even if the rules keep changing.

We now live in an information-based environment where we currently do not set the terms of the debate, let alone control its outcome. Unfortunately, style and image compete with substance as indicators of merit. Our industry is a part of this world, too.

A largely urban public, urged on by mainstream environmentalists, projects its perception of the world's condition onto our forestlands. They believe forests are there for their enjoyment, not to produce things they need for their way of life. They ignore economics, and the needs of the rural communities located adjacent to forestlands. Their demands for preservation cannot be denied since they represent the majority in our society.

We at SPI have always been adaptable, quick to meet challenges, and willing to try new things. Red, as the leader, demands nothing less. However, the challenge of environmentalism and a burgeoning population is far greater than past challenges. Environmentalism attempts to change our world view,

the things we value, and the way we live. It is largely succeeding.

While some of its goals have merit, the means to attain them are destructive. They focus on the preservation of natural resources at all costs, de-emphasizing human needs. Since SPI is resource-based, we sit directly in the line of fire.

Many of us now realize that the traditional weapons used to do battle with these proponents are largely ineffective. In the past, we most often fought from a defensive posture, trying to reason with them. We gathered facts, stressed accuracy, and responded with reasonableness. We met strident opposition, misinformation, and over-simplified statements of "fact." We always hoped the opposition would just go away.

As the controversy intensified, I spent a great deal of time talking to SPI's management, both present and past, in formulating strategies to deal with the situation. We discussed past battles, trying to determine what did or didn't work. We debated hiring the types of people who could help with solutions to the problems facing us. As a result, we built on the foundation laid out by Red and Bud in dealing with our transformation into a large, timberland-owning company.

There were two separate, but related, arenas we had to deal with: the operational and the environmental/political. In the operational, we had long recognized that in order for SPI to prosper, we had to increase the resource base "upstream" and expand product lines "downstream." The trick was to do this while still retaining the **hands-on** control and commitment to efficiency that had brought the company to its position of prominence.

As environmental restrictions decreased production from the land base, it was obvious that we would need to increase the size of our land base or begin to shut down sawmills. The steady and dramatic decline in Forest Service timber sales also made acquisition of additional timberland necessary. Consequently, we made two large purchases, along with several smaller ones, in late 1989 and in 1990.

The largest was the Fibreboard properties in the area north of Truckee and east of Quincy. These were primarily "checkerboard" lands that had been sold by the Southern Pacific Railroad many years ago. Fibreboard had owned them for over 30 years, then sold out to LP. Later, after LP spun off Fibreboard, the lands reverted. During this process, Fibreboard retained a sawmill at Truckee, and used the lands to "wood" a major portion of their mill's needs.

The lands northwest of Truckee contained significant volumes of larger dimension type True fir, and had been carefully managed for Fibreboard by Howard "Bud" Fish. The lands near Quincy supported primarily mixed conifer second-growth on good site, some of which Fibreboard had acquired from DiGiorgio, the Forest Service and High Sierra Pine Mills.

For many years, SPI purchased considerable volumes from Fibreboard's lands. In some cases, the sales were timber sales requiring SPI to do the logging. Thus, we were quite familiar with the tracts. The lands fit SPI's Quincy and Loyalton facilities very well, and augmented the declining Forest Service supply on the east side of the Sacramento Valley. This was critical, since a facility like Loyalton, situated facing the desert Great Basin to the east, had only half a working circle from which to draw timber.

In late 1989, we negotiated a complicated package with Fibreboard involving part exchange, part cutting contract with eventual purchase, and part outright purchase. Nego-

tiations were made more difficult since the respective CEOs, Red Emmerson and Larry Hart, are hard-nosed. They negotiated face to face, neither wanting to give an inch.

The lands are currently managed by our Grass Valley district. The 51,500 acres acquired from Fibreboard provide a good distribution of age classes to augment those on the rest of our timberlands.

In 1990, Don Curry, a former employee of Erickson Lumber Co., contacted us about our possible interest in the timberlands owned by Jack Erickson in the Interstate 80 corridor between Auburn and Donner Summit. Erickson had also owned and operated a sawmill in Marysville before selling out in 1989.

Red respected Jack Erickson as a tough competitor and hands-on operator. We had "bumped heads" with Erickson on timber sales ever since acquiring the DiGiorgio mills. At the same time, we often contracted with Erickson Air Crane for helicopter logging, a logging method pioneered by Jack. Red and Jack respected each other as survivors; and after some haggling over loggable volumes and prices, purchase of the 9700 acres was completed.

The Erickson lands had significant volumes of old-growth timber along with second-growth, and contributed to stability for SPI's east-side operations. With the Erickson purchase, total acreage acquired in 1989-1990 amounted to approximately 65,000 acres.

The second prong in our operational strategy was to expand downstream into secondary manufacturing with "value-added" products. The large millwork plant at Richfield, north of Corning, has been able to take advantage of specialty items using upper grades of lumber.

The Oroville millwork plant was sold in early 1991. SPI plans to consolidate millwork operations into two very large and modern facilities - the current Richfield facility, and a new state-of-the-art plant at Red Bluff. Many of the people, and most of the machinery in the current Chico facility, are moving to Red Bluff.

The Red Bluff plant came on-line in June 1991. It is housed in a building a half-mile in perimeter, and features completely computerized chop-saws and scanners. It optimizes the yield from each board, replaces the Chico facility and puts the company in an extremely competitive position in millwork. Eventually, it will allow expansion into new product lines.

After completion of the Red Bluff facility, the Richfield plant will undergo an upgrade with installation of the same type of equipment. The result will be two "next generation" plants that will replace those that are already competitive. These facilities will allow us to better and more profitably utilize our own raw materials, along with those purchased from others.

We have recently begun an expansion into the window business by manufacturing complete windows to be marketed as "SPI" windows. This represents a significant step to downstream products. While the old Answerman stores represented an attempt at the retail building products business, the marketing of SPI windows is something new and different.

In the meantime, sawmill modernization proceeds unabated. New kilns, sorters, optimizing edgers, etc. continue to make appearances. The Susanville plant, under George Emmerson, has recently undergone a major renovation that is boosting production and lowering costs. Trips to Canada and the Northwest to explore small-log-sawing technologies are ongoing; and plans are underway to renovate the current small-log mills to use "true" small logs.

On the resource side, production from commercial and pre-commercial thinnings that generate logs, hog fuel and chips is on the upswing. Cull logs are also produced, to be used for hog fuel and chips. A portion of these products goes to help fuel the cogeneration plants, while some is sold outside.

It has taken a long time and a lot of effort on Bud's part; but SPI now realizes the importance of participating in the environmental and political arena. Red takes a personal interest and an active role in these affairs; and the company generally supports those involved in these daily battles.

Red's political influence and expertise has grown to where he is viewed as a progressive leader by the media, the politicians, and most of the industry. SPI has benefitted immensely from his commitment in those areas.

The company now has a Director of Government Affairs, Ed Bond, something unheard of a few years ago. Since "line" people with operational authority are so effective in the political and regulatory areas, several persons within the company now spend part of their time representing SPI's view and protecting its interests. Tom Nelson, Ed Murphy and SPI's wildlife biologist, Steve Self, are examples. As before, their participation in this area is contingent upon getting their "regular" jobs done, hence their 14-hour days, and Saturday-Sunday stints.

Red's instincts in dealing with the media have always been to be low profile and let others do the talking and self-promotion. That is still his preference; but he has come to understand that he has no choice if he is to succeed in remaining in business. He is a leader whether he likes it or not. As such, his opinions are sought and valued. He worries about this constantly, wishing he could return to his low-profile approach. Under the circumstances, he probably can't.

We have given considerable thought to what must occur for SPI's long-term survival in the state of California. We in the industry tend to be quite localized in our thinking since we operate in primarily rural areas. We can be influential because we live, work, and play there, and contribute to the economic base of these communities.

Unfortunately, the majority of decisions that affect us are made by people in other parts of the state who don't represent us. They make decisions based on their own experience (which doesn't include exposure to us), and on what they hear and see on television (mostly from the environmentally influenced media). In those areas, the environmentalists are widely perceived to represent the public interest and serve as a check on corporate interests or "greed."

Our industry's communications effort, while improving, will take considerable time to change that perception. In the meantime, we need to use other means to communicate with the public.

We noted that a resource-based industry

is particularly vulnerable to public opinion because its operations can visibly alter the landscape, while its benefits, particularly in urban areas, are taken for granted. Since the environmental community has the media's (hence the public's) ear, it is difficult to insulate the industry from truly damaging events, such as a statewide initiative. To solve such problems, it has become necessary to begin an accommodation so that forestry "reform" can get under way.

It is clear that the environmental movement and its followers are not a temporary aberration. They have become "mainstream" and provide many with an alternative, albeit secular, form of religion.

It appeared to many of us that we needed to open a dialogue with the mainstream environmental groups, recognizing that they, too, are an industry with legitimate, if often misguided, interests. The continuing confrontation with no dialogue - each camp playing its respective roles - was slowly choking us to death.

The environmental movement had inherent advantages in terms of media appeal. It was easy to convince an urban public of environmental degradation in the rural areas since the urbanites were often surrounded by an exploding population in a deteriorating city environment. It was easy to extrapolate that picture to the rest of California.

It was painfully evident that the system of environmental laws set up to foster citizen participation in resource decisions was easily manipulated to subvert timely decisions and thwart business activity. Many new environmental groups sprang up to take advantage of the situation. Their rhetoric became ever more strident as they gained a larger following and more power.

Many of us thought a good-faith effort to reach accommodation with legitimate environmental groups might result in several things:

• Heightened credibility with politicians, agency staffs, and the media. SPI, and the industry, could soften the perception that our positions were knee-jerk, predictable and designed to delay. We would be in a better position to explain what we **really** can or can't do. It would also enhance our credibility when stating our position in future confrontations. We knew that the battle would never cease; but this effort would not hurt our position if we continued to fight.

• Help turn the environmentalists' black and white, good guy vs. bad guy world view into a grayer, more complicated place where there are several choices rather that just two. The movement has been able to focus their forces on a perceived faceless, monolithic industry. It is easy to portray us as an enemy - self-serving, and in need of increasing controls. With dialogue, a face is attached to the adversary. This small step could complicate efforts to shut us down.

We had found it easier to forestall threatened litigation on the local level when prospective plaintiffs had someone to talk to from which they could learn another side of the controversy. The image of detached, out-of-state, corporate interests was improper when faces of real people, with families and legitimate concerns, were seen across the table.

The industry only recently became involved in concerted scientific efforts to examine resource issues other than timber. The spotted owl research work being done by land-owning companies represents a major step in this direction. This gives us access to a process that, before, was limited exclusively to, and controlled by, State and Federal agencies. This began to produce positive results. We planned to conduct a series of field trips with those we could identify as key environmental leader. However, other events intervened; and the trips never occurred.

In 1990, we entered a new arena of conflict which we had not experienced before - that of the statewide initiative. The environmentalists filed several initiatives for the state ballot with one, "Forests Forever," directed specifically at forest practices. While very expensive and time-consuming, industry people found the resulting controversy to be an enlightening experience in how California's political and media processes work. We were exposed to the pollsters and the initiative campaign industry as well as the urban media. Nobody had a good time.

Because of depressed economic conditions, some effective media work on our side, some

Ed Murphy and Tom Nelson at seminar sponsored by California Forestry Association to explain SPI's spotted owl management program, 1991. Photo by author.

ineffective media work on the other side, and bond provisions included in the language, the initiatives were narrowly defeated. Some of us knew the "victory" was only a short reprieve.

Most believed the defeat of the initiatives would bring both sides to the next arena - the legislative. They also knew that if efforts failed there (perhaps even if they succeeded), one or more initiatives were probable in 1992.

In the winter of 1991, the majority of the industry decided to attempt formal negotiations with representatives of the environmental community. Even if unsuccessful, many thought it would help prioritize issues and promote better understanding. However, hopes for an agreement that could serve as the basis for legislation were not high.

Hal Arbit, manager of a fund for institutional investors, had spent over five-million dollars of his own money on the 1990 initiative campaign. He was the main financial proponent of the "Forests Forever" initiative. Several industry people attempted to meet

with him, but he insisted that Gail Lucas, of the Sierra Club, attend the meeting. Some of the industry members refused to meet under those circumstances.

Red, believing that a face-to-face meeting might help each understand the other's position, decided to contact Arbit himself. He also wanted to size up an individual who would commit such a huge sum of money to something so harmful to SPI.

Subsequently, several meetings took place, and the two gradually came to respect each other's views although there were certainly no agreed-upon solutions. Out of these contacts grew the original negotiation process with its various participants.

The industry designated four members for the negotiating team. However, Arbit suggested that there be only three members on each side, so the industry decided to select Bill Dennison, president of the California Forestry Association (then called Timber Association of California), to represent the industry in general; Dave Kaney, General Manager of Simpson Timber, to represent the coast; and either Larry Hart, of Fibreboard Corporation, or me, for the inland districts. Larry declined the honor since he knew the effort would take up much of his time for the next several months.

From the beginning, the formal negotiations were difficult, with neither side willing to move toward the other. Since the industry owned some of the resources, and the environmental community wanted to restrict the use of such resources, any industry compromise amounted to giving something away with nothing gained in return. Both sides viewed the negotiations as a politically necessary step prior to moving on to the legislature. The environmentalists felt the legislative effort would not result in a solution they could accept, and that all this was a necessary prelude to a 1992 initiative campaign.

As negotiations faltered, it became apparent to us at SPI that there could be grounds for general, if not specific, agreement. While certainly restrictive, much of what the environmental side was asking for was feasible in concept if we kept an open mind, and accepted the premise that forestry practices would become much more complex and expensive.

After five meetings, there seemed to be no movement either way. The other industry team members were not as willing to compromise as we were; and it was clear the process was about to grind to a halt. We, sensing that a compromise was possible, and convinced that a new initiative effort could be avoided, pressed on.

The other industry members eventually became adversaries to the process. Red, and the rest of us at SPI, were "high profile" more than ever. None of us were comfortable, or pleased, with our new role, but felt we had no choice but to proceed. Some in the industry thought that Red and SPI had sold them out, and that SPI had pulled out of the negotiating process to pursue their own agenda with the environmentalists. At the same time, it appeared to us at SPI that the industry members of the team would not budge; and that the process was about to fizzle. We could not let that happen.

In our view, we had several choices, none of them good. We could fall back, defend ourselves as best we could with facts, and die slowly as we had in the past. We could give up, cash out our assets at a loss, and look for something else to do. We could also join the dialogue, attempt to educate our adversaries, and get them personally acquainted with us, our problems, and our opportunities.

Hovering over everything was the initiative process which, in our opinion, could not be defeated by a weakened industry. There were some in the industry who had already given up and left California - some of the smarter members months ago - while some of the financially weaker ones were only beginning to talk about leaving. SPI chose to stay and see the battle through.

After several weeks of very intense effort between members of the original team of environmental negotiators and three SPI people, a proposal was produced. Interestingly, no face-to-face meetings took place during that time. The negotiating sessions took place as conference calls, some lasting six hours at a stretch. The three SPI participants were Tom Nelson, Redding District Timberland Manager; Ed Murphy, Inventory Systems Analyst; and myself. We kept the industry, through the Timber Association, informed of progress. Some in the industry urged us not to reach an agreement, while others encouraged us to persevere.

As agreement was reached, both sides took the draft proposal back to their respective camps in an attempt to gain support as a compromise legislative proposal. If broad agreement could be reached, there would be no mainstream environmental initiative, nor any new substantive legislation, or regulations introduced for five years, while everyone gave the package time to be adopted and monitored.

Many local environmental groups rejected the proposal as giving away too much; but most of the mainstream groups thought they could support it, although they, too, had reservations about selling out to the industry.

While some companies were in immediate support, the industry, in general, believed the proposal was too restrictive and that they could not be in compliance and remain in business. They believed it failed to account for regional differences in their respective operations and timberlands. While most were committed to the legislative process, they adopted a position of "oppose unless amended."

This effectively made the goals of the original agreement unattainable, particularly the five-year truce feature. We thought the agreement could provide the basis for legislation that could be accepted by most companies if amended to meet their concerns. We believed that approaching the legislature with a restrictive package would reverse the usual pattern of compromising downward in the face of environmentalists' demands, a process in which we always lost. We believed, too, that amendments would be used by legislators, the environmental community and ourselves to win support from various companies, forest landowners and other interested parties. The result would be legislation formed the way legislation is supposed to be formulated - through compromise.

The challenge would be to amend the proposal in such a way that the environmental groups could accept it, without drastically curtailing individual companies' operations.

This difficult, fractious process continues at this writing, with several proposed amendments to the bills moving through committee. The stakes are high; but SPI continues its efforts to build on the process so it may have a say in its future. There are no guarantees that the process will result in a satisfactory legislative solution. Alternatives are currently the subject of much discussion, in case legislation fails.

The strategy, of which the legislation is one part, can work only if the companies are involved on a daily basis in the political and regulatory process. It requires a credible and even-handed approach which recognizes the legitimacy of the other players' concerns in the process.

In some measure we are aided in this effort by SPI's high-tech computer system with mapping capabilities. It is evident that this sophisticated system is useful in making our timberland management credible. The con-clusions we draw concerning the effects of our management activities on the land are difficult to assail with the type of analysis and mapping we are able to perform. We can show our decisions are environmentally correct.

We are resolved to stay a step ahead of the regulators and others in the high-tech game. We have something they want, namely, better information. Since we know our resource better than anyone, we display our strengths in the negotiating process.

SPI's wildlife survey work has proven effective, and we are currently trying to gain a legislative solution that would show we are serious in seeking answers based on science, not perceptions. We are addressing other issues such as cumulative watershed effects due to different cutting methods, and the habitat needs of species assumed to be old-growth obligates.

The willingness to assess and analyze other resources has paid dividends as well. The company's spotted owl management plan is an example. With the concurrence of the U. S. Fish and Wildlife Service, the plan allows us to continue timber harvest while protecting owls on SPI lands. We are offering it as an example of how to plan and manage for wildlife species on Federal land as well as on State and private lands. It has met with some success.

The future is uncertain and full of dangers. Of course, it always is. SPI has faced trying times before and always prevailed. While the present era is more complicated than others, we have joined the fight with a clear vision and a plan suited to the times. So far, it seems to be producing some of the results we hoped for.

To stay in the business the Emmersons founded and nurtured requires dedicated people who know their business and who are unafraid of change. Such human resources are in abundance at SPI. While it is not easy to look forward with great confidence, Red's commitment and continued support provides hope for better times ahead. Perhaps, Bud's prediction of doom is premature.

Steve Self, SPI's wildlife biologist and the author enjoying a beer at SPI's annual forester's picnic at Anderson in 1991.   Photo by Pat McEuen.

APPENDICES

APPENDIX A

Postdate

As this manuscript was being sent to the printer in mid-August 1991, SPI was continuing to make news. An agreement to buy the California assets of Bohemia, Inc., a public company, was signed. The assets consisted of some 33,000 acres of timberland in the Sierra, an old-growth sawmill at Grass Valley, a small-log mill at Lincoln similar to SPI's Anderson mill, and a medium-density fiberboard plant at Rocklin, all in California.

On the front page of the August issue of *BoardTalk* there was a story of this acquisition, along with a letter from Red about the environmental problems and his view of the future. The announcement of Tom Nelson's appointment to the California Board of Forestry was also included.

The accommodation reached between SPI and the environmentalists was labeled by the media the "Sierra Accord," in reference to the name Sierra in SPI and the Sierra Club. The elements of this truce were included in four bills introduced in the California legislature, with a provision that all must pass or none of them would become law. After several months, Governor Pete Wilson's Resource Agency submitted their own amendments to the bills. These were labeled the "California Accord."

The coastal companies formed the "Coastal Working Group" which began to lobby and press for amendments to the bills; and the effort began to gobble up large sums of money. Paid lobbyists were hired to direct their efforts.

Thus, the timber industry became more fragmented than ever. Because of the deep division, Bill Dennison was finding it nearly impossible to keep the California Forestry Association (CFA) together. It was another instance in which the association could not take a stance. Bill was under immense pressure and was becoming frustrated and worried. He was directed to stay out of the controversy by the Board of Directors. He re-solved to persevere and said he would neither give up nor resign.

Some members of the industry were beginning to ponder the likelihood of forming separate associations - one for the coast, and one for the inland producers, or of having no association at all. With the industry in such disarray and CFA unable to bring its members together on such important issues, the California legislature was receiving mixed signals as amendments to the Sierra Accord were sought by the various factions. Those companies with operations in counties where unemployment was above the state average, or who were on "sustained yield," were exempted from the increased restrictions by some late amendments to the bills. That would effectively eliminate several large coastal companies from the new regulations.

Even if legislation is passed, there is no assurance that the Governor will sign the bills into law. Some of the industry members are considering their options if there is no law and the petition being circulated by the environmentalists becomes an initiative that appears on the 1992 ballot. Since many of them believe they cannot beat such an initiative, they are considering saving their money for the litigation that is sure to follow.

There is fear that the exemptions contained in the amendments have already caused the environmentalists to walk out on the Sierra Accord agreement, thus insuring that there will be an initiative. With the economic lives of so many citizens at stake, it was difficult for many to accept the division in the industry. In recent years, even a united industry had always battled tremendous odds to stay alive; and the new, deeper division seems to be a portent of doom.

In the third week of August 1991 the bills were still not in final form and were involved in partisan maneuvering in the capitol. Red's optimism was being tested as never before as he, Dan Tomascheski, Ed Bond, Tom Nelson

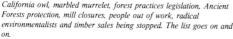

BoardTalk
SIERRA PACIFIC INDUSTRIES
Employees' Newsletter

Volume 12, Number 4   August, 1991

A Letter from Red...

Because of the many confusing timber supply issues that are going on, I feel it's necessary to once again tell you how I feel about the future of Sierra Pacific Industries' timber resource supply.

It seems that every day there are new stories related in some way to our industry's forest resources. They involve such things as the spotted owl, California owl, marbled murrelet, forest practices legislation, Ancient Forests protection, mill closures, people out of work, radical environmentalists and timber sales being stopped. The list goes on and on.

Some of the stories are factual, others are not. Some are pure rumors started and passed on by people with wild imaginations. And the rumors are usually nothing but doom and gloom. Even though those rumors are serious in nature, sometimes I have to laugh at how ridiculous they are.

In spite of these stories, this is how I feel about SPI's future and why I feel the way I do:

Over the years we have worked hard to be competitive in our industry. We've improved our mills, added co-gen plants, borrowed money to buy more forest lands, and hired, trained and developed good people. All of these things not only help us in present times, but will give us all a better foundation for the many years to come.

Even though we have our own lands we are very dependent on Forest Service timber sales and timber from other land owners. If the time comes when these sources are no longer available to us, then yes, we would probably have to consolidate some of our operations. BUT, and this is a big "but," as long as there is some outside source of timber, we will be aggressive in going after it. Let's be realistic about this. The United States and the world will always have a need for lumber and other wood products. Our goal is to make sure that Sierra Pacific Industries plays a major role in supplying that need.

Our foresters are good stewards of our lands. They're not thinking of only today. They are planning and renewing our resource for our wood fiber needs into the next century. And, they are committed to protecting the environment and wildlife as they go along.

With resources from our own lands and our competitiveness in buying timber from other landowners, including the Forest Service, I'm confident that SPI will be a major player in our industry for many years to come. I'm committed to this futuristic goal.

Sincerely,

Red

SPI Agrees to Buy Bohemia-California

Sierra Pacific Industries has reached an agreement in principle with Bohemia Inc. of Eugene, Ore., to buy Bohemia's California operations. Included in the purchase will be 33,000 acres of forest lands. Details and timing of the proposed sale are still being worked out between the two companies.

"We are interested in Bohemia because its California properties are near, and in some cases next to, land that we now own. They will fit right in with some of the things we're presently doing," said Red Emmerson about the proposed purchase. Red went on to say, "This is another commitment that we're making for the future of our company in California."

Bohemia is a public company which offered to sell its assets in Oregon and California. SPI is not involved in buying any of its Oregon operations.

Nelson Named To Board

SPI's Tom Nelson has just been appointed by Governor Pete Wilson to the California State Board of Forestry. Tom is one of three industry representatives on the nine member Board which oversees forest practices in the state, including review of timber harvest plans.

A University of Minnesota graduate in forestry, Tom is a licensed professional forester who has been with Sierra Pacific for seven years. In addition to his new civic duties, he will continue in his position as SPI's Redding Timber Manager.

"I look at my appointment to the Board as an opportunity to help resolve the critical forest practice reform issues in California. While I consider this as a personal honor, I, and the other Board members have a huge task ahead of us," Nelson said.

Congratulations to Tom on receiving this important appointment to the Board of Forestry.

TOM NELSON

Work With One Another
For the Safety of Each Other!

and Ed Murphy continued their efforts to protect SPI's interests. All of them were conducting the "high profile" activities that Red

hated; and he had no choice but to participate. The future remains in doubt.

APPENDIX B

Logging Contractors

Each year, logging and road construction for SPI is big business, employing nearly as many persons as SPI does in its sawmills. Thus, while the workers in the woods are not technically on the payroll, they are an integral part of the SPI operation. Without them, there would be no history of the company, indeed, there would be no future.

While there are many other kinds of contractors, such as construction, electrical and trucking, those who work in the woods can be considered part of the SPI family. Some are small outfits with few employees. Others are good-sized companies employing over a hundred persons.

Over the years, there have been many gyppo loggers who have come and gone at SPI. Those listed here are the principal contractors, both logging and road construction. As always, it is nearly impossible to include every deserving name. Deepest apologies to those inadvertently omitted.

Acord Logging Co.
Attebery & White
B & L Logging
Bear Cat Logging Corp.
Bear Creek Construction
Bennett Logging Co.
Bill Hannan Logging
Bill Schmitt Logging Co.
Blue Sky Trucking
Boak Logging Co.
Bollman Logging Co.
Bushnell Logging Co.
C & M Logging
Carter Chitwood Logging
Cascade Logging Co.
Chambers Logging Co.
Cheek Skyline Logging
Cheek Cat Logging
Chilcott Logging
Clover Logging Co.
Coffee Creek Sand & Gravel
Columbia Helicopters
D. C. Road Construction Co.
D. Dwyer Development
D. G. McDonald Construction
Davis Logging Co.
Don Cummins
Double T Logging Co.
Easter Logging
Ed Hood Logging
Emmett Baker Logging
Emmett Baugh
Erickson Air Crane
Ever Ready Construction Co.

F. W. Porteous Logging
Flintstones Logging Co.
Flying Eagle Logging Co.
Folchi Construction
Gene West Inc.
Gerschpacher Logging Co.
Gilbert Logging Co.
Glenbrook Lumber Co.
Glenn Schirman Logging
H & R Logging Co.
Hansen Enterprises
Harry McReynolds Logging
Headrick Logging Co.
Hollenbeak Logging
Holt Logging Co.
Huffman Logging
J. Wilcox Logging
J. W. Fisher Logging
J & K Logging
James & Nye Construction Co.
Jerry Watkins Logging
Jim Brewster, Jr.
John McGary Logging
Ken Pierce Logging
Larry Cyphers Logging
Leonhardt Construction Co.
Leroy Edwards Logging Co.
Little Bitty Logging Co.
Lonnie Johnson Logging
M. A. Fisher Logging Co.
McCaffrey Logging Co.
McElroy Bros. Logging Co.
McNight Redi-Mix
Medici Logging Co.
Michael Morgan Logging

Mitch Gray Logging
Monte West Construction
Neuenschwander Logging
Paul Warner Enterprises
Ramelli Logging Co.
Ranlee Logging Co.
Red McKenzie Logging Co.
Rex Gott Logging
Robinson Enterprises
Robinson Timber Co.
Ron Andrews Logging
Roper Logging Co.
Schwartz Logging Co.
South Siskiyou Logging
Stan Leach Timber Inc.
Steve Meilicke Logging
Steve Schmitt Logging
Ted Tyrell Logging
Thomas Creek Logging
Thomason Logging Co.
Timber Contractors
Timber Harvesters
Tom Craven Logging
Triangle Roads Inc.
Trinity River Logging Co.
Vanetti Logging
Vic Hamilton Logging
W. R. S. Consultants
West Side Logging
Westside Contractors
White Top Logging
Wold Logging Co.
Zane Butterfield Logging
Ziegler Logging

APPENDIX C

SIERRA PACIIFIC INDUSTRIES
Management Group Roster
(1991)

Division Managers

Amos, Gordon	Arcata
Armstrong, Ken	Hayfork
Coulter, George	Quincy
Dearman, Darrel	Redding (CV)
Harrington, Jerry	Anderson
Maciel, Larry	Trucking
Pierson, Kendall	Red Bluff
Pipkins, Dan	Loyalton
Rogers, Marlin	Anderson Millwork
Root, Dave	Burney
Sanguinet, Jay	Red Bluff
Schmidt, Mike	Richfield
Sisk, Stuart	Distribution Center
Taborski, Matt	Sloat

Accountants

Anderson, Paul	Richfield Controller
Bell, Alan	Corporate Auditor
McEuen, Pat	Timber Division Controller
Shifflet, Steve	Red Bluff Controller
Smith, Alan	Arcata Controller
Stanley, Jack	Susanville Controller

Forestry

Banka, Bill	Quincy
Dillard, Joe	Susanville
Feller, Tim	Tahoe District
Frost, Jack	Timberlands
Gromacki, Jerry	Redding (CV)
Hoover, Ron	Arcata
Nelson, Tom	Redding District
Ostrowski, Jim	Mt. Shasta District
Voss, Ron	Log Resources
Walz, Tom	Weaverville District

Sales

Ahrens, Bob	Millwork
Byrne, Dan	Lumber
Chase, Jack	Lumber
Collins-Lund, Lori	Lumber
Dean, Loyce	Millwork
Humphrey, Terry	Lumber
Johnson, Jim	Lumber
Kuehl, Terry	Lumber
Maciel, Wendie	Lumber
Majors, Mark	Lumber
McKenzie, Rich	Window
Preston, Rod	Window
Renlund, Sally	Millwork
Risinger, Charlie	Millwork
Schweitzer, Charlie	Lumber
Sharp, George	Lumber
Stolz, Rich	Lumber
Westlake, Mark	Millwork

Miscellaneous

Blanc, Gary	Lumber Buyer
Boyce, Byron	Quality Control
Fairchild, Deke	Purchasing Manager
Gaston, Steve	Data Processing Manager
Moore, Tracy	Personnel Manager
Rogers, George	Traffic Manager

Senior Management

Bond, Ed	Human Resources
Gartman, Jon	Taxes
Hoppe, Ron	Sales
Lowry, Ray	Controller
Smith, Dick	Director
Stevens, Ron	Operations
Tomascheski, Dan	Resources

GLOSSARY

Airport limo - An old automobile kept at various airports frequented by SPI personnel, and used to travel to SPI facilities and vicinity.

Big Five - During the 1980s, the senior management group of SPI.

Big Five II - The Big Five after the addition of several younger members in the late 1980s.

Big Red - The label given by environmentalists to a large redwood tree in Mendocino County, California.

Board foot - A piece of wood measuring 12" X 12" X 1".

BoardTalk - The name of SPI's company newspaper.

Brush mill - A small sawmill, constructed in the woods where logs were available close by. The mill was usually primitive, labor-intensive, and inefficient.

Bug - A stripped-down automobile chassis with a seat which Emily (Emmerson) Thorpe learned to drive.

California Pollution Control Financing Authority's variable-rate demand, pollution-control revenue bonds - Bonds backed by Barclay's Bank, sold to finance the construction of cogeneration facilities at Burney, Quincy and Susanville, and the black-topping of several SPI log yards.

California Wilderness Bill - A bill passed by Congress in 1984 which designated a number of areas in California as Wilderness, designated some areas for further study, and was supposed to "release" other areas for multiple-use activities. The "releases" never occurred.

Certified Lumber Grader - A person who, by demonstrating proficiency in grading lumber according to rules issued by various lumber grading organizations, is accredited to do so. Such rules are accepted in the trade as standards by which lumber is bought and sold.

Certified Tree Farm - a timbered property dedicated by the owner to the growing of successive crops of trees. If such lands meet certain criteria, Western Wood Products Association (formerly Western Pine Association) "certifies" them.

Clear-cut - A regeneration harvest system under which all trees are cut, the resulting slash may be reduced by burning, or a portion of it removed, in preparation for planting.

Co-op - In the wood products industry, those sawmills and/or plywood plants owned by the workers.

Cogeneration (cogen) - In the timber industry a facility that uses steam derived from burning wood-waste which is used to spin a turbine and a generator to produce electricity. Technically the word denotes a process by which steam at various pressure is drawn off at different stages to run other machines, or to dry lumber.

Conglomerate - A corporation which is made up of a number of companies operating in widely different fields.

Cruise, timber - A method of estimating the volume of wood in a stand of trees. Usually the trees are measured on only a portion of the property (sample) and volumes are calculated statistically. In a 100% cruise all the trees are measured.

Cut up plant - a plant using lumber as a raw material that cuts, rips, and trims it into smaller sizes, thus increasing the grade of each piece.

Depression - The great economic contraction suffered in the U. S. and eventually worldwide in the early 1930s.

depression - The economic contraction suffered in the period 1981-82 which hit the timber industry especially hard.

Dimension lumber - Construction lumber usually 2 X 4, 2 X 6, 2 X 8, etc., as opposed to boards, 1 X 4, 1 X 8, etc., and timbers, 6 X 8, 6 X 10, 10 X 14, etc.

Energy Czar - The name given to the employee in charge of SPI's cogen facilities.

environmentalist (l.c.) - label given by Ron Arnold, in his book *The Ecology Wars*, to the segment of the population that advocates the wise use of resources.

Environmentalist (u.c.) - label given by Ron Arnold, in his book *The Ecology Wars*, to those environmentalists and splinter groups who advocate preservation of resources at all costs.

Farmer logs - Logs purchased from small ranchers or other land owners. Such logs are usually small, low grade, and from young-growth trees.

Federal Timber Contract Payment Modification Act - An act passed by Congress that allowed purchasers of high-priced timber to return to the government all, or a portion, of such timber sales at a discount, while specifying stringent rules for harvesting the remainder.

Forest Service planning process - A slow procedure under which the agency attempts to prepare a detailed plan for managing the land in each National Forest.

Forests Forever Initiative - A 1990 ballot initiative submitted in California by environmentalists that, among other provisions, restricted the harvest of timber which had not reached the culmination of mean annual growth, eliminated clear-cutting, and eliminated cutting of "old-growth" timber.

Form class - The ratio of the tree diameter inside the bark at the top of the first 16-foot log to the diameter outside the bark at breast height (4 1/2') expressed as a whole number.

Four Wheeler - A small all-wheel-drive vehicle for off-road use by foresters, ranchers and recreationists.

G.I. Bill - A law passed by Congress after World War II that provided payment to qualified veterans for subsistence, and to qualified schools for books, supplies and tuition.

Geographic Information System (GIS) - A system designed to produce geographic mapping information. Data is usually gathered from satellite imagery and computer enhanced.

Gyppo logger - A contract logger employed to harvest an owner's timber. Originally a term used derisively, the name has grown to be accepted with pride by those in the profession.

Headwaters Forest - The label given by environmentalists to a portion of The Pacific Lumber Co. timberland in Humboldt County, California.

Incident Commander - Title given by the Forest Service to the individual placed in charge of the activities of the agency in dealing with emergencies such as wildfires and floods.

Inflation-fighting formula - A descriptive term derisively applied by SPI foresters to describe a timber appraisal technique designed to raise bid prices.

Initiative - In California a "ballot initiative" may be submitted to the voters for approval and, if passed, becomes law. To qualify for the ballot a petition must be signed by at least 5% of the number of qualified voters who voted for governor in the previous election; currently about 395,000.

Leveraged buyout (LBO) - A process by which companies are purchased with largely borrowed funds. Various assets of the acquired company are usually sold or liquidated to pay off the debt.

Log grades - Logs categorized by species and quality according to strict grading rules. Log scaling and grading bureaus and other organizations have developed a number of different criteria for use in various regions, most of which consider, among other things, the end use (sawlogs for making lumber, peelers for making veneer), knots, slope of grain, size, defects, etc.

Log scale - The volume of a log usually expressed in terms of board feet. There are many types of log scales, but the one commonly used in California is the Scribner Decimal C.

Luan - A tree species commonly known as Philippine mahogany.

Lumber tally - The volume of lumber expressed in terms of board feet.

Management Group - In SPI the group participating in the management profit sharing plan. See Appendix A for current members.

Mecca - SPI's Arcata sawmill, the "father" of them all.

Millwork plant - a "catch-all" term describing a facility that utilizes lumber as a raw material and produces a "finished" product such as door jambs, window parts, or some other product that is to be further manufactured.

Moulding plant - A facility utilizing lumber as a raw material to produce mouldings such as window trim, baseboard, picture framing, door trim, etc.

Multi-sale extension plan (MSEP) - In the early 1980s, a plan submitted by each timber purchaser to the Forest Service (or Bureau of Land Management) that, when approved, granted extensions of time for harvesting all timber sales in an operator's portfolio, but required strict payment and/or harvest schedules.

Old man's ground - Gentle topography.

Open market logs - Logs bought from suppliers who normally do not own manufacturing facilities, and who sell to those who offer the highest price.

Overrun - The number greater than one resulting when the difference between lumber tally and log scale is expressed as a percentage.

Owl, bad - A spotted owl found in a low-priced timber sale, thus requiring the timber operator to return the sale to the Government.

Owl, good - A spotted owl found in a high-priced timber sale, thus requiring the timber operator to return the sale to the Government with little cost to the operator.

Owl, Northern spotted (Strix occidentalis) - An owl inhabiting large areas of the western forest, believed by some to be dependent upon old-growth forests for survival, and recently placed on the Threatened and Endangered Species List.

Peelable mill - A log grade added to the rules of most scaling organizations several years after the original rules were promulgated. The original rules had only two broad classifications: peelers and sawlogs. The sawlog category was very broad and, as peeling technology improved, operators were peeling lower-grade logs. The peelable mill grade specified rules for grading such sawmill logs as "peelable."

Peeler logs - Logs suitable for manufacture into veneer. Such logs are graded #1, #2, or #3 Peelers based on size, quality, grain and freedom from certain defects.

Polish Pope - Name given to the author under which he "married" various couples attending SPI meetings or social functions.

Potter's wheel - A wheel that is spun and on which the potter turns vases, bowls, etc.

Pre-merchantable timber - Trees that are generally large enough to be measured in board feet, but too small for efficient use in sawmills. Diameter limits may vary from area to area depending upon types of local sawmills. Timber cruise specifications may or may not include pre-merchantable trees.

Public Utility Regulatory Policies Act (PURPA) - An act passed by Congress which required public utilities to pay private producers of electricity the cost of production at the same rate as if the utility had produced the electricity itself (avoided cost).

Push - The foreman or boss in charge of a crew.

Remanufacturing plant - a "catch-all" term describing a facility that utilizes lumber as a raw material. Lumber is cut, trimmed and ripped into various sizes and sold to others who make it into different end-products.

Select peelers - Another term for peelable sawmill logs, although usually indicating a log with strictly peeler qualities but lacking the size to be graded a peeler log.

Shasta salamander - A salamander believed by many biologists to be a distinct species living only in Shasta County.

Silvicultural activities - Establishing, growing and tending stands of trees. This may include such things as planting, pruning, weeding, thinning and utilization of harvesting systems to regenerate the stand.

Silviculturist - One who performs silvicultural activities.

Slow Down Hoedown - Party given for the author prior to his retirement from SPI in 1990.

Small logs - The term means different things in different regions. In California small logs are usually between 5" diameter inside bark (d.i.b.) at the small end, and 24" - 26" diameter outside bark (d.o.b.) at the big end.

Small log mill - A sawmill for sawing small logs but not large logs. Minimum/maximum log diameters for which the mill is designed may vary in different areas of the country.

Soft I and Soft II - Terms used to describe the procedures formulated by U.S. Forest Service to allow limited extensions of time for timber operators to harvest high-priced timber during the 1981-82 "depression." It was one form of contract relief.

Spotted owl management plan - A plan prepared by SPI's wildlife biologist and foresters that permits timber harvest while protecting the spotted owl and its habitat. The plan was ratified by the U. S. Fish and Wildlife Service and certifies that, if timber operations are conducted in conformance with it, there is no "taking" of the owl.

Tie mill - A small sawmill cutting railroad ties of several specified lengths which are sold rough-green, usually to be treated with a preservative later.

Timber sale contract relief - A term applied to various laws, rules and regulations promulgated to extend the time for harvest of high-priced timber, or to allow cancellation of all or part of such contracts. The term came into general use during the 1981-82 "depression" in the timber industry.

Timber Harvest Plan - A plan prepared by a California Registered Professional Forester for submission to the California Department of Forestry for approval before any timber harvesting can occur.

Underrun - The number less than one resulting when the difference between lumber tally and log scale is expressed as a percentage.

Wild and Scenic River - A river designated by the government under various laws and regulations meant to protect the rivers from degradation and to restrict use or development near them.

Young man's ground - A term coined by SPI foresters to describe steep and/or difficult topography, as opposed to more gentle ground (old man's ground).

INDEX

N

O

P